Sadye M. L. Logan, Editor
Ramona W. Denby
Priscilla A. Gibson
Co-editors

Mental Health Care
in the African-American
Community

Pre-publication
REVIEWS,
COMMENTARIES,
EVALUATIONS . . .

"**T**his book critically examines the historical roots of persistent disparities in mental health status and treatment of people of African descent in the United States. The book identifies current policies and practices that contribute to these disparities and advances innovative approaches to improve access, quality, and effectiveness of services. It will be particularly valuable for social workers and other practitioners to increase their cultural competence with African Americans, transform systems of care, and improve mental health care outcomes."

Salome Raheim, PhD, ACSW
Associate Professor,
School of Social Work,
The University of Iowa

"**M**ental Health Care in the African-American Community* provides insight and wisdom to benefit all who work with the mental health concerns of African Americans. Readers will find immense value in the sections exploring the most contemporary topics of professional and community concerns. This book brings erudition to current issues and intragroup concerns by edging the critical content with classroom and discussion activities for each topic. It is a valuable resource for students, teachers, and professionals."

Barbara W. White, PhD
Dean and Centennial Professor
in Leadership for Community,
Professional, and Corporate
Excellence, School of Social Work,
The University of Texas at Austin

HU

The Haworth Press
New York

Mental Health Care in the African-American Community

HAWORTH Social Work in Health Care
Gary Rosenberg and Andrew Weissman
Editors

A Guide to Creative Group Programming in the Psychiatric Day Hospital by Lois E. Passi

Social Work in Geriatric Home Health Care: The Blending of Traditional Practice with Cooperative Strategies by Lucille Rosengarten

Health Care and Empowerment Practice in the Black Community: Knowledge, Skills, and Collectivism by Sadye L. Logan and Edith M. Freeman

Clinical Case Management for People with Mental Illness: A Vulnerability-Stress Model by Daniel Fu Keung Wong

The Social Work–Medicine Relationship: 100 Years at Mount Sinai by Helen Rehr and Gary Rosenberg

Social Group Work with Cardiac Patients by Maurice Scott Fisher Sr.

Mental Health Care in the African-American Community edited by Sadye M. L. Logan, Ramona W. Denby, and Priscilla A. Gibson

Mental Health Care in the African-American Community

Sadye M. L. Logan
Editor
Ramona W. Denby
Priscilla A. Gibson
Co-editors

The Haworth Press
New York

For more information on this book or to order, visit
http://www.haworthpress.com/store/product.asp?sku=5364

or call 1-800-HAWORTH (800-429-6784) in the United States and Canada
or (607) 722-5857 outside the United States and Canada

or contact orders@HaworthPress.com

The Haworth Press, Inc. 10 Alice Street, Binghamton, NY 13904-1580.

PUBLISHER'S NOTE
The development, preparation, and publication of this work has been undertaken with great care. However, the Publisher, employees, editors, and agents of The Haworth Press are not responsible for any errors contained herein or for consequences that may ensue from use of materials or information contained in this work. The Haworth Press is committed to the dissemination of ideas and information according to the highest standards of intellectual freedom and the free exchange of ideas. Statements made and opinions expressed in this publication do not necessarily reflect the views of the Publisher, Directors, management, or staff of The Haworth Press, Inc., or an endorsement by them.

Library of Congress Cataloging-in-Publication Data

Mental health care in the African-American community / [edited by] Sadye L. Logan, Ramona W. Denby, Priscilla A. Gibson.
    p. ; cm.
    Includes bibliographical references and index.
    ISBN: 978-0-7890-2611-8 (hardcover : alk. paper)
    ISBN: 978-0-7890-2612-5 (softcover : alk. paper)
    1. African Americans—Mental health services. 2. Community mental health services—United States. I. Logan, Sadye Louise, 1943- II. Denby, Ramona W. III. Gibson, Priscilla A.
    [DNLM: 1. African Americans—psychology—United States. 2. Community Mental Health Services—methods—United States. WA 305 M54836 2007]

RC451.5.N4M445 2007
362.2089'96073—dc22

2007015793

CONTENTS

PART III: THE CONSUMERS OF MENTAL HEALTH SERVICES OVER THE LIFE COURSE

Chapter 8. Poverty, Special Education, and ADHD   139
Gwendolyn Perry-Burney

Chapter 9. War on African-American Girls: Overcoming Adversities   155
Tanya S. Brice

PART V: IMPLICATIONS FOR AN INTEGRATED, HOLISTIC APPROACH TO MENTAL HEALTH SERVICES

ABOUT THE EDITORS

Sadye M. L. Logan, DSW, ACSW, LICSW-CP, holds the I. DeQuincy Newman Endowed Professorship in Social Justice at the University of South Carolina College of Social Work. She teaches practice method and family treatment courses. Her research interests include social justice issues impacting families and children, culturally specific services for children and families of color, the psycho-spiritual dimensions of practice and education, addictive behaviors, and racial identity development. Dr. Logan has written and published extensively in these areas. Her most recent published books include *Social Work Practice with People of African Descent: An Annotated Bibliography*; *Reconceptualizing the Strengths and Common Heritage of Black Families: Practice, Research, and Policy Issues* ; *African American Families: Strengths, Self Help and Positive Change* ; and *Health Care in the Black Community: Empowerment, Knowledge, Skills, and Collectivism.*

Ramona W. Denby, PhD, ACSW, is Associate Professor at the University of Nevada Las Vegas School of Social Work. Dr. Denby has worked with children and families in a wide capacity for more than ten years. Her teaching interests include direct practice, human behavior, child welfare, and culturally specific service practice. Dr. Denby's research interests involve programming and treatment issues relevant to children and families. Specifically, Dr. Denby conducts research in the areas of child welfare, children's mental health, juvenile delinquency, and culturally specific service delivery. She has published extensively in the leading social work journals.

Priscilla A. Gibson, PhD, ACSW, LICSW, is an Associate Professor in the School of Social Work, College of Education and Human Development at the University of Minnesota. She is a licensed Independent Clinical Social Worker (LICSW) with over twenty-five years of direct social work practice experience with diverse populations. Her research interests include

Mental Health Care in the African-American Community
© 2007 by The Haworth Press, Inc. All rights reserved.
doi:10.1300/5364_a

African-American grandmothers and other older caregivers in kinship care arrangements, qualitative research methods, African-American adolescents and their families, and adoption. She has published in the leading social work journals.

CONTRIBUTORS

Carla Adkison-Bradley, PhD, is Professor and Director of Training, Doctoral Program in Counselor Education, Western Michigan University, Kalamazoo, MI.

Keith A. Alford, PhD, is Associate Professor, Syracuse University, School of Social Work, Syracuse, NY.

Donna Holland Barnes, PhD, is Research Associate and Professor, Howard University, Psychiatry Department, Washington, DC.

Elizabeth Bradshaw is a PhD candidate in the Counseling Psychology Department, Western Michigan University, Kalamazoo, MI.

Tanya S. Brice, PhD, is Associate Professor and MSW Program Director, Abilene Christian University, Abilene, TX.

Jesse A. Brinson, PhD, is Associate Professor, University of Nevada at Las Vegas, Department of Counseling, Las Vegas, NV.

Chandra F. Brown, PhD, is a program specialist at Charleston Place, Charleston, SC.

Anita-Yvonne Bryan, PhD, is Senior Coordinator of training programs and multicultural services liaison at Duke University, Chapel Hill, NC.

Nicholas Cooper-Lewter, PhD, is a visiting professor, University of South Carolina, College of Social Work, Columbia, SC.

Brenda K. J. Crawley, PhD, is Associate Professor, Loyola University, School of Social Work, Chicago, IL.

Andrea Dakin is an MSW candidate, University of Illinois at Chicago, the Jane Addams College of Social Work, Chicago, IL.

Mental Health Care in the African-American Community
© 2007 by The Haworth Press, Inc. All rights reserved.
doi:10.1300/5364_b

Kendra P. DeLoach is a PhD candidate at the University of South Carolina, College of Social Work, Columbia, SC.

Michele D. Hanna, PhD, is Assistant Professor, University of Denver, Graduate School of Social Work, Denver, CO.

Ruth G. McRoy, PhD, is Research Professor and a senior research fellow, Evan B. Donaldson Adoption Institute, School of Social Work, University of Texas, Austin, TX.

Elijah Mickel, DSW, is Professor of Social Work and Assistant Dean, College of Health and Public Policy, Delaware State University, Dover, DE.

Patricia O'Brien, PhD, is Associate Professor, University of Illinois at Chicago, Jane Addams College of Social Work, Chicago, IL.

Gwendolyn Perry-Burney, PhD, is Associate Professor, California University of Pennsylvania, Department of Social Work and Gerontology, California, PA.

Jo-Ann Lipford Sanders, PhD, is Director and Associate Professor of graduate studies in counseling at Heidelberg College, Tiffin, OH.

Carrie Jefferson Smith, PhD, is Associate Professor, School of Social Work, Syracuse, NY.

Elizabeth Waggoner is an MS candidate in marriage and family therapy and a graduate assistant in the Department of Counseling at the University of Las Vegas, Las Vegas, NV.

Gregory Washington, PhD, is Assistant Professor, University of Tennessee, College of Social Work, Knoxville, TN.

Foreword

Mental Health Care in the African-American Community is a beacon for social workers and other mental health providers. It signals alarms and offers both guidance and encouragement to contemporary practitioners who recognize the importance of their participation in transforming mental health services in the United States. The United States Department of Health and Human Services (USDHHS) is directing a federal initiative to transform public mental health services by promoting a recovery model. The USDHHS defines* mental health recovery as "a journey of healing and transformation enabling a person with a mental health problem to live a meaningful life in a community of his or her choice while striving to achieve his or her full potential" (USDHHS, n.d., Background). Although focusing on recovery in transforming the public mental health system may represent progress, it fails to adequately address how social and structural patterns in the United States perpetuate disparities in the qualities of mental health services for African Americans.

This book's comprehensive critique and analysis of the history, philosophy, policies, research, and practice modalities that undergird mental health care in the Black community address the antecedents and consequences of those disparities and offer holistic practice strategies for promoting wellness and recovery.

Nocona L. Pewewardy, PhD
Assistant Professor
California State University, Fresno
Department of Social Work
Fresno, CA

---

*U.S. Department of Health and Human Services (n.d.). National Consensus Statement on Mental Health Recovery. Retrieved April 28, 2006, from http://www.mentalhealth.samhsa.gov/publications/allpubs/sma05-4129.

Mental Health Care in the African-American Community
© 2007 by The Haworth Press, Inc. All rights reserved.
doi:10.1300/5364_c

Acknowledgments

This is a project born of intention, perseverance, and grace. Self-effort and much grace was required to bring it to fruition. We acknowledge all of our supporters and especially our families for their unfailing support and encouragement. Included in our gratitude are the contributing authors. We applaud their dedication and commitment to researching, advocating, and writing about the creation and sustainment of a mentally healthy world for all people but particularly for those of African descent. Deep appreciation is extended to Amy Cue, a University of South Carolina MSW graduate assistant, for her help in typing the manuscript. Finally, we wish to extend deepest appreciation to our publisher, The Haworth Press, for the patience and belief in this timely and important contribution to the literature on the mental health needs of people of African descent.

Mental Health Care in the African-American Community
© 2007 by The Haworth Press, Inc. All rights reserved.
doi:10.1300/5364_d

Introduction

The purpose of this book is twofold. First, it will provide a critique and analysis of the history, philosophy, policies, research, and practice modalities that undergrid mental health care in the Black community.* Second, the book will use a life course perspective and evidence-based practice not only to frame this critique and analysis but also to suggest new and expanded ways of conceptualizing the mental health needs and care of the Black community.

Given the focus of this book, a life course perspective serves to organize the concerns of Black families and communities. A life course perspective assumes that each person's life has a unique trajectory—a long-term pattern of stability and change—that is based on his or her own unique interactions with the environment overtime. This approach to understanding human behavior also recognizes the influence of age, history, culture, and unexpected life events. According to G. H. Elder (1998, p. 9), "life course theory and research alerts us to the real world in which lives are lived and where people work out paths of development as best they can. It tells us how lives are socially organized in biological and historical times, and how the resulting social pattern affects the way we think, feel and act" ("The life course as development theory," *Child Development, 69,* 1-12). Taken together, life course theory and evidence-based practice will serve as a framework for the topics of discussion in this book. The evidence-based approach is an expanded way of thinking and talking about our practice that allows us to individualize and translate evidence into a given practice situation.

Several edited textbooks have been written about mental health in the Black community, with some of the literature more current than others. Despite the overall usefulness of the literature—especially when it employs empirical data focusing on one research study—there is no direct link to the social work practice and education community. In this book we have attempted to make such direct links to social work. The chapters here will

---

*The terms *Black, African American,* and *people of African descent* are used interchangeably throughout the book, as are the terms *African-centered, Africentered,* and *Afrocentric.*

Mental Health Care in the African-American Community
© 2007 by The Haworth Press, Inc. All rights reserved.
doi:10.1300/5364_e

move us beyond a simple analysis of factors and issues affecting the mental health of Black people. As a groundbreaking book on mental health care in the Black community, this text will examine the mental health needs of the Black community from a social work perspective. The social work orientation will not only provide a context for all of the helping professions but will also enable current and historical analysis of the impact of mental health research, policy, community, and clinical practice on Black families.

An important aspect of the book is its emphasis on evidence-based practice with a life course orientation. It is increasingly recognized that professional interventions should be justified by empirical findings. Therefore, our intent is to place emphasis on the integration of practice and research as a means of improving practice effectiveness. The life course intervention is flexible in that it recognizes unique transactions and life course markers that are shared by particular cohorts as well as unexpected life events. This flexibility also allows for the critical analysis of practice approaches, research, and policy issues across the life course. Finally, as indicated previously, the life course orientation supports a holistic, integrated approach to mental health care. This approach addresses spiritual, physical, and emotional concerns as well as coping resources and help-seeking behavior.

The book is organized into five parts. Part I includes three chapters, which introduce readers to the conceptual factors and historical reviews that frame the remaining parts of the book. Part II (Chapters 4-7) focuses on the mental health service organizations and their responses to the mental health concerns experienced by African-American families.

Part III includes four chapters that focus on the consumers of mental health services over the life course: young children, teenagers, adults, and older African-American men and women. Part IV (Chapters 12-16) extends the discussion on mental health practice by focusing on research, policy, and practice. The book concludes by examining implications in Part V, which incorporates four chapters and the epilogue; this part presents an integrated, holistic approach that focuses on mental health services for individuals, families, groups, and communities.

It is the intent that this book to serve not only as a resource guide for the lay community but also as a textbook for the professional community. The impetus for addressing the lay community was motivated in part by the following questions and most especially by the expressed needs of African-American families for information that addresses these issues.

- How effective are drug treatment programs?
- Should family members expect a cure from mental illness?

- Should family members expect drug treatment programs to prevent recidivism?
- What kind of mental health treatment should families expect from the state hospitals, from group homes, or from private centers and prisons?
- What steps should families take to locate community support services when experiencing a mental health crisis?

In addition to using these questions as a guide to resource development, emphasis has also been placed on identifying the cultural resources upon which Black families draw to survive and even thrive within environments that are not always supportive of health, growth, and development. It is hoped that students in the helping professions, researchers, educators, practitioners, and mental health consumers and their families will find that this book facilitates our journies toward health and healing and helps us to better understand and navigate the various systems of mental health care.

PART I:
A HISTORICAL OVERVIEW
AND CONTEXTUAL FACTORS

Chapter 1

African-American Mental Health: A Historical Perspective

Priscilla A. Gibson
Ramona W. Denby

Mental health for African Americans is an intimately connected history. It can be translated into a survival mechanism with the influence of race as a driving factor (Hines-Martin, Brown-Piper, Kin, & Malone, 2002; McNeil & Kennedy, 1997). Historically, African Americans differ from every other group as they entered this country involuntarily and experienced demeaning systems to control their behavior through slavery (McNeil & Kennedy). The history of African Americans and their mental health needs is a difficult history indeed. Many scholars and researchers would argue that the social and psychological ills that African Americans face are directly related to various historical aspects of slavery. As indicated throughout the chapters in this book, it is evident that whether one is discussing teenage pregnancies, substance abuse issues, psychiatric problems, child welfare concerns, familial issues, or issues pertaining to gang violence, slavery continues to have an impact on the psychosocial lives of today's African-American population.

Although some may disagree about the influence of slavery on the mental health of African Americans, others espouse that this very denial influences the mental health of African Americans as well as those who deny the connection. For some African Americans, emotional stressors affect internal perceptions such as self-esteem and external behaviors that are compared to Whites (McNeil & Kennedy, 1997). Hines-Martin et al. (2002) note that, historically, African Americans experienced racism, intolerance, exclusion from quality health care, limited economic resources, and nega-

Mental Health Care in the African-American Community
© 2007 by The Haworth Press, Inc. All rights reserved.
doi:10.1300/5364_01

tive experiences with health care research. Other influential factors include devaluation and mistreatment (Boulware, Cooper, Ratner, LaVeist, & Powe, 2003). Wideman (1984) provides a detailed explanation on how these factors affect his daily life and sanity:

> It was a trick I'd learned early on. A survival mechanism as old as slavery. If you're born black in America you must quickly teach yourself to recognize the invisible barriers disciplining the space in which you may move. This seventh sense you must activate is imperative for survival and sanity. Nothing is what it seems. You must always take second readings, decode appearances, pick out the obstructions erected to keep you in your place. Then work around them. What begins as a pragmatic reaction to race prejudice gradually acquires the force of an instinctive response. A special way of seeing becomes second nature. You ignore the visible landscape. It has nothing to do with you. It will never change, so you learn a kind of systematic skepticism, a stoicism, and, if you're lucky, ironic detachment. I can't get to the mountain and the mountain ain't hardly coming to me no matter how long I sit here and holler, so mize well do what I got to do right here on level ground and leave the mountain to them folks think they own it. (p. 221)

There is no denying that the stress of racism and discrimination affect mental health (Hines-Martin et al., 2002; McNeil & Kennedy, 1997; U.S. Department of Health and Human Services, 2001).

The sociopolitical influence of race also affects the amount of literature on the mental health history of African Americans. There is a paucity of information. Another is the contemporary view of mental health services. In some segments of the African-American community, there is a stigma associated with the use of mental health services (Neighbors, 1985). What is even more of a compelling mental health issue is that many African Americans have been unwilling to discuss the topic of mental health as a major cultural topic. Historically, African Americans have maintained that deviant behavior, psychiatric disorders, and drug abuse issues were topics that were more closely aligned with the majority culture. African Americans, being a God-fearing people, would argue that one needs only to call upon the Lord thy God to solve all of one's worldly concerns. In fact, it has been noted that African Americans who do seek help with their mental health concerns are more likely to obtain the assistance of someone in their informal social network or church affiliation (Neighbors, 1985).

This chapter provides historical information on the mental health of African Americans. Included would be the role played by African Americans as well as a description of the major periods and important. The chapter also offers a new approach to view and work with the mental health concerns of African Americans in a culturally sensitive manner. The chapter concludes with a summary and ancillary classroom activities.

MAJOR PERIODS AND THEIR INFLUENCES

There are three major periods affecting African-American mental health. Those periods are slavery, emancipation, and systemic issues unique to twentieth-century America.

Slavery

Slavery was a defining period for African Americans. Whitaker (2002) calls the history of mental health for African Americans "shameful" and connected to the status of being free or being enslaved. As discussed later in the book, Samuel Cartwright, a doctor from the South, diagnosed slaves with two types of insanity, draptomania and dysaesthesia aethiopis. Draptomania described those slaves who attempted to escape. A diagnosis of dysaesthesia aethiopis was given to those seen as idle and disrespectful of the master's property (Whitaker, 2002). In the 1840 census, there was a higher percentage of insanity among slaves in the North as compared to their peers in the South (Whitaker, 2002). Whitaker attributes the increase to Whites telling census workers "all of the Negroes in their communities were crazy" (2002, p. 171). With this type of communication, Whites began to socially construct a view of African Americans that became fact, and thus institutionalized.

During this period, Africans used self-help for assistance with concerns in the form of the extended family (Martin & Martin, 1985). Older slaves were accorded with the status of being wise and consequently, sought out for advice. Early African Americans used spirituality and the Black churches for emotional relief from problems of oppression (Schiele, 2000). This furthered the misperception that African Americans lived a "trouble free existence" and that they received "special care and supervision" under the institution of slavery (Vega & Rumbaut, 1991).

Emancipation

Freedom from slavery did not remove the problems that African Americans encountered with mental health diagnoses. During this period, African

Americans became at-risk for being locked in asylums because of the definition of sanity (Whitaker, 2002). Sanity was defined by the behaviors that slave masters valued such as "docile, hardworking laborer who paid him proper respect" (Whitaker, 2002, p. 171). Those who eschewed this behavior found themselves in asylums, jails, and the poorhouse. Whitaker documents that the incidence of insanity for Blacks increased fivefold during emancipation. In addition, doctors continued to publish medical information that associated being Black with insanity or limited intelligence. For example, in 1886, J. M. Buchanan stated that the Negro had limited brain growth and in 1921, W. M. Bevis wrote that Negroes were "prone to psychotic illness . . . because they were descendents of 'savages and cannibals'" (p. 172). Whitaker notes that E. Franklin Frazier responded that Whites might be labeled as insane because of these assertions, which resulted in threats to his life. During emancipation there were other influential Blacks such as Frazier who disagreed with the prevailing notion of Blacks as inherently insane and/or of limited intellectual abilities.

Twentieth Century

Mental health of Blacks during this period was characterized by inferior treatment and severe mental health diagnoses. For instance, African Americans were diagnosed with schizophrenia instead of depression (Whitaker, 2002; see Chapter 3 for further discussion). The prevailing thought was that Blacks did not react to "grief, remorse, etc." and were "happy-go-lucky" (Whitaker, 2002, p. 172). By the 1930s, research on African Americans began showing they had "higher rates of insanity" than Whites (Vega & Rumbaut, 1991), which may be evidence of racist diagnostic patterns in response to increased resistance to adverse conditions faced by African Americans. Interestingly, children from poor families were more likely to have mental health issues than those children from wealthier families (McLeod & Shanahan, 1996). This seems to suggest that family poverty histories have an impact on children's mental health status. African-American children are more likely to live in poverty than other children, so they are more likely to receive a mental health diagnosis than other children.

THEMES FROM THE LITERATURE

Important themes provide additional historical perspective on the mental health of African Americans. These have been identified as (1) incidence of mental health disorder, (2) relationship with mental health service providers, and (3) service utilization.

Incidence of mental health disorder. When compared to other racial groups, African Americans had higher rates of psychiatric disorders but lower rates of comorbidity disorders (Fellin, 1996).

Relationship with mental health service providers. Historically, African Americans are less likely to enter the mental health system and when in that system, they are more likely to encounter difficulties with their service providers. Fellin (1996) found that African Americans are more likely to seek help from their informal social support systems. Homma-True, Greene, Lopez, and Trimble (1993) state that African Americans are fearful of the mental health system. Similarly, Collins et al. (2002) found that African Americans are less confident in their doctors and less likely to have health insurance. The lack of cultural knowledge and sensitivity by service providers has been listed as barriers to service utilization (McNeil & Kennedy, 1997). Starting in the 1970s, this area has received greater attention from service providers and their organizations (Parham, 2002).

Service utilization. McNeil and Kennedy (1997) identified the four As that affect mental health service usage. These are availability, accessibility, acceptability, and affordability. Community-based mental health service utilization by African Americans has been described as low to nonexistent (Snowden, 1998). Neighbors (1985) found that African Americans have a negative view of mental health services, seeing them as ineffective or unacceptable. Hines-Martin et al. (2002) state that African Americans face barriers to mental health services at the individual, environmental, and institutional levels.

Influencing factors may be that African Americans tend to get the most severe labels (McNeil & Kennedy, 1997). For example, Whitaker (2002) and others have been cited throughout this text indicating that African Americans and people with low incomes are more likely to be diagnosed with schizophrenia than those with higher incomes. Padgett et al. (1994) found that African Americans are less likely to use outpatient facilities but according to Snowden and Cheung (1990), they are more likely to be hospitalized in psychiatric facilities.

A RENEWED APPROACH

Adhering to two tenets of the life course perspective approach that incorporates history and culture (Hutchison, 2005), not repeating the difficulties of the past in the mental health area and embracing culturally sensitive services are essential. The general goal of the mental health system ought to be to assist African Americans in the most culturally sensitive manner possible

(Denby, Rocha, & Owens-Kane, 2004). Understanding the culture of African Americans will assist in providing culturally sensitive mental health services-when needed from the formal system. The following provides information about service delivery, research, and racism that might be helpful:

Service delivery. It is suggested that identifying the unique sociocultural needs of African Americans is important (Snowden & Hu, 1997; Wang, Berglund, & Kessler, 2001). Denby et al. (2004) suggest viewing environmental threats such as "poverty, discrimination, cultural bias, suicide, depression, physical health problems, substance abuse, and other more general factors that create stress" (p. 74). Gibson and McRoy (2004) recommend assisting clients with cultural maintenance, which values African and African-American's heritage. In addition, attending to language, behavior, coping style, and religious beliefs are essential (Wagner & Gartner, 1994). These authors note that the phrase "bad nerve" might be used to describe many thoughts, feelings, beliefs, and psychomotor states and behaviors. As stated previously, African Americans use their informal social support systems for mental health concerns. For example, those who are church-affiliated might use ministers who foster connections between mental health and spirituality (Mollica, Streets, Boscarino, & Redlich, 1986). Recent research has found that African Americans attributed spirituality as important in understanding and treating the cause of mental health difficulties (Millet, Sullivan, Schwebel, & Myers, 1996). Traditionally African Americans seek and obtain help for mental health problems from folk healers (Cheung & Snowden, 1990) and members of their families and church (Henderson & Primeaux, 1981).

Research. Studies on the mental health of African Americans must also take culture into account. Freeman and Logan (2004) list ten common errors made in research studies. Most of these are associated with using a dominant lens and ignoring cultural factors to assess people of African descent. Given the negative historical treatment to which African Americans were subjected, they ought not to be compared to other groups. Society's reliance on group comparative data is a flawed manner of conducting research. Yet it is currently seen as best practice and the gold standard. An alternative approach is to incorporate a cultural lens when studying African Americans that includes their values systems and respect within group diversity.

Racism. Racism continues to be a defining factor in mental health for African Americans. Rollock and Gordon (2000) list eight areas in mental health that are influenced by racism (pp. 7-8). These are:

1. The identification and interpretation of deviance and distress.
2. Definitions of psychological symptoms including the causes and cures.

3. Explanation of the etiology of mental disorder and deficiency.
4. Mental health evaluations that are designed to showcase the needs of disadvantaged groups.
5. Mental health service delivery lacking providers who are culturally similar to clients.
6. Racism that affects the institutional structure so that programs are designed without the economically disadvantaged in mind.
7. Diverse populations have been understudied in research projects.
8. Training in mental health services ignores social context and oppressed populations.

Being aware of how these eight areas continue to appear in the mental health service delivery system is important. In addition, Harrell (2000) identified six types of racism: Racism-related life events (significant life experiences that are time limited), vicarious racism experiences (observations and reports), daily racism microstresses (slights and exclusions), chronic-contextual stress (influence of social structures and political dynamics that must be coped with), collective experiences (observing the way in which racism affects the lives of those with whom we are connected), and transgenerational transmission (race-related stories that are passed down). Dealing with racism is a constant in the lives of African Americans. Finding ways to lessen its effects takes energy. Harrell (2000) suggest validating experiences of racism and using social support networks.

CONCLUSION

The information about the treatment of African Americans in the mental health system is parsimonious at best. What little information exists shows a history of exclusion and devaluation and their negative influences on the social construction of mental health. Attention to the historical underpinnings of how African-American mental health has been viewed, depicted, and postulated is crucial to supporting the renewed effort of greater cultural sensitivity in treatment approaches and practitioner attitudes.

CHAPTER SUMMARY

There are sociopolitical realities associated with race that are important to consider in any discussion of African-American mental health. Historically, slavery, emancipation, and the era of the twentieth century are defining periods influencing our understanding of African Americans and mental health. The degradation and humiliation of the slave era resulted in African Americans being viewed as inferior and mostly insane. This definition of sanity post-emancipation supported the notion that African Americans were of limited intelligence and docile behavior was the acceptable form of conduct. Thinking patterns of this nature only added to the racial disdain of the day. As time progressed in the twentieth century, socioeconomic conditions of African Americans became more visible; disparities in income, education, and mental health treatment were extreme. African Americans fell on the lower end of the socioeconomic scale in each of these areas.

A historical perspective of mental health of African Americans depicts the influence of race and race-related stress. African Americans have experienced difficulties in the mental health system: greater frequency of diagnosing disorders as severe, low utilization of services, and lack of culturally sensitive services. Hence, help-seeking behaviors on the part of African Americans continue to indicate a preference for using such informal social support systems as the church, friendship networks, and folk healers. Although these networks have sustained African Americans through the years, the need for service utilization of mental health professionals remains paramount but can only happen when cultural sensitivity is exercised. African-American consumers of mental health services have unique issues as members of a society where race continues to make a difference.

CLASSROOM ACTIVITIES

1. *Group activity: Measures of mental health*. Divide the class into four groups. Each group will list individual, family, community, and social factors that can negatively affect African-American families. Then, each group will list cultural values held by African Americans that might act as positive factors to strengthen families' abilities to cope. Instruct each group to discuss their lists. After all groups have reported, engage in a discussion about the process. What was new, encouraging, enlightening, and so on about the exercise?

2. *Entire class activity: Discussion on the contemporary influence of mental health history of African Americans*. List the following five questions on a board. Ask the students to take two minutes to review them and think/write responses to be discussed with the entire class. Discuss one question and students' responses before moving to the next.

Questions:
   a. Why were the behaviors of slaves associated with their mental health?
   b. What aspects of this conceptualization (behavior of slaves) continue for African Americans today?
   c. Consider responding to someone who states that African Americans are too aggressive. How would you respond in a way that would logically connect that view to the mental health history of African Americans?
   d. Sometimes, it is said that African Americans are too aware of slavery and ought not to revisit it as often as they do. In considering a historical perspective of mental health, provide a "yes—it is revisited too often" and "no—it is not revisited too often" response respectively.
   e. List the various types of racism and provide examples of them. What are other ways to intervene? Provide suggestions according to age, gender, geographical context, and so on.

3. *Class assignment: Increasing community-based mental health services to African Americans.* There is agreement in the literature that African Americans do not utilize mental health services at a high rate. While some use alternative approaches such as people in their informal social system, others go to their ministers. This assignment requires that you conduct research on this issue and develop a culturally sensitive program that might increase service utilization of this group. Students need to do the following steps, summarize them into a PowerPoint presentation, and present the project in class:
   a. Conduct a literature search on barriers to mental health use by African Americans including statistics (national, statewide, in your community of residence). Use no fewer than ten articles/chapters besides that chapter. What are the five major barriers? What is your interpretation of the statistics?
   b. Conduct a face-to-face or telephone interview with one person who is in an administrative position in the state and local mental health offices, respectively. What factors does each attribute to African Americans' low rate of mental health service utilization? What strategies have been tried to increase the utilization rate? If none, ask about the reasoning behind the inaction.
   c. From the information gathered, what aspects of a culturally sensitive service delivery system is needed to increase mental health service utilization by African Americans? What are the cost and benefits of your suggestions?
   d. Summarize the results of your work in a PowerPoint presentation. What did you learn from the literature and interviews?

REFERENCES

Boulware, L. E., Cooper, L. A., Ratner, L. E., LaVeist, T. A., & Powe, N. R. (2003). Race and trust in the health care system. *Public Health Report, 118*(4), 358-365.

Cheung, G. K., & Snowden, L. R. (1990). Community mental health and ethnic minority populations. *Community Mental Health Journal, 26,* 277-291.

Collins, K. S., Hughes, D. L., Coty, M. M., Ives, B. L., Edwards, J. N., & Tenney, K. (2002). *Diverse Communities, Common Concerns: Assessing Health Care Quality for Minority Americans.* New York: The Commonwealth Fund.

Denby, R., Rocha, C., & Owens-Kane, S. (2004). African American families, mental health, and living cooperatives: A program and research analysis. In E. M. Freeman & S. L. Logan (Eds.), *Reconceptualizing the Strengths and Common Heritage of Black Families: Practice, Research, and Policy Issues* (pp. 72-94). Springfield, IL: Charles C Thomas.

Fellin, P. (1996). *Mental Health and Mental Illness: Policies, Programs, and Services.* Belmont, CA: Thomson Brooks Cole.

Freeman, E. M., & Logan, S. L. (2004). Common heritage and diversity among black families and communities: An Africentric research paradigm. In E. M. Freeman & S. M. Logan (Eds.), *Reconceptualizing Strengths and Common Heritage of Black Families: Practice, Research, and Policy Issues* (pp. 5-24). Springfield, IL: Charles C Thomas.

Gibson, P. A., & McRoy, R. G. (2004). Cultural maintenance: Building on the common heritage of black families. In E. M. Freeman & S. M. Logan (Eds.), *Reconceptualizing the Strengths and Common Heritage of Black Families: Practice, Research, and Policy Issues* (pp. 237-265). Springfield, IL: Charles C Thomas.

Harrell, S. P. (2000). A multidimensional conceptualization of racism-related stress: Implications for the well-being of people of color. *American Journal of Orthopsychiatry, 70*(1), 42-57.

Henderson, G., & Primeaux, M. (1981). The importance of folk medicine. In G. Henderson & M. Primeaux (Eds.), *Transcultural Health Care* (pp. 59-77). Menlo Park, CA: Addison-Wesley Publishing.

Hines-Martin, V., Brown-Piper, A., Kin, S., & Malone, M. (2002). Enabling factors of Mental health service use among African Americans. *Archives of Psychiatric Nursing, 17*(5), 197-204.

Homma-True, R., Greene, B., Lopez, S. R., & Trimble, J. E. (1993). Ethnocultural diversity in clinical psychology. *The Clinical Psychologist, 46,* 50-63.

Hutchison, E. D. (2005). The life course perspective: A promising approach for bridging the micro and macro worlds for social workers. *Families in Society, 86*(1), 143-152.

Jones, B. E., & Gray, B. A. (1986). Problems in diagnosing schizophrenia and affective disorders among blacks. *Hospital and Community Psychiatry, 37*(1), 61-65.

Lewin, M. E., & Altman, S. (2000). *American's Health Care Safety Net: Intact But Endangered.* Washington, DC: National Academy Press.

Martin, J. M., & Martin, E. P. (1985). *The Helping Tradition in the Black Family and Community.* Washington, DC: National Association of Social Workers.

McLeod, J. D., & Shanahan, M. J. (1996). Trajectories of poverty and children's mental health. *Journal of Health and Social Behavior, 37,* 207-220.

McNeil, J. S., & Kennedy, R. (1997). Mental health services to minority groups of color. In T. R. Watkins & J. W. Callicutt (Eds.), *Mental Health Policy and Practice Today* (pp. 235-257). Thousand Oaks, CA: Sage.

Millet, P. E., Sullivan, B. F., Schwebel, A. I., & Myers, L. J. (1996). Black Americans' and white Americans' views of the etiology and treatment of mental health problems. *Community Mental Health Journal, 32*(3), 235-242.

Mollica, R. F., Streets, F. J., Boscarino, J., & Redlich, F. C. (1986). A community study of formal pastoral counseling activities of the clergy. *American Journal of Psychiatry, 143,* 323-328.

Neighbors, H. W. (1985). Seeking professional help for personal problems: Black Americans' use of health and mental health services. *Community Mental Health Journal, 21*(3), 156-166.

Padgett, S. K., Patrick, C., Burns, B. J., & Schlesinger, H. J. (1994). Ethnicity and the use of outpatient mental health services in a national insured population. *American Journal of Public Health, 84*(2), 222-226.

Parham, T. A. (2002). Counseling African Americans: The current state of affairs. In T. A. Parham (Ed.), *Counseling Persons of African Descent* (pp. 1-9). Thousand Oaks, CA: Sage.

Rollock, D., & Gordon, E. W. (2000). Racism and mental health into the 21st century: Perspectives and parameters. *American Journal of Orthopsychiatry, 70*(1), 5-134.

Schiele, J. H. (2000). *Human Services and the Africentric Paradigm.* New York: Haworth Press.

Snowden, L. R. (1998). Managed care and ethnic minority populations. *Administration and Policy in Mental Health, 25,* 125-131.

Snowden, L. R., & Cheung, F. K. (1990). Use of inpatient mental health services by members of ethnic minority groups. *American Psychologist, 45,* 347-355.

Snowden, L. R., & Hu, T. (1997). Use of impatient mental health services among the severely mentally ill. *Journal of Community Psychology, 25*(3), 235-247.

U.S. Department of Health and Human Services. (2001). *Mental Health: Culture, Race, and Ethnicity—A Supplement to Mental Health: A Report of the Surgeon General.* Rockville, MD: U.S. Department of Health and Human Services, Substance, Abuse and Mental Health Services Administration, Center for Mental Health Services.

Vega, W. A., & Rumbaut, R. G. (1991). Ethnic minorities and mental health. *Annual Review of Sociology, 17,* 351-383.

Wagner, J., & Gartner, C. (1994). Special Report: Highlights of the 45th Institute on Hospital and Community Psychiatry. *Hospital and Community Psychiatry, 45*(1), 11-16.

Wang, P., Berglund, P., & Kessler, R. (2001). Recent care of common mental disorders in the United States. *Journal of General Internal Medicine, 15*(5), 284-292.

Whitaker, R. (2002). *Mad in America: Bad Science, Bad Medicine, and the Enduring Mistreatment of the Mentally Ill.* Cambridge, MA: Perseus Publishing.

Wideman, J. E. (1984). *Brothers and Keepers.* New York: Holt, Rinehart and Winston.

Chapter 2

A Conceptual and Theoretical Framework for Understanding African-American Mental Health

Ramona W. Denby

As a cultural group, it could be argued that African Americans continue to experience more psychosocial stressors than any ethnic group in American society. Devalued social status, economic and resource deficiencies, limited access to health care, family structural changes, low-income neighborhoods, and the presence of racism and discrimination continue to plague the day-to-day existence of many African Americans. As these issues play themselves out in the lives of African Americans, many individuals cope very well while others fall prey to various mental health concerns. Mental health issues such as depression, suicidal ideation, and drug abuse are rising health concerns for many African Americans. Whereas one might speculate that these mental health issues are more prevalent among African-American young males, women, children, and the elderly are also experiencing more pervasive problems than ever before.

Prevalence rates of depressive symptoms among African Americans are beginning to outpace that of the general population (Miller et al., 2004). The well-known African-American psychiatrist James Comer (1974) noted that the level of individual apathy, "seemingly laziness," and community decay found among African Americans is the result of feelings of hopelessness and depression. Given the magnitude of the problem, researchers are beginning to address the differential manifestations of depressive illness (Baker, 2001). Studies on depression contain better epidemiologic data and are better able to discern subgroup differences within the African-American population. In other words, research now addresses the manner in which depression exists among males, females, children, and the elderly (Baker,

Mental Health Care in the African-American Community
© 2007 by The Haworth Press, Inc. All rights reserved.
doi:10.1300/5364_02

2001; Brown, 1990; Cochran, Brown, & McGregor, 1999; Gary & Yarandi, 2004; Lichtenberg, Brown, Jackson, & Washington, 2004). For example, Gary and Yarandi (2004) discovered that prevailing measures of depression (e.g., Beck Depression Inventory-II) can generate useful data about the manner in which symptoms are expressed in African-American women. The consequences of such mental health conditions as depression are profound. Depression is associated with physical health problems and it decreases one's overall functioning and level of productivity (LaVeist, Bowie, & Cooley-Quille, 2000; Olfson et al., 2002). (See Chapter 5 for further discussion on depression.)

Suicide, another mental health issue, has increased dramatically within the African-American community (Gary, Yarandi, & Scruggs, 2003; Smith & Johns, 1995). Suicide risk is greatest for African Americans aged twenty to twenty-four, followed by those aged twenty-five to thirty-four, and finally those aged thirty-five to forty-four (Gary, Yarandi, & Scruggs, 2003). Kimbrough, Molock, and Walton (1998) found that African-American college students with nonsupportive families and friends are more likely to express suicidal ideations and depression. Another African-American subpopulation of concern with respect to suicide is the elderly. Suicide rates for elderly Black men have increased (Alston, Rankin, & Harris, 1995). (See Chapter 10 for further discussion on suicide and Chapter 11 for information on the elderly.) In reference to alcoholism and/or drugs (see Chapter 7), many researchers cite overall negative consequences to African Americans (Boyd, Phillips, & Dorsey, 2003; Brinson, 1995; Fishbein & Perez, 2000; Gil, Vega, & Turner, 2002; Petry, 2002; Substance Abuse and Mental Health Services Administration [SAMHSA], 2004; Zule, Flannery, Wechsberg, & Lam, 2002). The rate of illicit drug use for African Americans is currently 8.7 percent of its population (SAMHSA, 2004). Drug use often involves needle sharing and illicit sexual activity in exchange for drug use. A potentially dire consequence of these behaviors is the contraction of HIV/AIDS. African-American women are one of the largest groups to contract HIV/ AIDS as a result of drug use (Beatty, 2003; also see Chapter 18). Finally, mental health problems and dysfunctions often coexist with other conditions, namely homelessness (Feitel, Margetson, Chamas, & Lipman, 1992), incarceration (Teplin, 1999), foster care (Garland, 2001), violence (Fitzpatrick & Boldizar, 1993), and substance abuse (SAMHSA, 2004).

To mitigate the affects of poor mental well-being and to restore overall functioning, African Americans have relied on their resiliency, coping skills, spirituality, and the support found in informal systems. The use of social supports, albeit sometimes intangible, has been a long-standing tradition that has preserved the psychological well-being of African Americans (Bailey,

Wolfe, & Wolfe, 1996). In addition, African Americans buffer their psyche through an intact sense of self and high self-esteem (Gray-Little & Hafdahl, 2000).

Despite the inherent abilities of African Americans and the resources that exist naturally within their communities, they sometimes seek professional mental health intervention from formal sources (Snowden, 1998). Still, many African Americans do not successfully complete their treatment in private agency settings.

Help-seeking patterns for African Americans tend not to mirror those of their European-American counterparts. Various reasons for African Americans' hesitancy to seek formal mental health services have been given, including cultural mistrust of White mental health clinicians (Whaley, 2001) and the manner in which services are structured, organized, and delivered (Diala et al., 2000). Given these findings and the mental health needs of the African-American community, it is paramount that investigation into the development of "alternative" mental health programming continues.

This chapter proposes an alternative approach to conceptualizing and structuring mental health programming that will meet the needs of African Americans. Depression, suicide, substance abuse, and other mental well-being threats provide the context for which the issue of alternative mental health programming for African Americans is explored. The conceptual framework offered in this chapter is undergirded by a major assumption. Threats to mental well-being are partly the result of social-environmental conditions that work counter to the needs of African Americans. With this assumption in mind, the chapter includes a critical analysis of four major mental health programming issues. First, a historical analysis of the problem of service "mismatch" is provided. Next, the author reviews the philosophical and theoretical underpinnings of traditional mental health programming. In addition, cultural competence is explored as a possible means of restructuring and reorganizing services within human service disciplines like social work. Finally, an alternative framework and conceptualization model for the development of mental health programs that specifically address the needs of African Americans is offered.

REVIEW OF THE LITERATURE

Mismatch Between Traditional Programming and African Americans' Mental Health Needs

This section contains a historical perspective of the problem of service "mismatch." This discussion is followed by a critical analysis of the philosophical and theoretical base upon which current mental health programming rests. This section concludes with a discussion of the implications and consequences of mismatched services.

The Historical Service Mismatch

Social work's departure from its historical service charge. The problem of inadequate service provisions to suit African Americans' social support needs is as old as the social work profession itself. Much of the African-American service needs surround environmental interventions. Although social workers are environmental change agents, they have historically concentrated much of their efforts toward "curing" the predicaments of "self" as opposed to eradicating socioenvironmental problems that compromised a client's internal self. Scholars such as Leiby (1978) have noted that early social work should not be characterized as the champion of reform and advocacy for the poor. Leiby believed that traditional social workers epitomized the virtues of social conformity and performed their duties on behalf of the ruling elite. Likewise, Lasch-Quinn (1993) blamed social work's turn-of-the-century focus on individual casework as a cause for the profession's neglect of the sociostructural issues that African Americans faced. Similarly, Specht and Courtney (1994) believe that "social work has abandoned its mission to help the poor and oppressed and to build communality" (p. 4).

Before social work can establish culturally responsive programming, it must fulfill its charge of advocacy and empowerment, and it must establish social reform, social justice, and social development. Historically, social work's charge was hindered because of its alliance to academic psychology, which proved culturally biased and heavily informed by social Darwinism. Guthrie (1991) states that four nativistic themes were created and that they cast African Americans negatively: (1) Darwin's origin of the species, which implied that African Americans were deficient and pathological, (2) Galton's eugenics, which maintained that African Americans were intellectually inferior, (3) McDougall's theory of instincts, which stereotyped African Americans as lazy and childlike, and (4) Mendelian genetics, which affected African Americans by providing a basis on which researchers could argue that genetic differences were attributable to psychological conditions.

Historical service provisions for African Americans. Historically, the true providers of services to African Americans were often outside the realm of formal social work. Lasch-Quinn (1993) has examined the use of settlement houses with African Americans and, in doing so, has challenged historical settlements in terms of their efficacy with African Americans. She has also chronicled settlement movements that African Americans developed and ran. Lasch-Quinn (1993) credits the South, Black churches, schools, and community groups as critical elements in carrying out a large portion of the settlement work for African Americans when traditional settlements (operated by movement leaders of the National Federation of Settlements) subscribed to the prevailing view of African Americans as culturally deficient. Moreover, Lasch-Quinn has established the fact that African Americans were largely rejected or segregated by traditional settlement movements. In her book, Lasch-Quinn recounts the Black settlements that did exist to serve African Americans. These settlements were largely borne of African Americans' own initiative and energy. Such settlements include Wharton Centre in Philadelphia; southern school settlements, such as Calhous School in Lowndes County, Alabama; the People's Village School in Mt. Meigs, Alabama; the Penn School on St. Helena Island, South Carolina; and the Tuskegee-Hampton model (Boris, 1995). Also significant to note is Lasch-Quinn's mention of African-American female activists in the establishment of social welfare provisions during the settlement-work era. These activists (under the auspices of such groups as the Women's Home Missionary Society of the Methodist Episcopal Church, South; the YWCA; and the Neighborhood Union in Atlanta) carried the initial battle cry for service provisions directed to African Americans.

Another early pioneer in settlement work with African Americans is Birdye Henrietta Haynes. Haynes was the lead settlement worker for two prominent social settlements for African Americans in the early 1900s. Her first assignment was the Wendell Phillips Settlement in Chicago. The second was the Lincoln House in New York. Haynes persevered and proved a strong advocate for African Americans even among the biased practices of the social reformers of the Progressive Era. Carlton-LaNey (1994) notes that this first-generation social worker's role in the settlement-house movement should be considered especially significant, given the limitations imposed by racism and segregation.

In an examination of social welfare services to African Americans during the antebellum period through the Progressive Era, Weaver (1992) finds that a mixture of White philanthropy and reliance on African-American mutual-aid networks abounded. For example, during the antebellum period, free African Americans' mutual-aid societies and some Northern White philanthropists served African Americans. Much of the work accomplished for African Americans during this era was carried out by church-based mutual-aid groups (e.g., the Free Africa Society, Philadelphia 1787) and fraternal orders (e.g., the Order of Masons, the first African-American fraternal order, established in 1775). In contrast, Weaver (1992) notes that while White philanthropic groups provided assistance to African Americans during this era, it was done in exchange for religious compliance. African Americans were often subjected to the religious teachings of the philanthropists, which Davis (1980) suggests eventually created African-American dependence on their White sponsoring agents and a subsequent disagreement among African Americans about the role that White philanthropy should occupy.

During the Civil War and Reconstruction Era, a great deal of social support to African Americans came via the Freedmen's Aid Society. The Freedman's Bureau was a resource base when the larger public domain concerned itself not with welfare relief, but with the establishment and continuation of agriculture and caste systems (Colby, 1984; Franklin, 1970; Rabinowitz, 1974). Weaver (1992) notes that specific to mental health–related services, the South, after much reluctance and government prompting, established the first service provisions for African Americans. Specifically, Tennessee established the first facility for African Americans in 1866 (Rabinowitz, 1974). Other states, such as Texas, followed suit through the provision of "separate but equal" lunatic asylums (Colby, 1984). However, these services were usually minimal, deplorable, and discriminatory. The Freedman's Bureau was still one of the key resources used by African Americans, because no adequate formal mental health services existed despite legislative prompting for such (Colby, 1984). During the Gilded Age, Weaver (1992) notes that public social services segregated African Americans and deemed them undeserving. As a result, organizations such as Northern White charitable groups, the African-American church, and fraternal orders became even more vigilant and relentless in their support of African Americans. It was during this era that groups like the Women's Club of 1870, and African-American agencies such as the Carrie Steele Logan Orphanage, the Good Samaritan Order, the Pickford Tuberculosis Sanitarium, and the Louisiana Association for the Benefit of Colored Orphans, were established (Weaver, 1992).

Finally, during the Progressive Era, fraternal orders, churches, and mutual-aid groups continued to be the basis of social support for African Americans. However, during this era, indigenous groups took on the agenda of pride, solidarity, and political reform (Weaver, 1992). Although this period was known for settlement work and charity organization societies, their work had little impact on African Americans and often disenfranchised them because of the social Darwinist perspective that was being embraced (Weaver, 1992). The National Urban League was a product of this era. This organization served the needs of African Americans and trained African-American social workers, but it was also subjected to the criticism that it alienated traditional mutual-aid groups as the result of its more contemporary methods of practice (Weaver, 1992).

PHILOSOPHICAL AND THEORETICAL UNDERPINNINGS OF TRADITIONAL MENTAL HEALTH PROGRAMMING

The literature review of traditional mental health programming was guided by a ten-question model developed by Denby, Rocha, and Owens-Kane (2004). In doing so, selected literature is discussed according to overall findings and implications for African Americans. The questions were selected because they frame the manner in which the current structure has evolved along fundamental service features. Further, the ten questions explore the philosophical and value base upon which traditional programs rest. Table 2.1 provides an overview of the findings related to the following questions: (1) How are individuals in need of services viewed? (2) What is the structure of program authority? (3) What is the value of expertise? (4) How is the need for assistance viewed? (5) What is the ideological base? (6) What is the role of authority? (7) How are problems viewed? (8) What is the nature of the worker-client relationship? (9) What assumptions are made about human nature? and (10) What is the purpose of classification?

How are individuals in need of services viewed? Traditional mental health programming takes a very "medical model" approach with individuals who are in need of help. Individuals seeking services are seen as patients. Indeed, it has been noted that at the turn of the century, individuals who required social, mental, or general supportive intervention were viewed as "social inferiors" (Abel, 1978). Historically, even the progressive reformers viewed those in need of services as irrational, failures, and childlike (Barnett, 1886, as cited in Abel, 1978; Karier, 1973). In general, individuals in need were unworthy and thought to be nonlegitimate citizens (Abel, 1978).

Particular to African Americans, it has been noted that turn-of-the-century sentiment viewed them generally negatively, often characterizing them as deviants, weak, dependent, and pathological (Martin & Martin, 1985; Snowden, 1998, 2001). As was the case historically, those individuals in need, and particularly African Americans, were viewed as being in need of a cultural rebirth (Abel, 1978). In other words, individuals were viewed as tabulae rasae (a blank slate on which middle-class values could be inscribed) (Abel, 1978).

What is the structure of program authority? Traditional mental health service programming closely adheres to distinct bureaucratic lines whereby decisions affecting service participants are imposed upon them by those "in charge." There exists a clear program hierarchy of administrators, supervisors, and clinical staff members who possess their own ruling domain and rarely relinquish their control to establish a more participatory process.

What is the value of expertise? In keeping with the formal structure found in traditional mental health services, programs employ recognized and

TABLE 2.1. Ten philosophical underpinnings that lead to a service—delivery mismatch.

	Traditional mental health programming	African Americans' service needs
How are individuals in need of services viewed?	viewed as patients	viewed as citizens
What is the structure of program authority?	distinct/hierarchical	democratic functioning
What is the value of expertise?	expert-role linking	peer-level linking
How is the need for assistance viewed?	individual self-help stressed	use of mutual aid stressed
What is the ideological base?	conservative values	service values
What is the role of authority?	paternalistic, governmental oversight	indigenous leadership and self-regulation
How are problems viewed?	attributed to individual dynamics	attributed to relational dynamics
What is the nature of the worker-client relationship?	directive	egalitarian
What is the assumption made about human nature?	fundamental belief in the sociological view of human nature	fundamental belief in the basic worth and inherent value of people
What is the purpose of classification?	provide a labeling scheme based on client behaviors, characteristics, and attributes	provide mutual recognition (groupings are based on common heritage and/or area of need)

legitimized experts. Practitioners, administrators, and other such "experts" receive legitimacy based on socially governed criteria, such as education, ranking, financial class, privilege, race, and cultural background.

How is the need for assistance viewed? Traditional mental health service programming emphasizes and values an individual's ability to help himself or herself. Independence is looked upon favorably, while non–self-sufficient individuals are blamed for their conditions.

What is the ideological base? The core ideological base of traditional mental health service programming is premised on the overall sociopolitical conservative value base. In a study of the relationship between ideology and service in social welfare in New York, Epstein (1988) found that 72 percent of the directors of the largest and most important service agencies characterized their political orientation as conservative. In this same study, Epstein could not find one respondent who could agree with the sentiment that agencies' missions should be to provide core services on the basis of a person's right to the service.

What is the role of authority? Traditional mental health service programs have historically embraced the role of the paternalistic, government overseer of public resources. Decisions related to service provisions and eligibility are generally made by legitimized program authorities as opposed to program beneficiaries.

How are problems viewed? In keeping with the "patient" depiction of individuals, the problems endured by those in need of services are often attributed to their own shortcomings, maladies, and personal dysfunction. The "disease model," whereby the root cause of symptomatology lies as biological phenomena, is a prevailing feature (DHHS, 2001).

What is the nature of the worker-client relationship? In traditional mental health service programming, service workers have often been quite directive and prescriptive in their approach to "clients." Clinicians sometime assess symptoms and treatment in a manner counter to the perceptions of their clients (DHHS, 2001).

What assumptions are made about human nature? Traditional mental health programming has by and large subscribed to the sociological view of human nature, which assumes inherent human deceit and weakness.

What is the purpose of classification? In traditional mental health programming, classification schemes establish a common language by which client behaviors, characteristics, and attributes become recognizable and uniform. This classification scheme has resulted in the labeling of those in need of intervention. Researchers have noted that the labeling of clients as mentally ill is possible because supposedly "normal" people have created symbolic structures to represent their view of people who present differently from themselves (DHHS, 2001; Foucault, 1965; Goffman, 1959; Helm, 1985).

PRESENT-DAY ATTEMPTS TO REFORM TRADITIONAL PROGRAM PHILOSOPHIES AND THEORETICAL UNDERPINNINGS

Organizational characteristics and culture have a profound impact on client outcomes (Glisson & Hemmelgarn, 1998; Glisson & James, 2002;

Kondrat, Greene, & Winbush, 2002; Yoo, 2002). One of the greatest consequences of using traditional mental health programming when treating African Americans can be viewed in service utilization patterns, where there is great disparity between African Americans and non-African Americans. It has been established that people of color are less likely than their White counterparts to seek or sustain involvement in traditional mental health programs, they are underrepresented in service delivery, and they are underserved (Kessler et al., 1996; Parham, White, & Ajamu, 2000; Vega et al., 1998; Zhang et al., 1998). There are many barriers to African Americans seeking mental health services, including mistrust and the mismatch of services to needs. Despite changes in the structure and organization of mental health service delivery, people of color (e.g., African Americans) continue to mistrust professionals and the organizations they represent (Cooper-Patrick et al., 1999; DHHS, 1999; Whaley, 2001). The reasons for this mistrust are varied but certainly stem from historical abuses and the mistreatment that African Americans receive currently in mental health programs (Bell, 1996; LaVeist, Diala, & Jarrett, 2000; Neal-Barnett & Smith, 1997).

The likelihood of differential diagnosis is another consequence that ensues from mental health programming that is based on traditional philosophical underpinnings. There is strong evidence to suggest the presence of differential diagnosis patterns among African-American clients (Baker & Bell, 1999; Borowsky et al., 2000; Neal-Barnett & Smith, 1997; Takeuchi & Uehara, 1996; Young et al., 2001. Also, see Chapter 3). Researchers (DHHS, 2001) attribute the disparate treatment that African Americans receive to four main reasons: (1) White therapists' lack of understanding of African-American social, economic, and cultural customs; (2) the therapist's lack of insight into his or her own feeling regarding the effects of race and class; (3) the use of theoretical underpinnings developed primarily for White clients; and (4) the denial of the existence of race and class differences.

There have been modest attempts to address African Americans' underutilization of mental health services. Specifically, researchers and practitioners have attempted to implement service-delivery models thought to be more culturally responsive (Singleton-Bowie, 1995; Segal et al., 1996; Sue & Sue, 1999). For example, there have been attempts to match clients to therapists of the same ethnic background (Sue, 1998) and some programs have provided counseling as opposed to drug treatment (Cooper-Patrick et al., 1997; Dwight-Johnson, Sherbourne, Liao, & Wells, 2000). The latest trend in mental health service provisions is what is referred to as *system of care* (Anderson, Wright, Kooreman, Mohr, & Russel, 2003; Brannan, Baughman, Reed, & Katz-Leavy, 2002; Pires, 2002; Stroul, 2002; Stroul & Friedman, 1986). The system of care framework represents a philosophical change in the organization and structure of mental health services for children. The components of the system of care model include community-based services, child-centered and family focused principles, cultural competence, comprehensive services, individualized services, least restrictive services, services that involve coordination and collaboration, child and family as partners, and early identification and intervention. The availability of federal funding has produced a major proliferation in the development of mental health services that are based on the system of care framework. Despite the prevalence of system of care models and the support of funding, there is little known about the effectiveness of this framework in producing positive outcomes for African-American clients.

Further, despite the recent efforts at mental health service reform, African Americans are reported to receive the least amount of benefit from services (Roth et al., 1996; Segal et al., 1996; Singleton-Bowie, 1995). It is obvious that further work is needed to develop and implement mental health program models that improve upon the failures of traditional approaches. Expanded and alternative mental health programming must match services with the specific needs of African Americans.

EXPANDED APPROACHES TO CONCEPTUALIZING MENTAL HEALTH PROGRAMMING FOR AFRICAN AMERICANS

The Current-Day Service Mismatch: Cultural Insensitivity

The preceding sections involved a review of the manner in which mental health services to African Americans have been unavailable, or at best, mismatched. Social work's departure from its charge and program developers' minimal attention to the importance of cultural values, ideologies, and the need for culturally specific programming has led to a mismatch of services to African Americans. The establishment of a fair and just system of care for people of color within the public mental health system continues to be elusive (Kondrat, Greene, & Winbush, 2002; Semke, 1999). Specific to children, there is clear evidence that the phenomenon of service mismatch is perpetuated through a practice of differential treatment (Barbell & Freundlich, 2001; Carrasco, 2004; Gary, Yarandi, & Scruggs, 2003; Gibbs, 1997; Gibbs & Bankhead, 2001; Gibbs & Fuery, 1994; Gibbs & Huang, 2003; Hawkins & Salisbury, 1983; Isaacs-Shockley, Cross, Bazron, Dennis, & Benjamin, 1996; McLoyd, 1990; Sheppard & Benjamin-Coleman, 2001; Slade, 2004; Stehno, 1990; Tharp, 1991).

How can services be structured in such a way that they are more culturally competent or culturally responsive? Defining what constitutes culturally responsive or competent service is not an easy task. What complicates this endeavor is the fact that there has been very limited attention devoted to this area of need. However, a handful of significant works, specific to mental health, have begun to identify a core set of values that enhance agencies' abilities to render culturally appropriate services (Benjamin & Isaacs-Shockley, 1996; Gibbs & Huang, 1990; Isaacs & Benjamin, 1991; Isaacs-Shockley et al., 1996). Isaacs and Benjamin (1991) conducted a national study of mental health programs to identify models that strive for cultural responsiveness. Salient findings relating to culturally competent programs or culturally responsive programs include the following provisions: (1) ensure participation of people of color at all organizational levels, (2) implement culturally responsive staffing patterns, (3) provide culturally responsive services, (4) work with natural informal support systems, (5) incorporate cultural knowledge into practice, and (6) acknowledge the issues and impacts of biculturalism.

The need for culturally specific programming, the benefits that result, and the methods of implementing such programming are well established (Benjamin & Isaacs-Shockley, 1996; Isaacs-Shockley et al., 1996). The efficacy of training mental health professionals about the importance of culturally appropriate services was revealed in an examination of a demonstration project in which Lefley (1984) found that such training resulted in a significant increase in minorities' use of services and a decrease in client dropout rates. Other examples of successful programs include Black Family Development, Inc. (premised on the principle of family empowerment) and Progressive Life Center, Inc. (founded on the principles of Nguzo Saba) (Benjamin & Isaacs-Shockley, 1996). Given that the needs of African Americans and the general population differ, programs should involve treatment specificity.

CONCEPTUALIZATION OF ALTERNATIVE MENTAL HEALTH PROGRAMMING: ESSENTIAL COMPONENTS

The chapters contained in this text involve a review and discussion of a range of threats to African Americans' mental well-being, including suicide, depression, substance abuse, youth violence, and child welfare system involvement. A culturally responsive framework for structuring services to address these needs is warranted. In this section the author offers an overarching three-pronged framework: a historical perspective, a theoretical and conceptual framework, and intervention strategies. This proposed mental health service framework, as illustrated in Exhibit 2.1, includes six major components: (1) cultural specificity, (2) strengths and empowerment orientation, (3) solution-focused intervention, (4) localized and indigenous regulations, (5) socioeconomic responsiveness, and (6) evidence-based cultural models.

Cultural Specificity

First, the vast majority of mental health programs are not culturally specific. Programs must be predicated on the needs, characteristics, and values of African-American individuals and families.

Strengths-Oriented, Empowerment-Based Intervention

Second, many programs designed to meet mental health needs operate from a deficit mode instead of a strengths-oriented empowerment base. Programs that adhere to a traditional philosophical base and work from a recognition of deficits are particularly bothersome where African Americans are concerned, because there can be a tendency to misinterpret African-American attributes and behaviors as problems when indeed they can be strengths. Because of the historical relationship that African Americans have had with traditional service structures, skills inherent in the "strengths perspective" (such as validation and acceptance) are of even greater importance.

Solution-Focused Intervention

Third, another shortcoming found in traditional mental health programming is the lack of solution-focused intervention. Traditional programming

---

EXHIBIT 2.1. Why Developmental Health Programming Specific to African Americans?

1. There is a lack of cultural specificity in current programming.
2. There is a need for strengths-oriented, empowerment-based programming.
3. There is a lack of solution-focused programming.
4. There is a need for localized and indigenously governed programming.
5. There is a need for socioeconomically responsive intervention.
6. There is a need for culturally specific models of intervention to become evidence based.

that concentrates heavily on intrapsychic self-reflection often omits practical means of alleviating areas of need. Skill-based and behavior-focused interventions are needed.

Localized and Indigenously Driven Regulations

Fourth, traditional mental health programming can be directed too much by the government, allowing little opportunity for self-regulation. Given the little autonomy and ownership that African Americans have in the shaping of societal structure, it is imperative that they share in the development of alternative mental health programming. As the architects of new programs, African-American clients may feel a sense of ownership and heightened investment and commitment to program goals.

Socioeconomically Driven Interventions

Fifth, there is a need to develop alternative mental health programming that addresses African Americans' needs, given the changing sociodemographic trends experienced by all age brackets and both genders within this population. Economic hardships prevent some African Americans from seeking needed mental health services. There is a need for African Americans and those social agents who have their best interests at heart to proactively develop programming whose survival is not solely contingent upon government funding patterns and whose eligibility criteria are not determined by those patterns.

Evidence-Based Cultural Models

Last, research is needed to examine the efficacy of mental health treatment models that purport to be culturally specific. Research should also include analyses of the costs and benefits of delivering culturally appropriate models of intervention (DHHS, 2001). Finally, mental health programming must support the training and development of staff so that evidence-based models can be delivered with high fidelity.

CONCLUSION

Given the current mental health and social support conditions of African Americans and the need for the development of alternative programming, the time for action has never been more pressing. However, prior to intervening, practitioners must first explore how and why traditional programming became seemingly nonresponsive to African-American clients' needs. In addition, practitioners must gain a full appreciation of the type of program structures that are better suited for African Americans. The preceding model contains conceptual points that attempt to better align programs to African-American clients' needs.

CHAPTER SUMMARY

Members of the African-American community, including children, adolescents, adults, and families, face tremendous social-environmental stressors and hardships that often lead to the need for mental health intervention. Although there are varied and significant mental health conditions experienced by African Americans, this chapter has used substance abuse, suicide, and depression, and their related consequences, as a point of reference and analysis. The major premise of the chapter is that the current mental health conditions and social support needs of African Americans are not adequately addressed by present-day programming and treatment models. An "alternative" approach to conceptualizing mental health programming, more conducive to the needs of African Americans, is needed. In support of these postulates, the author provides a critical analysis of four major mental health programming issues.

First, a historical analysis of the problem of service "mismatch" is provided, prompting the question: "How did mental health service provisions and African-American clients' needs become so mismatched?" Through a critical review of the literature, the author concludes that the social work profession departed from its original mission, which was to safeguard social justice and to advocate for service equity. Following this critique, the author surveys the literature and briefly summarizes the history of services that have been available to African Americans. This historical review spans the antebellum period through the Progressive Era.

Second, to establish the need for alternative mental health programming for African Americans, the author reviews the philosophical and theoretical underpinnings of traditional mental health programming. Ten fundamental service features are used to illustrate the disparity that exists between current mental health programming and the needs of African Americans.

Third, the service "mismatch" that has existed historically continues today in the form of "cultural incompetence." Today's practitioners must understand why the problem of service mismatch persists. To comprehend the problem as it exists today, practitioners must explore the issue of cultural competence within their respective disciplines.

Last, an alternative framework and conceptualization model for the development of mental health programs that specifically address the needs of African Americans is offered. A culturally responsive mental health program can be conceptualized along six essential elements: (1) cultural specificity, (2) strengths-orientation, (3) solution-focused intervention, (4) localized and indigenously driven regulation, (5) socioeconomically responsive intervention, and (6) evidence-based cultural models.

DISCUSSION QUESTIONS

1. It has been well established that the extraneous social-environmental conditions that African Americans face can sometimes lead to the need for mental health services. Discuss three of the most pervasive mental health conditions that exist in the African-American community today. Your discussion should include a review of trends, prevalence rates, and gender patterns.
2. The author argues that there is a "mismatch" between traditional mental health programming and the mental health needs of African Americans. The case for the mismatch assertion is supported through a critical analysis of social work's departure from its original service mission. In addition, evidence of the mismatch is found in the author's review of historical service provisions.

   Debate #1: Debate whether social work has departed from its historical charge, and in doing so abandoned the needs of such disenfranchised groups as the African-American mentally ill.

   Debate #2: Take and defend a position concerning the historical impact that African-American mutual-aid networks versus White philanthropic groups had in supporting the mental health needs of the African-American community.
3. The author makes the case that the philosophical and value base upon which mental health programs and services are structured can be assessed by considering ten major questions. Select a mental health agency within your local community. Assess your chosen agency on the basis of the ten questions listed in Table 2.1. Based on your analysis, to what extent do you think the selected agency is structured to address the needs of African-American clients?
4. Discuss some of the essential components inherent in a mental health program that is considered to be culturally competent.

5. Alternative mental health programming thought to be more responsive to the needs of the African-American community includes a strong focus on strength-based, empowerment-focused intervention. Discuss some of the strengths inherent in the African-American community that could serve as a springboard for the development of mental health programs.

REFERENCES

Abel, E. K. (1978). Middle-class culture for the urban poor: The educational thought of Samuel Barnett. *Social Service Review,* 596-620.

Alston, M. H., Rankin, S. H., & Harris, C. A. (1995). Suicide in African American elderly. *Journal of Black Studies, 26*(1), 31-35.

Anderson, J. A., Wright, E. R., Kooreman, H. E., Mohr, W. K., & Russell, L. A. (2003). The Dawn Project: A model for responding to the needs of children with emotional and behavioral challenges and their families. *Community Mental Health Journal, 39*(1), 63-74.

Bailey, D., Wolfe, D., & Wolfe, C. R. (1996). The contextual impact of social support across race and gender: Implications for African American women in the workplace. *Journal of Black Studies, 26*(3), 287-307.

Baker, F. M. (2001). Diagnosing depression in African Americans. *Community Mental Health Journal, 37*(1), 31-38.

Baker, F. M., & Bell, C. C. (1999). Issues in the psychiatric treatment of African Americans. *Psychiatric Services, 50,* 362-368.

Barbell, K., & Freundlich, M. (2001). Foster Care Today. Casey Family Programs National Center for Resource Family Support. Available at: www.casey.org/cnc. Accessed October 20, 2005.

Barnett, S. A. (1886). Barnett papers to Francis Gilmore Barnett, July 3, 1886. In E. K. Abel (Ed.). (1978), Middle-class culture for the urban poor: The educational thought of Samuel Barnett. *Social Service Review,* 596-620.

Beatty, L. A. (2003). Substance abuse, disabilities, and Black women: An issue worth exploring. *Women & Therapy, 26*(3/4), 223-257.

Bell, C. C. (1996). Pimping the African American community. *Psychiatric Medicine, 47,* 1025.

Benjamin, M. P., & Isaacs-Shockley, M. (1996). Culturally competent service approaches. In E. A. Stroul (Ed.), *Children's Mental Health: Creating Systems of Care in a Changing Society* (pp. 475-491). Baltimore: Paul H. Brookes.

Boris, E. (1995). Unwed and unwanted? New perspectives on social welfare. *Journal of Policy History, 7*(3), 356-375.

Borowsky, S. J., Rubenstein, L. V., Meredith, L. S., Camp, P., Jackson-Triche, M., & Wells, K. B. (2000). Who is at risk of non-detection of mental health problems in primary care? *Journal of General Internal Medicine, 15,* 381-388.

Boyd, M. R., Phillips, K., & Dorsey, C. J. (2003). Alcohol and other drug disorders, comorbidity, and violence: Comparison of rural African American and Caucasian women. *Archives of Psychiatric Nursing, 17*(6), 249-258.

Brannan, A. M., Baughman, L. N., Reed, E. D., & Katz-Leavy, J. (2002). System-of-care assessment: Cross-site comparison of findings. *Children's Services: Social, Policy, Research, and Practice, 5*(1), 37-56.

Brinson, J. A. (1995). Group work for black adolescent substance users: Some issues and recommendations. *Journal of Child & Adolescent Substance Abuse, 4*(2), 49-60.

Brown, D. R. (1990). Depression among blacks: An epidemiologic perspective. In D. S. Ruiz & J. P. Comer (Eds.), *Handbook of Mental Health and Mental Disorder Among Black Americans* (pp. 71-93). New York: Greenwood Press.

Carlton-LaNey, I. (1994). The career of Birdye Henrietta Haynes, a Pioneer settlement house worker. *Social Service Review, 254*-273.

Carrasco, M., (2004). African American Outreach Resource Manual. NAMI Multicultural Action Center.

Cochran, D. L., Brown, D. R., & McGregor, K. C. (1999). Racial differences in the multiple social roles of older women: Implications for depressive symptoms. *Gerontologist, 39*(4), 465-472.

Colby, I. C. (1984). *The freedman's bureau in Texas and its impact on the emerging social welfare system and black-white relations, 1865-1885.* Doctoral diss. University of Pennsylvania.

Comer, J. P. (1974). In black women's community development foundation. *Binding Ties, 2*(2), 11-12.

Cooper-Patrick, L., Gallo, J. J., Powe, N. R., Steinwachs, D. M., Eaton, W. W., & Ford, D. E. (1999). Mental health service utilization by African Americans and whites: The Baltimore Epidemiologic Catchment Area follow-up. *Medical Care, 37,* 1034-1045.

Cooper-Patrick, L., Powe, N. R., Jenckes, M. W., Gonzales, J. J., Levine, D. M., & Ford, D. E. (1997). Identification of patient attitudes and preferences regarding treatment of depression. *Journal of General Internal Medicine, 12,* 431-438.

Davis, L. G. (1980). The politics of black self-help in the United States: A historical overview. In L. S. Yearwood (Ed.), *Black Organizations* (pp. 37-50). Washington, DC: University Press.

Denby, R., Rocha, C., & Owens-Kane, S. (2004). African American families, mental health, and living cooperatives: A program and research analysis. In E. M. Freeman & S. L. Logan (Eds.), *Reconceptualizing the Strengths and Common Heritage of Black Families: Practice, Research, and Policy Issues* (pp. 72-94). Springfield, IL: Charles C Thomas.

Diala, C., Muntaner, C., Walrath, C., Nickerson, K. J., LaVeist, T. A., & Leaf, P. J. (2000). Racial differences in attitudes toward professional mental health care and in the use of services. *American Journal of Orthopsychiatry, 70*(4), 455-464.

Dwight-Johnson, M., Sherbourne, C. D., Liao, D., & Wells, K. B. (2000). Treatment preferences among primary care patients. *Journal of General Internal Medicine, 15,* 527-534.

Epstein, W. M. (1988). Our Town: A case study of ideology and the private social welfare sector. *Journal of Sociology and Social Welfare, 15*(3), 101-123.

Feitel, B., Margetson, N., Chamas, R., & Lipman, C. (1992). Psychosocial background and behavioral and emotional disorders of homeless and runaway youth. *Hospital and Community Psychiatry, 43,* 155-159.

Fishbein, D. H., & Perez, D. M. (2000). A regional study of risk factors for drug abuse and delinquency: Sex and racial differences. *Journal of Child and Family Studies, 9*(4), 461-480.

Fitzpatrick, K. M., & Boldizar, J. P. (1993). The prevalence and consequences of exposure to violence among African American youth. *Journal of the American Academy of Child and Adolescent Psychiatry, 32,* 424-430.

Foucault, M. (1965). *Madness and Civilization.* New York: Pantheon Books.

Franklin, J. H. (1970). Public welfare in the south during reconstruction era, 1865-1880. *Social Service Review, 44*(4), 379-392.

Garland, A. F., Hough, R. C., McCabe, K. M., Yeh, M., Wood, P. A., & Aarons, G. A. (2001). Prevalence of psychiatric disorders in youths across five sectors of care. *Journal of the American Academy of Child and Adolescent Psychiatry, 40,* 409-418.

Gary, F. A., & Yarandi, H. N. (2004). Depression among southern rural African American women. *Nursing Research, 53*(4), 251-259.

Gary, F. A., Yarandi, H. N., & Scruggs, F. C. (2003). Suicide among African Americans: Reflections and a call to action. *Issues in Mental Health Nursing, 24,* 353-375.

Gibbs, J. T. (1997). African-American suicide: A cultural paradox. *Suicide Life Threatening Behavior, 27*(1), 68-79.

Gibbs, J. T. (Ed.). (1988). *Young, Black and Male in America: An Endangered Species.* Dover, MA: Auburn House Publishing Company.

Gibbs, J. T., & Bankhead, T. (2001). *Preserving Privilege: California Politics, Propositions, and People of Color.* Westport, CT: Praeger.

Gibbs, J. T., & Fuery, D. (1994). Mental health and well-being of black women: Toward strategies of empowerment. *American Journal Psychology, 22*(4), 559-582.

Gibbs, J. T., & Huang, L. N. (1990). *Children of Color: Psychological Intervention with Minority Youth.* San Francisco: Jossey-Bass.

Gibbs, J. T., & Huang, L. N. (Ed.). (2003). *Children of Color: Psychological Interventions with Culturally Diverse Youth.* San Francisco: Jossey-Bass.

Gil, A. G., Vega, W. A., & Turner, R. J. (2002). *Early and Mid-Adolescence Risk Factors for Later Substance Abuse by African Americans and European Americans.* Public Health Report [suppl. 1]. Rockville, MD: U.S. Department of Health and Human Services.

Glisson, C., & Hemmelgarn, A. L. (1998). The effects of organizational climate and interorganizational coordination on the quality and outcomes of children's service systems. *Child Abuse & Neglect, 22,* 401-421.

Glisson, C., & James, L. R. (2002). The cross-level effects of culture and climate in human service teams. *Journal of Organizational Behavior, 23,* 767-794.

Goffman, E. (1959). *The Presentation of Self in Every Day Life.* Garden City, NY: Doubleday.

Gray-Little, B., & Hafdahl, A. R. (2000). Factors influencing racial comparisons of self-esteem: A quantitative review. *Psychological Bulletin, 126,* 26-54.

Guthrie, R. V. (1991). The psychology of African Americans: An historical perspective. In R. L. Jones (Ed.), *Black Psychology* (pp. 33-45). Berkeley: Cobb & Henry.

Hawkins, J. D., & Salisbury, B. R. (1983). Delinquency prevention programs for minorities of color. *Social Work Research and Abstracts, 19*(4), 5-12.

Helm, B. (1985). Social development and nation building. *Social Development Issues, 9*(1), 102-114.

Isaacs, M., & Benjamin, M. (1991). *Towards a Culturally Competent System of Care: Vol. II. Programs Which Use Culturally Competent Services.* Washington, DC: Georgetown University Child Development Center, National Technical Assistance Center for Children's Mental Health.

Isaacs-Shockley, M., Cross, T., Bazron, B. J., Dennis, K., & Benjamin, M. P. (1996). Framework for a culturally competent system of care. In E. A. Stroul (Ed.), *Children's Mental Health: Creating Systems of Care in a Changing Society* (pp. 23-39). Baltimore: Paul H. Brookes.

Karier, C. J. (1973). Liberalism and the quest for orderly change. In M. Katz (Ed.), *Education in American History: Readings on the Social Issues* (p. 306). New York: Praeger.

Kessler, R. C., Berglund, P. A., Zhao, S., Leaf, P. J., Kouzis, A. C., Bruce, M. L. et al. (1996). The 12-month prevalence and correlates of serious mental illness (SMI). In R. W. Manderscheid & M. A. Sonnenschein (Eds.), *Mental Health, United States* (Pub. No. [SMA] 96-3098). Rockville, MD: Center for Mental Health Services.

Kimbrough, R. M., Molock, S. D., & Walton, K. (1998). Perception of social support, acculturation, depression, and suicidal ideation among African American college students at predominantly black and predominantly white universities. *Journal of Negro Education, 65*(3), 295-307.

Kondrat, M. E., Greene, G. J., & Winbush, G. B. (2002). Using benchmark research to locate agency best practice for African American clients. *Administration and Policy in Mental Health, 29*(6), 494-518.

Lasch-Quinn, E. (1993). *Black Neighbors: Race and the Limits of Reform in the American Settlement House Movement, 1890-1945.* Chapel Hill, NC: University of North Carolina Press.

LaVeist, T. A., Bowie, J. V., & Cooley-Quille, M. (2000). Minority health status in adulthood: The middle years of life. *Health Care Financing Review, 21*(4), 1-13.

LaVeist, T. A., Diala, C., & Jarrett, N. C. (2000). Social status and perceived discrimination: Who experiences discrimination in the health care system, how, and why? In C. Hogue, M. Hargraves, & K. Scott-Collins (Eds.), *Minority Health in America* (pp. 194-208). Baltimore, MD: Johns Hopkins University Press.

Lefley, H. P. (1984). Cross-cultural training for mental health professionals: Effects on the delivery of services. *Hospital and Community Psychiatry, 35*(12), 1227-1229.

Leiby, J. (1978). *History of Social Welfare and Social Work in the United States.* New York: Columbia University Press.

Lichtenberg, P. A., Brown, D. R., Jackson, J. S., & Washington, O. (2004). Normative health research experience among African American Elders. *Journal of Aging and Health, 16*(5), 78S-92S.

Martin, J. M., & Martin, E. P. (1985). *The Helping Tradition in the Black Family and Community.* Washington, DC: National Association of Social Workers.

McLoyd, V. (1990). Minority child development: The special issue. *Child Development, 61,* 263-266.

Miller, D. K., Malmstrom, T. K., Joshi, S., Andresen, E. M., Morley, J. W., & Wolinsky, F. D. (2004). Clinically relevant levels of depressive symptoms in community-dwelling middle-aged African Americans. *Journal of the American Geriatrics Society, 52*(5), 1532-5415.

Neal-Barnett, A. M., & Smith, J. (1997). African Americans. In S. Friedman (Ed.), *Cultural Issues in the Treatment of Anxiety* (pp. 154-174). New York: Guilford Press.

Olfson, M., Marcus, S., Druss., B., Elinson, L., Tanielian, T., & Pincus, H. (2002). National trends in the outpatient treatment of depression. *Journal of American Medical Association, 287*(2), 203-209.

Parham, T. A., White, J. L., & Ajamu, A. (2000). *The Psychology of Blacks: An African-Centered Perspective* (3rd ed.). Upper Saddle River, NJ: Prentice Hall.

Petry, N. M. (2002). A comparison of African American and non-Hispanic Caucasian cocaine-abusing outpatients. *Drug and Alcohol Dependence, 69*(1), 43-49.

Pires, S. (2002, Spring). *Building Systems of Care: A Primer.* Washington, DC: Georgetown University Child Development Center, National Technical Assistance Center for Children's Mental Health.

Rabinowitz, H. N. (1974). From exclusion to segregation: Health and welfare services for southern blacks, 1865-1890. *Social Service Review, 48,* 327-354.

Roth, D., Lauber, B. G., Vercellini, J., Burns, G., Champney, T. F., & Clark, J. (1996). Services in systems: Impact on client outcomes. In D. Roth (Ed.), *New Research in Mental Health* (Vol. 12, pp. 388-401). Columbus: Ohio Department of Mental Health.

Segal, S. P., Bola, J. R., & Watson, M. A. (1996). Race, quality of care and anti-psychotic prescribing practices in psychiatric emergency services. *Psychiatric Services, 47*(3), 282-285.

Semke, J. (1999). Shifts in case mix locus of mental health care for Washington state adults with severe mental illness. *Administration and Policy in Mental Health, 26*(3), 191-205.

Sheppard, V. B., & Benjamin-Coleman, R. (2001). Determinants of service placements for youth with serious emotional and behavioral disturbances. *Community Mental Health Journal, 37*(1), 53-65.

Singleton-Bowie, S. M. (1995). The effect of mental health practitioners' racial sensitivity on African Americans' perception of service. *Social Work Research, 19*(4), 238-243.

Slade, E. P. (2004). Racial/ethnic disparities in parent perception of child need for mental health care following school disciplinary events. *Mental Health Services Research, 6*(2), 75-92.

Smith, J. C., & Johns, R. L. (Eds.). (1995). *Statistical Record of Black America.* New York: Gale Research Inc.

Snowden, L. R. (1998). Racial differences in informal help seeking for the mental health problems. *Journal of Community Psychology, 26*(5), 429-438.

Snowden, L. R. (2001). Social embeddedness and psychological well-being among African Americans and whites. *American Journal of Community Psychology, 29*(4), 519-536.

Specht, H., & Courtney, M. (1994). *Unfaithful Angels: How Social Work Has Abandoned Its Mission.* New York: The Free Press.

Stehno, S. M. (1990). The elusive continuum of child welfare services: Implications for minority children and youths. *Child Welfare, 69*(6), 551-562.

Stroul, B. (2002). *Issue Brief—Systems of Care: A Framework for System Reform in Children's Mental Health.* Washington, DC: Georgetown University Child Development Center, National Technical Assistance Center for Children's Mental Health.

Stroul, B., & Friedman, R. M. (1986). *A System of Care for Children and Adolescents with Severe Emotional Disturbance.* Washington, DC: Georgetown University Child Development Center, National Technical Assistance Center for Children's Mental Health.

Substance Abuse and Mental Health Services Administration. (2004). *Overview of findings from the 2003 National Survey on Drug Use and Health* (Office of Applied Studies, NSDUH Series H-24, DHHS Publication No. SMA 04-3963). Rockville, MD.

Sue, S. (1998). In search of cultural competence in psychotherapy and counseling. *American Psychologist, 53,* 440-448.

Sue, D. W., & Sue, D. (1999). *Counseling the Culturally Different: Theory and Practice* (3rd ed.). New York: John Wiley & Sons.

Takeuchi, D. T., & Uehara, E. S. (1996). Ethnic minority mental health services: Current research and future conceptual directions. In B. L. Levin, J. Petrila, & K. D. Hennessy (Eds.), *Mental Health Services: A Public Health Perspective* (pp. 63-80). New York: Oxford University Press.

Teplin, L. A. (1999). The prevalence of severe mental disorder among male urban jail detainees: Comparison with the Epidemiologic Catchment Area Program. *American Journal of Public Health, 80,* 663-669.

Tharp, R. G. (1991). Cultural diversity and treatment of children. *Journal of Consulting and Clinical Psychology, 59*(6), 799-812.

U.S. Department of Health and Human Services (DHHS). (1999). *Mental Health: A Report of the Surgeon.* Rockville, MD: DHHS.

U.S. Department of Health and Human Services (DHHS). (2001). *Mental Health: Culture, Race, and Ethnicity—A Supplement to Mental Health: A Report to the Surgeon General.* Rockville, MD: U.S. Department of Health and Human Services, Public Health Service, Office of the Surgeon General.

Vega, W. A., Kolody, B., Aguilar-Gaxiola, S., Alderate, E., Catalano, R., & Carveo-Anduaga, J. (1998). Lifetime prevalence of DSM-III-R psychiatric disorders among urban and rural Mexican Americans in California. *Archives of General Psychiatry, 55,* 771-778.

Weaver, H. (1992). African Americans and social work: An overview of the antebellum through the Progressive eras. *Journal of Multicultural Social Work, 2*(4), 91-102.

Whaley, A. L. (2001). Cultural mistrust of white mental health clinicians among African Americans with severe mental illness. *American Journal of Orthopsychiatry, 71*(2), 252-256.

Yoo, J. (2002). The relationship between organizational variables and client outcomes: Variable and client outcomes: A case study in child welfare. *Administration in Social Work, 26*(2), 39-61.

Young, A. S., Klap, R., Shelbourne, C. D., & Wells, K. B. (2001). The quality of care for depressive and anxiety disorders in the United States. *Archives of General Psychiatry, 58,* 55-61.

Zhang, A. Y., Snowden, L. R., & Sue, S. (1998). Differences between Asian and white Americans' help-seeking and utilization patterns in the Los Angeles area. *Journal of Community Psychology, 26,* 317-326.

Zule, W. A., Flannery, B. A., Wechsberg, W. M., & Lam, W. K. (2002). Alcohol use among out-of-treatment crack using African American women. *American Journal of Drug and Alcohol Abuse, 28*(3), 525-545.

Chapter 3

Mental Health Interventions and the Black Community

Sadye M. L. Logan

Given the unique niche that people of African descent occupy in the history of the United States and contemporary American society, it is critically important that the mental health needs of African Americans be discussed within this broad historical context (for more detail, see Chapter 1). Despite the laudable history of African-American survival, growth, and high degree of mental health, the long shadow of two centuries of enslavement continues, in some form, to haunt the mind and spirit of all African Americans (*Essence,* 2005; Meacham, 2000; Alter, 1997; Mumford, 1996).

The story of the survival and emancipation of the African-American people from slavery and plantation life is an old one. The impact of this transition and life beyond on their mental and physical health is a continuing saga. The characters tend to change, but the outcome has remained constant. The extraordinary 1999 report of the Surgeon General, referred to elsewhere in this book, served to refocus the nation's attention on the state of mental health in Black America. This landmark report also highlighted the type and quality of treatment services provided to Black service consumers (U.S. Department of Health and Human Services, 1999). Within this context, a discussion about mental health intervention designed to address the current needs of the Black community should be more than the regurgitation of old facts. This chapter provides, through an exploratory analysis, a contextual framework for examining and understanding the care and mental health needs of African Americans. In addition, a culturally responsive program, including practice guidelines and implications, is proposed. Finally, it is important to view this chapter as an extension of the two previous

Mental Health Care in the African-American Community
© 2007 by The Haworth Press, Inc. All rights reserved.
doi:10.1300/5364_03

chapters, which were designed to provide a historical overview and contextual framework for this book.

LITERATURE OVERVIEW

Although the history of mental health includes very limited references to the experiences of people of African descent, it is interesting to note that the prevailing ideologies and social policies that guided the mental health treatment of African Americans from the earliest recorded history still influence the treatment of African Americans today. (For further discussion on mental health policy, see Chapter 13 and Exhibit 3.1.)

EXHIBIT 3.1. A Chronology of Perceptions and Intervention of Mental Illness in People of African Descent

1619   The first African slaves, totaling twenty, arrive in Jamestown, Virginia (Bennett, 1993).

1745   South Carolina colonial assembly ruled that Kate, a slave woman who had killed her child, was "out of her senses" and her case was not adjudicated. The assembly passed an act giving each parish in the colony responsibility for care of lunatic slaves (Easterby, 1956).

1840   Epidemiological studies based on the sixth U.S. Census used to justify claim that Blacks were free of madness in a state of slavery but become mentally disturbed when set free (Anon, 1851; Thomas & Sillen, 1972).

1851   Cartwright, a physician, diagnosed all free Blacks as suffering from dysaethesia aethoiopis, a condition resulting from not having some White person to take care of them. He prescribed, as treatment of choice, hard work in the open air with rest periods and good wholesome food (Cartwright, 1851).

1893   South Carolina psychiatrist Babcock published "research" purporting that mental illness was almost nonexistent among "savage" tribes of Africa, but were on the encase among the emancipated African Americans (Babcock, 1895).

1914	Green, Director of Georgia State Sanatorium, believed that Southern Blacks were rarely, if ever, depressed because of what he described as their irresponsible, unthinking, childlike nature (Green, 1914).
1920-1930	Carl Jung, a psychiatrist, proposed a theory of "racial infection" to explain the mental and moral peculiarities of Whites. He contends that when a primitive race, that is, enslaved Blacks, outnumbers White people, the Whites become infected by association (Jung, 1930).
1950-1960	Carothers, a psychiatrist, and others believed that the absence of a sense of responsibility among Blacks accounted for the absence or rarity of depression (Carothers, 1947).
1973-1989	Leff, a British psychiatrist, and others theorized that Black Americans and people from industrially developing countries showed a lower level of intelligence and a lack of emotional differentiation (Leff, 1977).
1999	*Mental Health: A Report of the Surgeon General* underscores the relationship between a long history of oppression; the cumulative affect of economic hardship, homelessness, incarceration, and trauma; and the increased vulnerability to mental disorders among people of African descent. Calls for greater access and quality care (U.S. Department of Human Services, 1999).
2002	The President's New Freedom Commission on Mental Health confirmed significant barriers in access, quality, and outcome of care from people of African descent and calls for great access and quality care (U.S. Department of Health and Human Services, 2002).

Mental illness among the enslaved Africans was described by terms such as *negritude,* a condition thought to be a form of mild leprosy; *drapetomania,* a disease causing the slaves to run away; and *dysaethesia aethiopis* or *rascality,* defined as a "natural offspring of Negro liberty—the liberty to be idle, to wallow in filth, and to indulge in improper food and drinks" (Cartwright, 1851, pp. 548-597). However, Dr. Benjamin Rush, dean of the Medical School at the University of Pennsylvania and the father of American Psychiatry, believed that Africans became insane, in some instances, soon after they were enslaved in the West Indies (Fernando, 2002; Rush, 1812/1962).

Unfortunately, this valuable observation was overlooked by the mental health authorities and continues to be misplaced in understanding the impact of enslavement and ongoing oppression on the mental health of people of African descent (Null, 2002; Plummer, 1970; Jensen, 1969; Jung, 1930).

Numerous scholars and researchers on the Black experience have discussed the devastating impact of the slavery system on the mental health of African Americans. Three factors are thus noted about enslavement: (1) it was a form of forced dependence; (2) it created an enforced feeling of inferiority and a traumatized sense of self; and (3) it enforced a sense of helplessness and hopelessness about individual and group betterment (Willie, Rieker, Kramer, & Brown, 1995). These factors, coupled with premeditated violence and numerous racially motivated, legally sanctioned creative devices, were designed to destroy social, political, and economic cohesiveness among African Americans. It is not difficult to visualize the impact of such sociocultural and structural forces on the mind, body, and spirit of African Americans. In addition, these forces have also influenced the quality of our relationship with each other and with others in the society (Daniel, 2003; Smiley, 2001).

Despite the devastating impact of our social and cultural experiences, African Americans continued to tap into our inner resources such as faith, courage, steadfastness, tenacity, and remembrances of our strengths and cohesiveness, and of our African culture and heritage. These inner resources not only serve to sustain a sense of selfhood, but also support the development of protective institutions that have nurtured the social, psychological, and spiritual well-being of African Americans. These inner resources and the protective institutions served as buffers against economic and racial abuse in the broader environment outside of Black communities. However, life is not lived in a vacuum—it is interactive, progressive, and purposive. It was also very apparent, then and now, that a significant portion of the African-American population has not developed the same level of inner strengths, did not receive the same type and quality of services rendered by the protective institutions, and were differentially affected by the destructive societal structures and practices. These vulnerable groups constitute a growing number of families and children that are at risk for debilitating effects of mental health related problems.

This discussion underscores the belief that sociocultural structures and practices in this country play a significant role in level and quality of mental health and illness experienced by African Americans. At this point, it would be useful to define how this chapter is using the concept of mental health and illness. This discussion provides a broad conceptualization of mental health and mental health problems as the overarching framework for this and other chapters in this book.

THE EVOLVING CONCEPTION
OF MENTAL HEALTH PROBLEMS

It is generally agreed that conceptualizing mental health is a very complex and fuzzy matter. Much, if not all, of the fuzziness comes about because of a profound barrier in the mind-set of the general public regarding our sense of individuality and separateness. This individuality and separateness rest on a racialized foundation, rooted in a reluctance to recognize that we live in a diverse society. Semantics, or the power of words, further hampers this conceptualization.

Jahoda (1959), Gary (1978), and Ruiz (1990) at some level provided definitions of mental health. In their conceptualization, one might deduce that mental health is somewhat different from the absence of mental illness, but more a reflection of a stable internal state of mind regardless of the demands of environmental challenges and expectations. Gary (1978), however, placed emphasis on the individual's ability to control or modify his or her environment. One might also wonder about the construct of mental health as a stable internal state of mind as well as about the Surgeon General Report's conceptualization, which suggests that "mental health" and "mental illness" be thought of as points on a continuum—implying continuity and homogeneity. The report described *mental health* as the springboard of all that is necessary to become a fully functioning human being. It viewed mental health as indispensable to individual well-being in all interpersonal and intrapersonal relationships and in our contribution to society. *Mental illness,* on the other hand, refers collectively to all diagnosable mental disorders or health conditions that are characterized by alterations in thinking, mood, or behaviors associated with distress and/or impaired functioning. It is important, however, to note the report caution to readers regarding the many different interpretations of what it means to be mentally healthy—interpretations that are rooted in value judgments that vary across cultures (Cowan, 1994; Sue, Zane, & Young, 1994).

However, one wonders if the report should have raised the same precaution about all diagnosable mental disorders. It would be useful to pursue the construct of mental health as a stable internal state of mind. This conceptualization reduces the fuzziness and provides a specific, practical, achievable goal to work toward. This conceptualization also serves as a bridge in body-spirit connections. Therefore, it is intended here to connect this conceptualization and mental health with the emerging conceptualization of mind, body, and spirit as inseparable entities. It is also intended here to suggest that the way we conceptualize mental health is of critical importance because this conceptualization will guide how we intervene or treat mental illness and problems. Further, this conceptualization of mental health suggests that we must give great importance to keeping the mind healthy.

A great Indian sage once shared a story that illustrates the value of the mind to our mental health. He begins:

> If someone loses his hand, he can still live. If someone loses his leg, he can still live. If some loses his eyes, he can still live a very good life. However, if some has lost his mind, he is as good as dead.

> Then he goes on to tell a story about a very wealthy industrialist who had lost the use of his mind and was no longer aware of his surroundings or capable of caring for himself. The essence of the story is that it is impossible to live a quality life or to even exist as a productive human being without a strong, quiet or healthy mind.

This is a very practical, but powerful story about the great importance of an instrument that we neglect through abuse or misuse and know so very little about. Kshemaraja, a great eleventh-century Kashmiri scholar, in his book, *Pratyabhijnahridayam, or the recognition of one's own deepest nature,* describes the mind as the contracted form of the energy that is known by different names in different traditions. For example, the inner Self, God, Love, Buddha, the Truth and so on. Kshemaraja also describes how the mind contracts from being universal energy to the human mind. The implication of understanding and treating our minds as the contracted form of energy that creates and sustains the universe is simply awe-inspiring.

Swami Shantananda (2003) elaborates on the process. At the practical level, other scholars and researchers tell us that a steady, clear, and strong mind depends on a willingness to become aware of and letting go of old self-defeating thought patterns and feelings, and replacing these with uplifting thoughts and feelings (Dyer, 2004; Anantananda, 1996; Gillet, 1992). The bottom line is that how and what we think determines the quality and nature of our life and existence. There is little doubt that there will be many who will say that such a conceptualization about our mental health is some New Age thinking and will not work. Others will say that it does not address the real issues or that this conceptualization is not new, that it is already incorporated in the treatment services currently in use. Granted, some elements of truth will always exist in every argument against something that appears to be different than what is familiar and comfortable. However, what is different about this approach to creating and sustaining a strong healthy mind is that this becomes a way of life—a way of being in the world, a recognition that we create our realities based on how and what we think about our life (Gergin, 1985; Rorty, 1978).

It is important, however, to emphasize that this concept of a mentally healthy person is not to suggest that this person is not someone who does not behave appropriately in any given situation. The stable mind is strong and focused. A strong and focused mind transcends conditions and situations that generally create states of agitation and restlessness (Muktananda, 1986). This concept of mental health may also be applied to families and communities. It follows that individuals with stable minds will reverberate harmonious energy and relationships within their families and communities.

As is demonstrated in these discussions, this view of human beings is not new. It is also reflected in cultures of American Indians, Africans, and Eastern cultures and traditions. These cultural worldviews include an interconnectedness between mind, body, and spirit (Somé, 1992; Clifford, 1984; Haldipur, 1984; Kaker, 1984; Kaptchuk, 1983; Ademuwagun, Ayoade, Harrison, & Warren, 1979). Our more emergent views of human beings, especially as they relate to our service users, affirm that human beings have resources to cope, change, and find solutions to their problems; they are the experts on their lives (Lipchik, 2002). However, it is almost as if these beliefs stop short of purporting that these resources to cope, change, and find solutions to life problems are essentially innate and reside within the service users and that accessing those resources is intimately connected to the state of the service user's mind. If researchers, service providers, and educators push through the fears of what their peers and the general public would think or say and embrace such affirmation, this would bring these emergent views closer in alignment with a more holistic view of the human being. In the next section of this chapter, implications are addressed.

MENTAL HEALTH CARE FOR AFRICAN AMERICANS

According to current data, 36 million people, or 13 percent of the civilian noninstitutionalized population, identified themselves as African American or Black (McKinnon, 2003). Fifty-five percent of this population continues to be concentrated in the South, with 52 percent living in urban areas and 33 percent under eighteen, and 23 percent or 8.1 million living below the poverty level (see Chapter 14). It is estimated, however, that Black people account for 25 percent of the mental health needs in this country. According to the President's New Freedom Commission on Mental Health, approximately 5 to 7 percent of adults in a given year have a serious mental illness. *Serious mental illness* is a term used in federal regulations for any diagnosable mental disorder that affects work, home, or other areas of social functioning. Not unlike adults, approximately 5 to 9 percent of children have a *serious emotional disturbance,* or SED, a term used in federal regulations that refers to any diagnosable mental disorder in a child under age eighteen that severely disrupts social, academic, and emotional functioning. Available evidence suggests that our children are the most vulnerable and are grossly neglected in our current mental health system of care (The President's New Freedom Commission on Mental Health, 2003; see Chapter 8).

The World Health Organization (WHO, 2001) reported in a groundbreaking study of the United States, Canada, and Western Europe that mental illness ranks first in terms of causes of disability. Overall, the study found that mental illness accounts for 25 percent of all disability across the United States, Canada, and Western Europe. It is important to note that the percentages of mental illness across major industrialized countries are the same as the percentage of mental illness in Black America. The situation is grave and begs the questions of whether the problem can be reversed before reaching more severe proportions and what might be most efficacious and effective in addressing this very serious issue.

In reviewing the current conditions surrounding mental health care for African Americans, several recurring issues related to treatment or intervention and diagnoses emerged (see Exhibit 3.2). Intervention in these studies are referring to psychotherapy. Suffice it to say that the treatment outcomes were mixed. Beginning as early as 1972, treatment outcome results for Black service users were compared with treatment outcomes for White service users (Lerner, 1972). According to Sue, Zane, and Young (1994), three stud-

---

EXHIBIT 3.2. Issues in the Diagnosis and Treatment of African-American Mental Health Service Users

- Over- or underdiagnosed

- Dual diagnosis

- Sent to counseling by court (i.e., involuntary treatment)

- Lack of attention to contextual factors (i.e., poverty, cultural issues, spirituality/religion beliefs)

- Lack of attention for antipsychiatry or antimental health feelings

- Confusion around meaning and impact of racism

- Confusion around racial/ethnic identity issues

- Overdoses of medication

- Incarcerated as a form of intervention

- Not generally seen as good candidate for psychotherapy/individual treatment

ies, Lerner (1972) and Jones (1978 and 1982), reported improvements from pre- to posttreatment and no lack of ethnic differences in outcomes.

However, studies completed in 1985 and in 1991 found that service users of color, most particularly African Americans, reported significantly lower positive treatment outcomes. Further, specific client variables and therapist variables directly affected the treatment process. Client variables included expectations, preferences for ethnicity and therapist attitudes and levels of racial ethnic identity development. Therapist variables include ethnicity, style, and level of cultural sensitivity, attitudes, and background. Research on ethnic preference seems to underscore the importance of race, ethnicity, gender, values, and other favorable treatment outcome factors that affect the quality of life, but the research has not provided consistent results. Oftentimes, the inconsistency is attributed to methodological and conceptual limitations.

What seems evident is that despite the similarities in response rate between White service users and Black service users to interventions for some mental health disorders, effective treatment for Black service users must take into consideration the legacy of what has been referred to as the "chains of slavery" as well as the diverse nature of thirty-six million people that contribute to Black America (*Essence,* 2005). Some contextual factors that are critical to this process of effective service delivery include the health services delivery infrastructure or managed care, as well as the nature and quality of the environments where the service users reside. More often than not, African-American service users are living on marginal incomes in communities where violence, crime, and employment rates are high (see Chapter 7). In addition, substance abuse and dependence is endemic. Managed care, on the other hand, is concerned for the most part with cost containment and generating a profit for the insurance company (Cohen, 2003).

It goes without saying that effective treatment is dependent on accurate and responsible diagnosis. However, available data has consistently indicated that African Americans are accurately diagnosed less often than Caucasian service users when they are suffering from depression and seen in primary care (Baker & Bell, 1999; Sue, Zane, & Young, 1994) or when they are seen for psychiatric evaluation in an emergency room (Baker, Stokes-Thompson, Davis, Gonzo, & Hishinuma, 1999). Moreover, service providers and researchers have observed consistent patterns for many years whereby African-American service users presented higher than expected rates of diagnosed schizophrenia and lower rates of diagnosed affective disorders (Wang, Berglund, & Kessler, 2000). Baker and Bell (1999) report that when structured procedures were used for assessment, or when retrospective assessments were made via chart review, the disparities between African

Americans and Whites were nonexistent. Researchers have attributed this pattern of misdiagnosis or underdiagnosis to practitioner's bias. Unfortunately, practitioners in the mental health field make no concerted effort to allow for either racial bias, ethnocentrism, or some other factor(s) that support practitioners' predisposition to over- or underdiagnoses.

All evidence suggests that the mental health needs of African Americans are a complex situation of epidemic proportions. The landmark 1999 report *Mental Health: A Report of the Surgeon General* tells us that there are ranges of effective treatment for people with mental illness. However, the 2002 President's New Freedom Commission on Mental Health tells us that the nation's mental health service delivery system is in shambles. The President's New Freedom Commission on Mental Health also details the following systemic barriers to effective service delivery:

1. Failure to serve those with the most serious illness
2. Failure to intervene early in childhood
3. Failure to recognize mental health as a national priority

EVIDENCE-BASED TREATMENTS AND BEST PRACTICES

Available data suggest that African-American children as well as adults with mental health needs are unlikely to receive treatment that conforms to evidence-based recommendations (U.S. Department of Health and Human Services, 1999), or if they did receive treatment it would most likely be of an inferior nature. Evidence-based treatment is defined by the U.S. Department of Health and Human Services to mean treatment that adheres to official guidelines based on evidence from clinical trails (Wang, Berglund, & Kessler, 2000). These clinical trails included treatment in which medication from the appropriate care specialist is prescribed for the disorder plus at least four visits to the same provider or at least eight visits to either a psychiatrist or mental health specialist in the absence of prescribed medication.

The bottom line is that numerous factors mitigate against high-quality mental health care for African Americans (see Exhibit 3.2). These may include seeking help and lacking a usual source of health care as a focal point for health care, lack of access, symptom presentation, and the unavailability of alternative treatment.

The President's New Freedom report (2003) spoke of several stellar community-based approaches that are effectively and innovatively providing services despite the overwhelming barriers to mental health care. These programs are seen as guideposts to future service delivery. Two overreaching factors seem evident in this successful model of service delivery: commitment and compassion.

A complete paradigm shift is also necessary for ongoing and lasting change in the way this nation responds to mentally challenged individuals. This paradigm (see Exhibit 3.3) would begin with a national commitment to making the overall well-being of the nation's citizens a national priority. This focus must be emulated at all levels of government, and supported by a training culture for current and future mental health practitioners that imbues hope and recovery. To successfully make the shift, our thinking, doing, and acting must be a conscious and ongoing awareness that our approach to

EXHIBIT 3.3. A Proposed Approach for Mental Health Intervention with African Americans

Program: *Circles of Mental Health* are community-based services designed to evoke ownership and collaborative relationships. Different circles will be designed to address different levels of need and intensity.

Approach: An integrative, interdisciplinary framework with an assertive community treatment orientation takes what is useful from traditional approaches and combines with useful concepts from the emergent approaches. This would include the incorporation of ideas from solution-focused treatment, strength and empowerment orientations, multiculturalism, and postmodernalism. In this framework, helping would be collaborative, respectful, genuine, and inclusive of multiple forms and multiple means of providing access to services and benefits.

Goal: To create, in conjunction with other service programs, stigma free approaches to positive community based mental health and overall well being.

Features: Communities will be required as much as expected to commit and sustain with the necessary support the circles of mental health. Each circle will be designed and implemented by stakeholders in the community. Social policies and the necessary funding must be available to implement and maintain effective ongoing services.

Biggest Challenge: The implementation that would require a paradigm shift in the thinking of the service users (all community residents), the policy makers, and the collaborators designed to support community work groups.

mental health is based primarily on not viewing and understanding mental health problems in terms of the "illness" model. Prevention and intervention must be based on a conceptualization that factors in the human mind are central to securing and maintaining good mental health. Further, the development of strong, healthy mind, body and spirit must begin in infancy. Our tendency must be to work toward an antiracist world, to reject what is currently being referred to as "the new racism" (Allen, 2006; Hill Collins, 2004). It is necessary in this paradigm shift to conceptualize service as a holistic continuum of care in which service users are needed as respected collaborators in finding the best solutions to their mental health needs.

The promise of research into biological similarities and differences between African Americans and Whites is providing useful guidelines regarding dosage needs in certain medications. These findings will not only mitigate against current practices in which Black service users are overmedicated, thus creating increased risk of long-term severe side effects and serious physical reactions such as jitteriness and muscle cramps (Bell & Baker, 1994), but also increase the availability of more evidence-based best practices. However, in addition to the search for evidence-based practice, the overwhelming implications of this review and analysis of the mental health needs of African Americans suggest an approach to helping that would integrate what is useful from our traditional knowledge base with some emergent ideas (see Exhibit 3.3). These emergent ideas are based in empowerment concepts, with emphasis on strengths and solution focused interventions.

CONCLUSION

The health care needs of African Americans continue to be a national crisis. This is not surprising in that a significant portion of the thirty-six million African Americans in this country are suffering from some form of mental health problem and live on marginal incomes in communities where the crime and unemployment rates are high, and violence and drug abuse have become a way of life. Although contemporary mental health knowledge confirms that the degradation of two centuries of enslavement and the ongoing destructive consequences of its aftermath have been anything but friendly to the development of good mental health, there is still widespread denial that the lack of individual and family achievement is related to ongoing restrictive or oppressive societal structures and practices. A circular problem results from this action. There needs to be a paradigm shift in our thinking and action about the state of Black America in general, and the state of Black mental health in particular. In addition to creating a broad and expanded system of mental health care that addresses the needs of African Americans across the life cycle, it is imperative that our education, public welfare, and other related social systems develop programs, policies, and research agendas that are more responsive to the needs of African-American children and families.

CHAPTER SUMMARY

Central Ideas

The following central ideas serve as a summary of this chapter:

- African Americans constitute 13 percent (36 million) of the civilian noninstitutionalized population and account for 25 percent of the mental health needs in the United States.
- Sociocultural structures, policies, and practices in the United States significantly affect the level and quality of mental health and illnesses experienced by African-American families and children. The helping professions' emergent views of human beings as having resources to change and to find solutions to life challenges are reflected in the ancient wisdom of Africa and people of African descent.
- Treatment outcome for African-American service users across the life cycle has consistently reported from the early 1970s to present lower positive treatment results.
- African Americans in the mental health system are consistently diagnosed less accurately than Caucasians service users and prescribed inappropriate or ineffective treatments.
- Given the complexity and enormity of the challenge inherent in the mental health care of African Americans, an expanded paradigm of care is proposed.
- The expanded paradigm of care encourages traditional and emergent concepts that are based on a holistic nurturance from infancy to death of strong healthy mind, body, and spirit connections.
- Mental health prevention and intervention must be based on a conceptualization that factors in the human mind are central to securing and maintaining good mental health.

GROUP OR CLASSROOM ACTIVITIES

1. According to Gary Null (2002), the maximum legal length of commitment ranges from forty-five days in Arkansas to unlimited terms in Alabama, Mississippi, and South Carolina. Check with your state mental health system to determine the following:
   - What are the procedures used for commitment to the local state hospital?
   - What services are provided to patients once committed to the state hospital?
   - What role do social workers play in the delivery of services to patients in the state hospital?
   - What treatment modalities are utilized by the service staff?
   - What is the ethnic and gender status of the patients admitted?

2. Pomales, Claiborn, and LaFromboise (1986) reported in their research on the effects of Black students' racial identity on perceptions of White counselors' cultural sensitivity. Therapists who acknowledge and deal with the cultural issues raised by African-American clients are judged to be more culturally competent than are therapists who avoid such issues. In groups of five, brainstorm the possible cultural issues that may be raised in a treatment session with an African-American client. Once you have identified at least five possible treatment issues, prioritize the issues, then simulate a session in which at least two or three of the issues are addressed with the client(s).

3. Visit a local area mental health center with the intent of exploring the center's involvement in providing culturally responsive mental health services. In your contact with member(s) of the treatment staff, explore the following:
   - What is involved in the center's culturally responsive training?
   - What aspects of the culturally responsive training affect therapeutic processes and outcomes?
   - How often is staff engaged in culturally responsive training?

REFERENCES

Ademuwagun, Z. A., Ayoade, J. A., Harison, I., & Warren, D. M. (Eds.). (1979). Los Angeles: American Therapeutic Systems. Waltham, MA: Crossroads Press.

Allen, W. B. The New Racism. Available at: http://www.msu.edu/allen~wi/essays_and_misc/new_racism.PDF. Accessed March 12, 2006.

Alter, J. (December 8, 1997). The long shadow of slavery. *Newsweek*, CXXX, 58-63.

Anon. (1851). Startling facts from the census. *American Journal of Insanity, 8*(2), 153-155.

Babcock, J. W. (Ed.). (1895). The colored insane. *Alienist and Neurologist, 16*, 423-447.

Baker, F. M., & Bell, C. C. (1999). Issues in the psychiatric treatment of African American. *Psychiatric Services, 50*(3), 538-539.

Baker, F. M., Stokes-Thompson, J., Davis, D. A., Gonzo, R., & Hishinuma, E. S. (1999). Two-year outcomes of psychosocial rehabilitation of black patients with chronic mental illness. *Journal of General Internal Medicine, 50*, 535-539.

Bennett, L. Jr. (1993). *Before the Mayflower: A History of Black America.* New York: Penguin.

Carothers, J. L. (1947). A study of mental derangement in Africans and an attempt to explain it's peculiarities, more especially in relation to the African attitude to life. *Journal of Mental Science, 101*, 548-597.

Cartwright, S. A. (1851). Report on the diseases of physical peculiarities of the Negro race. *New Orleans Medical and Surgical Journal,* 691-715; reprinted in A. C. Caplan, H. T. Engelhardt, & J. J. McCartney (Eds.). (1981). *Concepts of Health and Disease.* Reading, MA: Addison-Wesley.

Clifford, T. (1984). *Tibetan Buddhist Medicine and Psychiatry: The Diamond Healing.* York Beach, ME: Samuel Weiser.

Cohen, J. A. (2003). Managed care and the evolving role of the clinical social worker in mental health. *Social Work, 48*(1), 34-43.

Cowan, E. L. (1994). The enhancement of psychological wellness: Challenges and opportunities. *American Journal of Community Psychology, 22*(2), 149-179.

Daniel, L. A. (Ed.) (2003). *The State of Black America.* New York: The National League.

Dyer, W. W. (2004). *The Power of Intention.* Carlsbad, CA: Hay House.

Easterby, J. H. (1956). The Journal of the Commons House of Assembly (September 10, 1743-June 17, 1946). Columbia, SC Archives Department, 43-45.

Essence (February 2005). *Breaking the chains, 35*(10), 150-153.

Fernando, S. (Ed.). (2002). *Mental Health, Race and Culture* (2nd ed.). New York: Palgrove.

Gary, L. E. (1978). *Mental Health: A Challenge to the Black Community.* Philadelphia, PA: Dorrance and Company.

Gergin, K. J. (1985). The social constructionist movement in modern psychology. *American Psychologist, 40*, 266-275.

Gillet, R. (1992). *Change Your Mind, Change Your World: A Practical Guide to Turning Limiting Beliefs into Positive Realities.* New York: Simon and Schuster.

Green, E. M. (1914). Psychoses among negroes—A comprehensive study. *Journal of Nervous and Mental Disorder, 41*, 697-708.

Haldipur, C. V. (1984). Madness in ancient India: Concepts of insanity in Charaka Samhita (1st Century A.D.). *Comprehensive Psychiatry, 25*, 335-343.

Hill Collins, P. (2004). *Black Sexual Politics: African American and the New Racism.* New York: Taylor and Francis.

Jensen, A. R. (1969). How much can we boost IQ and scholastic achievement? *Harvard Educational Review, 39,* 1-123.

Johodak, M. (1959). *Current Concepts of Positive Mental Health.* New York: Basic Books.

Jones, E. E. (1978). Effects of race on psychotherapy process and outcome: An exploratory investigation. *Psychotherapy: Theory, Research and Practice, 15,* 226-236.

Jones, E. E. (1982). Psychotherapists: Impressions of treatment outcome as a function of race. *Journal of Clinical Psychology, 38,* 722-731.

Jung, L. (1930). Your negroid and Indian behavior. *Forum, 83*(4), 193-199.

Kaker, S. (1984). *Shamons, Mystic and Doctors: A Psychological Inquiry into India and It's Healing Tradition.* London: Unwin Paperbacks.

Kaptchuk, T. J. (1983). *Chinese Medicine.* London: Century Paperback.

Kshemaraja (1990). *The Doctrine of Recognition: A Translation of Pratyabhijnahridayam.* Translated with an introduction and notes by Jaideva Singh. Albany NY: SUNY Press.

Leff, J. (1977). Culture and differentiation of emotional state. *British Journal of Psychiatry, 123,* 299-306.

Lerner, B. (1972). Therapy in the Ghetto: Political impotence and personal Disintegration. Baltimore, MD: The John Hopkins University Press.

Lipchik, E. (2000). *Beyond Technique in Solution Focused Therapy: Working with Emotions and the Therapist Relationship.* New York: Guilford.

McKinnon, J. (2003). *The Black Population in the United States: March 2002.* Current Population Reports, Series P20-541. Washington, DC: U.S. Census Bureau.

Meacham, J. (September 18, 2000). The new face of race. *Newsweek,* CXXXVI(12), 38-40.

Mumford, C. J. (1996). *Race and Reparations: A Black Perspective for the Twenty-First Century.* Trenton, NJ: Africa World Press.

New freedom commission on mental health, achieving the promise: Transforming mental health care in America: Final report (2003). DHHS pub. No. SMA-03-3832. Rockville, MD.

Null, G. (2002). *Pathologizing Life.* Available at http://www.whale.to/a/null.html. Accessed February, 4, 2006.

Plummer, B. E. (1970). Benjamin Rush and the negro American. *American Journal and Psychiatry, 127,* 793-798.

Pomales, J., Claiborn, C. D., & LaFromborse, T. D. (1986). Effects of black Students racial identity on perception of white counselors varying in cultural sensitivity. *Journal of Counseling Psychology, 33,* 57-61.

Rorty, R. (1978). Method, social science and social hope. In M. Gibbons (Ed.), *Interpreting Politics* (pp. 241-260). New York: NY University Press.

Ruiz, D. S. (Ed.). (1990). *Handbook of Mental Health and Mental Disorder among Black Americans.* New York: Greenwood Press.

Rush, B. (1812/1962). *Medical Inquiries and Observations Upon the Disease of the Mind.* NY: Hafner Publishing Company.

Smiley, T. (2001). *How to Make Black America Better.* New York: Doubleday.

Somé, M. P. (1992). *The Healing Wisdom of Africa: Finding Life Purpose through Nature, Ritual and Community.* New York: Jeremy P. Tarcher/Putnam.

Sue, S., Fujino, D. C., Hu, L. T., Takeuchi, D. T., & Zone, N. W. S. (1991). Community mental health services for ethnic minority groups: A test of the cultural responsiveness hypothesis. *Journal of Counseling Psychology, 59,* 533-540.

Sue, S., Zane, N., & Young, K. (1994). Research on psychotherapy with culturally diverse populations. In A. E. Bergin & S. L. Garfield (Eds.), *Handbook of Psychotherapy and Behavior Change* (4th ed., pp. 783-817). New York: John Wiley and Sons.

Swami Anantananda. (1996). *What Is On My Mind? Becoming Inspired with New Perception.* New York: SYDA Foundation.

Swami Muktananda. (1986). *Where Are You Going: A Guide to The Spiritual Journey.* Ganeshpuri, India: Guruda Siddhapeets.

Swami Shantananda. (2003). *The Splendor of Recognition.* New York: SYDA Foundation.

Thomas, A., & Sillen, S. (1972). *Racism and Psychiatry.* New York: Brunner/ Mazel.

U.S. Department of Health and Human Services (1999). *Mental Health: A Report of the Surgeon General.* Rockville, MD: Department of Health and Human Services, U.S. Public Health Services.

Wang, P. S., Berglund, P., & Kessler, R. C. (2000). Recent care of common mental disorders in the United States prevalence and conformance with evidence-based recommendations. *Journal of General Internal Medicine, 15,* 284-292.

Willie, C. V., Ricker, P. P., Kramer, B. M., & Brown, B. S. (1995). *Mental health, racism and sexism.* Pittsburgh, PA: University of Pittsburgh Press.

World Health Organization (WHO). (2001). *The World Health Report 2001—Mental Health: New Understanding, New Hope.* Geneva: World Health Organization.

PART II:
MENTAL HEALTH INTERVENTIONS FOR CURRENT ISSUES IMPACTING THE BLACK COMMUNITY

Chapter 4

Mental Health Services in Group Homes and Foster Care Services

Michele D. Hanna
Ruth G. McRoy

According to the U.S. Department of Health & Human Services (USDHHS, 2005a), there were an estimated 2.9 million child abuse and neglect referrals received by U.S. child protection agencies in 2003. Approximately 15.1 percent of the child victims were placed in foster care after a completed investigation of the allegations. Although many researchers have found no significant differences in incidence of child maltreatment between African Americans and Caucasians (Sedlak & Broadhurst, 1996), African-American children are 36 percent more likely to be removed from their homes and placed in foster care than Caucasian children (USDHHS, 2005a). As of September 30, 2003, approximately 35 percent of the 523,000 children in the foster care system were African American (USDHHS, 2005b). Studies have found that children involuntarily removed from their homes and placed in foster care are more likely to experience poor psychological well-being as compared to the general population (Kavaler & Swire, 1983; Garland, Landsverk, Hough, & Ellis-MacLeod, 1996; Farmer et al., 2001; Shin, 2005).

The majority of children who come into the system are from low-income families and are removed because of neglect, which often stems from poverty. Children who have been abused and/or neglected are at risk for depression, anxiety, substance abuse, personality disorders, violent behavior, and for abusing or neglecting their own children (Kessler, Davis, & Kendler,

Mental Health Care in the African-American Community
© 2007 by The Haworth Press, Inc. All rights reserved.
doi:10.1300/5364_04

1997; Clarke, Stein, Sobota, Marisi, & Lucy, 1999; Johnson, Cohen, Brown, Smailes, & Bernstein, 1999). Moreover, once they are removed and placed in out-of-home care, they encounter additional challenges including multiple moves, which can lead to developmental delays and affect their ability to form healthy attachments, relationships, and life skills (Werner & Smith, 1982; Casey Family Programs, 2001). Holland and Gorey (2004) also noted that "challenges within foster homes, such as conflicts between foster children and their foster parents and foster siblings, are strongly associated with mental health and behavioral problems" (p. 128).

Several studies have shown that children in foster care utilize mental health services at a higher rate than children in the general population (Blumberg, Landsverk, Ellis-McLeod, Ganger, & Culver, 1996; Garland et al., 1996; Haflon, Berkowitz, & Klee, 1992a; Takayama, Bergman, & Connell, 1994; Harman, Childs, & Kelleher, 2000). Even if youth have few mental health problems upon entry to out-of-home care, these issues can exacerbate over time if youth experience frequent moves and limited or no services (Hill, 2005).

In an analysis of the paid medical claims in California, Haflon, Berkowitz, and Klee (1992a) found that children in foster care were five times more likely to use mental health outpatient services and be hospitalized for mental illness. Garland et al. (1996) found that 56 percent of children in foster care receive some type of mental health service within the first six months of removal from their family of origin.

A number of factors seem to influence which children in care are more likely to receive mental health services For example, older children and males are more likely to receive mental health services (Blumberg et al., 1996; Garland et al., 1996; dosReis, Zito, Safer, & Soeken, 2001; Leslie, Hulbert, Landsverk, Barth, & Slymen, 2004; Thompson, 2005). Children who have been sexually or physically abused are more likely to use mental health services (Garland et al., 1996; Leslie et al., 2004). In fact, Shin (2005) found that foster children who were abused were about twenty-three times more likely to receive mental health services then foster children who did not have an abuse history.

As mentioned earlier, African-American children are disproportionately represented among the population of U.S. foster children and are therefore disproportionately impacted by the need for mental health services. However, African-American children in foster care are less likely to receive mental health services and when they do receive services, they tend to receive fewer services than Caucasian children (Close, 1983; Benedict, White, Stallings, & Cornely, 1989; Courtney et al., 1996; Tingus, Heger, Foy, & Leskin, 1996; Kolko, Selelyo, & Brown, 1999). Mental health services include diagnostic interviews, individual counseling or therapy, emergency or crisis care, family therapy, group therapy, hospitalization, residential care, medication management, and outpatient and inpatient care (Garland et al., 1996; Kolko et al., 1999; Leslie et al., 2004; Shin, 2005). In a review of a nationally representative cohort of children receiving specialty mental health care services during the first year after contact with child welfare services, African-American children were found to receive significantly fewer services than Caucasian children (Hurlburt et al., 2004).

This chapter presents a review of the literature on mental health utilization and service delivery issues for African-American children in general and for those in foster care and in group homes. Using a life course perspective and evidence-based practice approaches, suggestions are given for responding to the unique mental health needs of this overrepresented population of youth in care.

REVIEW OF THE LITERATURE

Mental Health Service Provision to African-American Youth

In the general population, African-American children are more likely than Caucasian children to have unmet mental health needs (USDHHS, 2001). Moreover, numerous studies have found racial disparities in access to mental health services. Using data from the National Survey on Child and Adolescent Well-Being, Leslie et al. (2004) found that African-American children were .34 times less likely to access mental health services than Caucasian children. Sheppard and Benjamin-Coleman (2001) examined the mental health services received by 2,803 African-American and Caucasian children between July 1993 and 1996 and they found that African-American children were more likely to be referred for services related to delinquency than mental health needs. Garland and Besinger (1997) found a trend for slightly lower recommendations for counseling services for African-American children than Caucasian children in a random sample of children in out of home care between May 1990 and October 1991.

Thompson (2005) reported that although there was no difference in the perceived need for services based on race, in a sample of predominantly low-income and minority children ages two to seven years, African-American children were less likely to receive services than Caucasian children specifically for behavioral and psychosocial problems. In this study 68 percent of the African-American children did not receive treatment for a parent-identified mental health need.

A number of factors have led to limited utilization of mental health services by African Americans. Partly because of historical experiences of race-based exclusion from health, educational, and social and economic resources; bias of providers; stigma in the community; poverty; cost of mental health care; and mistrust of systems (USDHHS, 2001), African Americans generally have not voluntarily sought mental health services.

Historically, society's response to the mental health problems of African-American children has been to institutionalize or incarcerate (Myers & King, 1983). For example, African-American youth are overrepresented in juvenile facilities as well as foster care. As many African-American youth are viewed stereotypically as being "aggressive," they are more likely to be diagnosed as schizophrenic, labeled as "aggressive," and prescribed psychiatric medications, and are also more likely to be labeled as being mentally or educationally retarded than Caucasian youth (Hill, 2005). Similarly, African-American youth are more likely to be identified for psychosocial problems and enter the juvenile justice system and less likely to receive the needed mental health and psychological interventions when behavioral problems arise (Gibbs, 2003).

ETHNIC DIFFERENCES IN UTILIZATION OF MENTAL HEALTH SERVICES

As noted earlier, findings vary on racial differences in mental health services provision to children in care. These differences tended to diminish as children's overall scores on the Child Behavior Checklist (CBCL) increased, indicating that as behaviors worsened access and use of services by Caucasian and African-American children became more comparable.

Tingus et al. (1996) found that a larger percentage of Caucasian children than African-American children received needed therapy within six months of being seen by county social services for sexual abuse evaluations. Haskett, Nowlan, Hutcheson, and Whitworth (1991) found that African-American children were less likely to attend therapy after a confirmed sexual abuse disclosure. Garland et al. (2000) found that when controlling for older age, severity of behavior problems, and type of maltreatment, African-American children were less likely to receive mental health services within the first six months of placement than Caucasian children. Burns et al. (2004) also found African-American school-age children in foster care were less likely to receive mental health services than Caucasian children of the same age.

Within a sample of 480 children in long-term foster care in a large metropolitan city, Leslie et al. (2000) found the number of outpatient visits reported by African-American children was comparable to Caucasian children. In this study 41.8 percent of the children had at least one outpatient mental health visit while in placement. The total number of outpatient services increased with age. Males and children in nonrelative foster care were also more likely to have an increased number of outpatient visits. Other studies have also found no significant differences based on race or ethnicity in the use of public mental health services by children in foster care (Blumberg et al., 1996; Risley-Curtiss, Combs-Orme, Chernoff, & Heisler, 1996).

However, in a recent study of Medicaid spending for children in foster care (Geen, Sommers, & Cohen, 2005), racial differences were noted. Using data from all fifty states and the District of Columbia, these researchers found that more Medicaid dollars were spent on Caucasian than on African-American or Hispanic children, on boys than girls, and on infants, adolescents, and older adolescents than on other children. The authors also found that the amount of spending per child varied from a high of $19,408 in Maine to a low of $1,309 in Arizona (Geen et al., 2005, p. 1).

MENTAL HEALTH DIAGNOSES OF CHILDREN IN CARE

The four leading diagnostic categories for children in foster care are adjustment disorders, conduct disorders, anxiety disorders, and emotional disorders (Haflon, Berkowitz, & Klee, 1992b). As mentioned earlier, a higher percentage of children in foster care receive a mental health diagnosis than children who receive other social services (dosReis et al., 2001; Farmer et al., 2001; Shin, 2005). After a review of Medicaid claims, Harman et al. (2000) found that children in foster care were three to ten times more likely to receive a mental health diagnosis. These children have been found to have a higher incidence of depression, anxiety disorders, and lack of behavioral or emotional control that has resulted in a higher rate of mental health service needs than children in the general population (Shin, 2005). In fact, Garland et al. (2001) found that 42 percent of children involved in child welfare meet the criteria for a mental disorder according to the *Diagnostic and Statistical Manual of Mental Disorders* (DSM-IV).

Ethnic differences have also been reported in research analyzing types of mental health diagnoses of children in foster care. In a study comparing children in foster care to children receiving SSI for disabilities, Caucasian children were found to be two times more likely than African-American children to be diagnosed with attention-deficit/hyperactivity disorder (ADHD), adjustment disorders, or depression (DosReis et al., 2001). Within the SSI group, however, African-American children were 3.6 times more likely to be diagnosed with ADHD and 2.9 times more likely to be diagnosed with developmental disorders. Other researchers have found that African-American youth are significantly more likely to be diagnosed with solitary conduct disorders and psychosis and less likely to be diagnosed with mood and anxiety disorders, substance abuse, and personality disorders (Pumariega, Rogers, & Rothe, 2005).

IMPACT OF TYPE OF PLACEMENT SETTING ON MENTAL HEALTH SERVICE PROVISION

Children removed from the home are placed in a variety of placement settings including kinship care, nonkinship foster care, therapeutic foster care, and residential care including group homes. The type of setting can influence likelihood of receiving mental health services. For example, children in kinship care placements have been found to use fewer mental health services than children in nonkinship foster care (Leslie et al., 2000; Burns et al., 2004; McMillen et al., 2004). African-American youth are about twice as likely as Caucasian children to be placed with kin rather than in nonrelated foster care (USDHHS, 2000). Despite the advantages of the stability of relative placements, many of these youth are living with older kin care providers "who are less likely to receive foster parent training, respite care, and children are less likely to receive educational or mental health assessments, counseling, or tutoring" (Hill, 2005, p. 8).

Children who were receiving mental health services prior to being removed from their homes are less likely to be placed in traditional foster care and more likely to be placed in residential group homes, a shelter, or the hospital (Blumberg et al., 1996). Some children are placed in therapeutic foster care (TFC), often seen as an alternative to a more restrictive residential placement (Curtis, Alexander, & Lunghofer, 2001; Buddle et al., 2004). Residential care includes community-based group homes and residential treatment centers. Children placed in both TFC and residential care often have significant behavioral, emotional, or mental problems that make it difficult for the child to maintain a placement in kinship or nonkinship foster care (Bryant & Snodgrass, 1990; Curtis et al., 2001).

The likelihood of placing African-American youth in residential versus other placement settings seems to vary. In one study of residential care in Illinois, African-American youth had a lower risk of being placed in residential care as their first out of home placement than Caucasian youth (Buddle et al., 2004). Shin (2005) found that 84 percent of foster youth who were diagnosed with a mental health disorder received at least one mental health service, with the most frequently used services being diagnostic interview (50 percent) and individual therapy (49 percent). Shin did not find any significant differences in service use between racial groups or type of placement. However, another study in Virginia reported that placement rates were higher for African Americans in all placement types including foster care, residential, hospitalization, and detention (Sheppard & Benjamin-Coleman, 2001). Some studies published in the early 1990s found that although 30 percent of the children in both TFC and residential care were African American, the majority of the children in these types of placements were older, Caucasian males (Curtis et al., 2001).

One study of a Pittsburgh-based TFC agency, found that 65 percent of the children served were African American (Timbers, 1990). Long-term outcomes for children who have been in residential settings also differ. African-American children are significantly more likely to be discharged from residential care to foster care as opposed to a more permanent setting such as reunification with parent or adoption (Buddle et al., 2004).

Children who move experience more out-of-home placements, often exhibit more disturbing behaviors, and, as a result, utilize more mental health services (James, Landsverk, Slymen, & Leslie, 2004; Hussey & Guo, 2005). In a sample of children with both psychotic and aggressive behaviors, children in TFC were more likely to use services such as respite care, in-home counseling, after-school programs, crisis intervention services, medical doctors, and mentor or therapeutic mental health services (Breland-Noble, Farmer, Dubs, Potter, & Burns, 2005). In the same study, children in group homes were more likely to work with a mental health professional, serve time in detention, have a probation officer, have an emergency room visit, and attend a special school than children in TFC.

BARRIERS TO MENTAL HEALTH SERVICE DELIVERY TO CHILDREN IN FOSTER CARE: IMPACT OF MANAGED CARE

Identified barriers to adequate mental health services for children in foster care include legal requirements that biological parents must consent to any care other than routine mental health; caseworkers relying on foster care givers to identify need for services; foster care givers not having the right to consent for mental health services; a lack of comprehensive mental health programs for foster children; and the advent of managed care (Simms, Dubowitz, & Szilagyi, 2000). Children in foster care do not experience the needed continuity of overall medical care under managed care (DiGiuseppe & Christakis, 2003).

Under managed care, African Americans have been found to receive less follow-up care after hospitalization for mental illness than Caucasians (Virnig et al., 2004). Snowden, Cueller, and Libby (2003) explored the impact of managed care on access to mental health services for minority children in foster care. Under managed care, overall, African-American children were found to receive less mental health care; however, they were found to have significant increases in residential treatment usage. Garland, Landsverk, and Lau (2003) identify possible explanations for racial disparities in the mental health services to African-American children, including cultural differences in help-seeking patterns; systemic bias in referral and service delivery; lack of minority health providers; and biased assessment techniques, resulting in triage to alternative services. All of these factors combined can result in African-American children receiving inequitable services while in the system.

Moreover, children who have been abused or neglected have been found to be more likely to engage in delinquent behavior that may lead to later incarceration (Wiebush, Freitag, & Baird, 2001). Those youth who are experiencing major behavioral problems are least likely to achieve permanence through adoption. About 20,000 youth never achieve permanency and "age out" of the foster care system each year or exit through running away or incarceration (General Accounting Office, 2004). In fact, studies have shown that high percentages of incarcerated felons in many states had at some time been in foster care (Hill, 2005).

NEW AND EXPANDED APPROACHES

Much evidence of mental health disorders among foster youth has been provided. However, a number of factors have been found that have limited the likelihood of treatment of these disorders. According to Austin (2005), "the inadequate training and experience of mental health professionals, child welfare staff, and foster families; limited collaboration between providers and biological parents, failure of the child welfare system to conduct regular assessments and lack of financial resources" are all barriers to service delivery (p. 8). Austin calls for better service coordination, intensive case management, and wraparound services that can lead to a reduction in placement changes (p. 12).

It is critical to design programs that address barriers to treatment and to develop evidence-based treatment approaches to provide quality care to

African-American youth and their families. Marsenich (2002) reported the effectiveness of wraparound and therapeutic foster care services, and called for proven effective models such as cognitive behavior therapy for depression and anger control therapy to be adapted for use with foster children and their families. Moreover, it is important to examine differential referrals of African Americans to other systems, including mental health and juvenile justice. As noted earlier, research has shown that disparate outcomes have been found to decrease when there is greater interagency collaboration between local child welfare and mental health agencies (Hurlburt et al., 2004). More research is needed that explores the use of alternative models of health care delivery and specific mental health interventions for children in foster care (Simms et al., 2000).

A number of suggestions are found in the literature for innovative approaches to address the mental health needs of African-American youth in the system. For example, Utsey, Howard, and Williams (2003) suggest an alternative therapeutic group mentoring model for working with African-American male adolescents in foster care. This model is designed to incorporate the significance of extended family, including fictive kin within the African-American community. A case study of six adolescents and mentors provided anecdotal evidence that with positive mentoring relationships, the group model is "effective in facilitating change in attitudes and behavior of several group members" (p. 138).

Gibbs (2003) recommends that in treating African-American youth, mental health clinicians need to "evaluate their exposure to traumatic events, their experiences with racial integration, their access to opportunities in the community, as well as current symptomatology and history of behavior problems" (p. 93). Clinicians need to take into consideration the family environment of the African-American youth including family structure and socioeconomic status.

Other scholars, such as Dupree, Spencer, and Bell (1997), discuss the importance of understanding the child's psychological disturbance from a life span developmental perspective. While emphasizing that the basic development of the African-American child is no different than that of other children, Dupree et al. (1997) identify sources of stress resulting from racism and discrimination that are important to consider when treating some African-American children. These sources of stress include poverty, low socioeconomic status, and environmental dangers such as neighborhood violence. With these stresses in mind, the clinician is encouraged to help the child to develop resilient coping strategies for survival.

Gibbs (2003) identifies family therapy as a primary treatment modality for African-American youth given the strong value African Americans place on family ties, including a large network of relatives and fictive kin children in out-of-home placements receiving mental health services that have been found to have very little involvement with their families (Duchnowski, Hall, Kutash, & Friedman, 1998). In a multiple-site study of children placed in an Alternative to Residential Treatment Study (ARTS), Duchnowski et al. found that many of the children receiving mental health services were reported to have been approximately six years old at problem onset and, on average, 8.7 years old at the time of receipt of their first mental health service. These children tend to have a high number of out-of-home placements and the severity of their problems tend to worsen over time. Family involvement in treatment had diminished considerably prior to the children's entry into the study, suggesting that failing to support families early on when the child's behavior first manifests leads to long-term involvement with the mental health system for the youth.

For African-American adolescents, Gibbs (2003) recommends that the mental health clinician understand that the youth may enter therapy with a great deal of anxiety and superstition. African-American youth are reported to be sensitive to the initial interactions with the therapists, looking for signs of respect as opposed to patronization or overfamiliarity. Clinicians are cautioned not to use ethnic slang or an oversimplified vocabulary with the youth. However, clinicians should recognize African-American youth's need to be seen as "cool" and understand that many of the street smart behaviors the youth exhibit are coping strategies that the child has used to survive chaotic and stressful environments.

Gibbs' recommendations are similar to those of Jackson and Westmoreland (1992), who identified the need for the therapist to be seen as trustworthy and credible by African-American children and youth. Jackson and Westmoreland noted that African-American children in foster care often come from an environment of deprivation and powerlessness. Placement in foster care compounds feelings of helplessness and lack of control that the child may already have experienced. Developing a therapeutic relationship with an African-American child may prove to be difficult given the child's suspicion of social workers, police officers, and others in a position of power and may have resulted in negative interactions with them or their biological family. This can also hinder the therapist's ability to engage the child's family in therapy. Jackson and Westmoreland recommend that the therapist working with African-American children in foster care be able to integrate knowledge of the normal childhood and development with knowledge of African-American culture and the impact of societal, economic, and political conditions on the circumstances that lead to the child entering care.

CONCLUSION

Much more research is needed on appropriate interventions for African-American youth in out-of-home care. However, the first step is to acknowledge that disparate service provision and utilization exists and then to bring mental health, child welfare, and juvenile authorities to the table in communities throughout the nation to begin to examine the data and make a plan to address the intersystemic issues that are disproportionately affecting African-American children. Staff should receive mandatory training in culturally competent service delivery and agencies should be evaluated and funded based upon their ability to provide equitable service delivery to all children and youth.

Agencies must begin to examine front-end decision making to identify ways to prevent children from coming into care by providing family based services in the home. Funding is needed to enable foster care, juvenile justice, and mental health staff to receive "undoing racism" training, to learn more about the structural factors that may have led to disparate treatment of African-American children and families. In addition, culturally appropriate parent skills training, job training, and subsidized housing are needed to address an underlying problem that leads to children entering the system—poverty. By reducing disproportionate poverty, many of the long-term negative outcomes resulting from neglect, abuse and placements may be avoided.

CHAPTER SUMMARY

Children in foster care have typically experienced a variety of losses, involuntary removal from their family of origin, neglect, and often abuse, and are highly likely to have a mental health diagnosis such as depression, anxiety disorder, psychoses, conduct disorders, attention deficit hyperactivity disorder, and/or developmental disorders. Research has shown that African-American children are disproportionately represented among the population of children in care, tend to enter care at younger ages, stay for a longer period of care, and are therefore likely to experience significant mental health needs.

However, the majority of studies have documented disparate mental health service utilization and delivery to African-American children in the foster care system. This finding seems consistent with the U.S. Surgeon General's report (USDHHS, 2001) on mental health outcomes, which stated, "racial and ethnic minorities bear a greater burden from unmet mental health needs and thus suffer a greater loss to their overall health and productivity" (p. 3).

A number of barriers to mental health treatment exist including differential referral and service delivery bias, lack of minority health providers, cultural differences in help-seeking, and lack of coordinated services between mental health and local child welfare offices. When services are provided, clinicians should design culturally appropriate interventions that take into consideration African-American life experiences and recognize and involve members of the extended family including fictive kin. Family treatment approaches should examine sources of stress in the family and community and emphasize the need to develop resilient coping strategies for survival.

Agencies must become aware of the impact of disparate service delivery on African-American youth in foster care. Increasing interagency collaboration between mental health services and child welfare services must occur and strategies for addressing differential referrals are essential. As much is known about the typical problems experienced by children in care, agencies should be proactive and provide foster parents with culturally appropriate training on these unique mental health needs as well as on strategies for accessing services. Moreover, training is needed for judges as well as child welfare agency staff on mental health needs and resources for the population of children in care. Finally, additional research is needed to develop more ethnically and developmentally appropriate, evidence-based mental health services for African-American youth and their families.

SUGGESTED GROUP AND CLASSROOM ACTIVITIES

1. Visit a local public child welfare agency and interview staff about the types of mental health problems that African-American foster children are experiencing. Collect data on mental health service providers and interview staff about the agency's needs to enhance service provision to African-American families.
2. Interview African-American community leaders and pastors to assess their perceptions of mental health needs of families and youth. Explore their awareness of the unique needs of children in foster care. Provide a copy of the list of mental health service providers as a resource for these community leaders.
3. Interview the directors of several mental health, juvenile justice, and child welfare agencies to determine what types of ongoing collaboration is occurring to address the needs of African-American children in care.

4. Review the literature on culturally competent mental health service provision for youth and develop an annotated bibliography of references that can be shared with local agency providers.
5. Identify social and economic strategies for preserving families and preventing the need for foster care placement.

REFERENCES

Austin, L. (2005). Unlocking mental health services for youth in care. *Children's Voice, 14*(3), 6-13.

Benedict, M. I., White, R. B., Stallings, R., & Cornely, D. A. (1989). Racial differences in health care utilization among children in foster care. *Children and Youth Services Review, 11,* 285-297.

Blumberg, E., Landsverk, J. L., Ellis-McLeod, E., Ganger, W., & Culver, S. (1996). Use of the public mental health system by children in foster care: Client characteristics and service use patterns. *Journal of Mental Health Administration, 23*(4), 389-405.

Breland-Noble, A. M., Farmer, E. M. Z., Dubs, M. S., Potter, E., & Burns, B. J. (2005). Mental health and other service use by youth in therapeutic foster care and group homes. *Journal of Child and Family Studies, 14*(2), 167-180.

Bryant, B., & Snodgrass, R. D. (1990). Therapeutic foster care: Past and present. In P. Meadowcroft & B. A. Trout (Eds.), *Troubled Youth in Treatment Homes: A Handbook of Therapeutic Foster Care* (pp. 1-20). Washington, DC: CWLA.

Buddle, S., Mayer, S., Zinn, A., Lippold, M., Avrushin, A., Bromberg, A., et al. (2004). *Residential Care in Illinois: Trends and Alternatives* (Final Report). Chicago, IL: Chapin Hall Center for Children at the University of Chicago.

Burns, B. J., Phillips, S. D., Wagner, H. R., Barth, R. P., Kolko, D. J., Campbell, Y., et al. (2004). Mental health need and access to mental health services by youth involved with child welfare: A National survey. *Journal of the American Academy of Child & Adolescent Psychiatry, 43*(8), 960-970.

Cappelleri, J., Eckenrode, J., & Powers, J. (1993). The epidemiology of child abuse: Findings from the second national incidence and prevalence study of child abuse and neglect. *American Journal of Public Health, 83*(11), 1622-1624.

Casey Family Programs. (2001). It's My Life. Casey Family Programs.

Clausen, J. M., Landsverk, J., Ganger, W., Chadwick, D., & Litrownik, A. (1998). Mental health problems of children in foster care. *Journal of Child and Family Studies, 7*(3), 283-296.

Clarke, J., Stein, M. D., Sobota, M., Marisi, M., & Lucy, H. (1999). Victims as victimizers: Physical aggression by persons with a history of childhood abuse. *Archives of Internal Medicine, 159,* 1920-1924.

Close, M. M. (1983). Child welfare and people of color: Denial of equal access. *Social Work Research and Abstracts, 19,* 13-20.

Courtney, M. E., Barth, R. P., Berrick, J. D., Brooks, D., Needell, B., & Park, L. (1996). Race and child welfare services: Past research and future directions. *Child Welfare, 75,* 99-135.

Curtis, P. A., Alexander, G., & Lunghofer, L. A. (2001). A literature review comparing the outcomes of residential group care and therapeutic foster care. *Child and Adolescent Social Work Journal, 18*(5), 377-392.

DiGiuseppe, D., & Christakis, D. A. (2003). Continuity of care for children in foster care. *Pediatrics, 111*(3), 208-213.

DosReis, S., Zito, J. M., Safer, D., & Soeken, K. L. (2001). Mental health services for youths in foster care and disabled youth. *American Journal of Public Health, 91*(7), 1094-1099.

Duchnowski, A. J., Hall, K. S., Kutash, K., & Friedman, R. M. (1998). The alternatives to residential treatment study. In M. H. Epstein, K. Kutash, & A. Duchnowski (Eds.), *Outcomes for Children and Youth with Emotional and Behavioral Disorders and their Families: Programs and Evaluations Best Practices* (pp. 55-80). Austin, TX: PRO-ED.

Dupree, D., Spencer, M. B., & Bell, S. (1997). African American children. In G. Johnson-Powell & J. Yahamoto (Eds.), *Transcultural Child Development* (pp. 237-268). New York: John Wiley & Sons, Inc.

Farmer, E. M. Z., Burns, B. J., Chapman, M. V., Philips, S. D., Angold, A., & Costello, E. J. (2001). Use of mental healthy services by youth in contact with social services. *Social Service Review, 75,* 605-624.

Garland, A. F., & Besinger, B. A. (1997). Racial/Ethnic differences in court referred pathways to mental health services for children in foster care. *Children and Youth Services Review, 19*(8), 651-666.

Garland, A. F., Hough, R. L., Landsverk, J. A., McCabe, K. M., Yeh, M., Ganger, W. C., et al. (2000). Racial and ethnic variations in mental health care utilization among children in foster care. *Children's Services: Social Policy, Research, and Practice, 3*(3), 133-146.

Garland, A. F., Hough, R. L., McCabe, K. M., Yeh, M., Wood, P. A., & Aarons, G. A. (2001). Prevalence of psychiatric disorders in youths across five sectors of care. *Journal of the American Academy of Child & Adolescent Psychiatry, 40*(4), 409-418.

Garland, A. F., Landsverk, J. L., Hough, R. L., & Ellis-MacLeod, E. (1996). Type of maltreatment as a predictor of mental health service use for children in foster care. *Child Abuse & Neglect, 20*(8), 675-688.

Garland, A. F., Landsverk, J. A., & Lau, A. S. (2003). Racial/Ethnic Disparities in mental health service use among children in foster care. *Children and Youth Services Review, 25*(5/6), 491-507.

Geen, R., Sommers, A., & Cohen, M. (2005). *Medicaid Spending on Foster Children.* Washington, DC: Urban Institute.

General Accounting Office. (November 2004). *Foster Youth: HHS Actions Could Improve Coordination of Service and Monitoring of States' Independent Living Programs.* GAO-05-25. Washington, DC: General Accounting Office.

Gibbs, J. T. (2003). Part Two: African American and racially mixed population groups. In J. T. Gibbs, L. N. Huang, & Associates (Eds.), *Children of Color; Psychological Interventions with Culturally Diverse Youth* (pp. 91-182). San Francisco: Jossey-Bass.

Haflon, N., Berkowitz, G., & Klee, L. (1992a). Children in foster care in California; An examination of Medicaid reimbursed health services utilization. *Pediatrics, 6*(89), 1230-1237.

Haflon, N., Berkowitz, G., & Klee, L. (1992b). Mental Health Service Utilization by Children in Foster Care. *Pediatrics, 6(89), 1238-1244.*

Harman, J. S., Childs, G. E., & Kelleher, K. J. (2000). Mental health care utilization and expenditures by children in foster care. *Archives of Pediatrics and Adolescent Medicine, 154*(11), 1114-1117.

Haskett, M. E., Nowlan, N. P., Hutcheson, J. S., & Whitworth, J. M. (1991). Factors associated with successful entry into therapy in child sexual abuse cases. *Child Abuse & Neglect, 15,* 467-475.

Hill, R. (2005). Disproportionality of Minorities in Child Welfare: Synthesis of Research Findings. Race Matters Consortium. Available at: www.racematters .org. Accessed March 5, 2006.

Holland, P., & Gorey, K. M. (2004). Historical, developmental, and behavioral factors associated with foster care challenges. *Child and Adolescent Social Work Journal, 21*(2), 117-135.

Hurlburt, M., Leslie, L. K., Landsverk, J., Barth, R. P., Burns, B. J., Gibbons, R. D. et al. (2004). Contextual predictors of mental health service use among children open to child welfare. *Archives of General Psychiatry, 12*(61), 1217-1224.

Hussey, D. L., & Guo, S. (2005). Characteristic and trajectories of treatment foster care youth. *Child Welfare, 84*(4), 485-506.

Jackson, H. L., & Westmoreland, G. (1992). Therapeutic issues for black children in foster care. In L. A. Vargas & J. D. Koss-Chiono (Eds.), *Working with Culture: Psychotherapeutic Interventions with Ethnic Minority Children and Adolescents* (pp. 43-62). San Francisco: Jossey-Bass.

James, S., Landsverk, J., Slymen, D. J., & Leslie, L. K. (2004). Predictors of outpatient mental health service use—The role of foster care placement change. *Mental Health Services Research, 6*(3), 127-141.

Johnson, J. G., Cohen, P., Brown, J., Smailes, E. M., & Bernstein, D. P. (1999). Childhood maltreatment increases risk for personality disorders during early childhood. *Archives of General Psychiatry, 56,* 600-606.

Kavaler, F., & Swire, M. R. (1983). *Foster-Child Health Care.* Lexington, MA: Lexington Books.

Kessler, R. C., Davis, C. G., & Kendler, K. S. (1997). Childhood adversity and adult psychiatric disorder in the US national Comorbidity Survey. *Psychological Medicine, 27,* 1101-1119.

Kolko, D. J., Selelyo, J., & Brown, E. J. (1999). The treatment histories and service involvement of physically and sexually abusive families: Description, correspondence, and clinical correlates. *Child Abuse & Neglect, 23*(5), 459-476.

Leslie, L. K., Hurlburt, M. S., Landsverk, J., Barth, R., & Slymen, D. J. (2004). Outpatient mental health services for children in foster care: A national perspective. *Child Abuse & Neglect, 28,* 697-712.

Leslie, L. K., Landsverk, J., Ezzet-Lofstrom, R., Tschann, J. M., Slymen, D. J., & Garland, A. F. (2000). Children in Foster Care: Factors influencing outpatient mental health service use. *Child Abuse & Neglect, 24*(4), 465-476.

Lisette, A. (2005). Unlocking mental health services for youth in care. *Children's Voice, 14*(3), 6-13.

Marsenich, L. (2002). *Evidence-Based Practices in Mental Health Services for Foster Youth.* Sacramento California Institute for Mental Health.

McMillen, J. C, Scott, L. Zima, B., Ollie, M. Munson, M., & Spitznagel, E. (2004). Use of mental health services among older youths in foster care. *Psychiatric services: A Journal of the American Psychiatric Association, 55*(7), 811-817.

Myers, H. F., & King, L. M. (1983). Mental health issues in the development of the black American child. In G. J. Powell (Ed.), *The Psychosocial Development of Minority Group Children* (pp. 275-306). New York: Brunner/Mazel.

Pumariega, A. J., Rogers, K., & Rothe, E. (2005). Culturally competent systems of care for children's mental health: Advances and challenges. *Community Mental Health Journal, 41*(5), 539-555.

Risley-Curtiss, C., Combs-Orme, T., Chernoff, R., & Heisler, A. (1996). Health care utilization by children entering foster care. *Research on Social Work Practice, 6*(4), 442-461.

Rubin, D. M., Alessandrini, E. A., Feudtner, C., Mandell, D. S., Localio, A. R., & Hadley, T. (2004). Placement stability and mental health costs for children in foster care. *Pediatrics, 113,* 1336-1341.

Sedlak, A., & Broadhurst, D. (1996). *Executive Summary of the Third National Incidence Study of Child Abuse and Neglect.* Rockville, MD: U.S. Department of Health and Human Services.

Sedlak, A., & Schultz, D. (2001). *Race Differences in Child Protective Services Investigation of Abuse and Neglected Children.* Paper presented at The Race Matters Forum sponsored by the University of Illinois at Urbana-Champaign and Westat, January 9-10, 2001.

Sheppard, V. B., & Benjamin-Coleman, R. (2001). Determinants of service placements for youth with serious emotional and behavioral disturbances. *Community Mental Health Journal, 37*(1), 53-65.

Shin, S. H. (2005). Need for and actual use of mental health services by adolescents in the child welfare system. *Children and Youth Services Review, 27,* 1071-1083.

Simms, M. D., Dubowitz, H., & Szilagyi, M. A. (2000). Health care needs of children in the foster care system. *Pediatrics, 106*(4), 909-918.

Snowden, L. R., Cueller, A. E., & Libby, A. M. (2003). Minority youth in foster care: Managed care and access to mental health treatment. *Medical Care, 41*(2), 264-274.

Spearly, J., & Lauderdale, M. (1983). Community characteristics and ethnicity in the prediction of child maltreatment rates. *Child Abuse & Neglect, 7*(1), 91-103.

Takayama, J. I., Bergman, A. B., & Connell, F. A. (1994). Children in foster care in the state of Washington. Health care utilization and expenditures. *The Journal of the American Medical Association, 271*(23), 1850-1855.

Thompson, R. (2005). The course and correlates of mental health care received by young children: Descriptive data from a longitudinal urban high-risk sample. *Children and Youth Services Review, 27,* 39-50.

Timbers, G. (1990). Describing the children served in treatment homes. In P. Meadowcroft & A. Trout (Eds.), *Troubled Youth in Treatment Homes: A Hand-Book of Therapeutic Foster Care* (pp. 1-20). Washington, DC: CWLA.

Tingus, K. D., Heger, A. H., Foy, D. W., & Leskin, G. A. (1996). Factors associated with entry into therapy in children evaluated for sexual abuse. *Child Abuse & Neglect, 20*(1), 63-68.

U.S. Department of Health and Human Services. (2001). *Mental Health: Culture, Race and Ethnicity—A Supplement to Mental Health: A Report of the Surgeon General.* Rockville, MD: U.S. Department of Health and Human Services, Substance Abuse and Mental Health Services Administration, Center for Mental Health Services.

U.S. Department of Health and Human Services, Administration for Children and Families, Administration on Children, Youth and Families, Children's Bureau. (2000). *Report to Congress on Kinship Foster Care*. Available at: http://aspe .hhs.gov/hsp/kinr2c00/index.htm. Accessed February 3, 2006.

U.S. Department of Health and Human Services, Administration for Children and Families, Administration on Children, Youth and Families, Children's Bureau. (2005a). *Child Maltreatment 2003.* Washington, DC: U.S. Government Printing Office.

U.S. Department of Health and Human Services, Administration for Children and Families, Administration on Children, Youth and Families, Children's Bureau. (2005b). The AFCARS Report: Preliminary FY 2003 Estimates as of April 2005. Available at: www.acf.hhs.gov/programs/cb. Accessed March 16, 2006.

Utsey, S. O., Howard, A., & Williams, O. (2003). Therapeutic group mentoring with African American male adolescents. *Journal of Mental Health Counseling, 25*(2), 126-139.

Virnig, B., Huang, Z., Lurie, N., Musgrave, D., McBean, M., & Dowd, B. (2004). Does medicare managed care provide equal treatment for mental illness across races? *Archives of General Psychiatry, 61*(2), 201-205.

Werner, E. E., & Smith, S. (1982). *Vulnerable but Invincible: A Study of Resilient Children.* New York: McGraw-Hill.

Wiebusch, R., Freitag, R., & Baird, C. (2001). *Preventing delinquency through improved child protection services.* Office of Juvenile Justice and Delinquency Prevention, Juvenile Justice Bulletin. Washington, DC: U.S. Department of Justice.

Chapter 5

African-American Women and Depression: The Intersection of Race and Gender

Carla Adkison-Bradley
Elizabeth Bradshaw
Jo-Ann Lipford Sanders

It is estimated that 17.5 million Americans suffer from clinical depression. Women experience depression twice as often as men (NIMH, 2000). The demographics for Black women who are depressed are noteworthy. For example, of the women between the ages of thirty and thirty-nine who are diagnosed as depressed, 58 percent are African American while only 20 percent are White American (Jones-Webb & Snowden, 1993).

As a society, we know little about the psychology of African-American women who comprise 7 percent (19 million people) of the U.S. population (United States Census, 2004). Specifically, many academic researchers and therapists have ignored the intersection of race, gender, and mental health. Several African-American women scholars (Greene, 1994; Jackson & Greene, 2000; Sanchez-Hucles, 1997) have attributed the absence of the African-American female perspective in the psychological literature to her dual identity as a member of a racially oppressed group and as a woman. Although other cultural identities such as ethnicity, gender, sexual orientation, spirituality, and class have been recognized and incorporated into discussions of client diversity, the saliency of race continues to be minimized within the counseling profession. For example, in the psychology profession,

Mental Health Care in the African-American Community
© 2007 by The Haworth Press, Inc. All rights reserved.
doi:10.1300/5364_05

the *Handbook for Counseling Women* (Kopala & Keitel, 2003) has been described as a definitive text for addressing the counseling needs of women. However, out of the thirty-three chapters contained in the book, there is not one chapter or major discussion on the mental health needs of African-American women.

When African-American women are the focus of research attention in regards to mental health and/or depression, the articles mainly focus on issues such as poverty (de Groot, Auslander, Williams, Sherraden, & Haire-Joshu, 2003; Kohn, Oden, Munoz, Robinson, & Leavitt, 2002), drug abuse (Boyd, Henderson, Ross-Durow, & Aspen, 1997; Ross-Durow & Boyd, 2000), or HIV (Johnson, Cunningham-Williams, & Cottler, 2003; Moneyham, Sowell, Seals, & Demi, 2000). The academic research is also limited in its sampling of African-American women. Most of the research is done with low-income (Jones, O'Connell, Gound, Heller, & Forehand, 2004; Ialongo et al., 2004) and single-parent women (Lehrer, Crittenden, & Norr, 2002; Ritter, Hobfoll, Lavin, Cameron, & Hulsizer, 2000), leaving the perspectives of other African-American women (e.g., working and middle class) out of the discourse. The not-so-hidden message is that the behaviors and cognitions demonstrated in "at-risk" African-American women are descriptive of the experiences of all African-American women. As a result, clinicians are left with a very narrow view of how African-American women cope with life circumstances in general and how they experience depression in particular. This narrow view could lead clinicians to underdiagnose or overpathologize the emotional concerns of African-American women.

Exploring the life course issues and concerns of women in general, and women between the ages of thirty and thirty-nine in particular, has become central in understanding women who struggle with depression. According to most developmental theories, individuals work their way through one developmental stage or life event to the next by solving problems that are met at each stage (Thomas, 1985). Life events and challenges such as childbirth and child rearing, marriage, divorce, and career and financial concerns pose the greatest impact on the lives of women. Several African-American scholars have contended, however, that African-American women have the additional responsibility and often stressor of preparing African-American children to exist in a hostile and racist society. African-American women are also the lowest paid in comparison to White American men, White American women, and African-American men.

To work effectively and competently with African-American women, helping professionals need to have a more accurate and informed understanding of the aspects of depression in African-American women and the clinical challenges that arise in addressing the counseling needs of this particular population. Hence, the overarching theme of this chapter is to describe and clarify issues and information regarding African-American women and depression. More specifically, this chapter presents and explains images and perceptions of African-American women. With knowledge of these critical issues, practitioners are in a better position to establish rapport, obtain accurate information, and formulate strengths-based intervention strategies. Characteristics and symptoms of depression along with treatment issues are presented. Implications for effective therapeutic practice is also discussed.

REVIEW OF LITERATURE

Contextual Dimensions: Images and Perceptions of African-American Women

A discussion of the emotional experiences of African-American women is complex because society has portrayed this population in constraining and degrading ways. Three of the most well-known stereotypes of African-American women are Mammy, Sapphire, and Jezebel. The Mammy persona originated from the days where African female slaves were used to clean house and tend to the master's children. This figure is "depicted as a bandanna clad, obese, dark complexioned woman with African features" (West, 1995, p. 459). Historically, the media has portrayed her as happy and always easy to soothe everyone's hurt and service their needs.

An example of the Mammy stereotype in action can be seen outlined in Bell and Nkomo's (2001) book *Our Separate Ways*. The authors conducted a study of White female professionals and asked them to discuss their perceptions of their Black female counterparts. The authors quote one specific White female professional in her description of Black female managers:

> I've watched how the senior women look out for the younger Black women and men in the company. There is always one who will organize a group, make sure they meet, and be responsible for their welfare. She is always available for consultation and willing to lend a hand if help is needed. Management looks to her when there are minority problems. And they better listen to her, because she doesn't take excuses from anybody. I think their behavior is partially based on the fact that they come from a matriarchal society where women run things. (p. 245)

Mitchell and Herring (1998) stated that the Mammy stereotype is so ingrained into American culture "that we expect some aspects of mammy like behavior from all Black women, whether they fit the physical description of Mammy or not" (p. 54).

The Mammy stereotypical image has implications for psychological distress in African-American women. The Mammy stereotype can bring about issues of appearance and the workhorse mentality for African-American women. The image of the "bandanna clad, obese, dark complexioned woman with African features" (West, 1995, p. 459) does not match with the White, thin, blond, and blue-eyed image of American female beauty (hooks, 2003). This disconnect can cause African-American women to question their physical attractiveness and desirability. The realization that they will never measure up to this White ideal can cause serious psychological distress.

Another stereotype of African-American women is Sapphire. This portrayal of African-American women is often traced back to the character of "Sapphire" from the 1950s television show of Amos & Andy (Mitchell & Herring, 1998; West, 1995) Sapphire depicts African-American women as "loud, obnoxious, and nagging" (Mitchell & Herring, 1998, p. 57). Several African-American women scholars (Benjamin, 1997; Smith, 1999; Turner, 2002) have espoused that African-American women who are confident, intelligent, and assertive in their professional responsibilities can be perceived as being a "Sapphire." The following narrative from an African-American woman professor illustrates this tendency:

> I am an educated African American female who is a law professor. As such, I am a Sapphire. I am a Sapphire not because I choose to be or because I actually am. I am a Sapphire because of an inflexible characterization about Black women that concludes that I am angry, threatening, and unintelligent. As a Sapphire, I am not regarded as entirely unintelligent, but intelligent enough to use my wit in angry and threatening ways. My status and effectiveness as a law professor and my potential career opportunities are diminished by my identity as a Black woman, i.e., as a Sapphire. (Smith, 1999, p. 32)

The Sapphire stereotype perpetuates the falsehood that African-American women are one-dimensional: they are either selfless nurturers like Mammy or loud and argumentative like Sapphire.

West (1995) discussed the stereotype of Jezebel as having come from the days of slavery when "white slave owners exercised almost complete control over Black women's sexuality and reproduction" (p. 462). Black female sexuality has become distorted by these violent roots and is still often seen as "bestial, and sexually out of control" (Greene, 2000, p. 241). In reality, a 1997 study (Wyatt, 1997) of the sexual behaviors of women revealed that White American women were more sexually active than African-American women.

The continuance of the Jezebel image can negatively affect African-American women. African-American women may feel that they are to be blamed for sexual assaults and more globally feel that they should not have control over their own sexual choices.

CHARACTERISTICS AND SYMPTOMS OF DEPRESSION

The most well-known and documented symptoms of depression include depressed mood for majority of the day, almost every day, little or no interest in normal activities (especially those that used to bring pleasure), loss of energy, and feelings of worthlessness or excessive or inappropriate guilt (American Psychiatric Association, 2000).

There are also differing degrees of intensity when it comes to depression. Depression can range from experiencing dysthymia to major depression. Dysthymia is a chronic disorder where people experience depressive symptoms but at a lesser intensity. A unique aspect of dysthymia is that the symptoms can seem to be just part of the person's personality (Mitchell & Herring, 1998). Major depression is the most severe form of depression. This form of depression involves symptoms that are usually present for at least two weeks in what is referred to as a depressive episode. Individuals with this disorder often feel as though they live in a world of complete darkness and think that they will never be happy again.

According to Jones and Shorter-Gooden (2003), however, a classic expression of depression often unique to African-American women is the sisterella complex. The sisterella complex is a constellation of depressive symptoms that have been described as unable to relax, works very hard (job tasks, household, child care), and is disconnected from one's own personal needs, suffers quietly, experiences excessive guilt, feels worthless and unworthy (Jackson & Greene, 2000; Jones & Shorter-Gooden, 2003). Several scholars have asserted that the "busyness" clinical feature is a coping mechanism for African-American women to keep their minds off feelings of sadness that have arisen. This expression of depression has proven problematic for African-American women because clinicians often evaluate depression based on the traditional symptoms identified in the DSM-IV, putting African-American women at risk for being underdiagnosed or perceived as not having clinical issues.

One of the barriers to effective and proper diagnosis and treatment of depression in African-American women is that they tend to shy away from receiving professional treatment for their depression. Several African-American clinicians have asserted there is a stigma attached to counseling in the African-American community. Specifically, seeking counseling is often seen as "being weak" or confirmation that an individual is "crazy" or out of control. Moreover, many African-American women may feel that their depressive symptoms or depressed mood is not anything to complain about. For instance, Danquah (2003) stated in an *Essence* magazine article, "my hardships were nothing in comparison with those that generations of Black women before me had faced" (p. 50). Danquah also acknowledged that "I saw therapy as an indulgence, a luxury I couldn't afford, and the idea of antidepressants frightened me. Taking medication would seem to confirm I was crazy" (p. 1). According to Jones and Shorter-Goodson (2003), too often African-American women dismiss their symptoms to just the "way of life" and attempt to go on as best they can until the symptoms become so debilitating that they are no longer able to function. As a result, many African-American women may be diagnosed with depression during medical visits or routine examinations. Hines-Martin, Malone, Kim, and Brown-Piper (2003) theorized that recognizing somatic symptoms associated with depression (e.g., backaches, shoulder pain, and headaches) may be the initial step in identifying depression in African-American women.

CASE STUDY: JUANITA

In an effort to illustrate the complexities and experiences of African Americans with depression, we will consider the case of Juanita. Juanita is a composite of African-American women that have been treated for emotional issues by the authors of this chapter.

Juanita is a fifty-year-old woman referred to the counseling agency by her girlfriend who was concerned about Juanita's emotional state. Juanita is an attractive, well-dressed professional woman working on a master's degree in marketing. She is the middle child and eldest daughter with an older brother and younger sister. Juanita's father was physically abusive to her mother and brother. After attempting to murder his wife, he was imprisoned when Juanita was sixteen years old. He also sexually abused Juanita for several years during her early teens. She has had no contact with him since her teens other than a chance meeting. Juanita has a very fragile relationship with her mother who seems to have displaced her anger toward her husband onto Juanita. Her brother has also been involved in the penal system for the majority of his life; and her younger sister, married and divorced in her early twenties, seems very dependent on Juanita for financial and emotional support.

Juanita is very active in her church. She is a minister, leader of the young people's auxiliary, and a Sunday school teacher. Many of the younger women refer to her as "mother."

Juanita has also played the role of "mother" to her siblings beginning as early as sixteen years old when her mother was hospitalized. During the months of rehabilitation, Juanita and her siblings were moved from relative to relative. During these times Juanita reports, "I had to learn to be strong, who else was going to take care of us." Juanita assumed the role of "mother" again when her younger sister asked Juanita to raise her five-year old.

Juanita has been married twice. Her first marriage occurred when she was in her early twenties; there were no children born to this union. Due to marital infidelity, with the approval of the church, she divorced him. Juanita busied herself in the church for almost eight years before she met her second husband. She has recently learned that her second husband has also been having an affair and he has filed for a divorce. Although she had suspected that he was being unfaithful, she had never approached him about it. Instead she prayed and believed that God would "fix it." Just before her husband left the family home, he told her that he never loved her but was fascinated by her involvement in the church. Since he filed for divorce she has been inconsolable, crying, and unable to attend her college classes. She is a full-time student very worried about her financial state. Juanita begged her husband to go into counseling, called her minister, her mother-in-law, and many family friends to talk with him, but he adamantly refused. Juanita shared with the intake counselor, "I don't understand why this keeps happening to me. I don't understand why I can't get it together; I'm a strong woman."

NEW OR EXPANDED APPROACHES IN WORKING WITH AFRICAN-AMERICAN WOMEN WITH DEPRESSION

How we think about African-American women and their lives affects the way we therapeutically respond to them. An overarching theme evident in this body of work is that African-American women have historically been portrayed as unintelligent, harsh, promiscuous, and physically and emotionally strong. When African-American women are viewed in this manner, it becomes easier for society to deny their intentional, creative, spiritual, and intellectual qualities, all qualities that are associated with being a women.

Utilizing a contextualized approach in the treatment of depression among African-American women can offer an important corrective in understanding the subjective experiences of African-American female clients (Johnson, 2006).

In the case study, Juanita displays characteristics typically associated with depression in African-American women. She was operating from the strong Black women myth as evidenced by her preoccupation with getting things done. She stated, "I have a lot of responsibility; people depend on me, it makes sense that I am tired all the time. So what if I don't seem to be happy all the time; who really is? What I know is that I need to get it together because I have a lot of things to do." What we really found interesting was her desire to discuss how "people" would be affected by her divorce. Juanita, seeming more concerned about the affect of her divorce on her teenagers, her church, and her family, failed to recognize how very much she was being affected. She stated, "This is going to hurt my church and embarrass my God. This cannot be happening to me again; I'm a minister." As a result, she has developed depressive symptoms such as being persistently sad, anxious, and tired "all my life," and having difficulty concentrating.

As suggested by Johnson (2004), resiliency in African-American women cannot be fully understood without appreciating the intentional and creative qualities of their behavior. In his contextual humanistic model, he advances the notion that the continual bombardment of barriers such as racism, family violence, and other hostile environmental forces may make it difficult to exercise those capacities for Black women. Warren (1995) suggested that clinical interventions for women with depression need to utilize a contextual depression model to accurately address a woman's total health status. A contextual depression model considers such factors as neurochemical, genetics, psychosocial, social support systems, ethnical and cultural influences, economics, loss, stress, and coping strategies. Practitioners must also consider a resilient perspective endemic in the myth of the strong Black woman. Although the nature of the myth can be destructive, certain components may be useful.

When deciding on a culturally responsive treatment method, we were guided by the work of Johnson (2004, 2006) and Warren (1995). The first step was to have Juanita have a complete physical. Next, using a resiliency perspective, Juanita was asked to explore how her various coping skills were in fact strengths to be used in self-help. This was especially difficult for her because she continued to state, "I am just doing what I have to do." Her church family and the values of her religion were important to her so we identified some individuals from her congregation who could serve as social supports. During one session, she invited three women from her congregation into our session.

Taking a cultural assessment is also very important because it allows one "to find out what is important for the woman in the areas of her ethnic, racial, and cultural background." It was during this assessment that we began to demystify the myth of the "strong Black woman." She was given reading materials specifically addressing depression in African-American females. This information also included information on etiology, medications, and various treatments. We needed to help Juanita understand that in combination these symptoms could be categorized as clinical depression not weakness.

To assess her level of depression, she was given several depression inventories. Juanita continued in individual therapy for several weeks where she continued to examine her coping strategies, learned alternative strategies, and practiced relaxation skills and crises management. We used her favorite music and bibliotherapy. Although the rates of suicide for African-American women are low, Juanita was evaluated for suicide potential on an ongoing basis. When Juanita felt ready, she was referred to a therapy group.

It is important to note that there are particular strategies that have been acknowledged as effective in the treatment of depression in African-American women. For instance, African-American women have historically used spirituality to explain and help with psychological distress. This strong reliance on spirituality can be traced back to slavery where many African-American women leaned on their strong sense of faith to help them endure being raped by slave owners and witnessing the children and loved ones being sold into slavery. Today, a large number of African-American women continue to use spirituality as a sense of support. For instance, the use of prayer as an active agent to bring physical, mental, emotional, and spiritual relief and revitalization is liberally employed in the worship services of most Black churches. Particularly, Franklin (1995) asserted that altar prayer and pastoral prayer are significant therapeutic tools. These activities permit congregants to have their personal and collective concerns named and absolved by the pastor or prayer leader. Often in this setting, emotional license is given to each praying person to do grief work, weep, and express vulnerability (Franklin, 1995). Several researchers have affirmed that prayer is an important coping strategy for many African-American females (Paragament et al., 1990).

Group counseling and support groups have also been regarded as the treatment of choice for African-American females. The experience of "bonding" among African-American women has been associated with the alleviation of feelings of isolation and guilt (Brown, Lipford, & Sanders, 1995; Jordan,

1991). Because depression is not necessarily discussed freely in the African-American community, hearing other women who look like them discuss their struggles with depression can help to normalize symptoms.

Positive affirmations of African-American women's appearance and feminine qualities can be another powerful tool in treating depression. hooks (1993) stated, "Within white-supremacist patriarchal society, it is very difficult to find affirming Black femaleness" (p. 83). Creating an atmosphere in counseling where African-American women can comfortably discuss their frustrations and pain with society's portrayal of them as women is extremely important. Iijima-Hall (1995) suggested that encouraging African-American women to seek out environments that are more accepting of differences in standards of beauty can help in fostering positive mental health.

CONCLUSION

This analysis of the writings and research on African-American women with depression provides a synopsis of information available to the helping profession. Perhaps the most salient theme evident from this body of work is the absence of an evidence-based psychosocial approach to treatment for African-American women. Emphasis on normalizing the validity of the African-American woman experience and life can be a start. Given the uncharted nature of many African-American female clients' lives, humanistic questions regarding what life goals they are trying to accomplish and identifying environmental, family, and cultural barriers will assist these clients in reawakening their creative capacities to achieve their desired objectives.

Culturally responsive counselors need to have the ability to hear, receive, and honor the stories that African-American women tell about their lives. This ability to embrace the client's worldview will create conditions for empowerment and healing for African-American women within the counseling relationship.

KEY WORD SUMMARY

Symptoms of Depression: depressed mood for the majority of the day, almost every day, little to no interest in normal activities (especially those that used to bring pleasure), loss of energy and feelings of worthlessness, or excessive or inappropriate guilt.

Dysthymia: chronic disorder where people experience depressive symptoms but at a lesser intensity. A unique aspect of dysthymia is that the symptoms can seem to be just part of the person's personality.

Major Depression: the most severe form of depression. This form of depression involves symptoms that are usually present for at least two weeks in what is referred to as a depressive episode. Individuals with this disorder often feel as though they live in a world of complete darkness and think that they will never be happy again.

Sisterella Complex: a constellation of depressive symptoms that have been described as unable to relax, works very hard (job tasks, household, child care) and is disconnected from one's own personal needs, suffers quietly, experiences excessive guilt, feels worthless and unworthy.

CHAPTER SUMMARY

This chapter explores the reasons underlying the differences in educational outcomes of African-American students in predominantly White universities. Drawing upon the research studies, the chapter examines the stereotype threat, recent contribution on achievement/performance gap, stereotyping as academic environmental stressor, quantitative and qualitative assessment of the power of stereotyping, role of anxiety as a mediating variable in the psychosocial research and its major effects on African-Americans clients, ways of coping with stereotype threat, examples from a case study, and assessment and treatment implications.

Stereotyping in predominantly White academic settings serves as an environmental warning for African-American students. Examples of stereotyping statements are (1) African-American students are less intelligent than their peers, (2) African-American students are lazy or unmotivated, and (3) African-American students were admitted into the university solely based on race or affirmative action. These stereotypical statements define their status in university academic ladder as well as show the perceived intellectual inferiority from the faculty and classmates. However, stereotyping of this magnitude is shown to result in anxiety when an African-American student is exposed to many of these stereotype activations. In addition, anxiety exerts a great effect on performance and health outcomes of African-American students.

Strategies such as interactive model of coping, altering performance expectations, and cognitive reframing are very useful in developing a clinical framework that addresses threat, anxiety, and coping responses. A case study showing the academic experiences of an African-American student and an expanded approach for assessing and treating stereotype threat is also discussed in the chapter.

SUGGESTED CLASSROOM ACTIVITIES

Discussion and/or Test Questions

1. The authors discuss three of the most well-known stereotypes (i.e., Mammy, Sapphire, Jezebel) of African-American women. Given today's cultural climate and the strides that have been made by African-American women, discuss whether these stereotypes are still pervasive in today's society.
2. Discuss some of the conditions and experiences that can lead to African-American women being underdiagnosed with respect to depression.
3. What are some of the coping skills and resiliency factors evident in the "Juanita" case vignette? How might these skills and factors guide a practitioner's work?
4. Discuss some of the strategies that the authors highlight as effective treatment approaches for African-American women who are suffering with depression.
5. Propose a research design that could be used to test the efficacy of the treatment approaches recommended by the authors.

REFERENCES

Adams, J. M. (2000). Individual and group psychotherapy with African Americans: Understanding the identity and context of the therapist and patient. In L. C. Jackson & B. Greene (Eds.), *Psychotherapy with African American Women: Innovations in Psychodynamic Perspectives and Practice* (pp. 33-61). New York: Guilford Press.

American Psychiatric Association (APA). (2000). *Diagnostic and Statistical Manual of Mental Disorders* (4th ed.). Washington, DC: APA.

Bell, E. L. J. E., & Nkomo, S. M. (2001). *Our Separate Ways: Black and White Women and the Struggle for Professional Identity.* Boston, MA: Harvard Business School Press.

Bender, M. (2000). Suicide and older African-American women. *Mortality, 5*(2), 158-170.

Benjamin, L. (1997). *Black Women in the Academy: Promises and Perils.* Gainesville: University Press of Florida.

Boyd, C., Henderson, D., Ross-Durow, P., & Aspen, J. (1997). Sexual trauma and depression in African-American women who smoke crack cocaine. *Substance Abuse, 18,* 133-141.

Brown, C., Abe-Kim, J. S., & Barrio, C. (2003). Depression in ethnically diverse women: Implications for treatment in primary care centers. *Professional Psychology: Research and Practice, 34*(1), 10-19.

Brown, S. P., Lipford-Sanders, J., & Shaw, M. (1995). Kujichagulia—Uncovering the secrets of the heart: Group work with African American women on predominately white campuses. *Journal for Specialists in Group Work, 20,* 151-158.

Costen, M. W. (1993). *African American Christian Worship.* Nashville, TN: Abingdon Press.

Danquah, M. N. (1998). *Willow Weep for Me: A Black Woman's Journey Through Depression.* New York: W. W. Norton & Company, Inc.

Danquah, M. N. (2003, December). Out of the blues. Essence, 34, 50. Available at: http://firstsearch.oclc.org. Accessed February 12, 2004.

de Groot, M., Auslander, W., Williams, J. H., Sherraden, M., & Haire-Joshu, D. (2003). Depression and poverty among African American women at risk for type 2 diabetes. *Annals of Behavioral Medicine 25,* 172-181.

Ennis, N. E., Hobfoll, S. E., & Schroder, K. E. E. (2000). Money doesn't talk, it swears: How economic stress and resistance resources impact inner-city women's depressive mood. *American Journal of Community Psychology, 28*(2), 149-173.

Franklin, R. M. (1995). Defiant spirituality: Care traditions in the black churches. *Pastoral Psychology, 43,* 255-267.

Goodman, S. H., Cooley, E. L., Sewell, D. & Leavitt, N. (1994). Locus of control and self-esteem in depressed, low-income African-American women. *Community Mental Health Journal, 30*(3), 259-269.

Greene, B. (1994). Diversity and difference: Race and feminist psychotherapy. In M. P. Mirkin (Ed.), *Women in Context: Toward a Feminist Reconstruction of Psychotherapy* (pp. 333-351). New York: Guilford Press.

Hines-Martin, V., Malone, M., Kim, K., & Brown-Piper, A. (2003). Barriers to mental health care access in an African American population. *Issues in Mental Health Nursing, 24,* 237-256.

hooks, B. (1993). *Sisters of the Yam: Black Women and Self-Recovery.* Boston, MA: South End Press.

hooks, B. (2003). *Rock My Soul: African American People and Self-Esteem.* New York: Atria Books.

Ialongo, N., McCreary, B. K., Person, J. L., Koenig, A. L., Schmidt, N. B., Poduska, J., et al. (2004). Major depressive disorder in a population of urbam, African-American young adults: Prevalence, correlates, comorbidity and unmet mental health service need. *Journal of Affective Disorders, 79*(1-3), 127-136.

Iijima-Hall, C. C. (1995). Beauty is in the soul of the beholder: Psychological implications of beauty and African American women. *Cultural Diversity and Mental Health, 1*(2), 125-137.

Jackson, L. C., & Greene, B. (2000). *Psychotherapy with African American Women: Innovations in Psychodynamic Perspectives and Practice.* New York: Guilford Press.

Johnson, P. (2004, October). *Incorporating a Contextual Humanistic Approach into Counseling Theories Courses.* Paper presented at the 2004 North Central Counselor Education and Supervision Conference. St. Louis, Missouri.

Johnson, P. D. (2006). Counseling African American men: A contextualizes humanistic perspective. *Counseling and Values, 20,* 187-196.

Johnson, S. D., Cunningham-Williams, R. M., & Cottler, L. B. (2003). A tripartite of HIV-risk for African American women: The intersection of drug use, violence, and depression. *Drug & Alcohol Dependence, 70,* 169-175.

Jones, C., & Shorter-Gooden, K. (2003). *Shifting: The Double Lives of Black Women in America.* New York: Harper Collins.

Jones, D. J., O'Connell, C., Gound, M., Heller, L., & Forehand, R. (2004). Predictors of self-reported physical symptoms in low-income, inner-city African American women: The role of optimism, depressive symptoms, and chronic illness. *Psychology of Women Quarterly, 28*(2), 112-121.

Jones-Webb, R., & Snowden, L. (1993). Symptoms of depression among blacks and whites. *American Journal of Public Health, 83*(2), 240-244.

Jordan, J. M. (1991). Counseling African American women: Sister friends. In C. C. Lee & B. L. Richardson (Eds.), *Multicultural Issues in Counseling: New Approaches to Diversity* (pp. 51-63). Alexandria, VA: American Counseling Association.

Kohn, L. P., Oden, T., Munoz, R. F., Robinson, A., & Leavitt, D. (2002). Adapted cognitive behavioral group therapy for depressed low-income African American women. *Community Mental Health Journal, 38,* 497-504.

Kopala, M., & Keitel, M. (2003). *Handbook for Counseling Women.* Thousand Oaks, CA: Sage Publications.

Lehrer, E., Crittenden, K., & Norr, K. F. (2002). Depression and economic self-sufficiency among inner-city minority mothers. *Social Science Research, 31,* 285-309.

Mitchell, A., & Herring, K. (1998). *What the Blues is All About: Black Women Overcoming Stress and Depression.* New York: Berkley Publishing Group.

Moneyham, L., Sowell, R., Seals, B., & Demi, A. (2000). Depressive symptoms among African American women with HIV disease. *Scholarly Inquiry for Nursing Practice, 14*(1), 9-39.

National Institute of Mental Health. (2000). Depression. Available at: http://www.nimh.nih.gov/publicat/depression.cfm. Accessed June 24, 2004.

Paragament, K., Ensing, D., Falgout, K., Olsen, H., Reilly, B., Van Haitsma, K., et al. (1990). God help me: Religious coping efforts as predictors of the outcomes of significant negative life events. *American Journal of Community Psychology, 18,* 693-824.

Reed, M. K., McLeod, S., Randall, Y., & Walker, B. (1996). Depressive symptoms in African-American women. *Journal of Multicultural Counseling & Development, 24*(1), 6-14.

Ritter, C., Hobfoll, S. E., Lavin, J., Cameron, R. P., & Hulsizer, M. R. (2000). Stress, psychosocial resources, and depressive symptomatology during pregnancy in low-income, inner-city women. *Health Psychology, 19,* 576-585.

Romero, R. E. (2000). The icon of the strong black woman: The paradox of strength. In L. C. Jackson & B. Greene (Eds.), *Psychotherapy with African American Women: Innovations in Psychodynamic Perspectives and Practice* (pp. 33-61). New York: Guilford Press.

Ross-Durow, P. L., & Boyd, C. J. (2000). Sexual abuse, depression, and eating disorders in African American women who smoke cocaine. *Substance Abuse, 18,* 79-81.

Sanchez-Hucles, J. V. (1997). Jeopardy not bonus status for African American women in the work force: Why does the myth of advantage persist? *American Journal of Community Psychology, 25,* 565-580.

Smith, P. (1999). Teaching the retrenchment generation: When Sapphire meets Socrates at the intersection of race, gender and authority. *William and Mary Journal of Women and the Law, 53,* 1-141.

Taylor, J., Henderson, D., & Jackson, B. B. (1991). A holistic model for understanding Predicting depressive symptoms in African-American women. *Journal of Community Psychology, 19,* 306-320.

Thomas, R. M. (1985). *Comparing Theories of Child Development.* Belmont, CA: Wadsworth Publishing.

Turner, V. (2002). Women of color in academe: Living with multiple marginality. *Journal of Higher Education, 73,* 74-94.

U.S. Census Bureau. (2004). Statistical abstract of the United Sates: 2004-2005 (124th ed). Washington, DC: Author.

Warren, B. J. (1995). Examining depression among African American women from a psychiatric mental health nursing perspective. *Womanist Theory and Research, 1*(2), 34-36.

West, C. M. (1995). Mammy, Sapphire, and Jezebel: Historical images of black women and their implications for psychotherapy. *Psychotherapy, 32*(3), 458-466.

Wyatt, G. (1997). *Stolen Women: Reclaiming Our Sexuality, Taking Back Our Lives.* New York: Wiley & Sons.

Chapter 6

Mental Health Challenges for Incarcerated African-American Women

Patricia O'Brien
Andrea Dakin

It's hard coming out here. We got a lot of obstacles. [Points to her hand] We got this. Just our color is a problem, on top of being an ex-offender. I had doors shut in my face all the time. I cried almost every day. But you know what, you just got to be diligent. Take that energy you were using to look for drugs and try to find a job. I refused to use drugs. If you use, you'll still be jobless. They might want you to pass a drug test. I was diligent.

(O'Brien & Lee, 2006)

What does it mean for the formerly incarcerated woman quoted above to be diligent when the odds are stacked against her? Nationally, women represent a growing corrections population. According to the Bureau of Justice Statistics (Glaze & Palla, 2005; Harrison & Beck, 2005), more than 1.1 million women are currently under criminal justice supervision in the United States with 91 percent of those on probation or parole. The percentage of

The research described in this study was made possible by Grant Number R01-DA013943 from the National Institute of Drug Abuse and its contents are solely the responsibility of the authors and do not represent the official views of the National Institute of Drug Abuse. In addition, this research was approved by the UIC Institutional Review Board, #2003-00234.

women entering U.S. prisons in the last twenty years has increased almost 400 percent, while male incarceration rates increased at less than half that rate. The incarceration of African-American women in state prisons rose 828 percent between 1986 and 1991 and it continues to rise (Bush-Baskette, 2000). The likelihood that a woman will go to prison during her lifetime has increased from a 0.3 percent chance in 1974 to a 1.8 percent chance in 2001 (Bonczar, 2003); however, the likelihood of an African-American woman going to prison is much higher than that of White women: 5.6 percent chance as compared to less than 1 percent, respectively. Finally, although African-American women make up 13 percent of the female population in the United States (U.S. Census, 2004), they are composed of 37 percent incarcerated women (Harrison & Beck, 2005).

Because of the social and economic context of exclusion of poor women of color coupled with violence against women, African-American women housed in the nation's state and federal facilities are also more likely to be undereducated and low income, and have experienced fewer opportunities for vocational and employment development prior to involvement with the criminal justice system. Approximately 70 percent of women under correctional sanction have minor children and, of those in prison, 64 percent lived with their children prior to incarceration (Mumola, 2000). Although a history of abuse by no means dictates subsequent involvement in a life of crime, 44 percent of women under correctional authority reported that, at some point during their lives, they had been physically or sexually assaulted (Greenfeld & Snell, 1999).

Several findings show that women are more likely than men to use drugs, to use more serious drugs, and to use them more frequently (Kassebaum, 1999). In state prisons, about half of the women had been using drugs, alcohol, or both at the time of the offense for which they had been committed (Greenfeld & Snell, 1999). By the end of 2003, almost 65 percent of Black women in federal prisons were incarcerated for drug offenses (Pastore & Maguire, 2005).

For African-American women, the intersection of race, gender, drugs, and public policy creates multiple obstacles to desistance from further criminal problems and return home to family and community. This chapter describes some of the theoretical and empirical correlates of African-American women and their involvement in the criminal justice system. Drawing from interviews with thirteen drug-convicted African-American women, an opportunity was created that enabled them to share their stories of returning to an economically disinvested community in a large, urban Midwestern city and the resiliencies and strengths they employed to negotiate their freedom. Within the overall context, best practices are identified and discussed.

LITERATURE REVIEW
AND THEORETICAL UNDERPINNINGS

Most policy analysts describe the massive increase of incarcerated women as "collateral damage" in America's drug wars. President Reagan's Comprehensive Crime Control Act of 1984 was aimed not at big dealers but at the street-level users who, as "small fish," could rat out the big fish or major dealers. Mandatory minimum sentences in the federal system and then those implemented in every state system added additional fuel to get and keep women locked up. Analogous with women's positions in the "legitimate" labor force, women within illegitimate drug operations often had little power and therefore little information they could sell to reduce their sentences, or chose to resist those demands because of their relationship with their partners or family members who may have also been involved in drug operations.

Correctional policy affects African-American women differently than it does Black men and White women. Criminal statues reflect society's view of both the offense's seriousness and offenders' deservedness for various forms of punishment. Golden (2005) discusses the multiple stigmas and categories assigned to poor, Black women such as "unfit" or "unworthy" that separate individual women from the mainstream culture. Worthiness is related to what Ramsey (1980) and others refer to as the triple oppression of race, gender, and class that converges in what Golden labels as "social exclusion." Daly (1997) makes use of the term "class-race-gender" (p. 33) to conceptualize such inequalities "not as additive and discrete, but as intersecting, interlocking and contingent." By this she does not mean that there is a hierarchy of oppressions but rather because "everyone is located in a matrix of multiple social relations" (p. 35), to theorize and analyze inequality one should focus on "mapping the salience and contingency of gender, class, race-ethnicity . . . both separately and together" (p. 34).

Within the literature, there exists a consensus that structural and environmental forces have an impact on the pathways to crime for African-American women. Arnold (1990) asserts that the incarcerated Black women she studied "were victims of class, gender, and race oppression who were structurally dislocated from the major social institutions of women in the society: the family, the school, and work" (p. 163). Hill and Crawford (1990) support the theory that the unique position of Black women in the structure of power relations in society has profound effects not shared by their White counterparts and suggest that "a search for a social explanation of female crime must consider that the criminality of black and white women may be tied to different experiences and/or to different ways of responding to similar experiences" (p. 621).

Henriques and Manatu-Rupert (2001) examined the multiple issues that contribute to the incarceration of African-American women and threaten to render these women recidivists. These issues include but are not limited to substance abuse, sexual abuse, fractured female relations, and abusive intimate relationships. Collins (1997) asserts that for the African-American women born into and continuing to live in poverty, the situation is created in which the impetus is provided for many to trade sex for money and/or drugs.

Gender also interacts with race, class, ethnicity, sexual orientation, and other aspects of culture to give shape to a woman's life, and thus the prison inmate population is not uniformly disempowered. According to McQuaid and Ehrenreich (1998), the differential effects of gender, race, and class of the outer prison world penetrate the prison walls; these relationships are re-enacted between guards and prisoners and may contribute to defining the prisoners' relations with their world outside of prison.

Ramsey (1980) and Richie (1996) have completed complementary analyses regarding how the gender socialization of African-American women (as compared to that of White women) has an impact upon their entry into crime. According to Ramsey, Black women have bought into the socially constructed male supremacy model. For Black women, this model is often a myth. The problem occurs when the male cannot economically support the family and the Black woman must do so. She is the visible and economic support of the family, but "defers to the dominant male model by always preserving the psychological power of the Black male" (1980, p. 360). This double bind then creates a sense of confusion and guilt over her role. Poor Black women can become trapped in the social expectations of larger society, making it difficult for them to escape the perceived need for criminal activity.

These expectations are also suggested by the "gender entrapment model" (Richie, 1996). Gender entrapment, according to Richie (1996), is "the socially constructed process whereby African American women who are vulnerable to men's violence in their intimate relationships are penalized for behaviors they engage in even when the behaviors are logical extensions of their racialized gender identities, their culturally expected gender roles, and the violence in their intimate relationships" (p. 4).

The model of gender entrapment among battered Black women illustrates how gender, race/ethnicity, and violence intersect to create an effective system of organizing women's behavior that makes them vulnerable to social exclusion, private and public subordination, and participation in illegal activities as a means of negotiating their identities, and, as a consequence, mass incarceration. The gender-entrapment theory helps to explain how some women who participate in illegal activities do so in response to violence, the threat of violence, or coercion by their male partners. Poverty seriously limits the options of African-American women in response to intimate and systemic abuse by a partner. They choose survival strategies that further exacerbate the impact of social marginalization, such as criminal behavior.

INCARCERATION DISPARITIES

Overwhelmingly, research focused on race and the criminal justice system has focused on men (Daly, 1994). There is considerably less research on women and prison than men regarding who is sent to prison, but it is increasing in number. "Within this growing body of research, the issue of race is not routinely addressed, either. When race is assessed, the comparisons are generally limited to African Americans and whites" (Walker, Spohn, & DeLone, 1996, p. 222).

> Gender and racial stereotypes play a part in the incarceration process. Flavin (2001) found that among women, the likelihood of incarceration is greatest for those women with a lack of ties to children, spouses, and/or family. She hypothesizes that these women most threaten conventional gender role expectations because they putatively fail to care for dependents or to be dependent on someone else. The disproportionately high incarceration rates, the automatic assumption of mothers' responsibility and fathers' presumed lack thereof has shortchanged both Black men and women. "Black men offenders do not have their responsibilities for others taken into account, while Black women offenders are subjected to a double-edge sword, rewarded if they are perceived as good parents but punished more severely if they are not." (Walker et al., 1996, p. 630)

In Golden's (2005) description of the correctional system as a "war on the family," she raises the "pregnant Black crackhead" as the archetypal unfit mother who has been criminalized "for their failure to represent maternal integrity and family values" (2005, p. 46), regardless of the actual impact of the drug use and other ways that women have attempted to parent their children. The point she makes is not that drug use during pregnancy is safe, but rather that crack babies, identified exclusively with poor, African-American mothers, became a racialized gloss for punishing Black women and shaping public support for "throwing away the key."

EXPANDED APPROACHES AND BEST PRACTICE

Examining studies from the mid-1980s to the mid-1990s, Bush-Baskette (2000) concluded that "the greater rate of increase in the incarceration of women . . . is driven exclusively by the War on Drugs . . . and that there should be further study of the effects on women, with special attention to the displacement of their dependent children" (p. 924). Delgado (2001) argued that "women, particularly those of color, have borne a disproportionate burden in the sentencing process when drugs were involved" (p. 53) as a result of involvement in drug sales or possession through a significant other.

Arvanites (1994) collected self-report data from a sample of approximately 1,600 individuals receiving treatment for drug and/or alcohol addiction and examined patterns in female drug use and criminal activity. Criminal activity was most frequently related to the use/abuse of alcohol in combination with at least one illicit drug. Females were more likely to report using cocaine than males (73 percent to 65 percent). Among those reporting that a single drug was their major problem, females identified cocaine while males reported alcohol. Prendergast, Wellisch, and Falkin (1995) argued that to address criminal behavior, drug abuse must be addressed in a holistic way.

It is not enough to simply provide substance abuse programs; they must be designed for women. Langan and Pellissier (2001) studied gender differences among federal prisoners (1,326 men and 318 women) enrolled in substance abuse treatment programs during the 1990s. These were prison-based substance abuse treatment programs that had been generally designed for men but were being administered to women as well. The authors concluded that treatment programs designed for men are inappropriate for women.

Holtfretter and Morash (2003) argued that a sizeable group of women have co-occurring needs in the areas of substance abuse and mental disorders. Thus, treatment for substance abuse must also address emotional stability, mental health, and parenting needs. This study used the technique of cluster analysis to provide a more comprehensive picture of the characteristics associated with women who exhibit specific needs and are at differing levels of risk for recidivism. The authors concluded, consistent with previous studies, that "to be effective in reducing recidivism and improving women's lives, programs must be gender responsive" (p. 150). Prendergast et al. (1995) reported from their nationwide survey of community-based and corrections-based treatment programs for women offenders on the program characteristics that pose obstacles to women's reentry and successful involvement in treatment. These include:

- Absence of child care
- Restrictive screening instruments that deny access to, for example, pregnant women and women with mental impairment
- Needs assessment protocols that lack comprehensive standards, resulting in a failure to properly perceive women's needs and provide, or refer to, appropriate services

Gender differences were observed in the predictors of treatment entry and completion by Pellissier (2004). Although women had more problems in employment and depression and were more likely to have a history of physical abuse, they also had higher levels of internal motivation. Women with "average/good" family ties were more likely to enter treatment. Women planning to live with their minor children after release were also more likely to enter treatment. Pellissier concluded that as motivation leads to change, for women, "motivational programs and treatment programs will need to clearly emphasize the role of substance abuse treatment in alleviating depression and other psychological distress" (2004, p. 1423).

Few studies focus only on African-American women, drug abuse, and prison. However, Holtfretter and Morash (2003) explored the likelihood of recidivism between women with different characteristics. The authors found that those at the highest risk for recidivism are more likely to have substance abuse, mental health, and child-related needs, and are most likely to be women who are African American or Hispanic. They are also most likely to have additional needs, such as those related to employment or educational services. The authors asserted that programs providing wrap-around services that organize access to a great many different program elements tailored to each woman, or programs that are holistic in providing many services at one location, would be helpful for this group of women who are more likely to experience recidivism. They also emphasized that the program should offer culturally appropriate services.

Mary Lou Ramsey was Director of Genesis, the first federally funded therapeutic community for incarcerated women in the United States. From her observations over many years of work with "female drug offenders" (1980), she found that women did not respond well to the "humiliation tactics of traditional drug treatment programs to sensitize women to their errors" (p. 367), because of their real status of powerlessness in the world. She also found that Black female drug abusers differ from White female drug abusers in their greater ability, by virtue of their minority subculture experiences, to perceive themselves as members of a group, thereby making group therapy potentially more effective with them. Experiences of prejudice or racism also adversely affect Black female drug offenders, and similar to the "entrapment model" theorized by Richie (1996), Ramsey argued that Black women experience a double bind related to their role of being the major economic provider of the family but subject to physical and psychological control and violence by male partners. Ramsey also believed that "Black women need to develop a greater sense of personal awareness regarding the feelings and reactions that have led to their use of drugs" (p. 364) to "move out of their positions of marginal power and to experience leadership and power over others" (p. 365). Of the many articles on treatment of former drug-affected women, Ramsey is unique in indicating that as women become cognizant of their internal issues related to addiction, a part of their "recovery" could include empowering themselves through education in social systems, politics, and economics to advance their leadership potential.

Classification of women in prison continues to be based upon men's level of risk and does not reflect the various needs of women (for treatment and connection with children or family members) (Farr, 2000; Van Voorhis, 2001). Women have additional needs once they enter prison. In a study of fifty-four parolees who discussed their retrospective experiences of incarceration, Pogrebin and Dodge (2001) found that institutional adjustment was difficult for the women because of the hostility with which they were treated by correctional officers, harassment by other inmates, the trauma experienced by first-time inmates, and separation from family members, especially minor children. The authors do not indicate the composition of the sample; however, in the prison facility from which the women were released, 32 percent of the population was Black and 18.4 percent was Hispanic. They concluded that an important "element of prison life for many women was dealing with the fear and violence" (p. 540), which might be addressed by better assessment of a need for mental health services.

Recent studies suggest an increasing recognition for services targeting women's specific issues are increasingly recognized. Green, Miranda, Daroowalla, and Siddique (2005) examined trauma exposure, mental health problems, and substance abuse issues among a sample of 100 female jail detainees in a county facility. Black women made up 81 percent of the sample. Women identified their biggest problems as: substance abuse (45 percent), family issues (22 percent), lack of skills and direction (12 percent), and lack of job or appropriate training (9 percent). They were interested in job training (93 percent), problem-solving skills (91 percent), stress management (88 percent), communication-skills building (83 percent), and drug education/treatment (75 percent). Nearly all of the women had been exposed to a traumatic event (98 percent), 90 percent reported at least one interpersonal trauma, and 71 percent reported being exposed to domestic violence.

Gray, Mays, and Stohr (1995) indicated that there is a discrepancy between what types of services women need versus what they are able to obtain. The authors conducted interviews and surveys at five jails that serve women only. One-third of the respondents were Black, one-third White, one-fifth Hispanic, and the remainder were Native American or from other ethnic groups. Inmates rated work training as the single most needed program, but less than 3 percent were participating in work training. Only 35 percent of women were employed prior to incarceration, although 57 percent said that they were the economic provider of their family. Of those who reported using alcohol frequently, 80 percent reported participating in alcohol programming, but only 42 percent of the offenders who reported frequent drug use were involved in treatment. Few programs were directed at repairing the damage done by victimization, and of those that were available, less than 4 percent of respondents were participating in those programs.

Mullings, Pollock, and Crouch (2002) reviewed data from 1,198 newly admitted female prisoners in Texas to assess relationships between childhood and adult characteristics and drug use, as well as the relationship between drug use and type of crime. Of the sample, 44 percent were Black, 39 percent White, and 13 percent Hispanic. The findings revealed that women prisoners with drug problems have extensive histories of childhood maltreatment, adult victimization, mental health problems, and greater involvement in criminal activity than prisoners without drug problems. Findings indicated that female inmates have complex and multifaceted needs for effective and innovated programs extending beyond drug treatment. For incarcerated women, their research emphasizes the "need for correctional treatment and programming that address gender-specific issues such as victimization, post traumatic stress disorder, depression, and parenting" (p. 91).

O'Brien (2002), reporting from an evaluation of a residential program for women exiting prison in a large urban city, found a high level of success for women who had longer than average stays at the program and at the point of departure had employment, housing, and an assigned mentor. Johnson (2003) reported from her study of formerly incarcerated African-American women at the same program that the "structured support provided by a halfway house can enable women to develop skills for self-sufficiency as well as skills to understand and cope with past histories of physical or sexual abuse, and of substance abuse" (p. 275).

REINTEGRATION/RECIDIVISM

Overall, studies show that women who receive treatment for substance abuse experience less recidivism and have better outcomes than those who do not receive treatment. Identification at intake (Dowden & Blanchette, 2002), indicators of social support (Farrell, 2000), a history of mental health treatment (Pellissier Camp, Gaes, Saylor, & Rhodes, 2003), communication training (Englander-Golden, Gitchel, Henderson, Golden, & Hardy, 2002), and community-based treatment immediately after discharge (Hall, Baldwin, & Pendergast, 2001) have been found to positively affect a woman's ability to avoid return to prison.

Jones and Sims (1997) found in their study of released men and women from prison in North Carolina (68 percent of whom were African-American women) that unstable employment (prior to incarceration) was a significant predictor of rearrest for women. In addition, race was a significant predictor of rearrest for specific crimes (e.g., African Americans, male and female, were more likely to be rearrested for violent/sexual offenses). Finally, this study supports the notion of "aging out" of crime; women commit less crime as they grow older.

In her study of the relationship between use of community-based social services by female parolees and subsequent recidivism, Pearl (1998) found that the use of certain types of community-based social services is associated with lower rates of recidivism. Women who participated in community-based social services have improved outcomes. The more access a woman has to services, the longer she will be able to remain in the community. Women who completed a drug-treatment and/or employment program had the lowest number of rearrests.

Stuart and Brice-Baker (2004) studied sixty women and explored twenty-six variables related to recidivism. They concluded that the current model of correction is not effective in reducing recidivism for all women, especially those whose primary criminal involvement is drug related. Gender-specific treatment approaches are clearly called for since several issues have been determined to affect female prisoners disproportionately or exclusively (sexual abuse, sexual assault, domestic violence, depression, pregnancy, and motherhood). There is also a need for an increased rehabilitation that should include preventive, community-based treatment; a refocusing of treatment when imprisonment occurs; and adequate follow-up care.

Findings from the Harm and Phillips study (2001), consistent with the experimental study in California (Prendergast et al., 1995), emphasize the need for drug-affected women to have access to both prison- and community-based drug treatment programs. Women often cited their children as a motivation for abstaining from drugs. Relationships with children, however, were tempered with guilt, conflict, and role reversal. Employment alone was not enough to prevent some women in the sample from returning to prison. Women who were successful in finding employment often reported that their incomes were insufficient to meet their basic needs or to support their children. This finding was echoed by a recent study of the relationship between incarceration and employment rates among former female state prisoners from Illinois. The study found that while women were able to find employment after release from prison, they were not able to earn sufficient wages to ensure the family lives above poverty (Cho & LaLonde, 2005).

Freudenberg, Wilets, Greene, and Richie (1998) examined women who enrolled in residential programs with on-site drug treatment and other social services after release as compared to women who enrolled in less comprehensive services. The residential treatment group participated in the program significantly longer than women in other types of services. Women who participated in post-release services were significantly less likely to be re-arrested in the year after release than a comparable group of women who participated in jail services, but were not eligible for postrelease services.

Race, class, and gender affect women before they enter prison, while they are incarcerated, and after they are released. Many of the studies cited earlier produce themes that resonate through both descriptions of before and after prison experiences, including inadequate and uncaring counsel, extremely harsh sentences for nonviolent offenses, and racially discriminatory treatment in the court system and in prison facilities. In addition, there is the observable disproportionality of African-American women at the highest level of punishment (prison) and a general conclusion that community-based treatments are needed to treat women prior to incarceration and support them in their attempts at re-entry and to remain drug-free.

BACK TO THE NEIGHBORHOOD   .

In 2004, the lead author, O'Brien, conducted an interview study with thirteen women returning to a community on the west side of Chicago with the intent of examining both how the individual women addressed their needs and how the community assisted these women. The women involved in the study were all African American with an average age of 38.7, all had been committed for drug offenses, and all had children under the age of 18. The women were interviewed two times, about three and six months after release from prison or the county detention center. We attempted to understand both the critical life events that related to initiation and continuation of alcohol and drug use, the need for drug treatment and other forms of treatment and services, and the use of treatment and services, particularly among women returning to a neighborhood where they had resided prior to incarceration.

This neighborhood where the women had chosen to return is one of seven (out of seventy-seven neighborhoods) in the Chicago metropolitan area where over half of former prisoners return. Although Golden (2005) refers to this neighborhood (which between 1991 and 2000 lost nearly 3,000 jobs) as "abandoned by hope" (p. 24), it is also a community of visionaries and warriors who will not give up on the dream of a revitalized and safe neighborhood.

Women's Survival and Postprison Resilience

Women identified an average of 5.23 critical life events prior to incarceration (range of 2 to 13). These events included child molestation, unplanned pregnancy, abusive relationships as adults, extreme physical harm by fire during childhood, unexpected loss of children, death of a parent or significant other family members, death of an intimate partner or spouse, multiple suicide attempts, and multiple incarcerations. At the first interview, two of the thirteen women reported high psychological distress and four women reported a moderate degree of psychological distress.

Nine of the thirteen women were using either alcohol or illicit drugs at the time they were first interviewed about three months after release. When asked why they were still using at the risk of having their parole revoked or being sent back to prison, women described their addiction:

> Heroin can be like your boyfriend. Whatever you're missing, heroin can take their place. It makes me feel like I'm able to do whatever I'm set out to do.

> If I don't get no heroin round here I can't function. My mind wasn't made up to just leave it alone—that's the whole thing.

Another woman referred to the community that triggered her use:

> Drugs, shooting, and other things that are going on. It's really not a good neighborhood, like it was when I first moved there.

Beyond the continuing drug use, women talked about "nothing to do" and their fear of getting caught up in activities in the community. They also identified as their greatest challenge getting a job and believed that their drug use and criminal record prevented them from even being considered. Employment symbolized not only legitimate income, but also "something to do" that enabled them to manage boredom or loneliness.

> Life is staring at me. It's bleak. When they find out you've been locked up, I never get people to answer me back.

At the time of the first interview, all of the women were living in someone else's home, very often the caregiver of the women's children. If family or friends cannot provide housing, there are few alternatives for women, especially transitional shelters where they can stay with their children.

By the time of the second interview, six months after release, only four women were still using illegal substances. Four of the women were employed at least part time. Two of the women were enrolled in employment training or a job readiness program. As one woman said,

> I'm healthy. I'm young. I'm able to do a lot of things. I have a lot of skills. I like just knowing that I can get the job done and be satisfied and the person I'm doing the job for is satisfied with me.

The one woman who was in a combination GED/job training program talked about a new-found relief she felt in delaying her job search:

> That was my main problem, by my wanting a job so bad. Now I know I have to be patient and to wait on the job I want. If the job that I want don't come along and another job comes, ok, I'll go for that job until the I get the job I really want because I know now that I need more computer training and I really need my GED and that's one thing I'm trying to get right now.

Most of the women did not enroll in drug treatment or use the social services that were available to them. Seeking drug treatment or follow-up may have been a court condition but both because there is a scarcity of drug treatment options (and none in the immediate neighborhood where the women resided) and because there seemed to be a lack of follow-up by parole officers or court personnel, only three of the women were in some type of treatment program by the second interview. The services women used provided immediate and concrete goods such as food and clothing in the early days after release. Several women engaged in peer groups that may have also supported their efforts to stay clean.

What else accounted for desistance for those who reported they were no longer using? For some, it may have been the fact that they had something else "to do" such as employment or training. Several others had moved outside of the neighborhood and believed they had some new opportunities. For others it was a combination of "being sick and tired of the same situation" and wanting something better for themselves. Several women mentioned the importance of their children having a model for not using drugs especially when they recognized with some pride that their children had not gotten "caught up" so far in drugs or other problems. Women also described increased relational competence in making choices about when and how they spent time with others, and a sense of efficacy in being able to resist further illicit activities.

CONCLUSION

This chapter provides a synthesis of literature that describes the critical and complex issues that African-American women involved with the criminal justice system experience as well as findings from a study with women in one neighborhood in a large, urban city heavily marked by the issues of continuing illicit drug use, low education and employment rates, and a high proportion of formerly incarcerated community members. The chapter and the experiences of this sample of women trying to reconnect to family and community point out the need for specific research on African-American females in the criminal justice systems, the lack of which limits our understanding of what changes need to be made to reduce women's incarceration. Strides are being made in important areas. The impact of a mother's incarceration on children is just beginning to be known, with almost 1.5 million minor children having a parent in state or federal prison (Mumola, 2000). Although Enos (1997) showed that African-American children were more likely to stay with grandparents and White children were more likely to stay with fathers or enter foster care, the long-term effects of these placements and a mother's incarceration still needs to be explored.

Finally, we do not yet know the full impact of the collateral consequences of laws for ex-offenders (Finzen, 2005). Collateral consequences law makes rehabilitation challenging for former prisoners; collectively, these laws make reintegration even more difficult, if not impossible, when they intersect to exert an impact on African-American women's economic and social choices. These laws, such as restrictions on employment, public housing, and access to public benefits, adhere as a result of a criminal conviction and continue to civilly punish ex-offenders long after their sentences have ended. Without access to food, housing, employment, or education, it becomes nearly impossible for a formerly incarcerated woman, regardless of race, to successfully reintegrate into society and turn away from criminal activities. Even more important is for us to consider the opportunities for support and attention to identified mental health and substance abuse concerns prior to the warehousing of so many women and men in a putative war on crime or drugs that no one wins.

CHAPTER SUMMARY

This chapter provides a glimpse into lives of incarcerated African-American women and the many structural and personal challenges that they experience. More than 50 percent of the more than 1.1 million women in federal prisons were incarcerated for drug offenses. However, multiple interlocking conditions (class, race, gender) contribute to their incarceration.

Available research suggests that women at higher risk for recidivism are likely to have the triple threat of substance abuse, mental health, and child-related needs. The following supports should be in place prior to release:

1. a comprehensive and multidimensional assessment of psychological, social/relational, and educational/vocational needs prior to release;
2. identification of a coach/case manager who can assist women in linking with the appropriate level of drug treatment or aftercare in the community;
3. assistance with identifying family issues for family conferencing and negotiation;
4. closer attention to job placement that enables women to gain income and gradual experience in the labor market but also enables them the flexibility for addressing other post-release expectations or needs.

Best practices for incarcerated Black women include but are not limited to group therapy and programs and services emphasizing a greater sense of personal awareness and self-reflections. In addition, women are responsive to services that provide immediate and concrete goods, such as food and clothing, in the early stage of release. It appears that desistance results as much from informal and natural supports as from the more traditional approaches. Overall, one might conclude that the women in this study made a choice regarding destinies. It becomes important to these women to rethink their life purpose.

SUGGESTED GROUP/CLASSROOM ACTIVITIES

Discussion Points

1. What are the key resources that should be developed to facilitate African-American women's reentry from prison to the community?
2. How can linkages between mental health care in prison and in the community be fostered?
3. How can family be both a help and a challenge to women trying to desist from crime and/or recover from addiction?
4. What are some cultural supports that you think could be helpful?
5. The women in the study indicated difficulty in trying to find employment and/or "something to do" with their time. What might be specific ways that the Black community could be supportive of women who need to gain experience while at the same time regaining their place in the community?

Activity: World Without Prisons

Break into small groups. Each group is responsible for describing their vision of what a world without prisons would look like. Groups can draw, list out bullet points, or create a song. After about fifteen minutes, have members report back to the larger group. The facilitator should highlight common themes or big differences between people's visions. Did some people draw apocalyptic nightmares, while others drew visions of perfection? What key concerns are people expressing?

Next, brainstorm to answer two questions written on flipchart paper or chalkboard: "How is prison MEDICINE?" and "How is prison POISON?" Review brainstorms and ask how could we heal our communities without using poisons? What might be ALTERNATIVE MEDICINE to the problems that people have that often leech out in the community to threaten property and life?

REFERENCES

Arnold, R. A. (1990). Processes of victimization and criminalization of black women. *Social Justice, 17*(3), 153-166.

Arvanites, T. M. (1994). *Female Drug Use and Crime.* Presented at the American Society of Crimininology, Miami, FL, November 11, 1994.

Bonczar, T. P. (2003). *Prevalence of Imprisonment in the U.S. Population, 1974-2001.* Washington, DC: Bureau of Justice Statistics (NCJ197976).

Bush-Baskette, S. R. (2000). The war on drugs and the incarceration of mothers. *Journal of Drug Issues, 30*(4), 919-928.

Byrne, J. M., & Taxman, F. S. (1994). Crime control policy and community corrections practice: Assessing the impact of gender, race, and class. *Evaluation and Program Planning, 17*(2), 227-233.

Cho, R., & LaLonde, R. (2005). The Impact of Incarceration in State Prison on the Employment Prospects of Women. Unpublished report. Chicago, IL: University of Chicago.

Collins, C. F. (1997). *The Imprisonment of African American Women.* Jefferson, NC: McFarland & Company, Inc.

Daly, K. (1994). Criminal law and justice system practices as racist, white and racialized. *Washington and Lee Law Review, 51,* 431-464.

Daly, K. (1997). Different ways of conceptualizing sex/gender in feminist theory and their implications for criminology. *Theoretical Criminology, 1*(1), 25-51.

Delgado, M. (2001). *Where are All the Young Men and Women of Color? Capacity Enhancement Practice and the Criminal Justice System.* New York: Columbia University Press.

Dodge, M., & Pogrebin, M. R. (2001). Collateral costs of imprisonment for women: Complications of reintegration. *The Prison Journal, 81*(1), 42-54.

Dowden, C., & Blanchette, K. (2002). An evaluation of the effectiveness of substance abuse programming for female offenders. *International Journal of Offender Therapy and Comparative Criminology, 46*(2), 220-230.

Englander-Golden, P., Gitchel, E., Henderson, C. E., Golden, D. E., & Hardy, R. (2002). "Say It Straight" training with mothers in chemical dependency treatment. *Journal of Offender Rehabilitation, 35*(1), 1-22.

Enos, S. (1997). Managing motherhood in prison: The impact of race and ethnicity on child placements. *Women & Therapy, 20*(4), 57-73.

Farr, K. A. (2000). Classification for female inmates: Moving forward. *Crime & Delinquency, 46*(1), 3-17.

Farrell, A. (2000). Women, crime, and drugs: Testing the effects of therapeutic communities. *Women & Criminal Justice, 11*(1), 21-48.

Finzen, M. E. (2005). Systems of oppression: The collateral consequences of incarceration and their effects on black communities. *Georgetown Journal on Poverty Law & Policy,* 12, 74-86.

Flavin, J. (2001). Of punishment and parenthood: Family-based social control and the sentencing of black drug offenders. *Gender & Society, 15*(4), 611-633.

Freudenberg, N., Wilets, I., Greene, M. B., & Richie, B. (1998). Linking women in jail to community services: Factors associated with rearrest and retention of drug-using women following release from jail. *Journal of the American Medical Women's Association, 53*(2), 89-93.

Glaze, L. E., & Palla, S. (2005). *Probation and Parole in the United States, 2004.* Washington, DC: Bureau of Justice Statistics (NCJ 210676).

Golden, R. (2005). *War on the Family: Mothers in Prison and the Families They Leave Behind.* New York: Routledge.

Gray, T., Mays, G. L., & Stohr, M. K. (1995). Inmate needs and programming in exclusively women's jails. *The Prison Journal, 75*(2), 186-202.

Green, B. L., Miranda, J., Daroowalla, A., & Siddique, J. (2005). Trauma exposure, mental health functioning, and program needs of women in jail. *Crime & Delinquency, 51*(1), 133-151.

Greenfeld, L. A., & Snell, T. L. (1999). *Women Offenders.* Washington, DC: Bureau of Justice Statistics (NCJ 175688).

Hall, E. A., Baldwin, D. M., & Prendergast, M. L. (2001). Women on parole: Barriers to success after substance abuse treatment. *Human Organization, 60*(3), 225-233.

Harm, N. J., & Phillips, S. D. (2001). You can't go home again: Women and recidivism. *Journal of Offender Rehabilitation, 32*(3), 3-21.

Harrison, P. M., & Beck, A. J. (2005). *Prisoners in 2004.* Washington, DC: Bureau of Justice Statistics (NCJ210677).

Herniques, Z. W., & Manatu-Rupert, N. (2001). Living on the outside: African-American women before, during, and after imprisonment. *The Prison Journal, 81*(1), 6-19.

Hill, G. D., & Crawford, E. M. (1990). Women, race, and crime. *Criminology, 28*(4), 601-626.

Holtfreter, K., & Morash, M. (2003). The needs of women offenders: Implications for correctional programming. *Women and Criminal Justice, 14*(2/3), 137-160.

Johnson, P. C. (2003). *Inner Lives: Voices of African American Women in Prison.* New York: New York University Press.

Jones, M., & Sims, B. (1997). Recidivism of offenders released from prison in North Carolina: A gender comparison. *The Prison Journal, 77*(3), 335-348.

Kassebaum, P. A. (1999). *Substance Abuse Treatment for Women Offenders: Guide to Promising Practice.* Rockville, MD: U.S. Department of Health and Human Services, Center for Substance Abuse Treatment.

Langan, N. P., & Pellissier, B. M. M. (2001). Gender differences among prisoners in drug treatment. *Journal of Substance Abuse, 13,* 291-301.

McQuaide, S., & Ehrenreich, J. H. (1998). Women in prison: Approaches to understanding the lives of a forgotten population. *AFFILIA, 13*(2), 233-246.

Mullings, J. L., Pollock, J., & Crouch, B. M. (2002). Drugs and criminality: Results from the Texas women inmates study. *Women & Criminal Justice, 13*(4), 69-96.

Mumola, C. J. (2000). *Incarcerated Parents and Their Children.* Washington, DC: Bureau of Justice Statistics (NCJ182335).

O'Brien, P. (2002). *Evaluation of Grace House: Using Past Experience to Inform Future Results.* Chicago, IL: Jane Addams College of Social Work.

O'Brien, P., & Lee, N. (2006). Moving from needs to self-efficacy: A holistic system for women in transition from prison. *Journal of Women and Therapy, 29*(3/4), 261-284.

Pastore, A. L., & Maguire, K. (2005). *Sourcebook of Criminal Justice Statistics.* Washington, DC: U.S. Department of Justice, Bureau of Justice Statistics (NCJ 208756).

Pearl, N. R. (1998). Use of community based social services to reduce recidivism in female parolees. *Women & Criminal Justice, 10*(1), 27-52.

Pellissier, B. (2004). Gender differences in substance use treatment entry and retention among prisoners with substance use histories. *American Journal of Public Health, 94*(8), 1418-1425.

Pellissier, B. M. M., Camp, S. D., Gaes, G. G., Saylor, W. G., & Rhodes, W. (2003). Gender differences in outcomes from prison-based residential treatment. *Journal of Substance Abuse Treatment, 24,* 149-160.

Pogrebin, M. R., & Dodge, M. (2001). Women's accounts of their prison experiences: A retrospective view of their subjective realities. *Journal of Criminal Justice, 29,* 531-541.

Prendergast, M. L., Wellisch, J., & Falkin, G. P. (1995). Assessment of and services for substance-abusing women offenders in community and correctional settings. *The Prison Journal, 75*(2), 240-256.

Ramsey, M. L. (1980). Special treatment and treatment needs of female drug offenders. *Journal of Offender Counseling, 4*(4), 357-368.

Richie, B. E. (1996). *Compelled to Crime: The Gender Entrapment of Battered Black Women.* New York: Routledge.

Stuart, B., & Brice-Baker, J. (2004). Correlates of higher rates of recidivism in female prisoners: An exploratory study. *Journal of Psychiatry & Law, 32*(1), 29-70.

U.S. Census Bureau. (2000). Census 2000 Summary File. Available at: http://factfinder.census.gov. Accessed November 11, 2005.

Van Voorhis, P. (2001). *Classification of Women Offenders: A National Assessment of Current Practices.* Washington, DC: U.S. Department of Justice.

Walker, W., Spohn, C., & DeLone, M. (1996). *The Color of Justice: Race, Ethnicity, and Crime in America.* Belmont, CA: Wadsworth Publishing.

Chapter 7

Prevalence of Substance Abuse Within the African-American Community: Mental Health Implications and Interventions

Elizabeth Waggoner
Jesse Brinson

Aside from the continued increase in HIV/AIDS cases among African Americans, a concomitant public health concern is the increased prevalence rates of psychoactive substance use in the African-American community. A growing body of epidemiological data suggests that within many inner cities, substances such as alcohol, tobacco, marijuana, cocaine, and heroin have had a profound negative impact among ethnic minorities, particularly African Americans (Beauvais & Oetting, 2003; Lewin & Altman, 2000). For example, the use and abuse of crack cocaine accounts for much of the violence-related trauma that we see among and between African-American youth gangs in many U.S. inner cities. Moreover, the use of psychoactive substances, such as heroin, is associated with the increase of HIV infections in many African-American women and men between the ages of eighteen and twenty-five (Boyd et al., 2004; Centers for Disease Control, 2003).

More than 50 percent of African-American children grow up in a home with one parent; the parent that is noticeably absent tends to be the African-American male. When looking at absent fathers, the nonparticipation in the lives of their families is inextricably linked to their substance use and abuse (Brinson, 1994). Child welfare research with African-American children reveals that cases involving child abuse are often directly related to one or more individuals being involved in the use of licit or illicit drugs (Barth, Courtney, Berrick, & Albert, 1994; Carten, 1996; Daro & McCurdy, 1991;

Mental Health Care in the African-American Community
© 2007 by The Haworth Press, Inc. All rights reserved.
doi:10.1300/5364_07

Gregoire & Schultz, 2001; Gruber, Fleetwood, & Herring, 2001; Jackson, 1995; Maluccio & Ainsworth, 2003; McAlpine, Marshall, & Doran, 2001; McNichol & Tash, 2001).

An examination of the research pertaining to African-American men who are incarcerated reveals that most of them committed the criminal offense for which they were convicted while under the influence of some type of drug (Brinson, 1995). A review of the increase of such mental health problems as depression, stress-related disorders, and phobic disorders within the African-American community reveals that symptoms of mental disorders are more likely to be attributed to substance use and abuse (Zhang & Snowden, 1999). The data are clear: drug abuse undermines motivation, influences juvenile crime, interferes with cognitive processes, contributes to debilitating mood disorders, and increases risk of family problems (Hawkins, Catalano, & Miller, 1992). As the proliferation of gang violence, health problems, family problems, incarceration rates, and depressed attitudes become increasingly evident in many African-American communities, there will be greater awareness and appreciation of the impact that drugs are having upon individuals, families, and communities.

Given that African Americans come from a spiritual culture, practitioners, educators, and researchers alike often ponder the question: "Why do African Americans seem to have such a problem with the abuse of substances?" Although the answers to this question are rather complex, this chapter includes a discussion of several scholarly explanations that may help to place this issue into a larger sociocultural context.

As a result of the discussions contained in this chapter, readers will develop their own answers to the preceding question as they are guided through a review of several cultural factors that could have an impact on the substance use of African-American individuals. The writers approach the topic from a life course perspective and a developmental analysis of substance use among African Americans.

REVIEW OF THE LITERATURE

Who Is an African American?

At first glance, this may not seem to be an important issue. However, it is an important issue for several reasons. First, it is important to remember that immigrants from North, South, and Central America, the Caribbeans, and Africa do not consider themselves to be African American. Yet, for ease of counting purposes, demographers in the United States automatically include them in the African-American category. Second, researchers often use this shorthand approach when studying participants for various research projects. Consequently, when members of these groups seek out treatment for issues pertaining to substance use and abuse, the statistics for the African-American category may become artificially inflated with members that do not personally identify themselves as such. Third, and this may sound somewhat convoluted, but people have been known to claim African-American heritage when they believe it is in their best interests to do so. In other words, a person of mixed race may self-identify as a White person when things are going great for him or her, then claim the African-American part when faced with some type of adversity, such as seeking treatment for substance abuse. Ultimately, it is imperative that readers understand that African Americans are a varied group and any statistical conclusion must be examined within the context of the diversity of the population.

HISTORICAL CONTEXT OF ALCOHOL, TOBACCO, AND OTHER DRUG USE AMONG AFRICAN AMERICANS

Tribal Life

The overwhelming majority of today's African-American population traces its ancestry to the slave trade from Africa (Williams & Jackson, 2000). Various cultures in Africa have a long history of incorporating beer, wine, marijuana, and other herbal hallucinogens such as *qat* into daily life (Brinson & Fisher, 1999). Some areas used maize or millet to brew beer; others tapped palm trees to make wine. South of the Sahara, Arab traders who introduced ganja products such as marijuana and hashish to the region influenced many tribes. The stimulant *qat,* another Arabic influence, was either chewed or brewed into a tea. In most cases, these fairly mild intoxicants and stimulants were incorporated into tribal culture, often used as a part of group, medicinal, or religious activities, and had established norms governing their use and misuse (James & Johnson, 1996).

Slavery

The cultural uprooting of slavery changed the social patterns for alcohol and drug use among African Americans (Tseng, 2003). Because most slaves were involved in agriculture, drinking was often limited to weekends, holidays, harvest rituals, and celebrations. Women abstained at a higher rate than men because of traditional African tribal sanctions against women drinking, and because of their high visibility as caretakers of the slave holders' children (James & Johnson, 1996). Drinking changed from a social ritual to an escape from the hard labor, demoralization, dispossession, and oppression of captive life.

Abolitionist and Prohibition Movements

The temperance movement that began in the mid-1800s began to change African-American beliefs about drinking. At first, Northern abolitionists viewed the practice of giving alcohol to slaves as an attempt to keep slaves docile and passive. For many African Americans, temperance became a tool toward abolition. But in the South, slave owners who supported temperance did so because they believed alcohol unleashed dangerous and rebellious impulses in slaves. After the Civil War, many Southern Whites saw the Prohibition Movement as another way to control the behavior of African Americans. Racist beliefs about the sexual dangers presented to White women and children by drunk and uninhibited Black men led to strong support of temperance in this region (Fisher & Harrison, 2000). Preserving their right to drink alcohol became a way for some African Americans to demonstrate their defiance against segregation and limited legal rights.

Post–Civil War Era

At the end of the Civil War, many African Americans started to migrate northward from the South in search of jobs. They left rural communities behind and moved primarily to urban centers. Although African Americans were underrepresented in the growing number of citizens addicted to opium and cocaine in various forms at the end of the nineteenth century, their use and abuse of alcohol became more intensified at this time. Whereas in the South many African Americans had limited social outlets to congregate for alcohol use, urban life offered many opportunities to drink at taverns and clubs, and drinking switched from celebrations and special occasions to more frequent consumption of alcohol that often led to excess and abuse. In essence, the pattern of alcohol use that formerly was used as an escape from the oppression of slavery now was used as an escape from prejudice, low wages, violence, and racial segregation (James & Johnson, 1996).

Post–World War I

By the end of World War I, the federal government had become very concerned about the social ills caused by widespread addiction and habit-forming drugs. Federal regulations such as the Harrison Narcotics Act of

1914 placed governmental controls over the sale and distribution of narcotics. Almost overnight, an illegal drug trade developed that led to dramatically higher prices for heroin, opium, and cocaine. Prohibition led to large profits from the sale of bootleg liquor. At this time, "African American communities increasingly became the place where whites practiced their vices . . . and law enforcement often ignored alcohol and other drug sales in these communities" (James & Johnson, 1996, p. 16). Urban African Americans, denied higher education and employment by segregation and discrimination, soon became a target for the purchase, sale, and use of illicit drugs and alcohol. By the 1930s, this population started to become disproportionately represented as drug addicts in major American cities, a trend that has · continued to this day.

Post–World War II

After World War II, marijuana use previously restricted to subculture groups, such as prisoners, pimps, prostitutes, and military personnel, started to spread throughout the African-American middle class. Alcohol abuse continued to increase, especially in rural African-American communities where many farm workers had lost their jobs because increased mechanization. Heroin usage rates continued to rise among urban African Americans and had reached epidemic levels by the 1960s. The growth of syndicates to control the production and distribution of drugs created a new class of criminal in African-American society, the drug dealer, and led to intergenerational addiction with entire families involved in the drug trade (James & Johnson, 1996). The Vietnam War left many returning African-American veterans addicted to opium, heroin, or morphine and helped spread the use of heroin from urban areas to the whole country. The counterculture community in the 1960s and 1970s introduced common use of marijuana, hallucinogens, amphetamines, and cocaine in powder form to high school and college youth throughout the country, including African Americans.

1980s

In 1985, a new, cheap, and smoke form of cocaine called crack was introduced into the American market by the Colombian drug cartel. In two or three short years, the low price and intense but brief euphoric high of crack made this the drug of choice, other than alcohol, for many African Americans living in inner-city communities. African-American gangs quickly became involved in crack distribution and sales, and battles over sales territory led to a dramatic escalation in neighborhood violence. Increases in crack cocaine use also led to escalating use of alcohol and heroin to control the restlessness, alertness, and acute paranoia experienced when coming down from a crack high (Fisher & Harrison, 2000). By 1995, 22 percent of cocaine users nationwide were African American, 62 percent were Euro-American, and 16 percent were Hispanic. But in many major cities, such as Los Angeles, almost 60 percent of cocaine users were African American (Strickland, 2001).

Many of the family and social support networks of urban African-American communities crumbled under the intense financial burden of crack addiction, which often left addicts destitute and homeless in just a few months. Women users often turned to prostitution to support their habit, exposing them to violence and risky sexual behavior (Wechsberg, Lam, Zule, & Bobashev, 2004). Children were often neglected, abused, or abandoned by their crack-using parents (Okundaye, Lawrence-Webb, & Thornton, 2004). Infants exposed to crack in utero often suffered severe withdrawal symptoms after birth and became cranky and difficult to care for (Boyd, Phillips, & Dorsey, 2003).

Twenty-First Century

By the beginning of the twenty-first century, new trends in substance abuse were emerging in the United States. Crystal meth, a new, cheap, and easy-to-make version of methamphetamine, was developed in a crystalline form that could be smoked. This stimulant offered a much longer and more intense high than cocaine. Hallucinogens became more popular with the import of club drugs from Europe, such as Ecstasy, and resurgence in the use of LSD. Unlike crack cocaine, crystal meth and club drugs had a minimum impact on African Americans because of the drugs initial use and availability in predominately Caucasian communities (Yacoubian & Peters, 2004). Another trend in substance abuse was a significant increase in the nonmedical use of pain relievers such as Vicodin or Lortab. In fact, by 2003, more Americans were abusing pain relievers than cocaine, presaging a major shift in nationwide substance abuse.

USE AND ABUSE OF ALCOHOL, TOBACCO, AND OTHER DRUGS

According to the National Institute on Drug Abuse (NIDA) report *Drug Use among Racial/Ethnic Minorities* (2003), approximately 12.2 percent of the U.S. population is comprised of non-Hispanic African Americans. Fifty-three percent of this group lives in the South, 37 percent live in metropolitan areas of the Northeast and Midwest, and only 10 percent live in the West. Just over 6 percent of Americans with African ancestry qualify as active and current users of illegal drugs. Looking across all age ranges, this usage rate is comparable to rates for non-Hispanic Whites and Hispanics; is higher than rates for Asian/Pacific Islanders; and lower than rates for American Indian/ Alaskan Natives. Historically African Americans have had a lower rate of substance abuse than Caucasians. Only in the past few years has the African-American prevalence rate of abuse started to equal the Caucasian rate.

Drinking rates for African-American men are higher than the rates for adolescents and women, but overall African Americans drink less than non-Hispanic Whites. Adults from age eighteen to thirty-five have the highest prevalence rate for alcohol use, just over 50 percent, while youth twelve to seventeen drink at a 13 percent rate, and adults over thirty-five drink at a 38 percent rate (NIDA, 2003). Single and newly divorced people drink more heavily than do married people. Geographic location also affects alcohol use rates. African Americans who live in the western United States and in large metropolitan areas drink more heavily than residents in eastern and rural areas (Strickland, 2001). African Americans are less likely to drink daily and more likely to binge drink on the weekends or at special occasions, a pattern established centuries ago during slavery. They are also more likely than Caucasians to experience medical consequences from alcohol use, such as cirrhosis, heart disease, and mouth, lung, and esophageal cancers (Petry, 2003).

African Americans are less likely to be heavy smokers than Caucasians, prefer to smoke menthol cigarettes, and are less likely to smoke light or low-tar cigarettes. Smoking rates steadily increase with age. Only about 14 percent of adolescents smoke, and this rate has been steadily declining (Wallace et al., 2002). But by age twenty-five a little over 30 percent of African-American adults smoke and this rate increases about 1 percent for every decade of age (NIDA, 2003). As with alcohol and illegal drugs, women smoke less than men. African Americans process nicotine differently than other groups, as they take longer to clear nicotine from their system, and show higher serum levels of nicotine metabolites, despite smoking fewer cigarettes per day (Resnicow, Soler, Braithwaite, Ahluwalla, & Butler, 2000).

Substance abuse among Americans of African descent follows a pattern distinct from other ethnic groups. For African-American youth in the lower grades and in high school, the prevalence rate for alcohol, tobacco, and other drug use (except for marijuana) has consistently shown to be lower than that for the majority population of non-Hispanic Whites (Fishbein & Perez, 2000; Gil, Wagner, & Tubman, 2004; Wallace et al., 2002). However, after age twenty-five the African-American abuse rate gradually exceeds the majority rate, especially among men (NIDA, 2003). For most African Americans, substance abuse becomes problematic later on in life, while with most other ethnic groups, abuse problems start at a much earlier age. Research to date has not yet found a cause for this postadolescent increase in substance use, but many theories exist. Some researchers speculate that African-American family values such as kinship bonds, work orientation, educational achievement, and religious commitment provide a strong, effective control over African-American youth and partially shelter them from the stresses of racism, financial disadvantages, and social limitations. During the transition to adulthood, however, many African Americans lose these family based protections and start to use alcohol and drugs to cope with the challenges of racism (Beauvais & Oetting, 2003). Other researchers hypothesize that differences in socioeconomic and demographic factors, such as discrimination, poverty, high unemployment, and disadvantaged neighborhoods, place African-American adults at greater risk for substance abuse than the majority population (Gil et al., 2004).

THE EFFECTS OF DRUG AND ALCOHOL USE

Certain subgroups within the African-American population are more adversely affected by drugs and alcohol than others. For example, African-American women in general rarely abuse drugs and have a 5.2 percent prevalence rate of use compared to 12 percent for African-American men (NIDA, 2003). For substance abusers over twenty-five, the preferred substances are tobacco and alcohol while those under twenty-five prefer marijuana. Women aged twenty-five to thirty-five prefer cocaine (Beatty, 2003). Yet low-income African Americans who live in urban areas represent one of the highest risk groups for alcohol and illicit drug use (Kim, Han, Hill, Rose, & Roary, 2003). Women who live in these communities abuse cocaine while pregnant at a rate disproportionate to the rest of the population. Consequently, these same women are overrepresented in criminal justice facilities and substance abuse treatment centers (Lewis, 2004). Infants exposed to cocaine before birth are at greater risk for physical and psychological impairment, and are often lethargic, prone to overstimulation and irritability, and difficult to care for (Porter & Porter, 1998). Maternal substance abuse in this group is associated with greater risks of poverty, homelessness, mental illness, violence, trauma, child abuse, and placement of children in foster care, and exposure to sexually transmitted diseases, such as HIV (Connors, Bradley, Whiteside-Mansell, & Crone, 2001; Wobie, Eyler, Garvan, Hou, & Behnke, 2004).

Because of illegal drug use, HIV infection rates among African Americans, especially women, have risen sharply in the past decade. In 2003, 49 percent of people with AIDS were African American, compared to 35 percent in 1993 (Boyd et al., 2004; CDC, 2003). According to the Centers for Disease Control (2003), during 2000-2003 the HIV/AIDS rates for African-American females were nineteen times the rates for White females and five times the rates for Hispanic females. Over two thirds of the children born in 2003 who tested positive for HIV were African American (CDC, 2003). More than 60 percent of the AIDS cases among African Americans can be traced to injection drug use by the patient or the patient's sexual partner. Risky sexual behavior, another cause of HIV, is also linked to substance abuse, as addicts often trade sex for money or drugs and are more likely to have increased sexual activity, unprotected sex, and multiple partners (Boyd et al., 2004). HIV prevalence rates among African-American women who use drugs range from 1.7 percent among noninjecting users to 54 percent among homeless women trading sex for drugs (Wechsberg et al., 2004).

African Americans, like most groups of color, experience more serious and lasting negative consequences from alcohol and drug abuse than Caucasians do. Many social and cultural factors contribute to this unequal burden on minorities. Legal penalties for the use of powder cocaine, primarily used by Caucasians, are much lighter than penalties for crack cocaine, primarily used by African Americans (U.S. Sentencing Commission, 1995). Ethic groups of color are more likely to be targets of racial profiling, are more likely to be arrested, and often receive stiffer sentencing than Caucasians for the same crime (Beauvais & Oetting, 2003). Once incarcerated for drug-related crimes, African Americans are less likely than the majority to be treated for substance abuse (BJS, 1999).

Social economic status (SES) is another factor that makes the consequences of drug use worse for groups of color. Low-income, unemployment, limited educational opportunities, and higher dropout rates make it difficult for many African Americans to access the basic health care, health insurance, and treatment programs available to more affluent populations. Lower SES and substance abuse also damage family structure. Alcoholism and heavy drinking within urban and poor African-American families create problems that include: physical and sexual abuse of children, spouses and partners; drinking-related violence; marital difficulties; financial and health problems; child neglect; and inappropriate sharing of alcoholic beverages with infants and children (Harper, 2001). African Americans are also at higher risk for the toxic effects of cocaine. Cocaine toxicity affects both the sympathetic nervous system and the cardiovascular system. Since hypertension and heart disease are common among African Americans, cocaine use exacerbates these health problems (Boyd et al., 2003). This fact alone suggests that African Americans could suffer a potentially lethal consequence from the use of cocaine.

African-American adolescents as well as adults undergo stresses unique to their community that are linked to substance abuse. These youth are more likely than Caucasian youth to witness, take part in, or be victim to violence from gang activity; to observe drugs being sold in their neighborhood; to have a parent, sibling, or friend die; and to be arrested, incarcerated, or somehow involved with the criminal justice system (Brinson, 1995; Moore, Madison-Colmore, & Moore, 2003; Resnicow et al., 2000). Family disruptions related to alcohol and drug abuse often lead to homelessness and placement in kinship or foster care and expose many African-American children to HIV, trauma, neglect, and abuse (Okundaye et al., 2004). Adolescent girls are usually initiated into drug or alcohol abuse by their boyfriends and are more likely than Caucasian girls to proceed from marijuana use into abuse of cocaine, heroin, and heavy alcohol use (Guthrie & Low, 2000).

LIFE COURSE ANALYSIS AND CURRENT SUBSTANCE ABUSE TREATMENT APPROACHES FOR AFRICAN AMERICANS

Infancy

The first step in a life course analysis of substance abuse and its impact on African-American communities would be to examine how prenatal drug exposure affects the growth and development of infants. Cocaine exposure before birth leaves infants lethargic, unresponsive, irritable, and difficult to nurture. Care for these infants is difficult and unrewarding and the mother often becomes frustrated, detached, and avoidant. These maladaptive parenting behaviors can often lead to impaired infant development and stunted growth, and also risk the entry of the child into foster care.

Porter and Porter (1998) offer a theoretical model called the Infant Massage Parenting Enhancement Program (IMPEP) that blends infant massage into a planned parenting program for substance-abusing mothers. The massage builds maternal sensitivity to infant needs and strengthens the maternal bond with the child, which increases the mother's desire to participate in the parenting classes and seek out drug treatment. The pilot studies of this model, targeted mainly toward African-American women, support the feasibility of using IMPEP as an intervention with substance-abusing mothers. Another study identified specific risks that could lead to out-of-home placement for cocaine-exposed newborns born to African-American women.

Wobie et al. (2004) found that the closer to giving birth that a mother used cocaine significantly reduced the chances of her retaining custody of her child. In addition, the higher the education level and number of positive life experiences of the mother then the higher the probability that she would retain custody.

Childhood

The majority of research on African-American adolescent drug and alcohol abuse focuses on males rather than females, which is consistent with the low prevalence of substance abuse among females. However, some work is being done on developing culturally appropriate substance abuse prevention programs for African-American girls. Guthrie and Low (2000) propose a prevention model that incorporates gender socialization and self-efficacy as key prevention factors along with the influences of racism, sexism, classism, and ageism. Belgrave (2002) notes that effective prevention programs for this group have incorporated protective factors such as strengthening ethnic identity, building self-esteem, and cultivating positive peer support and skill enhancement.

Adolescence

Culturally appropriate prevention programs targeted at African-American boys have also been studied. Harvey and Hill (2004) examined the effects of an Africentric youth and family rites of passage program on at-risk boys with no history of substance abuse. They found that the young boys exhibited gains in self-esteem and accurate knowledge of the dangers of substance abuse, while the parents showed improvements in parenting skills, racial identity, cultural awareness, and community involvement. Moore et al. (2003) discuss the need for more Africentric-directed drug treatment programs for African-American teenage boys that are strength based and emphasize the interpersonal relationships and survival mechanisms that exist among African-American culture.

Another main focus of research on adolescent males is early initiation of alcohol and drug use. African-American teenage boys who use substances before high school are at a heightened risk for developing substance abuse and psychiatric disorders by early adulthood (Gil et al., 2004). Early substance use by this group also exerts a direct influence on the failure to graduate from high school (McCluskey, Krohn, Lizotte, & Rodriguez, 2002).

Current research aimed at both adolescent boys and girls covers a wide range of topics. Robbins et al. (2002) examined whether psychiatric disorders contribute to substance abuse among minority youth, including African Americans. For Hispanics, substance abuse appears to occur more often with problem behavior, whereas for African Americans substance abuse often occurs on its own.

Several studies identified early and midadolescence risk factors for substance abuse by African Americans. For some African-American youth very high exposure to cumulative risk factors from the personal, familial, and social context realm is the primary pathway for alcohol and marijuana dependence. Early adolescent exposure is more important for alcohol dependence and midadolescent exposure is more important for marijuana abuse or dependence (Gil, Vega, & Turner 2002). These risk factors grouped together must be high enough to overcome the very protective effect of African-American family values. Fishbein and Perez (2000) found that lack of prosocial values, poor attitudes toward police, and perceived limited opportunities predicted drug use for high-risk African-American youth. For males, a poor relationship with the father and a good relationship with the mother predicted higher levels of involvement with drug sales. The study posited that since mothers of these high-risk youth often engaged in deviant behavior themselves they did not view their sons' drug involvement as problematic. Being traumatized by the death of a friend is another substance abuse risk factor for teenage African Americans (Caldwell et al., 2006).

Only one study focused on the efficacy of publicly funded substance abuse treatment programs for adolescents. A study of sex and ethnic differences on treatment referrals and outcomes reveals that compared to Caucasian adolescents, African Americans and Hispanics were primarily referred into treatment from criminal justice; usually mandated to treatment; reported marijuana as the primary drug; and were much less likely to be injection drug users. Minority adolescents were more likely than their Caucasian counterparts to have unsuccessful treatment outcomes even though Caucasian teens have more severe alcohol and drug abuse problems (Shillington & Clapp, 2003).

Potts (2003) discusses the benefits of developing school-based interventions in African-American communities with ideas from emancipatory and African-centered education. This approach "looks at social problems within the context of the historical processes and social forces that have transformed communities of people of African descent" (Potts, 2003, p. 178). By reconnecting students with African and African-American history, traditions, values, and principles, the students will be empowered to deal with community problems such as "resource asymmetries, structures of domination, and the forced rupture with African cultural traditions and healing resources" (Potts, 2003, p. 178).

Adulthood and Family Life

One focus of family systems research was residential substance abuse programs that housed African-American women along with their children. A joint federal-state project called Arkansas CARES was developed to provide residential care for low-income pregnant and parenting women and dependent children. Though this project was not specifically targeted toward African Americans, a majority of the participants were African-American women who abused crack cocaine. Women who completed the program had a 15 percent relapse rate one year later and had positive outcomes in employment, self-sufficiency, family interaction skills, and increased knowledge of the negative consequences of substance abuse (Connors et al., 2001).

Lewis (2004) took a different approach to family systems and examined the experiences of African-American women with children in formal substance abuse programs. The study used an Afrocentric, feminist approach and grounded theory to identify specific themes that benefited these women in treatment and could be applied in the development of new, culturally appropriate treatment programs. The specific themes identified by the women were: basing treatment on a complete life history; being allowed to distance themselves from their children to focus on their treatment; knowing that their children were in a safe space during this distancing; feeling that child care with little or no African-American staff was not a safe space; having access to caring, credible counselors and therapists; wishing more counseling staff were African American; and using spirituality as a support during recovery.

Family systems research also included a study of family based prevention counseling that supports a customized prevention planning program for families of at-risk youth (Hague, Liddle, Becker, & Johnson-leckrone, 2002). The goal is to target the specific risk and protective factors in each family that may lead to or prevent substance abuse and antisocial behavior, and then offer specialized counseling to address these factors. Results among African-American families noted gains in global self-worth, family cohesion, and bonding to school, and a decrease in peer antisocial behavior.

Perrino, Coatsworth, Briones, Pantin, and Szapocznik (2001) examined the factors that drive families to initially engage and participate in family based substance abuse prevention programs. The only significant factor that proved to be an overwhelming barrier for engagement by African-American families was a low level of family organization. For all ethnic groups the strongest predictor of engagement was a high level of family organization, family communication, and family cohesion.

Even though men have the highest prevalence rates for substance abuse in the African-American community, very little research is directed specifically toward this group. Rich (2001) notes that our current health care system is biased against and resists socioeconomic differences among African-American men and leaves them disenfranchised and marginalized. African-American concepts of masculinity, experiences of violence in the urban landscape, and negative and often traumatic experiences with institutions such as the criminal justice system shape the health risk and health-seeking behaviors of these men. African-American men "develop ways of coping that exemplify their resilience but . . . are formed by a basic acceptance of their circumstances" (Rich, 2001, p. 5).

A review of the current literature on substance abuse among African-American men reveals a similar bias in the mental health care system. Research data for these men must be extrapolated from substance abuse studies of the general population that include racial and ethnic demographics. Results from a study of young adult probationers referred to treatment for substance abuse show that this population was more likely to be African American with a significantly earlier age of primary substance abuse. These youth were also more likely to use marijuana than older adults, who preferred alcohol (Sinha, Easton, & Kemp, 2003). These results are similar to studies done on African-American adolescents.

The Federal Bureau of Prisons (BOP) collected data on the differing behaviors of African-American and Caucasian participants in prison-based substance abuse treatment programs. A follow-up study examined treatment outcomes in this population. Rounds-Bryant (2004) noted that in general African-American men in substance abuse treatment are less likely than Caucasian men to be employed before or after treatment; to have more economic difficulties; and to have more exposure to drug use in their social environments. Results of the study indicated that African Americans had a higher relapse rate than Caucasians (67 and 47 percent, respectively) after release from prison and a shorter time to resuming drug use (5.7 and 8 months, respectively). BOP data also shows that 66 percent of state prisoners were released in metropolitan areas that are socially chaotic and have few resources to address the needs of returning offenders (Rounds-Bryant, 2004). The higher incarceration rate of African-American men and their increased exposure to drugs, alcohol, crime, poverty, and unemployment makes it extremely challenging for them to abstain from drug and alcohol use.

EXPANDED APPROACHES IN THE TREATMENT
OF SUBSTANCE ABUSE AMONG AFRICAN AMERICANS

In considering intervention strategies for working with African Americans who suffer from alcohol and drug addiction, it is important to search the literature for empirically supported models. For example, Washington and Moxley (2003) developed group interventions based on increasing self-efficacy and a sense of empowerment by using gestalt experiments; engaging in prayerful homework and meditation; sharing powerful stories of people overcoming obstacles; discussing the lives of successful African Americans; and exploring visual art. According to the reported findings, these interventions helped participants develop a sense of community, reduce stress, develop positive outcomes, and improve self-efficacy and the ability to think positively.

Wechsberg et al. (2004) examined an intervention that includes culturally enriched content that is grounded in empowerment theory and African-American feminism. After completion, program participants showed a significant reduction in cocaine use, unprotected sex, trading sex, and homelessness. They also showed significant improvement in finding full-time employment.

Wright (2003) discussed how important spirituality can be in treating substance abusers. The author examined narrative stories from African Americans recovering from substance abuse and identified how these individuals incorporated spirituality into their recovery. Spirituality was important in each stage of change and linked to themes of abandonment, surrendering, reconnecting, transformation, and maturity.

Milligan, Nich, and Carroll (2004) conducted a study that examined two treatment approaches: behavioral treatments such as cognitive-behavioral therapy and twelve-step facilitation, and pharmacotherapy such as desipramine and disulfiram. Overall results revealed that African Americans could benefit from these interventions. Although such approaches as individual, group, and family therapy are the prevailing methods for working with substance abusers in treatment programs, alternative strategies should be examined when working with African Americans. African Americans are thought to make extensive use of alternative treatments for health and mental health problems. This preference is deemed to reflect African-American cultural traditions developed partly when African Americans were systematically excluded from mainstream health care institutions (Smith Fahie, 1998). Therefore, the writers postulate that the heavy use of facilitative communication methods and nontraditional therapeutic approaches that emanate from the arts, spiritual-based interventions, and network-interventions are also worthwhile considerations whether in an agency or individual treatment setting. The next section considers the aforementioned expanded approaches to working with African Americans who suffer from drug and alcohol addictions.

SPIRITUALITY AND RELIGION
AS A CLINICAL INTERVENTION

Given that many African Americans tend to have strong religious orientations, it could be helpful to have a spiritual counselor, guide, mentor, or even minister be part of the therapeutic team. Many African Americans value the wisdom of ministers and other religious figures and may find the inclusion of such a person in clinical sessions and activities quite comforting. Some African-American clients may have exhausted traditional intervention strategies and programs. The use of spirituality as an intervention might create a sense of hope for the client who has encountered other therapeutic approaches with limited success.

In addition it is important to note that the meaning a client ascribes to spirituality and religion may be quite different from convention and what is considered the norm by mainstream culture. With that said, practitioners should empower clients to lead the way in introducing spirituality into the clinical setting.

NETWORK INTERVENTION

Many African Americans were raised in a collectivist culture. This means that many individuals have extended family members that support their overall well-being. These individuals are considered family, as the result of long-standing relationships, but may not be linked directly by blood lines. These individuals are often willing to help in any manner or even be responsible for the family member that is directly affected by a substance abuse problem. It could be useful to have weekly therapy sessions with the client and the extended family, with the hope that the extended family may exert a measure of influence over the individual to disrupt nonproductive ways of thinking and behaving.

Facilitative Communication Methods

Given that many African Americans live in a society that does not reinforce their cultural identity and value system, it is extremely important to show respect to them in clinical settings to establish rapport and give them confidence that they can overcome their addictive behaviors. This includes, at a minimum, using respectful titles (e.g., Mr., Mrs.) unless they give the clinician and staff permission to do otherwise. In other words affirmations, validation, and character restoration should be strategies employed by practitioners.

In addition, providers of clinical services should be encouraged to examine their attitudes and perceptions of African Americans, especially in light of the fact that most service providers are non-African American. If the service provider finds that he or she may be bound with cultural stereotypes of the African-American client, then the provider must attempt to rid himself- or herself of those views immediately. Otherwise, the provider will most likely relate to the client in a manner that will encourage resistance toward the provider. The manifestation of respect allows the client to feel safe enough to open a window into his or her inner experience, allowing the provider to see the client's hurts and pains. Research on respect shows a relationship between the show of respect and positive client outcomes (Pope & Kline, 1999).

CREATIVE ARTS THERAPY

To promote the free expression of identity development issues, which can be linked to the abuse of substances, the writers often encourage the use of creative arts in therapy (e.g., paintings, music, videos, television shows). In one study, African-American youth rated a multicultural drug prevention video intervention program as having a great impact on decreasing their behavioral intention of using substances (Freimuth, Plotnick, Ryan, & Schiller, 1997). Practitioners are well served by keeping in mind that the use of the "arts" should be culturally informed and suggested therapeutic activities must be conducive to the client's values and beliefs.

CONCLUSION

It is important to contextualize African Americans' substance use within the broader framework of the U.S. society. The psychosocial factors under which many African Americans live their lives may put many of them at greater risk for substance use and for such alcohol and drug-related conditions as gang violence, HIV/AIDS exposure, and other psychiatric disorders. Nonetheless, human service professionals must not discount the fact that as a cultural group, African Americans continue to defy the odds. An overwhelming majority of African Americans are not using drugs, do not commit crimes, are emotionally stable, take good care of their physical health, and are not undergoing psychotherapy.

Service providers working with African Americans in treatment settings must be aware of various interventions that could be effective with the African-American client. Although it is helpful to use interventions that have empirical support, it is also a worthwhile consideration to examine approaches that have shown promise. Moreover, any intervention should be tailored with the concept of cultural sensitivity in mind. Many of the strategies that are offered in this chapter have proven to be beneficial approaches for work with African Americans.

CHAPTER SUMMARY

The authors note that African Americans in treatment are likely to come from several different ethnic groups, which could ultimately have an impact on the extent to which substance use rates are deemed reliable. Next, the authors discuss African Americans' substance use and abuse patterns detailing the current use and abuse of alcohol, tobacco, and other drugs. It is emphasized that by the year 2003, the data revealed that more African Americans were moving away from hard drug use, but a trend was developing with respect to more frequent use of prescription pain medication. Near the end of the chapter, the authors include a discussion of treatment approaches that have shown to be effective when working with African-American substance users. Immediately following the discussion of traditional therapeutic approaches, a summary of alternative treatment interventions that hold promise is offered as viable strategies in working with African Americans.

The chapter concludes with a discussion of the resilient nature of African Americans. This resiliency has resulted largely because African Americans continue to live their lives under more adversity than any other group in the United States. The economic and social disparity that exists for African Americans has been shown to be linked to behavioral problems of substance abuse. Nonetheless, most African Americans function at a high psychological level in American society.

DISCUSSION QUESTIONS

1. How would you describe an African American?
2. A number of reasons are given as to why people may consider alcohol and drug use. What are some reasons African-American children and adults may consider the use of alcohol or drugs?

3. What treatment intervention might you consider in working with African Americans who are struggling with a substance abuse issue?
4. Which developmental period had the most impact on African Americans' substance use? Explain why.

REFERENCES

Barth, R. P., Courtney, M., Berrick, J. D., & Albert, V. (1994). *From Child Abuse to Permanency Planning: Child Welfare Services, Pathways, and Placements.* Hawthorne, NY: Aldine de Gruyter.

Beatty, L. (2003). Substance abuse, disabilities, and Black women: An issue worth exploring. *Women & Therapy, 26*(3/4), 223-236.

Beauvais, F., & Oetting, E. (2003). Drug abuse: Etiology and cultural considerations. In G. Bernal, J. E. Trimble, A. K. Burlew, & F. T. Leong (Eds.), *Handbook of Racial & Ethnic Minority Psychology* (pp. 448-461). Thousand Oaks, CA: Sage Publications.

Belgrave, F. (2002). Relational theory and cultural enhancement interventions for African American adolescent girls. *U.S. Department of Health and Human Services: Public Health Reports, 117,* S76-S81.

Boyd, C., & Holmes, C. (2002). Women who smoke crack and their family substance abuse problems. *Health Care for Women International, 23*(6/7), 576-586.

Boyd, M., Philips, K., & Dorsey, C. (2003). Alcohol and other drug disorders, comorbidity, and violence: Comparison of rural African American and Caucasian women. *Archives of Psychiatric Nursing, 17*(6), 249-258.

Boyd, S., Thomas-Gosain, N., Umbricht, A., Tucker, M., Leslie, J., Chaisson, R., et al. (2004). Gender differences in indices of opioid dependency and medical comorbidity in a population of hospitalized HIV-infected African Americans. *American Journal of Addictions, 13*(3), 281-292.

Brinson, J. A. (1994). The incarceration of African American males: Unsettled questions. *Journal of Offender Rehabilitation, 20*(3), 85-95.

Brinson, J. A. (1995). Group work for black adolescent substance users: Some issues and recommendations. *Journal of Child & Adolescent Substance Abuse, 4*(2), 49-60.

Brinson, J. A., & Fisher, T. (1999). Ho'oponopono: A Group Work Conflict Resolution for School Counselors. *Journal for Specialists in Group Work, 24*(4), 369-382.

Bureau of Justice Statistics (BJS). (1999). Substance abuse and treatment, state and federal prisoners, 1997. *Bureau of Justice Statistics Special Report, January 1999* (No. NCJ 172871). Washington DC: BJS.

Caldwell, R., Sturgess, S., Silver, N. C., Brinson, J., Denby-Brinson, R., & Burgess, K. (2006). An examination of the influence of perceived parenting practices on depression and substance use among African American juvenile offenders. *Journal of Forensic Psychology Practice, 63* (3), 31-50.

Carten, A. J. (1996). Mothers in recovery: Rebuilding families in the aftermath of addiction. *Social Work, 41*(2), 214-223.

Centers for Disease Control (CDC). (2003). *HIV/AIDS Among African Americans.* Available at: http://www.cdc.gov/hiv/pubs/Facts/afam.htm. Accessed April 25, 2005.

Connors, N., Bradley, R., Whiteside-Mansell, L., & Crone, C. (2001). A comprehensive substance abuse treatment program for women and their children: An initial evaluation. *Journal of Substance Abuse Treatment, 21*(2), 67-75.

Daro, D., & McCurdy, K. (1991). *Current trends in child abuse reporting and fatalities: The results of the 1989 annual fifty state survey.* Chicago: National Center on Child Abuse Prevention Research.

Fishbein, D., & Perez, D. (2000). A regional study of risk factors for drug abuse and delinquency: Sex and racial differences. *Journal of Child & Family Studies, 9*(4), 461-480.

Fisher, G., & Harrison, T. (2000). *Substance Abuse* (2nd ed.). Boston, MA: Allyn & Bacon.

Freimuth, V. S., Plotnick, C. A., Ryan, C. E., & Schiller, S. (1997). Right turns only: An evaluation of a video-based, multicultural drug education series for seventh graders. *Health Education & Behavior, 24*(5), 555-567.

Gil, A., Vega, W., & Turner, R. (2002). Early and mid-adolescence risk factors for substance abuse by African Americans and European Americans. *U.S. Department of Health and Human Services; Public Health Report, 117,* 15-29.

Gil, A., Wagner, E., & Tubman, J. (2004). Associations between early-adolescent substance use and subsequent young-adult substance use disorders and psychiatric disorders among a multiethnic male sample in Florida. *American Journal of Public Health, 94*(9), 1603-1610.

Gregoire, K. A., & Schultz, D. J. (2001). Substance-abusing child welfare parents: Treatment and child placement outcomes. *Child Welfare, 80*(4), 433-452.

Gruber, K. J., Fleetwood, T. W., & Herring, M. W. (2001). In-home continuing care services for substance-affected families: The Bridges Program. *Social Work, 46*(3), 267-277.

Guthrie, B., & Low, L. (2000). A substance use prevention framework: Considering the social context for African American girls. *Public Health Nursing, 17*(5), 363-373.

Hague, A., Liddle, H., Becker, D., & Johnson-Leckrone, J. (2002). Family-based prevention counseling for high-risk young adolescents: Immediate outcomes. *Journal of Community Psychology, 30*(1), 1-22.

Harper, F. (2001). In R. L. Brathwaite & S. E. Taylor (Eds.), *Health Issues in the Black Community* (pp. 403-415). San Francisco, CA: Jossey-Bass.

Harvey, A., & Hill, R. (2004). Africentric youth and family rites of passage program: Promoting resilience amongat-risk African American youths. *Social Work, 49*(1), 1-12.

Hawkins, J. D., Catalano, R. F., & Miller, J. Y. (1992). Risk and protective factors for alcohol and other drug problems in adolescence and early adulthood: Implications for substance abuse prevention. *Psychological Bulletin, 112,* 64-105.

Jackson, M. S. (1995). Afrocentric treatment of African American women and their children in a residential chemical dependency program. *Journal of Black Studies, 26*(1), 17-30.

James, W., & Johnson, S. (1996). *Doin' Drugs: Patterns of African American Addiction.* Austin: University of Texas Press.

Kim, M., Han, H., Hill, M., Rose, L., & Roary, M. (2003). Depression, substance use, adherence behaviors, and blood pressure. *Annals of Behavioral Medicine, 26*(1), 24-32.

King, A., & Canada, S. (2004). Client related predictors of early treatment dropout in a substance abuse clinic exclusively employing individual therapy. *Journal of Substance Abuse Treatment, 26*(3), 189-195.

Lewin, M. E., & Altman, S. (2000). *America's Health Care Safety Net: Intact but Endangered.* Washington, DC: National Academy Press.

Lewis, L. (2004). Culturally appropriate substance abuse treatment for parenting African American women. *Issues in Mental Health Nursing, 25*(5), 451-473.

Maluccio, A. N., & Ainsworth, F. (2003). Drug use by parents: A challenge for family reunification practice. *Children and Youth Services Review, 25*(7), 511-533.

McAlpine, C., Marshall, C. C., & Doran, N. H. (2001). Combining child welfare and substance abuse services: A blended model of intervention. *Child Welfare, 80*(2), 129-149.

McCluskey, C., Krohn, M., Lizotte, A., & Rodriguez, M. (2002). Early substance use and school achievement: An examination of Latino, White and African American youth. *Journal of Drug Issues, 32*(3), 921-943.

McNichol, T., & Tash, C. (2001). Parental substance abuse and the development of children in family foster care. *Child Welfare, 80*(2), 239-256.

Milligan, C., Nich, C., & Carroll, K. (2004). Ethnic differences in substance abuse treatment retention, compliance, and outcome from two clinical trials. *The Journal of Neuropsychiatry and Clinical Neurosciences, 55,* 167-173.

Moore, S., Madison-Colmore, O., & Moore, J. (2003). An Afrocentric approach to substance abuse treatment with adolescent African American males: Two case examples. *Western Journal of Black Studies, 27*(4), 219-231.

National Institute of Drug Abuse (NIDA). (2003). *Drug Use Among Racial/Ethnic Minorities, Revised, September 2003* (No. 03-3888). Washington, DC: NIDA.

Okundaye, J., Lawrence-Webb, C., & Thornton, P. (2004). Substance abuse, homelessness, HIV/AIDS, and African American children. In J. E. Everett, S. P. Chipungu, & B. R. Leashore (Eds.), *Child Welfare Revisited: An Africentric Perspective* (pp. 197-211). New Brunswick, NJ: Rutgers University Press.

Perrino, T., Coatsworth, J., Briones, E., Pantin, H., & Szapocznik, J. (2001). Initial engagement in parent-centered preventive interventions: A family systems perspective. *The Journal of Primary Prevention, 22*(1), 21-44.

Petry, N. (2003). A comparison of African American and non-Hispanic Caucasian cocaine-abusing outpatients. *Drug and Alcohol Dependence, 69*(1), 43-49.

Pope, V. T., & Kline, W. B. (1999). The personal characteristics of effective counselors: What 10 experts think. *Psychological Reports, 84,* 1339-1344.

Porter, L., & Porter, B. (1998). A blended infant massage-parenting enhancement program for recovering substance-abusing mothers. *Pediatric Nursing, 30*(5), 363-401.

Potts, R. (2003). Emancipatory education versus school-based prevention in African American communities. *American Journal of Community Psychology, 31*(1/2), 173-183.

Resnicow, K., Soler, R., Braithwaite, R., Ahluwalia, J., & Butler, J. (2000). Cultural sensitivity in substance use prevention. *Journal of Community Psychology, 28*(3), 271-290.

Rheingold, A., Smith, D., Ruggiero, K., Saunders, B., Kilpatrick, D., & Resnick, H. Loss (2004). Trauma exposure, and mental health in a representative sample of 12-17 year-old youth: Data from the National Survey of Adolescents. *Journal of Loss & Trauma, 9*(1), 1-19.

Rich, J. (2001). Primary care for young African American men. *Journal of American College Health, 49*(4), 183-187.

Robbins, M., Kumar, S., Walker-Barnes, C., Feaster, D., Briones, E., & Szapocznik, J. (2002). Ethnic differences in comorbidity among substance-abusing adolescents referred to outpatient therapy. *Journal of the American Academy of Child & Adolescent Psychiatry, 41*(4), 394-401.

Rounds-Bryant, J. (2004, August). Correlates of drug treatment outcomes for African American and white male federal prisoners: Results from the TRIAD study. *American Journal of Drug and Alcohol Abuse,* 1-18.

Shillington, A., & Clapp, J. (2003). Adolescents in public substance abuse treatment programs: The impacts of sex and race on referrals and outcomes. *Journal of Child & Adolescent Substance Abuse, 12*(4), 69-91.

Sinha, R., Easton, C., & Kemp, K. (2003). Substance abuse treatment characteristics of probation-referred young adults in a community-based outpatient program. *American Journal of Drug & Alcohol Abuse, 29*(3), 585-597.

Siqueland, L., Crits-Christoph, P., Gallop, R., Barber, J., Griffin, M., Thase, M., et al. (2002). Retention in psychosocial treatment of cocaine dependence: Predictors and impact on outcome. *American Journal on Addictions, 11*(1), 24-40.

Smith Fahie, V. P. (1998). Utilization of folk/family remedies by community-residing African American elders. *Journal of Cultural Diversity, 5,* 19-22.

Strickland, T. (2001). Substance abuse. In R. L. Braithwaite & S. E. Taylor (Eds.), *Health Issues in the Black Community* (pp. 384-402). San Francisco, CA: Jossey-Bass.

Substance Abuse and Mental Services Administration (SAMSA). (2004). *Overview of Findings from the 2003 National Survey on Drug Use and Health* (Office of Applied Studies, NSDUH Series H-24, DHHS Publication No. SMA 04-963). Rockville, MD: SAMSA.

Tseng, W.-S. (2003). *Clinician's Guide to Cultural Psychiatry.* San Diego, CA: Academic Press.

United States Sentencing Commission (1995). Special Report to Congress: Cocaine and Federal Sentencing Policy. Washington, DC: GPO.

Wallace, J. Jr., Bachman, J., O'Malley, P., Johnston, L., Schulenberg, J., & Cooper, S. (2002). Tobacco, alcohol and illicit drug use: Racial and ethnic differences among U.S. high school seniors. *U.S. Department of Health and Human Services; Public Health Reports, 117,* S67-S75.

Washington, O., & Moxley, D. (2003). Group interventions with low-income African American women recovering from chemical dependency. *Health & Social Work, 28*(2), 146-157.

Wechsberg, W., Lam, W., Zule, W., & Bobashev, G. (2004). Efficacy of a women-focused intervention to reduce HIV risk and increase self-sufficiency among African American crack abusers. *American Journal of Public Health, 94*(7), 1165-1174.

Williams, D. R., & Jackson, J. S. (2000). Race/ethnicity and the 2000 census: Recommendations for African American and other black populations in the United States. *American Journal of Public Health, 90,* 1728-1730.

Wobie, K., Eyler, F., Garvan, C., Hou, W., & Behnke, M. (2004). Prenatal cocaine exposure: An examination of out-of-home placement during the first year of life. *Journal of Drug Issues, 34*(1), 77-95.

Wright, V. (2003). A phenomenological exploration of spirituality among African American women recovering from substance abuse. *Archives of Psychiatric Nursing, 17*(4), 173-185.

Yacoubian, G. Jr., & Peters, R. (2004). Exploring the prevalence and correlates of methamphetamine use: Findings from Sacramento's ADAM Program. *Journal of Drug Education, 34*(3), 281-293.

Young, A., Boyd, C., & Hubbell, A. (2000). Prostitution, drug use, and coping with psychological distress. *Journal of Drug Issues, 30*(4), 789-801.

Zhang, A. Y., & Snowden, L. R. (1999). Ethnic characteristics of mental disorders in five U.S. communities, *Cultural Diversity and Ethnic Minority Psychology, 5,* 134-146.

Zule, W., Flannery, B., Wechsberg, W., & Lam, W. (2002). Alcohol use among out-of-treatment crack using African American women. *American Journal of Drug & Alcohol Abuse, 28*(3), 525-545.

PART III:
THE CONSUMERS
OF MENTAL HEALTH SERVICES
OVER THE LIFE COURSE

Chapter 8

Poverty, Special Education, and ADHD

Gwendolyn Perry-Burney

As an individual moves through the life course, she or he encounters increasing biological, psychological, and social problems that can affect quality of life. Lack of fit between an individual and the environment can negatively affect a person's mental health. For children, their experiences in school affect their mental health. In addition, African-American youth experience complex mental health disadvantages that are compounded by a combination of poverty, environmental toxins, racial bias, and lack of access to quality health services and preventive services, and disproportionate placement in special education.

The middle childhood period is characterized by rapid physical development and cognitive skills. During this stage of childhood, family, peers, and teachers greatly influence the child's development. Moreover, success and failure in the classroom play an important role in the individual's development. According to Zastrow and Kirst-Ashman (2004), "children who experience failure in school, or even in peer relations, may develop a sense of inferiority" (p. 255).

Recently, media attention has focused on the inequality in public schools accumulating from the historic landmark decision by the U.S. Supreme Court, *Brown v. Board of Education* ruling that ended legal segregation of schools, and the No Child Left Behind Act. In addition, there has been a decade of media attention given to attention-deficit/hyperactivity disorder (ADHD) for children with problems of inattention, impulsivity, and/or hyperactivity.

The author wishes to acknowledge Margaret Smith, PhD, Edinboro University of PA for her assistance with this chapter.

This chapter examines the placement of African-American children in special education, and a review of the literature with an emphasis on ADHD and poverty. It then discusses a new expanded approach using the life course perspective. It ends with a conclusion and suggested ancillary activities for the classroom.

LITERATURE REVIEW

Special Education

In 1991, Congress renamed the Education of All Handicapped Children Act as the Individuals with Disabilities Education Act (IDEA) (P.L. 101-476). IDEA was amended in 1997 and 2004. The act expanded services for disabled children by supporting students in obtaining a free and appropriate public education (Turnbull & Turnbull, 2000). The types of disabilities that qualify a child for special education include specific learning disabilities, speech or language impairments, combined deafness and blindness, emotional disturbance, mental retardation, hearing impairments, autism, multiple disabilities, visual impairments, traumatic brain injury, orthopedic impairments, and other health impairments. African-American children are referred to special education programs because of learning disabilities, severe emotional or behavioral disabilities, and mental disabilities (Patton, 1998) in disproportionate numbers. In order to raise awareness about the overrepresentation of African Americans placed in special education classes, the National Association for the Education of African American Children with Learning Disabilities held a meeting in Washington, DC, with parents and representatives from over twenty national organizations, including the National Alliance of Black School Educators and the Children's Defense Fund. Elsie Blount, the board president for the association stated, "African-American students are facing discrimination for both the color of their skin and for having learning disabilities" (Goldstein, 2003, p. 6). Goldstein also reports that in the National Research Council study (2002), more than 14 percent of African-American students were in special education classes as compared to 13 percent American Indians, 12 percent White, 11 percent Hispanics, and 5 percent Asian Americans.

The overrepresentation of African-American children in special education is socially constructed and perpetuates the inequality and oppression of placing children in a devalued position. Patton (1998) stated, "special education, grounded in structured power relationships, is designed to serve the interests of the dominant, social, political, and economic classes" (p. 27). Research indicates gender differences in learning styles and maturity (Hale,

2001; Irvine, 1990). Boys' attention spans are much shorter than girls, and girls mature much faster than boys. In the classroom, teachers tend to rate African-American boys higher on externalizing behavior like conduct and hyperactivity problems.

HISTORY OF ADHD

In the early 1900s, one of the first attempts to describe the symptoms of attention deficit disorders came from George Still, a physician. Dr. Still portrayed these children as having a "morbid defect in moral control" (Barkley, 1990, p. 4) caused by a genetic dysfunction. In 1968, the second edition of the *Diagnostic and Statistical Manual of Mental Disorders* (DSM-II) identified it as hyperkinetic reaction of childhood (Barkley, 1990; Lerner, Lowenthal, & Lerner, 1995). In 1980, the DSM-III was published and the term "attention deficit disorder" was established, and the focus shifted to problems with attention rather than activity problems. Attention-deficit/hyperactivity disorder is the most recent term given by psychiatrists in the DSM-IV that require behaviors appear before age seven and continue for at least a six-month period. It strengthens the need of professionals to provide evidence of system-related impairments in at least two settings (i.e., school, work, and/or at home) and that these impairments interfere with developmentally appropriate functioning (Anastopoulos & Shelton, 2001).

Since the 1980s, ADHD is the most commonly diagnosed childhood psychiatric disorder affecting between 4 and 12 percent of school-age children (Valente, 2001). In 1991, African-American children constituted 16 percent of the nation's school population and 35 percent of the special education population. Data seem to support gender differences in the prevalence of ADHD. Boys are diagnosed with ADHD two to three times more than girls. On average, at least one child in every classroom in the United States needs help for this disorder (NIMH, 1994). The disorder is characterized by inattention, hyperactivity, and impulsivity and is detected more often and in greater numbers of young children. The ADHD child is often diagnosed impressionistically and subjectively without objective measures criteria. A common scenario is that the teacher informs the parents that their child is not paying attention as much as the other children and suggests that they consult a family physician. In addition to the complaint of "not paying attention teachers may cite noncompliance, emotional immaturity, or unsatisfactory academic progress" (Anastopoulos & Shelton, 2001, p. 25) as behaviors that lead them to believe that a child might have ADHD. Descriptions of children with ADHD often include complaints of not listening or following directions, rushing through their work with little attention to neatness or accuracy (Barkley, 1990), not finishing assigned work, daydreaming, and becoming easily bored. The second behavior used in diagnosing a child with ADHD is impulsivity or lack of self-control. Newman and Newman (1995) define self-control as the ability to comply with a request, to modify one's behavior, to postpone action, and to behave in a socially acceptable way on one's own. The third behavior is hyperactivity. Children who exhibit this behavior are those in constant motion, moving in and out of their seats when others are seated, and speaking when others are talking during classroom sessions (Diller, 1998; NIMH, 1994).

Assessment, treatment, and follow-up of ADHD have become a balance of science and clinical judgment. Currently, there are five professionals who can make the diagnosis of ADHD: Clinical social worker, neurologist, pediatrician/family physician, psychiatrist, and psychologist. In addition to their ability to diagnose ADHD they carry other roles in working with the child. The clinical social worker and psychologist provide counseling, the psychiatrist prescribes medication and can also provide counseling, whereas the pediatrician/family physician and neurologist prescribes medication, only. The following is the percentage of children diagnosed and prescribed medication by profession. Physicians estimated that they prescribed medication for 77 percent of children diagnosed with ADHD. The physicians' specialty had a significant effect on how medication was prescribed to children. Child psychiatrists prescribed medication for 88 percent of children diagnosed with ADHD; pediatricians, 77 percent, and family physicians, 72 percent (Sax & Kautz, 2003).

RITALIN

The most frequently prescribed medication is Ritalin, given to children six years and older. Studies suggest that psychostimulant medication improves the child's ability to follow rules and decreases emotional over-reactivity. Psychostimulants used for the treatment of ADHD are methylphenidate (Ritalin, Concerta, and Metadate), and amphetamine (Dexedrine and Adderall). However, some doctors are concerned that psychostimulants affect the child's developing brain and emotional skills, which do not fully mature until age thirty (Kluger, 2003).

African-American children diagnosed with ADHD and placed on psychostimulation medication led many scholars and clinical social workers to believe that there were racial disparities in treatment and overmedication of the drug. These concerns led to an investigation and panel discussion by the

Congressional Black Caucus. In March 2004, a panel of child psychiatrists presented scientific evidence that African-America children with ADHD were not overmedicated as suspected, but were often undertreated and often denied appropriate access to care (Benoit, 2004). To date, no lifetime longitudinal studies have been done on the effectiveness, side effects, and long-term use of psychostimulation medication on African-American children.

MIDDLE CHILDHOOD DEVELOPMENT

As African-American children mature, great stress is placed on developing self-management and coping skills. Stress comes in many forms such as the experience of racism, oppression, and discrimination as a result of race (West, 1993), socioeconomic status (Land & Legters, 2002), and ethnicity within the school environment. They are cognitively aware of the need for adaptation to social pressures and norms about "fitting in" with their peers and social environment. For children, a sense of belonging to a peer group is an important aspect of their development and it is reported that students with more friends at school tend to be more connected to the school (McNeely, Nonnemaker, & Blum, 2002). A student's self-evaluation is related to the kind of peer relationships he or she has throughout the school experience. Peer relationships contribute to the social and emotional development of youth and are important in self-evaluation and self-esteem. If peer relationships and attachments are limited with students identified as popular, athletic, and smart, then the student in special education may become isolated and alienated from their non-peers while in special education. The student segregated in special education may become disengaged and disconnected from the traditional social experiences in the school, as it becomes a source of negative identification. Patton (1998) notes that African-American males placed in special education often have segregated classrooms and buildings. This type of segregation sends the message of being labeled "dumb," or "unmanageable." It is important to understand the school as a system that influences not only the educational achievement and performance of students, but also their social and mental health status as well.

Mental health is a dynamic process. Much of the research and measures used in middle childhood were designed for Whites using traditional theories such as Eric Erickson's psychosocial theory of "industry versus inferiority," and Jean Piaget's cognitive development of "concrete operations" during this period. One of the criticisms throughout the literature is the absence of multiculturalism and the use of culturally specific assessment instruments in the diagnosis and treatment of African-American children. Jones, Brown, Davis, Jeffries, and Shenoy (1998) note "the assumption that treatment modalities generated by these theories are equally effective for this group has often gone uncontested" (p. 425). This is especially detrimental to African-American children, because in their communities they are taught to be themselves and are allowed the capacity for self-determination (Hale, 2001; Lawson, 1998). Clearly, the lack of quantitative and qualitative clinical research trials conducted exclusively on African-American children and the exclusion of using the world-view of African Americans diminishes the potential for understanding ADHD itself and results in inadequate information and poorer outcomes.

POVERTY, SCHOOL, AND PARENTAL INVOLVEMENT

Conceptualizing the etiology of mental health in African-American children is complex but one central factor that is consistently recognized as having an impact is poverty (Orfield & Lee, 2005; U.S. Department of Health and Human Services, 2001). Poverty located at the family and community level have a significant influence on the mental health outcome and school performance of low-income children in general and in particular, African-American children.

African-American children living in the social context of poverty are at risk for negative social, emotional, physical, and mental development. From an environmental context, poverty is a contributing factor in divorce, violence, crime, substance abuse, suicide (Sheafor & Horejsi, 2003), and teen pregnancy. Poverty is disproportionately experienced by children of color; 31 percent of African-American children lived in poverty in 2000, while 28 percent of Hispanics and 9 percent of White non-Hispanics were identified as living in poverty (Nation Center for Educational Statistics, 2003).

Outside of the family, the school environment presents the second most important social context for children (Dryfoos, 1990; McWhirter et al., 2004) and public education as a social institution is influenced by the cultural values of the larger society. The impact of poverty is critical for African-American children within the school context because the child's adaptive responses and behaviors to external conditions may lead to their misidentification and misclassification as displaying maladaptive behavior at home and school (Obi & Obiakor, 2001). Poverty recognized at the school level relates to the number of students receiving free lunches (Land & Legters, 2002). In addition, high poverty area schools have lower achievement performance scores in reading and mathematics (U.S. Department of Education, 2000). In fact, one in six African-American students attends totally segregated schools compared to 1 percent of Whites (Orfield & Lee, 2005), thus the quality and level of education students receive is influenced by the financial status of the school.

Parental involvement has been identified as a critical factor in the success and progress of children. Often schools do not treat African-American parents as an asset in the educational process, but as causes for their children's failure (Thompson, 2003). An important mandate in IDEA is parental involvement, although there is no formal training for low-income parents to become knowledgeable about the special education process and procedures nor the long-term consequences on the child's education if they are placed in special education. Many parents perceive involvement in the school as negative, based in part on their own past school experiences, and also because they do not feel welcome to question the decisions of school personnel. Parents complain that teachers and administrators talk down to them rather than giving them tools to assist their children. The parents' normal reaction is to defend and protect the integrity of their home and their child's behavior.

NEW EXPANDED APPROACH

Self-Efficacy

Receiving specialized services and placement in special education class can be a social and emotional cost to the African-American students' mental health, which results in low self-concept and negative self-esteem. Self-concept reflects the individuals' overall assessment of themselves and their values, abilities, and skills, whereas self-esteem reflects how they value themselves and whether they regard themselves as important to others or as able to make positive contributions to their environment (McWhirter et al., 2004). Placement into a special education class for African-American children, in particular males, can lead to a negative response to the educational experience. Arbona (2000) reports that there is in fact a strong relationship between a student's self evaluation and school performance.

When a teacher identifies an African-American student as being unable to meet the behavioral and academic tasks in a general education class, the student is likely to be referred for evaluation of need for specialized support services. The process of labeling the student's learning style and performance as a problem, and the resulting inference that he or she may have a mental disorder or disability, can have a profound impact on how he or she responds to the learning environment (Lloyd, Kaufmann, Landrum, & Rose, 1991; Quinn, 1998).

Life Course Perspective

Additional insight regarding factors that influence the development of African-American children's mental health development can be understood through the life course perspective. The "life course concept assumes that individual development processes take place in the context of families and other groups but considers the meaning of race, ethnicity, social class, and gender socialization as well as sexual orientation and disability" (Devore & Schlesinger, 1999, p. 64). Three recommendations must be addressed regarding the factors that influence African-American children's mental health through the life course perspective, and their placement in special education. First, students must see teachers that look like them in the classroom. Second, parents must become active partners with the school. Third, the school must have a cultural knowledge of working with low-income African-American children.

Students rarely see teachers who look like them in the classroom, even though research shows that African-American children tend to do better in the classroom setting and meet higher expectations when taught by teachers from their ethnic group. Teachers must be prepared for working with African-American low-income children, in particular boys who are overrepresented in special education. Hale (2001) asserts that "African American children, particularly boys, should not be required to sit for long periods of time . . . learning activities should be designed that enable children to move as they learn" (p. 118). Teachers must get involved and evaluate the situation of the student more holistically by evaluating their "learning styles, their values, language, and history, as well as the many resources in the home and the community" (Irvine, 1990, p. 114).

Schools in poverty areas that lack an equitable share of learning resources have a greater number of inexperienced teachers. Often, teacher preparation does not mandate or include in the curriculum that student teachers obtain an urban field practice experience. Although there is increasing ethnic diversity in school-age children, teaching personnel are becoming more homogeneous. White females tend to be the majority of school personnel in the elementary, middle, and high schools. In special education, African-American teachers in both the elementary and secondary level represent less than 7 and 10 percent, respectively (Jones et al., 1998; U.S. Department of Education, 2003). Hale (2001) notes that the scarcity of African-American teachers limits the opportunity for African-American children to have positive role models. Also, fewer knowledgeable teachers are available to respond to cultural behaviors that may impact the children's mental health and academic progress. A lack of cultural competence and teaching experience, as well as racial bias by school personnel regarding the students they teach, may account for the overrepresentation of African-American students in special education whom are "misidentified, mis-categorized, misplaced, and misinstructed" by teachers who lack cultural knowledge to understand the impact of the student's cultural of origin (Grossman, 1998; Obiator & Schwenn, 1996).

It is imperative that parents become active partners with the school in the planning and implementation of special education services for their child, and not merely act as cosigners. Once a child is recommended for special education, parents must proactively call the school and set up a meeting to discuss the child's behavior. Prior to the parent-teacher meeting, teachers must prepare an agenda and obtain the child's work assignments from several classes. During the meeting, teachers must be patient and unhurried and disseminate materials that can be utilized by both the parent and the child to correct the behavior. Especially important is the need for teachers to be prepared to effectively communicate with African-American parents and make them feel comfortable at the school. This can be accomplished by having a designated place for parents and school personnel to meet and discuss the child's progress and behavior. With notice, parents should be allowed to sit in on their child's classes. If parents are dissatisfied with the outcome of the meeting, they have a right to have someone outside the school system perform an Independent Educational Evaluation (IEE) at no cost by the school district.

The last recommendation is a need for cultural competence in working with low-income African-American children at the community level. Life experiences of African-American children cannot be separated from their ethnic group membership and history. From a historical context, racism, discrimination, and oppression are parts of the cultural climate in which development takes place. Similarly, institutional racism has a profound impact on the major systems by which African-American children interface throughout their life journey. Thus, for African-American children, Artiles (1998) indicates that ethnic group membership, economic class, and issues related to family influence are factors that influence placement in special education, and, as Kunjufu (2005) notes, result in the diagnosis of ADHD.

Practice, Policy, and Research Recommendations

For two decades there have been publications on the overrepresentation of African-American children diagnosed with ADHD, and their enrollment in special education. There appears to be disconnections among the African-American child diagnosed with ADHD, the school, parents, and special education staff. This author suggests that a collaborative effort between social workers, teachers, and parents might result in better educational and mental health outcomes for the child.

Social workers can play a significant role in helping parents, children, and the school to combat some of the negative consequences of special education. Social workers can empower and guide parents in obtaining for their children a complete physical, vision, and hearing screening prior to special education evaluation. Children with vision and hearing impairments have difficulty in school performance and engage in behavior that is disruptive as a result of their inability to participate in the educational process. During the referral and evaluation process, the parent's information about the psychosocial development and life events experienced by the child should be taken into consideration as an initial step in modifying the behavior intervention. Social workers should assist parents in understanding the long-range advantages and disadvantages of special education as it relates to future goals and outcomes.

Policymakers must recognize the achievement gap between African-American and Caucasian children. In 2004, the government increased funding for Title 1 and IDEA by $1 billion while decreasing funds for the No Child Left Behind Act. This decease in educational programs came at a time when state and local communities were struggling with budget cuts in the public sector. The common theme is "do more with less," while increasing accountability. The No Child Left Behind Act requirements mandate state and local equality in public schools and strategies to raise student performance. The increase in funding for Title 1 and IDEA has eliminated funding to public educational programs like music, gym, and after school programs. Yet it appears that the competitiveness of the U.S. society occurs simultaneously with a thrust toward streamlining education (Searight & McLaren, 1998) and mental health care, and drugging children for societal compliance. The cost of streamlining programs places African-American children at risk of low-paying jobs at a time when business leaders and corporations are looking for self-directed and creative individuals to meet the growing global demands of high-tech jobs.

The literature review and new approaches using the life course perspective suggest the need for further research into the effectiveness of student-parent-teacher communication. The use of social work counseling, cooperative teamwork, and medication needs to be explored in longitudinal studies on the long-term effects of placement of African-American children in special education.

CONCLUSION

African-American low-income children who attend school in high-level poverty areas are at risk for placement in special education. Poverty at the family level and attending a school with a high concentration of poverty predisposes children to conditions that may lead to adaptive responses that are incongruent with school expectations and behavior. Biological, environmental, and social contexts, including the family, school, and community, influence mental health and school performance, but this is especially true for African-American children in relation to self-identify and self-concept. Children struggle to develop coping and adaptive skills to address the trauma that result from poor school performance, poverty, and environmental toxins. Community and family violence are major factors impacting the psychosocial development and mental health of children and youth. Children and youth who witness violence are at risk for developing aggressive and defiant behavior, which crosses all social contexts.

Children under psychosocial stresses are more likely to have mental health problems and tend to perform poorly in school as well. The influence of their environmental and social contexts contributes to the behavioral symptoms that are often identified as ADHD. African-American children misplaced and misidentified for special education programs experience isolation from peers and a watered-down curriculum.

The misidentification and misclassification of African-American children from low-income families into special education has been a concern for the past twenty years. Children in special education have poor social and economic outcomes. Future economic costs are incurred for children in special education, for they are not academically prepared for future employment and productivity.

Distinction between behavioral patterns that warrant mental health intervention and special education should be addressed in the referral process. Refinement of the referral process must include consideration of cultural variables that influence behavioral patterns sustaining the child's social and emotional identity. Families should be counseled about mental health treatment as a plausible resource to help children in the development of age-appropriate behaviors that have been impacted by social or physical stressors.

Lastly, the school must begin to address the stigma about special education and the students who are placed in the program. Isolation and alienation of these students place them at risk for poor peer relationships, negative self-concept, and low self-esteem, as well as low school performance. Transitional planning for students should not be limited to vocational training and employment, but also college as well.

CHAPTER SUMMARY

This chapter provides a view on the influence of poverty on African-American children in special education. Information includes statistics on the overrepresentation of African-American children in special education, and content on Ritalin, middle school development, and parental involvement. African-American children are often misdiagnosed with ADHD, which results in psychosocial stress and implications for mental health interventions. Strategies are recommended for parental empowerment and intervention at the pubic policy level.

ANCILLARY ACTIVITY

Experimental Exercise and Case Analysis

Two exercises are described in this chapter. The first increases awareness of labels assigned to gender differences in the classroom behavior.

Exercise Number 1

A. Brief description
   You will interview two individuals of opposite genders and ethnicity to gather information, which is shared in class.
B. Objectives
   1. Identify gender differences of behavior in the classroom.
   2. Describe various consequences of negative and positive behaviors.
   3. Discuss the implications of middle-childhood on adult development.
C. Procedure
   1. Talk to a friend or relative about his or her middle-childhood school experiences. Ask about (a) peer involvement, (b) teacher's teaching styles, (c) what they did when "bored," and (d) consequences that occurred from positive and/or negative behaviors.
   2. Form subgroups of four or five persons. Describe the challenges of being middle-school aged from your questions above. Make a list of gender and ethnic differences in classroom treatment.
   3. Discuss the strengths and challenges that being labeled ADHD might have on life course development from middle childhood through adulthood.

4. A representative from each group presents a summary of their findings. Include in the summary what behaviors would have been labeled ADHD and why.

5. List at least three occupational jobs that a person with ADHD might pursue.

Exercise Number 2

Ms. Akilah is a social worker at John F. Kennedy Middle School. One day she is asked to attend a conference with a teacher, parent, and student. The goal of the meeting is to discuss the behavior of Hasson, an eleven-year-old African-American male who passes notes and throws spitballs at his classmates. Hasson is constantly in and out of his desk during class. His teacher, Ms. Adams, has Hasson in several of her classes where he exhibits these behaviors. Ms. Adams, a recent graduate from state college, wants Hasson evaluated for medication.

During the meeting, Ms. Mohammad, Hasson's mother, described her son as smarter than average and active in sports. Hasson plays football and basketball at the community park. During the parent-teacher conference, Ms. Mohammad informed Ms. Adams that "this is the first time I'm hearing of Hasson's classroom behavior." The mother began to question the teachers' classroom management skills and her inability to positively interact with Hasson. She stated, "When Hasson is interested in his work, there is no disruptive behavior problems." The mother also voiced concerns that the school does not allow Hasson to bring home textbooks, and that he has no homework assignments. Hasson plays outside from 4:00 p.m. until 9:00 p.m. daily.

Questions for Discussion:

1. Identify the problem. How should the social worker handle the problem between the teacher, parent, and student?

2. What life transition is relevant for Hasson? For the teacher?

3. Are culture and the inexperience of the teacher an issue? Explain fully.

4. How would you analyze this case and what actions would you recommend?

5. What possible consequences might ensue with your recommended plan?

REFERENCES

Anastopoulos, A. D., & Shelton, T. L. (2001). *Assessing Attention-Deficit/Hyperactivity Disorder.* New York: Plenum Publishers.

Arbona, C. (2000). The development of academic achievement in school aged children: Precursors to career development. In R. Lent & S. Brown (Eds.), *Handbook of Counseling Psychology* (3rd ed., pp. 270-309). New York: John Wiley & Sons.

Artiles, A. (1998). The dilemma of difference: Enriching the disproportionality discourse with theory and debate. *Journal of Special Education, 32,* 32-36.

Barkley, R. A. (1990). *Attention Deficit Hyperactivity Disorder: A Handbook for Diagnosis and Treatment.* New York: Guilford Press.

Benoit, M. (2004, April 8). Experts address influence of AD/HD in Black community. *Black Issues in Higher Education, 21,* 2.

Devore, W., & Schlesinger, E. G. (1999). *Ethnic-Sensitive Social Work Practice* (5th ed.). Boston: Allyn & Bacon.

Diller, L. H. (1998). *Running on Ritalin.* New York: Bantam Books.

Dryfoos, J. G. (1990). *Adolescents at Risk: Prevalence and Prevention.* New York: Oxford University Press.

Goldstein, L. (2003, November 12). Group targets racial disparities in Special Education. *Education Week, 23,* 11.

Grossman, H. (1998). *Ending Discrimination in Special Education.* Springfield, IL: Charles C Thomas.

Hale, J. E. (2001). *Learning While Black: Creating Educational Excellence for African American Children.* Baltimore, MD: Johns Hopkins University Press.

Irvine, J. J. (1990). *Black Students and School Failure: Policies, Practices, and Prescriptions.* Westport, CT: Greenwood Press.

Jones, R. T., Brown, R., Davis, M., Jeffries, R., & Shenoy, U. (1998). African Americans in behavioral therapy and research. In R. J. Jones (Ed.), *African American Mental Health* (pp. 413-450). VA: Cobb & Henry Publishers.

Kluger, J. (2003). Medicating young minds. *Time, 162,* 48-58.

Kunjufu, J. (2005). *Keeping Black Boys Out of Special Education.* Chicago, IL: African American Images.

Land, D., & Legters, N. (2002). The extent and consequences of risk in U.S. Education. In S. Stringfield & D. Land (Eds.), *Educating At-Risk Students.* Chicago, IL: University of Chicago Press.

Lawson, W. B. (1998). Psychopharmacology and African American mental health. In R. J. Jones (Ed.), *African American Mental Health* (pp. 303-314). VA: Cobb & Henry Publishers.

Lerner, J. W., Lowenthal, B., & Lerner, S. R. (1995). *Attention Deficit Disorders: Assessment and Teaching.* Pacific Grove, CA: Brooks Cole Publishing.

Lloyd, J. W., Kauffman, J. M., Landrum, T. J., & Rose, D. L. (1991). Why do teachers refer pupils to special education? An analysis of referral records. *Exceptionality, 2,* 115-126.

McNeely, C. A., Nonnemaker, J. M., & Blum, R. W. (2002). Promoting Student Connectedness to School: Evidence from the National Longitudinal Study of Adolescent Health. *Journal of School Health, 72*(4) 138-146.

McWhirter, J. J., McWhirter, B. T., McWhirter, E. H., & McWhirter, R. J. (2004). *At-Risk Youth: A Comprehensive Response.* Belmont, CA: Brooks Cole.

National Institutes of Health. National Institute of Mental Health (1994). *Attention Deficit Hyperactivity Disorder.* United States Department of Health and Human Services. National Institutes of Health. Abstract obtained from CINAHL database.

Newman, B. M., & Newman, P. R. (1995). *Development Through Life: A Psychosocial Approach* (6th ed.). Belmont, CA: Brooks Cole.

Obi, S. O., & Obiakor, F. E. (2001). Empowering African American exceptional learners: A vision for the new millennium. *The Western Journal of Black Studies, 5,* 93-100.

Orfield, G., & Lee, C. (2005, January). Why segregation matters: Poverty and educational inequality. The Civil Rights Project: Harvard University Press. Retrieved September 15, 2005, from www.civilrightsproject.harvard.edu/research/deseg/why_segreg_matters.pdf.

Patton, J. M. (1998). The disproportionate representation of African American in special education: Looking behind the curtain for understanding and solutions. *Journal of Special Education, 32,* 25-31.

Quinn, P. (1998). *Understanding Disability: A Lifespan Approach.* Thousand Oaks, CA: Sage Publications.

Sax, L., & Kautz, K. J. (2003). Who first suggests the diagnosis of attention-deficit/hyperactivity disorder? Annuals of Family Medicine, 1, 3. Retrieved from EBSCO on October 18, 2004.

Searight, H. R., & McLaren, A. L. (1998). Attention-deficit hyperactivity disorder: The medicalization of misbehavior. *Journal of Clinical Psychology in Medical Settings, 5,* 467-495.

Sheafor, B. W., & Horejsi, C. R. (2003). *Techniques and Guidelines for Social Work Practice* (6th ed.). Boston: Allyn & Bacon.

Thompson, G. L. (2003). *What African American Parents Want Educators to Know.* Westport, CT: Praeger Publishers.

Turnbull, H. R. III, & Turnbull, A. P. (2000). *Free Appropriate Public Education: The Law for Children with Disabilities* (6th ed.). Denver, CO: Love Publishing Co.

United States Department of Education (2000, February). *A 5 Year Report Card on American Education.* Washington, DC: Author.

United States Department of Health and Human Services (2001, August). *Mental Health: Culture, Race and Ethnicity. A Supplement to Mental Health: A Report of the Surgeon General.* Washington, DC: Author.

Valente, S. M. (2001). Treating attention deficit hyperactivity disorder. The nurse practitioner. *American Journal of Primary Health Care, 26,* 14-15, 19-20, 23-29. Abstract obtained from CINAHL database.

West, C. (1993). *Race Matters.* New York: Vintage Books.

Zastrow, C. H., & Kirst-Ashman, K. K. (2004). *Understanding Human Behavior and the Social Environment* (6th ed.). Belmont, CA: Brooks Cole.

Chapter 9

War on African-American Girls: Overcoming Adversities

Tanya S. Brice

> Like a plastic ball,
> I toss between myself
> and the various identities
> I have been assigned.
> Look out—I fell in the mud.
> Look out—I opened my mouth,
> and out came ideas
> you don't think are pretty.
> I suppose it would be scary
> to be a ventriloquist who found out
> her dummy could talk,
> to find the doll had a brain
> and opinions that will bite
> when provoked.

This poem was written by a sixteen-year-old female member of "Recess!," a literary program that is one component of the University of Florida's Center for the Study of Children's Literature and Media. The tenor of this poem speaks to the struggles experienced by African-American girls who are under attack by the media, social institutions, and policymakers. They are often portrayed in the media as hypersexualized. African-American girls are more often portrayed on television and in movies as aggressive, vixen-like characters. Furthermore, a simple Internet search with keywords "Black

Mental Health Care in the African-American Community
© 2007 by The Haworth Press, Inc. All rights reserved.
doi:10.1300/5364_09

girls" yields pages of pornographic sites. On the other hand, a search with "White girls" as the keywords yields pages of popular self-help style sites. This mischaracterization creates adversities which these young girls must overcome.

In social institutions, African-American girls are characterized as difficult to control (Lei, 2003; Paul, 2003). In response, mental health policymakers develop policies that penalize African-American girls by pathologizing normalized adolescent behaviors based on misperceptions and misunderstandings (Aneshensel & Sucoff, 1996; Bui, Kim, & Takeuchi, 1993; Washington, 1982). Consequently, the community responds to these young girls as if the misperceptions are true.

Interestingly, African-American girls are often neglected in the literature. Black boys are often the focus in delinquency literature. White girls are often the focus in adolescent literature. Black girls tend to be relegated as the referent population when addressing inherent pathologies in adolescent girls. This chapter addresses this disparate view of African-American girls and the impact on the mental health status of this population. In addition, it explores the historical context of these disparate views as a lens by which to provide strategies to address contemporary issues. This exploration is guided by Africentric and life course frameworks. Finally, this chapter examines the manifestation of compromised mental health among African-American girls, and offers novel approaches to address their unique needs. This chapter concludes with an ancillary section intended to provoke applicable discussions as they relate to African-American girls.

LITERATURE REVIEW

African-American girls are faced with many obstacles. They are at an increased risk for pregnancy and sexually transmitted diseases. In addition, African-American girls are at an increased risk for low academic achievement and expectations. Finally, African-American girls are faced with conflicting role expectations, which creates obstacles to achievement. These obstacles are entrenched in a historical response to African-American girls. An understanding of the historical context will provide insight to the contemporary manifestation of attitudes and behaviors among African-American girls.

Historical context. In the United States, women of African decent have been portrayed historically as "innately promiscuous" and as "erotic icons" (Brice, 2005). Further, these women were believed to be sexually unrestrained (Brice, 2005; Gutman, 1976). These portrayals and beliefs served as justification for the repeated rape and molestation endured by African-American women and girls by White men and boys (Accomando, 1998), and for the forgiving of this criminal behavior by White women of their men (Lerner, 1972). Persistent denial of the severity of this sexual violation perpetuated continued degradation of African-American women.

For more than four centuries, African women and girls learned to adapt to this constant threat of sexual victimization by developing protective processes for enduring this atrocity. It is plausible that mothers would prepare their young, often pre- or early pubescent daughters for the impending thievery of their sexual innocence by instructing them not to resist. Resistance would result in further physical punishment, the threat of being separated from the family unit, or death. These mothers might have instructed their daughters how to position their bodies so as to not endure too much pain or tearing. Most disturbingly, these young girls learned that if they were passive in the face of sexual violation, they might earn special favor with the perpetrator, including economic and perceived social benefits.

There was no protection for African-American girls. African-American men who sought to protect these young girls from sexual exploitation often risked severe punishment or death (A Negro Nurse, 1912). Furthermore, there was no law prohibiting the perpetration of rape against a Black woman. No man, African American or White, could be charged with the offense of rape against an African-American woman until the mid-twentieth century (Accomando, 1998; Lerner, 1972). This lack of protection resulted in the institutionalized devaluation of African-American women and, unfortunately, the participation in this degradation by young African-American girls as the only means to improve economic and social circumstances.

INFLUENCE OF SEXUAL BEHAVIOR .

This institutionalized devaluation of African-American women has contemporary implications for mental health issues. African-American girls are at increased risk for early initiation of sexual activity (Brown, 1985; East, Felice, & Morgan, 1993; French & Dishion, 2003), placing them at an increased risk for pregnancy and for contracting sexually transmitted diseases. In fact, African-American girls are more likely to experience at least one pregnancy during adolescence than any other ethnic group in the United States. Although 35 percent of all adolescent girls experienced at least one pregnancy, 57 percent of all African-American girls experienced at least one pregnancy during adolescence (Miller, Forehand, & Kotchick, 1999; The National Campaign to Prevent Teen Pregnancy, 2004).

There are dismal economic implications for adolescent pregnancy, particularly for African-American girls. Teen mothers are most likely to live in poverty (Maynard, 1997), and poor children are more likely to have a mental health diagnosis (McLeod & Shanahan, 1996). In addition, adolescent mothers and their children are at an increased risk to experience school failure (Maynard, 1996; National Campaign to Prevent Teen Pregnancy, 1997) resulting in increased rates of school drop-out (The National Campaign to Prevent Teen Pregnancy, 2003). Consequently, this lack of formal education guarantees decreased wage earnings, further perpetuating a life of poverty for these young mothers and their children. This cycle almost guarantees mental health involvement for these adolescent mothers and their children.

Second, there are health implications of adolescent pregnancy. The children of adolescent mothers are more likely to be of low birth weight (Maynard, 1996), resulting in long-term health concerns. In the United States, health concerns are directly related to economic concerns. Furthermore, these children are at an increased risk of child abuse as these young mothers struggle to address mounting health and economic concerns.

Finally, there are social implications for teen pregnancies. Girls born to teen mothers are at an increased risk to become teen mothers. On the other hand, boys born to teen mothers are at an increased risk to become involved in the criminal justice system (Maynard, 1996; The National Campaign to Prevent Teen Pregnancy, 2002, 2003). For youth in the juvenile justice system, the rates of mental health diagnoses are two to three times higher than for youth in the general population. This may suggest that the experiences of the adolescent mother are often transmitted to her child(ren) in conscious and unconscious modes of communication, often resulting in negative contact with mental health systems.

In addition, sexually engaged African-American girls are at an increased risk of contracting sexually transmitted diseases. For instance, African-American girls are more likely to contract HIV than adolescent girls of all other ethnic/race groups. Further, they are significantly more likely to contract HIV than all adolescent boys (DiClemente et al., 2004). This is also true for other sexually transmitted diseases, such as syphilis and gonorrhea. Surprisingly, this population is least likely to use condoms, despite being aware of the increased risk of contracting disease (Gage, 1998; Terry & Manlove, 2000; Weisman et al., 1991). This risky behavior may indicate a sense of helplessness, often characteristic of a diagnosis of depression, further confirming the historical message of devaluation of this group.

ACADEMIC ACHIEVEMENT

African-American girls are more likely to experience low academic achievement than their White counterparts, despite the strong value placed on education in the African-American community (Martin & Martin, 1985). This behavior has been described as achievement avoidant (Feld & Ruhland, 1977). Specifically, African-American girls are more likely to avoid academic activities perceived as more difficult, thus not achieving their full potentials. Although they may make adequate grades, and are more likely to graduate high school and attend college than African-American boys, they are least likely to work at a maximum level of ability (Feld & Ruhland, 1977).

This may be explained by the perception that there are no apparent rewards for successful academic achievements in the girl's community and society as a whole. Children are taught to do well in school, to get as much education as is feasible, and then they will be rewarded with career (economic) successes. African-American children are more likely to live in low-income, racially homogenous neighborhoods. These neighborhoods often have poorly funded schools where children are consistently undereducated (Eamon, 2002). Poorly educated children, despite the successes achieved within that system, are least likely to find adequate employment as adults to support themselves and their families. Consequently, there is often chronic unemployment and underemployment in these communities. Children of these communities often see no connection between academic achievement and economic successes. Middle-class African Americans, on the other hand, may live in racially mixed communities, and may attend schools of better quality. However, given the same educational achievements, they make less money than their White counterparts (Sirin & Rogers-Sirin, 2004). There is a dissonance between the notion of academic achievement and economic success.

MISPERCEPTIONS

African-American girls are often characterized as "being loud" and uncouth. This behavior is seen as threatening to authority figures and to males (Lei, 2003). This characterization of African-American girls is an obstacle of misperception. Being loud and uncouth may actually be an act of resistance against historical and contemporary adversities (Schilt, 2003). Being loud may serve as a protective barrier against perceived impending danger. If a message of devaluation is being transmitted to African-American girls, the natural resistance to that message may be to communicate their value in dramatic ways. Being loud is an attempt to make one visible when otherwise treated as if invisible.

Conflicting Role Expectations

African-American girls are faced with conflicting role expectations. They are often portrayed as promiscuous by the media (Gandy, 2001; Milkie, 1999). This media expectation is in conflict with African-American family and community expectations (Brown, 1985; East, 1998; East et al., 1993). The African-American family, the smallest unit of the African community, expects chastity, often discouraging sexual behavior until social maturity or marriage. This creates conflict in the African-American girl.

This conflict often results in a lowered self-concept among African-American girls. They are inundated with Eurocentric ideals of beauty, such as lighter skin, Nordic facial features, long hair, and a thin body structure. These standards of beauty are in direct conflict with Afrocentric standards, which are to embrace divinely bestowed natural features (Milkie, 1999; Rosenberg, 1987; Slaughter, 1972; Steward, 1927). The African-American family strives to assist the young girl to appreciate her beauty, despite conflicting messages from the media.

There are mental health implications for overcoming adversities faced by African-American girls. The strategies used to cope with perceived attacks are often characterized as pathological by mental health providers. African-American adolescents are most likely to be referred to community mental health centers for treatment (Takeuchi et al., 1993), rather than inpatient treatment facilities. Furthermore, coercive methods, such as court orders, are typically the conduit of the referral. This is typically because African-American children are disproportionately placed in out-of-home placement arrangements (Takeuchi et al., 1993).

SUCCESSFUL, STRENGTH-BASED MODEL

Sensitive programs that incorporate social support systems into the curriculum and are culturally competent must address obstacles faced by African-American girls. Carlton-LaNey and Burwell (1996) suggests that a successful program model include the following components:

1. *The model must respect the African-American culture.* Successful programs recognize the inherent strengths of the African-American culture, and attempt to draw on those strengths to address the needs of

young girls. Because the story of African Americans is one of over-coming adversities in spite of structural barriers, programming should operate with the fundamental belief that young girls will overcome their adversities.

2. *The model must "begin where the community is."* It must demonstrate an understanding of the African-American community in order to de-velop appropriate programs, provide sensitive service delivery, and to advocate for the community in a meaningful way. The goal is to culti-vate social and political power in the community. The underlying as-sumption is that by strengthening the community, the individual girl is strengthened.

3. *The model should focus on the collective group identity that flows from the African tradition.* The collective identity of the African-American community is one of survival. Appropriate programming that ad-dresses the needs of African-American girls should remind them that they are an integral part of the community.

NEW EXPANDED APPROACH

Although adolescent girls may be at an increased risk for social ills, the characterizations of African-American girls should be viewed as attacks. In a strong African-centered community, the adversities faced by these girls are also the concern of the community. For instance, adolescent pregnancy does not have to translate to decreased educational opportunities and pov-erty. There is a need to reconceptualize success from an African-centered perspective. In an African-centered community, a child born is viewed as a blessing from God, regardless of the status of its parents. This child should not be viewed as an obstacle, but an opportunity. From this perspective, ad-olescent pregnancy is not viewed as a hindrance to predetermined goals, but an enhanced trajectory towards those goals. In addition, we must seek to discover the structural explanations for the war against these girls.

ATTEMPTS TO ADDRESS THESE OBSTACLES

There have been several attempts to address obstacles faced by African-American girls. These attempts include mentoring, life skills enhancement, emphasis on academic achievement, and/or spiritual and moral development. The most common approach is mentoring programs (Jekielek, Moore, & Hair, 2002).

Mentoring programs tend to focus on enhancing academic performance, as is evidenced by improved study habits and grades. These programs also focus on improving personal outcomes for participants, such as improved interpersonal interactions and enhanced community volunteerism. In addition, effective mentoring programs emphasize positive adult-youth relationships (Belgrave et al., 2004; Hirsch et al., 2000; Jekielek et al., 2002; Monges, 1999). These programs tend to seek a developmental approach with adolescents, rather than a deficit approach. This approach encourages a focus on the strengths of the participant within the context of adolescence. Mentoring programs are usually conducted in supervised after-school programs, school-aged child care programs, YMCA/YWCA programs, scouting programs, and in Boys and Girls Clubs of America (Hirsch et al., 2000).

In addition, there are programs that encourage life-enriching skills among its adolescent participants. The programs that focus solely on African-American girls often focus on improved communication skills, age-appropriate styles of dress, increasing the self-esteem of participants, and developing leadership skills. These programs were often developed by African-American clubwomen (Brown-Moses, 1923; Carlton-LaNey & Hodges, 2004; Gilmore, 1994; Guttierez & Lewis, 1994; Henry, 1981), such as the National Council for Negro Women, who have been doing this type of programming since the 1920s, or other community organizations in the African-American community. These programs were founded in racial uplift ideology, which posits that improving the lot of the least in our community, improves the lot of the entire community.

There are also programs that focus on the spiritual and moral development of African-American girls. These programs, such as the Candace Rites of Passage (Monges, 1999) and the Sisters of Nia (Belgrave et al., 2004), use African traditions, customs, and components of various African religions and mythologies, to enhance the life skills of African-American girls. The conceptual framework of these programs is that spiritual and moral avenues of increased awareness of self will enable the young girl to connect the spiritual to the material (Billingsley & Caldwell, 1991; Gavazzi, Alford, & McKenry, 1996). This, in turn, enables the participant to understand her greater purpose on this earth. This understanding increases the likelihood that she will not engage in behaviors detrimental to that greater purpose.

Each of these types of programs has proven to be anecdotally effective. They have been effective in delaying the initiation of sexual behaviors, thus decreasing adolescent pregnancy, and the contracting of sexually transmitted diseases. They have been effective in increasing academic achievement and expectations. Finally, each of these programs has proven anecdotal effectiveness in reducing role conflicts and improving self-concept among

African-American girls. However, few programs have engaged in empirical studies of effectiveness (Belgrave et al., 2004; Hirsch et al., 2000; Jekielek et al., 2002; Monges, 1999; Spoth, Guyll, Chao, & Molgaard, 2003). Consequently, there is little in the literature to counter the deficit-laden, pathological characterizations of African-American girls.

CONSEQUENCES OF PAST PRACTICES

Unfortunately, strategies developed to address the needs of African-American girls are scarce. Of those established to meet this population, the focus is on the perceived pathologies of the individual girl. Public policy has sought to address the needs of African-American girls from a deficit-based perspective (Chesney-Lind, 1999; East, 1998; Grant, 1984; Hunt & Hunt, 1977; Macke & Morgan, 1978). For instance, academic deficits and moral concerns (sexuality), and the consequences of such, have traditionally been addressed through welfare policy. The development and enhancements of social supports are an integral part of practice with African-American girls. A strong social support network serves as a protective factor for these young girls (Farrell & Barnes, 1993; Wasserman, 2003).

IMPACT ON OTHERS

The community and family are integral to the struggle of African-American girls to overcome adversities. In addition, the misperception of African-American girls by others has a negative impact on the African-American community, families, and individuals. This war on African-American girls also impacts family, economic, and social structures. The role of the African-American family adapts to counter the attacks on the young girl. The family structure shifts to accommodate the needs of its members in need.

Community

The African-centered community is vital to the survival of all of its members. This community has historically provided the context for overcoming adversities in a spirit of collectivity. There is a framework of group survival (Asante, 1990; Bekerie, 1994; Bell, Bouie, & Baldwin, 1990; Blackwell, 1975), which provides the assurance to its members that the entire community will overcome together. Specifically, there is assurance that the survival of one member is necessary for the survival of the community.

This group survival framework was most evident in history during the struggle to overcome the Maafa holocaust, which is the disaster of forced kidnapping and enslavement of African people (Ani, 1994), and subsequent chattel slavery, Jim Crow policies, and the continued struggle for full civil rights in America.

In this context, African-American girls should experience the assurance that their struggle to overcome adversity is a communal struggle to overcome adversity. When these girls are misperceived, the community is misperceived. Consequently, there is an investment by the African-centered community to provide adequate support to its members, including African-American girls (Diop, 1974; Dove, 1998).

Family

The African-American family is the smallest unit in the African-centered community. It is the strongest, most functional institution in the African-centered community (Hill, 1971.). The individual family members function as a component of the family unit. There is an expectation that the individual member uplifts the community by uplifting the family.

The African-American family is characterized as highly adaptive to societal adversities (Gutman, 1976; Hill, 1971). It has diverse compositional and functional structures. The family may be in various forms such as nuclear, extended, and augmented families. The African-American family is also characterized by diverse family ties (Hill, 1971; Martin & Martin, 1985). These families claim relationships by blood, by marriage, formal and informal adoptions, or by simply assimilating into the family life (Billingsley & Caldwell, 1991), thus lending to the notion of communal interconnectedness.

The African-American family has a strong achievement orientation (Billingsley, 1968; Billingsley & Caldwell, 1991), which is essential to the survival of the community. An African-American girl who is not living up to her fullest academic and social potential is, in essence, threatening the survival of the African-American family and community. African-American girls get primary socialization from their mothers (Dickson, 1993) regarding role expectations.

There may be several explanations for this phenomenon. Poor, young African-American girls often see their mothers coping "successfully" as single parents. This misperception often leads these young girls to underestimate the enormity of parenting (Hare, 1987), so they are not deterred from engaging in risky sexual behaviors that may result in pregnancy. In addition, African-American girls may view motherhood as a means of attaining adult status (Mayfield, 1982). Consequently, tensions between mother and daughter are amplified as they struggle to adapt to these new familial roles. At a time when these young girls should be transitioning from total dependence on parents to dependence on self and peers, these young mothers find themselves transitioning from total dependence on parents to having someone totally dependent upon them, forcing a shift in the family structure.

FORMAL SOCIAL STRUCTURES

Social structures are made relevant by the adversities affecting African-American girls. Social structures in this society are in place to address the needs of society members. Social organizations such as schools, social service institutions, and even correctional institutions exist solely to serve those in need. So, without adversities, these structures would not exist (Nagel, 1974; Pontara, 1978; Snyder, 1978). These structures depend on the maintenance of chaos in society (Baecker, 2001; Grusky, 1994).

Consequently, these structures may act as instruments of oppression. For instance, the education system through which these girls matriculate may be an example of an oppressive social structure (Sedlak, 1983; Wald & Losen, 2003). Although public education is accessible to all American children, all American children do not receive adequate or equal education. In a way, the American education system serves a need to have undereducated members of society. Undereducated members perform menial, yet necessary societal tasks. In addition, the undereducated members will consume the services of the other social institutions. This system continues to commit violence against its target members through policy development and service provision (Fields & Smith, 1998; Russett, 1964) that fosters dependence on those institutions.

It is important that we explore mental health treatment within the context of the target population. African-American girls often gain a mental health diagnosis based on misperceptions, which is usually a manifestation of their active resistance against structural adversities. We must develop and implement approaches that are relevant to the specific needs of adolescent African-American girls.

LIFE COURSE PERSPECTIVE

The examination of African-American girls is most appropriately viewed from a life course perspective, which recognizes the influence of age, history, culture, and unexpected life events on individual and family development (Hutchison, 2005). This perspective is often characterized as event history, such as the sequence of events, individual experiences, or life transitions from birth to death. Life course perspective posits that culture and social institutions also influence event history of individuals and families.

There are five basic components of the life course perspective: cohort, transitions, trajectories, life events, and turning points. Each component provides some insight into the impact life events have on the individual and family. Cohort refers to a group of people born at the same historical time period, thus experiencing particular social changes within a given culture in the same sequence and at the same age (Hutchison, 2005). This cohort's event history shapes opportunities for education, work, and family life. Consequently, strategies are developed to cope with shared circumstances. For instance, African-American adolescents who grew up in the 1960s responded to the social transitions of the era by becoming involved in their communities through political action and social programs. As a result, this cohort has experienced a significant increase in political participation through elected offices and appointments, as well as electoral activities such as voter registration and partisan campaign activities. This involvement has ultimately strengthened the autonomy of the African-American community, enabling it to continue to support the development of African-American girls.

Transitions in the life course perspective recognize that individuals experience a number of events, such as births, marriages, divorces, and deaths. There are socially constructed roles that individuals are expected to play as they move through life transitions. This component is concerned with macro-level issues involving structural impacts on role expectations. For instance, there is an expectation that women adhere to a Victorian standard of womanhood, an ideology socially constructed for White women. However, African-American girls are often judged by this standard. So, when a young girl is assertive in articulating her needs, she is deemed "unladylike" by the majority society. This may negatively affect her educational and employment opportunities. It is necessary that African-American girls be provided family and community supports to ease their transition to a culturally constructed definition of womanhood. Transitions in event history recognize that the structural expectations of womanhood (macro-level) would be in conflict with the African-American girl's ability to transition to womanhood (micro-level).

There are long-term patterns of stability and change in an individual's life course, usually characterized by multiple transitions. This continuity of direction is expressed in the trajectories component of the life course perspective. Although individuals comprise a family, each individual has a unique trajectory, such as educational, occupational, and health. Each family is a collection of intersecting trajectories, often setting families on a collective trajectory. For instance, an African-American girl who experiences academic success has a positive impact on the well-being of the family unit. The collective nature of these families is supported by this component of the life course perspective. The action of one unit of the family impacts the entire family unit, and one family unit impacts the entire community unit.

Life events are another component of the life course perspective. This component is described as a significant occurrence involving a relatively abrupt change that may produce serious and long-lasting effects on an individual's life course. As a result of the stress invoked by life events, adaptive skills are required. For instance, adolescent pregnancy is a life event that produces long-lasting effects on the life course of the adolescent, the family, and on the community. Roles and relationships are changed, and adaptations are made to accommodate this shift. The pregnant adolescent is expected to shift from an egocentric world view typical of this developmental stage, to a world view that places the child as a prominent concern. The family views this adolescent as one requiring more responsibility. This life event creates stress in the family system as they strive to adapt.

The final component of the life course perspective is characterized as turning points. This component is a special life event that produces a lasting shift in trajectory, not a temporary detour. Turning points are typically realized in hindsight. For instance, the sexual victimization of prepubescent girls has proven to have a significant impact on their life trajectory. Although the immediate response may be to ensure the physical well-being of the young girl, the lasting effects may include depression manifested through sexual promiscuity and delinquency (Chesney-Lind & Shelden, 2004). Consequently, the long-term response to this victimization may be through mental health and juvenile justice systems.

It is important to note that life course trajectories are not smooth and predictable, but often results in twists and turns or even reversals in life course. Life events may open or close opportunities, often make a lasting change on one's environment, and have an impact on one's self-concept, beliefs, or expectations.

African-American girls face adversities that are historically grounded in a tradition of mistreatment and devaluation. As a result of this history, African-American families have adapted child-rearing practices to overcome this adverse treatment. These practices are reflected in the messages transmitted to African-American girls regarding role expectations and behaviors. It is important to recognize the influence of this historical context on the contemporary manifestations of adaptation and survival in the African-American community, and specifically among African-American girls.

AFRICENTRIC PERSPECTIVE

An Africentric framework also influences the conceptualization of this chapter. This view posits interconnectedness between humanity and nature. All modalities and realities are viewed as one. There is no demarcation between the spiritual and the material, thus to destroy one part is to destroy the whole (Asante, 1990; Schiele, 2000). This continuity from the material to the spiritual is the universal basis of the Africentric viewpoint (Asante, 1990). Group survival is another important tenant of this framework. Because there is an interconnection of humans and the environment, the survival of the group is paramount to individual survival. Group survival prioritizes the survival of the community throughout the African diaspora. The community is connected by common cultural values, such as interdependence, cooperation, unity, mutual responsibility, and reconciliation (Bell et al., 1990).

An attack on African-American girls is an attack on the African-American community. The African-American woman is the bearer of life to the community. She is also responsible for shaping the community through her mothering and nurturing of that new life. If one aims to destroy the African-American community, one would seek to destroy the source of that community's life—the female, the mother, the bearer of life. African-American girls are the future bearers of life in this community. African-American girls are plagued with many obstacles, which may negatively impact their ability to uphold their responsibility of shaping the community through the mothering and nurturing of new life.

SUGGESTED MENTAL HEALTH
INTERVENTION STRATEGIES

These components may be incorporated in a variety of settings involved in the delivery of services to African-American girls. Whatever the setting, service providers should validate African-American culture, and communicate that acknowledgment in their service delivery to African-American girls. This would translate into defining norms as set by the African-American community. For instance, adolescents may be expected to take on more mature roles at a younger age in the African-American community than in other communities (e.g., "latch key" responsibilities, higher degree of household chores, caring for younger siblings). These expectations should be viewed as normative behaviors within the context of the African-American community. In addition, the service provider must establish and maintain connections with the African-American community to serve as experts and consultants to the service providers when addressing the needs of African-American girls.

PUBLIC POLICY

Policy development and analysis should explore issues affecting African-American girls through a cultural lens of awareness and competency. It is difficult to truly examine issues of people of African descent through a European lens without viewing the target as pathological. First, policy practitioners should respect African-American culture as a legitimate culture, not a counterculture. This requires an awareness of the historical and contemporary components of this culture, particularly as it relates to African-American girls. Only after gaining this awareness will policy practitioners realize the impact of policy on the African-American community. The culturally sensitive policy practitioner should then develop policy that would empower the community to support the development of the young girl as a potential conduit of life. For instance, policy that addresses delinquency should include identified social support systems for the adolescent girls, in the implementation of the policy. This approach builds on the collective nature of the African-American community. In addition, the policy should be empowering, not punitive to the community, to the family, and to the adolescent. This empowered community would then assist in developing policy that addresses other issues of concern, such as under-education, and chronic under-employment and unemployment.

SOCIAL SUPPORTS

The social support systems of African-American girls should also use an African-centered lens by which to view issues of concern to this population, as they transition through significant life events. In the African-American community, the social support system goes beyond the immediate family. This support system may include extended family members (e.g., multiple level cousins, aunts, uncles, great-relatives) and nonblood-related kin (e.g., neighbors, ministers, family friends). These support systems must realize that their life course trajectories are intimately connected to that of the young girl.

PROGRAMMING

Clinical practitioners must also view the African-American girl from an African-centered lens. There are a number of successful historical models that serve as contemporary examples of successful programming. African-American women have struggled to address the needs of African-American girls, particularly through the Negro club women's movement, since the early 1900s (Carlton-LaNey & Hodges, 2004; Dill, 1979; Hodges, 2001; Kogut, 1970; Lasch-Quinn, 1993; Lerner, 1974; Martin & Martin, 1985; Neverdon-Morton, 1982). These practice models epitomized the following principles:

1. *Young girls who are labeled as wayward are redeemable.* A culturally competent practitioner must view these young girls as redeemable. This requires that the practitioner define the young girl by her potential, not by her past struggles. For instance, an adolescent mother should be provided options regarding her future (e.g., higher education), just as if she had no child. However, the planning should incorporate appropriate support for the mother and child as she strives for her goals.
2. *Focus on the spiritual centeredness of each young girl.* The practitioner must tune into the spiritual centeredness of each girl, with the understanding that everything is spiritual as is expressed in the African tradition. This is not to be confused with religiosity. Spiritual centeredness is an acknowledgment that each individual has a purpose in the larger cosmos. This ideology provides a life purpose to each young girl. As the adolescent girl is supported in identifying this aspect of her current life and the planning of her future, she should be assisted in identifying the purpose of her goals, with the anticipation of those plans placing her on a trajectory towards reaching a full understanding of her life purpose.
3. *Equip each young girl with necessary tools for survival.* The practitioner must equip each young girl with the necessary tools for survival. It is not enough to explore the perceived struggles, but the practitioner must provide culturally specific strategies by which these girls can overcome adversities and the dominant society's role in maintaining these adversities. For instance, if an adolescent girl in high school states that she has no plans for higher education, even if she has the grades to do so, it is important that she is supported in developing other appropriate career goals.
4. *Utilize the principle of interconnectedness.* The practitioner must frame all interventions with the principle of interconnectedness. This

principle reiterates the importance that each individual has to larger society. It also posits that the community cannot be uplifted unless every member of that community is uplifted. The uplift of the community ensures the success of every member of that community. Adolescent girls should be encouraged to participate in structured community services, such as reading to children, feeding the homeless, sitting with the sick, and visiting the elderly. This provides a sense of community for the young girl, which instills connectedness to members of the community.

DISSEMINATION STRATEGIES

Suggestions for new approaches enabling African-American girls to overcome adversities are not effective unless the information is disseminated and accepted as relevant by stakeholders. The following strategies seek to make previous strategies relevant.

Educators. Educators should acknowledge different world views to examine social problems, and should expose their students to those different world views. It is important that educators have access to this information through professional meetings and scholarly journals.

Researchers. An African centered lens should be used to evaluate program effectiveness for those programs designed to address the needs of African-American girls. This requires quasi-experimental and experimental designs comparing these programs to others. The results of these program evaluations should be used to strengthen existing programs and for the development of new programs. Secondly, there should be empirical exploration added to the literature examining the impact of social structures on the mental health of African-American girls. This exploration should use an African-centered framework by which to examine potential research questions. In addition, research results should be disseminated at professional meetings and in scholarly, peer-reviewed journals, so that the African-centered approach to research becomes normative.

Social supports. Community programs tailored for potential members of support networks that reintroduces and acknowledges African-centered traditions should be a necessary component of the community. Community organizers should use these traditions as they implement programs. These programs should be a balance between arts, sciences, and history. Practitioners, policy makers, and researchers should use these community members as consultants to their practice.

CONCLUSION

African-American girls are under attack. When they attempt to resist those attacks, they are at risk of a mental health diagnosis. It is important that we explore issues faced by African-American girls from life course and African-centered perspectives. These perspectives will provide explanations for particular reactions and potential solutions to adversities faced by this population. It is the responsibility of the community to help these girls overcome adversity. It is the responsibility of practitioners, researchers, and policy makers to acknowledge the importance of the community, as well as to assist the community in helping African-American girls. Ultimately, providing uplift to African-American girls provides uplift to our society.

CHAPTER SUMMARY

Themes gleaned from this chapter include historic and current obstacles faced by African-American teens and resulting behaviors responses. African-American girls are under attack, which generally pathologizes their behaviors. These obstacles are reframed with suggested mental health intervention strategies. The communities can assist these girls through the adoption of culturally sensitive public policies and the development of social programs in the girls' communities.

CLASSROOM ACTIVITIES

Case study: Kineesha J.

Kineesha is fifteen years old and in the eleventh grade at Milltown High School. She is an honor student and is academically gifted in math and the sciences. Kineesha has just been referred to you because she has reportedly threatened to kill her AP Calculus teacher. This is your first meeting with her. Kineesha reports the following on her intake form:

> My calculus teacher keeps messing with me. He kept standing too close to me in class. I told him that if he don't get out of my way, that I would kill him. He was looking for the chance to get me out of his class and I gave it to him. Now we are all happy. And, no, I am not crazy!!!!!

Kineesha comes to her appointment with you as scheduled. She is dressed in a miniskirt and halter top. She does not look at you. She keeps her arms and legs crossed throughout the entire session.

Kineesha is the oldest of three siblings. She has a sister, Sharday, age two; and a brother, Raykwan, age four. Kineesha's mother, age twenty-nine, is incarcerated on drug charges. Kineesha reports that her mother was "set up" by her boyfriend, and is serving a fifteen-year sentence "for not knowing where her boyfriend hid the drugs." She reports that Sharday was born in prison. Kineesha and her siblings are in the legal custody of their maternal grandmother who is currently hospitalized for complications with diabetes and hypertension. Kineesha's twenty-three-year-old aunt also lives in the home. Kineesha's aunt and mother are owners of a popular hair salon. Since her grandmother's recent hospitalization, Kineesha has become the primary caregiver for her siblings.

Kineesha reports that she "used to like school," but now it "seems more of a hassle." She reports that she wants to get her GED and "get on with [her] life." Despite having a 4.2 GPA, Kineesha finds all of her classes boring and a "waste of time." Kineesha reports that she plans to be a cosmetologist.

Questions for Discussion

1. Using the Carlton-LaNey & Burwell model as a framework, what information would you need from Kineesha to help her define the main issue? Discuss the obstacles currently faced by Kineesha and determine which issues are primary. Provide your rationale.
2. What role would the following players have in helping Kineesha overcome obstacles:
   a. Kineesha
   b. Family
   c. Community
   d. Schools
   e. Policymakers
   f. Service providers
3. Describe a community program that would help Kineesha overcome adversities.
4. Describe how you would assess the strengths possessed by Kineesha and her family.
5. Discuss how you would talk to Kineesha about the adversities that she is facing and their influencing factors.
6. If you were to develop a support group for girls who have similar problems such as Kineesha, what would be the eight most important topics to discuss? Describe some exercises that you might try with this group.

REFERENCES

A Negro Nurse. (1912). More slavery at the South. *The Independent, 72*(3295), 197-200.

Accomando, C. (1998). "The laws were laid down to me anew": Harriet Jacobs and the reframing of legal fictions. *African American Review, 32*(2), 229-245.

Aneshensel, C. S., & Sucoff, C. A. (1996). The neighborhood context of adolescent mental health. *Journal of Health and Social Behavior, 37,* 293-310.

Ani, M. (1994). *Let the Circle Be Unbroken: The Implications of African Spirituality in the Diaspora.* Trenton, NJ: Red Sea Press.

Asante, M. K. (1990). *Kemet, Afrocentricity, and Knowledge.* Trenton, NJ: Africa World.

Baecker, D. (2001). Why systems? *Theory, Culture, and Society, 18*(1), 59-74.

Bekerie, A. (1994). The four corners of a circle: Afrocentricity as a model of synthesis. *Journal of Black Studies, 25*(2), 131-149.

Belgrave, F. Z., Reed, M. C., Plybon, L. E., Butler, D. S., Allison, K. W., & Davis, T. (2004). An evaluation of Sisters of Nia: A cultural program for African American girls. *Journal of Black Psychology, 30*(3), 329-343.

Bell, Y. R., Bouie, C. L., & Baldwin, J. A. (1990). Afrocentric cultural consciousness and African-American male-female relationships. *Journal of Black Studies, 21*(2), 162-189.

Billingsley, A. (1968). *Black Families in White America.* Englewood Cliffs, NJ: Prentice-Hall.

Billingsley, A., & Caldwell, C. H. (1991). The church, the family, and the school in the African American community. *The Journal of Negro Education, 60*(3), 427-440.

Blackwell, J. (1975). *The Black Community: Diversity and Unity.* New York: Harper & Row Publishers, Inc.

Brice, T. S. (2005). "Disease and delinquency know no color": Syphilis and African American female delinquency. *Affilia: Journal of Women and Social Work, 18*(10), 300-314.

Brown-Moses, C. H. (1923, April). An appeal to Negro women. *Asheville Daily News.*

Brown, S. V. (1985). Premarital sexual permissiveness among Black adolescent females. *Social Psychology Quarterly, 48*(4), 381-387.

Bui, K. V. T., Kim, L., & Takeuchi, D. T. (1993). The referral of minority adolescents to community mental health centers. *Journal of Health and Social Behavior, 34,* 153-164.

Carlton-LaNey, I., & Burwell, Y. (1996). Introduction: African American community practice models: Historical and contemporary responses. *Journal of Community Practice, 2*(4), 1-6.

Carlton-LaNey, I., & Hodges, V. (2004). African American reformers' mission: Caring for our girls and women. *Affilia, 19*(3), 257-272.

Chesney-Lind, M. (1999). Challenging girls' invisibility in juvenile court. *Annals of the American Academy of Political and Social Science, 564,* 185-202.

Dickson, L. (1993). The future of marriage and the family in Black America. *Journal of Black Studies, 23*(4), 472-491.

DiClemente, R. J., Wingood, G. M., Harrington, K. F., Lang, D. L., Davies, S. L., Edward, W., et al. (2004). Efficacy of an HIV prevention intervention for African American adolescent girls: A randomized controlled trial. *Journal of the American Medical Association, 292*(2), 171.

Dill, B. T. (1979). The dialectics of Black womanhood. *Signs: Journal of Women in Culture and Society, 4*(3), 543-555.

Diop, C. A. (1974). *The African Origin of Civilization: Myth or Reality?* (M. Cook, Trans.). New York: Lawrence Hill.

Dove, N. (1998). African womanism: An Afrocentric theory. *Journal of Black Studies, 28*(5), 515-539.

Eamon, M. K. (2002). Effects of poverty on mathematics and reading achievement of young adolescents. *The Journal of Early Adolescence, 22*(1), 49-74.

East, P. L. (1998). Racial and ethnic differences in girls' sexual, marital, and birth expectations. *Journal of Marriage and the Family, 60,* 150-162.

East, P. L., Felice, M. E., & Morgan, M. C. (1993). Sisters' and girlfriends' sexual childbearing behavior: Effects on early adolescent girls' sexual outcomes. *Journal of Marriage and the Family, 55,* 953-963.

Farrell, M. P., & Barnes, G. M. (1993). Family systems and social support: A test of the effects of cohesion and adaptability on the functioning of parents and adolescents. *Journal of Marriage and the Family, 55*(1), 119-132.

Feld, S., & Ruhland, D. (1977). The development of achievement motivation in Black and White children. *Child Development, 48,* 1362-1368.

Fields, J. M., & Smith, K. E. (1998). *Poverty, Family Structure, and Child Well-Being: Indicators from the SIPP.* Washington, DC: Population Division, U.S. Bureau of the Census.

French, D. C., & Dishion, T. J. (2003). Predictors of early initiation of sexual intercourse among high-risk adolescents. *The Journal of Early Adolescence, 23*(3), 295-315.

Gage, J. A. (1998). Sexual activity and contraceptive use: The components of the decision making process. *Studies in Family Planning, 29*(2), 154-166.

Gandy, O. H. (2001). Racial identity, media use, and the social construction of risk among African Americans. *Journal of Black Studies, 31*(5), 600-618.

Gavazzi, S. M., Alford, K. A., & McKenry, P. C. (1996). Culturally specific programs for foster care youth: The sample case of an African American rites of passage program. *Family Relations, 45*(2), 166-174.

Gilmore, G. E. (1994). North Carolina federation of colored women's clubs. In D. Hines, E. Brown, & R. Terborg-Penn (Eds.), *Black Women in America: A Historical Encyclopedia* (pp. 882-884). Bloomberg: Indiana University Press.

Grant, L. (1984). Black females "place" in desegregated classrooms. *Sociology of Education, 57*(2), 98-111.

Grusky, D. B. (1994). The contours of social stratification. In D. B. Grusky (Ed.), *Social Stratification: Class, Race, and Gender in Sociological Perspective* (pp. 3-36). Boulder, CO: Westview Press.

Gutman, H. G. (1976). *The Black Family in Slavery and Freedom: 1750-1926.* New York: Pantheon Books.

Guttierrez, L., & Lewis, E. A. (1994). Community organizing with women of color: A feminist approach. *Journal of Community Practice, 1*(2), 23-43.

Hare, B. R. (1987). Structural inequality and the endangered status of Black youth. *Journal of Negro Education, 56*(1), 100-110.

Henry, L. J. (1981). Promoting historical consciousness: The early archives committee of the National Council of Negro Women. *Signs: Journal of women in culture and society, 7*(1), 251-259.

Hill, R. (1971). *The Strengths of Black Families.* New York: National Urban League.

Hirsch, B. J., Roffman, J. G., Deutsch, N. L., Flynn, C. A., Loder, T. L., & Pagano, M. E. (2000). Inner-city youth development organizations: Strengthening programs for adolescent girls. *The Journal of Early Adolescence, 20*(2), 210-230.

Hodges, V. G. (2001). Historical development of African American child welfare services. In I. B. Carlton-LaNey (Ed.), *African American Leadership: An Empowerment Tradition in Social Welfare History* (pp. 203-213). Washington, DC: National Association of Social Workers.

Hunt, J. G., & Hunt, L. L. (1977). Race, daughters and father-loss: Does absence make the girl grow stronger? *Social Problems, 25*(1), 90-102.

Hutchison, E. D. (2005). The life course perspective: A promising approach for bridging the micro and macro worlds for social workers. *Families in Society, 86*(1), 143-152.

Jekielek, S., Moore, K., & Hair, E. (2002). *Mentoring Programs and Youth Development: A Synthesis.* Washington, DC: Child Trends.

Kogut, A. (1970). The Negro and the charity organization society in the progressive era. *Social Service Review, 44,* 11-21.

Lasch-Quinn, E. (1993). *Black Neighbors: Race and the Limits of Reform in the American Settlement Movement, 1890-1945.* Chapel Hill: University of North Carolina Press.

Lei, J. L. (2003). (Un)necessary toughness: Those loud Black girls, and those quiet Asian boys. *Anthropology & Education Quarterly, 34*(2), 158-181.

Lerner, G. (Ed.). (1972). *Black Women in White America: A Documentary History.* New York: Pantheon Books.

Lerner, G. (1974). Early community work of Black club women. *Journal of Negro History, 59*(2), 158-167.

Macke, A. S., & Morgan, W. R. (1978). Maternal employment, race, and work orientation of high school girls. *Social Forces, 57*(1), 187-204.

Martin, J. M., & Martin, E. P. (1985). *The Helping Tradition in the Black Family and Community.* Washington, DC: National Association of Social Workers, Inc.

Mayfield, L. (1982). *Status Transition of Black Teenage Mothers.* City University of New York Graduate Center, New York.

Maynard, R. A. (1997). The costs of adolescent childbearing. In R. A. Maynard (Ed.), *Kids Having Kids: Economic Costs and Social Consequences of Teen Pregnancy* (pp. 285-338). Washington, DC: The Urban Institute Press.

McLeod, J. D., & Shanahan, M. J. (1996). Trajectories of poverty and children's mental health. *Journal of Health and Social Behavior, 37,* 207-220.

Milkie, M. A. (1999). Social comparisons, reflected appraisals, and mass media: The impact of pervasive beauty images on Black and White girls' self-concepts. *Social Psychology Quarterly, 62*(2), 190-210.

Miller, K. S., Forehand, R., & Kotchick, B. A. (1999). Adolescent sexual behavior in two ethnic minority samples: The role of family variables. *Journal of Marriage and Family Therapy, 61*(1), 85-98.

Monges, M. M. A. K. R. (1999). Candace rites of passage program: The cultural context as an empowerment tool. *Journal of Black Studies, 29*(6), 827-840.

Nagel, J. (1974). Inequality and discontent: A nonlinear hypothesis. *World Politics, 26,* 453-472.

Neverdon-Morton, C. (1982). Self-help programs as educative activities of Black women in the South, 1895-1925: Focus on four key areas. *Journal of Negro Education, 51*(3), 207-221.

Paul, D. G. (2003). *Talkin' Back: Raising and Educating Resilient Black Girls.* Westport, CT: Praeger.

Pontara, G. (1978). The concept of violence. *Journal of Peace Research, 15*(1), 19-32.

Rosenberg, R. (1987). Seeds in hard ground: Black girlhood in the bluest eye. *Black American Literature Forum, 21*(4), 435-445.

Russett, B. M. (1964). Inequality and instability: The relation of land tenure to politics. *World Politics, 16,* 442-454.

Schiele, J. H. (2000). *Human Services and the Afrocentric Paradigm.* Binghamton, NY: The Haworth Press.

Schilt, K. (2003). "I'll resist with every inch and every breath": Girls and Zine making as a form of resistance. *Youth Society, 35*(1), 71-97.

Sedlak, M. W. (1983). Young women and the city: Adolescent deviance and the transformation of educational policy, 1870-1960. *History of Education Quarterly, 23*(1), 1-28.

Sirin, S. R., & Rogers-Sirin, L. (2004). Exploring school engagement of middle-class African American adolescents. *Youth Society, 35*(3), 323-340.

Slaughter, D. T. (1972). Becoming an Afro-American woman. *School Review,* 299-318.

Snyder, D. (1978). Collective violence: A research agenda and some strategic considerations. *The Journal of Conflict Resolution, 22*(3), 499-534.

Spoth, R., Guyll, M., Chao, W., & Molgaard, V. (2003). Exploratory study of a preventive intervention with general population African American families. *The Journal of Early Adolescence, 23*(4), 435-468.

Steward, G. A. (1927). The black girl passes. *Social Forces, VI*(1), 99-103.

Takeuchi, D., Bui, K. V. T., & Kim, L. (1993). The referral of minority adolescents to community mental health centers. *Journal of Health and Social Behavior, 34,* 153-164.

Terry, E., & Manlove, J. (2000). *Trends in Sexual Activity and Contraceptive Use Among Teens.* Washington, DC: The National Campaign to Prevent Teen Pregnancy.

The National Campaign to Prevent Teen Pregnancy. (2003). *Fact Sheet: A Look at the Real Costs of Teen Pregnancy.* Washington, DC: Author.

The National Campaign to Prevent Teen Pregnancy. (2004). *Teen Sexual Activity, Pregnancy and Childbearing Among Black Teens.* Washington, DC: Author.

Wald, J. M., & Losen, D. J. (2003). *Deconstructing the School-to-Prison Pipeline.* San Francisco: Jossey-Bass.

Washington, V. (1982). Racial differences in teacher perceptions of first and forth grade pupils on selected characteristics. *The Journal of Negro Education, 51*(1), 60-72.

Wasserman, G. A. (2003). *Risk and Protective Factors of Child Delinquency.* Washington, DC: United States Office of Juvenile Justice and Delinquency Prevention.

Weisman, C. S., Plichta, S., Nathanson, C. A., Chase, G. A., Ensminger, M. E., & Robinson, J. C. (1991). Adolescent women's contraceptive decision making. *Journal of Health and Social Behavior, 32*(2), 130-144.

Chapter 10

Suicide and Young
African-American Males

Gregory Washington
Donna Holland Barnes

It is not well known that the incidences of suicide among African-American male youth recently took an uncharacteristic turn. From 1980 to 1995, the suicide rates for Black youth ages 10 to 19 increased from 2.1 to 4.5 per 100,000, an increase of 114 percent. The rate increased the most for Blacks ages 10 to 14 years (233 percent) compared with a 120 percent increase for Whites. Among Blacks aged 15 to 19 years the suicide rates increased 128 percent, compared with 19 percent for Whites (CDC, 1998). According to Barnes and Bell (2003) by 1998, the rates for Black males aged 15 to 24 decreased from the 1994 rate of 21 per 100,000 to 15 per 100,000. This current decrease is reflective of an early 1980s level. The reasons for this unprecedented increase in the 1980s and early 1990s are unknown but by 1998, it had subsided. Currently, the suicide rates for African-American males between the ages of 15 and 24, is the third-leading cause of death (after homicide and unintentional injuries).

The impact of any increase in suicidal behavior in African-American communities is compounded by the fact that among the male population many of these communities have high rates of homicide, drug abuse, and alcoholism. Often, young children growing up in these communities have witnessed violence, been victimized, or grieved the loss of a parent, sibling, or friend. Social ills that are not managed properly, such as thwarted grieving processes and post-traumatic stress disorder, can develop into untreated mental disorders that in turn may lead to suicidal behavior.

Mental Health Care in the African-American Community
© 2007 by The Haworth Press, Inc. All rights reserved.
doi:10.1300/5364_10

Although the rates of suicide in the United States among all pre-adolescents and adolescents increased dramatically during the last few decades, the unique interactions African-American males have with societal realities such as unemployment, crime, poverty, and oppression may influence responses that are sometimes self-destructive. Numerous African-American communities in the 1980s and 1990s experienced very high rates of young African-American male unemployment and some research scholars suspect that this and the corresponding crack cocaine epidemic influenced the increase in suicide among African-American youth (Lester, 1998).

According to Wallace, Brown, Bachman, and Laveist (2003), suicide rates of young African-American youth have historically been lower than European-American youth. Others, especially scholars and practitioners, are presently wondering if historical protective factors such as family, community collectivity, and other cultural strengths eroded or simply became ineffective. For example, between 1980 and 1995, a total of 3,030 African-American males aged 10 to 19 years suicided (CDC, 1998). The troubling nature of this sudden increase was made more mysterious by recent research findings of the Institute of Medicine that suggest that the rates have stabilized (Goldsmith, Pellmar, Kleinman, & Bunney, 2002). Currently, little or no empirical literature exist for addressing specific risk factors of African-American suicidal behavior or evidence-based prevention literature that addresses potential protective factors. It is generally argued that we need more knowledge about the significance of cultural differences, protective factors, and unique risk factors related to externally directed violence among young African-American male youth (Poussaint & Alexander, 2000). This chapter critiques our knowledge of the history, philosophy, policies, research, and practice of suicide prevention and treatment as it relates to young African-American males. We plan to pose questions for further review.

REVIEW OF THE LITERATURE

The historical review of people of African descent and suicide needs to include the transition from overtly racist and biased scientific literature to literature that is more based on accurate interpretation of empirical data. Historically, and as recently as the 1960s, mental health professionals believed that people of African descent did not have the psychological complexity to commit suicide or to experience mental illness (Chapters 1, 2, and 3) (Lawson, 2002). This was professed by many, but in reality, suicide among Africans and African Americans is not new and is documented back to the times of the transatlantic slave trade (Owens, 1976). Slavery has important implications in terms of how we approach mental illness and how we understand suicide. In the 1800s, Black culture was considered inferior and there was an active attempt to get slaves to reject, remove, and disown their culture. And most important, slaves were not believed to have a psychological life; it was considered to be nonexistent (Lawson, 2002).

It is well documented that some slaves would choose suicide rather than leave Africa and experience the unknown. It is argued that early historical reports of suicide among African Americans were grossly underreported because it was believed that Blacks do not kill themselves (Poussaint & Alexander, 2000). Coroners and other death certifiers were not classifying Black deaths, especially the young, as suicides even when the evidence was clear. Consequently, suicide among African Americans was rarely discussed or talked about in the scholarly and local communities. Among the early and recent scholars and clinicians who wrote about African Americans and suicide were Prudhomme (1938), who wrote about the characteristics of suicide in the American Negro, and Poussaint, who wrote about Black suicide and its relationship to mental illness in African Americans (Poussaint, 1975; Poussaint & Alexander, 2000).

Currently, the literature on Black suicide provides several theories that attempt to explain the increase in suicide among African Americans. They include a breakdown of traditional support systems (Lester, 1998); too many guns in the Black communities (Joe & Kaplan, 2001); transitioning to the middle-class or predominantly White neighborhood (Holmes, 1977) and moving away from the church (Early, 1992).

These explanations have the potential to enhance the understanding of those interested in clarifying factors related to the complex phenomenon of Blacks and suicide. But, no single theory is capable of explaining this phenomenon conclusively. Was it the underreporting, the flawed tracking systems, or the lack of discussion about suicide that kept the reported rates low? Scholars and clinicians continue to wonder about the cause of the increase in the past two decades and explore the demographics and risk factors related to these reported suicides. Unfortunately, we know very little. More research on the risk factors that lead to suicide and the protective factors that guard against suicide is needed. But what we do know is that families who experience the loss of a family member as a result of suicide have two major concerns. The first concern relates to locating pre- and post-community support when experiencing a suicidal family member (Poussant & Alexander, 2000). The second concern relates to the nonexistent or inconsistent levels of safety within hospitals or other institutions providing care to suicidal family members (The President New Freedom Commission on Mental Health, 2002). The importance of expanding the explanations for suicide among young African-American males is salient as a result of the scarcity of suicide research studies and treatment and prevention programs that address the unique needs of African Americans (CDC, 1992; Gibbs, 1997; Joe & Kaplan, 2001). It is increasingly evident that cultural differences and institutions of social interaction that include racism, oppression, and discrimination need to be researched (Clark, Anderson, Clark, & Williams, 1999; Poussaint & Alexander, 2000). Despite the alarming rise in suicidal behaviors among African-American male adolescents, only a few contextually grounded studies that incorporate ecological factors relevant to the experiences and circumstances of African-American youth have been conducted (Willis et al., 2003).

Recommendations from these contextually grounded studies and other studies suggest a broader and more efficient identification and treatment of at-risk youth (Garland & Zigler, 1993). In addition, studies examining the influence of conditions such as extreme poverty and urban stress are also important. Researchers such as Miller, Webster, and MacIntosh (2002) believe that the daily stressful experiences of urban African-American adolescents can contribute to detrimental outcomes and the development of maladaptive response patterns that could include self-harming behavior. This research appears to support the argument that young African-American males in poor and oppressed communities may be at greater risk for suicide. In addition, more research on risk factors that lead to suicidal behavior is needed, such as the disproportionate availability of drugs and the related family instability that often includes domestic violence and abuse in many poor urban African-American communities.

Although it is true that African-American and other male youth share depression and aggressive behavior as risk factors, it is necessary to identify risk factors that may be uniquely associated with African-American males, such as low social economic status, low education, crime, difficulties in interpersonal relationships, stressful life events, chronic stress, and poor health (Primm, 2005). In discussing some of these risk factors Barnes and Bell (2003) identify several inconsistencies and paradoxes related to African-American suicide rates, including the relatively low suicide rates for African-American incarcerated males. Suicide rates for White incarcerated men are approximately nine to fifteen times higher than for those of the same race on the outside and prison suicide rates are approximately one and a half times higher than in the general population. Similarly, youth in detention and correctional facilities are four times more likely to complete suicide than youths in the general population. In spite of the fact that African-American males are a much larger percent of this population the suicide rates for European-American males are much higher. It would be important to examine through future research the factors related to the low African-American male suicide rates in the context of an apparent risk such as incarceration.

In addition to traditional criteria for assessing suicide risk in youth, shared risk factors for interpersonal violence and other self destructive behavior among African-American boys require investigation and incorporation into risk assessment protocols (Joe & Marcus, 2003). This is suggested, in part, by a result of the similarity in contextual conditions that frequently include familial instability, poverty, and exposure to violence and substance abuse behavior.

RISK FACTORS

There are some general biopsychosocial risk factors for suicide that social workers and other practitioners working with African Americans in general, and young African-American males in particular, should consider when engaging these populations. These include markers such as purchasing a gun, traits that demonstrate a change in behavior, or correlates, for example, factors that relate to suicidality, such as a major loss, clinical depression, and substance abuse. All can lead to self-destructive behavior and self-inflicted injuries. Other risk factors include environmental/societal factors, spiritual alienation or lack of a belief systems, poverty, and biopsychosocial factors.

Environmental/Societal Factors

African-American youth environmental factors that can lead to suicidality often generate from social structures that are not meeting the needs of African-American youth such as inadequate education or mis-education and their connection to the limited vocational options these youth can visualize. Risk factors also include the absence of family, and peers that are disconnected from the life-affirming morals of their community of origin (Gibbs, 1997). Environments such as this lead to stressful events, loneliness, social isolation, and feelings of loss. Environmental risk factors also include those that present barriers to accessing mental illness health care, such as cultural stigma associated with help-seeking behavior, distrust of the health care system, and living in underserved communities with few Black health care providers. In addition, lack of social support in the African-American community and a sense of isolation is a critical risk factor for suicide (Nisbet, 1996).

Spiritual Alienation or Lack of a Belief System

The absence of spirituality being displayed in the lives of some African-American males is believed to result in a condition of spiritual alienation that could contribute to risks of self- and externally-directed violent behavior. Spiritual alienation is defined here as the inability to internalize the spiritual concept of self and others, for example, the inability to acknowledge the importance of a higher power or force, and disproportionate associations of self-worth with materialism (Schiele, 2000). It is further theorized that there is an increased likelihood that individuals with high spiritual alienation will develop unhealthy attitudes toward drug use as a result of their disconnectedness from self, others, and a higher power or force. Although there is little research in this area, some of these conditions have been observed as prerequisites for suicide.

Poverty

It is believed by many scholars in the field of juvenile delinquency that young African-American males in poor and oppressed communities may be at greater risk for self-destructive behavior because many of these youth feel desperate, angry, worthless, hopeless, or helpless and this ultimately distorts how they make decisions. Some of these youth decide to pursue lifestyles or engage in illegal behaviors because they perceive that these are the best options. It is suggested these decisions are made because of the lack of jobs, disproportionate availability of illicit drugs and their distribution, and related family instability in many poor urban African-American communities (Schiele, 2000; Washington, 2003). The absence of healthy adult African-American males as role models has also been suggested as a risk factor for poor educational success and behavior problems, and a contributor to children having a more "externalized loci of control" (Rodney & Mupier, 1999; Rodney, Tachia, & Rodney, 1999; Wilson, 1978). In addition, many men in poor African-American communities are impacted by social problems that include homicide and incarceration. The results are a void of available healthy adult African-American males as role models in these communities.

Cultural, economic, and psychological differences, which include the mechanisms that allow racism to impact mental health, thereby increasing suicide risk, need to be researched because some studies indicate that mental health among Blacks is significantly affected by racism (Clark et al., 1999; Poussaint & Alexander, 2000).

Biopsychosocial Factors

Untreated and undetected mental disorders can lead to suicide (Goldsmith et al., 2002). If detected and treatment is indicated, there may be provider access and patient noncompliance issues. In fact, there is a 15 percent chance of suicide when major depressive disorder is diagnosed and left untreated (Clark & Fawcett, 1991; Fawcett, Clark, & Scheftner, 2002). Depression is a frequently unrecognized problem among young adolescents at the middle school level and is the leading cause of suicidal behavior in young adolescents (Saluja et al., 2004; Shelton, 2002). Signs of depression can sometimes be displayed differently among African-American males than the majority population. Young Black males who witness violence or victimization can develop a depressive illness. Expressions of anger or aggressive behavior that is sometimes viewed as normal behavior in the Black communities can be signs of suicide (Okwumabua & Wong, 2003; Poussaint & Alexander, 2000). This aggressive behavior often results in young Black males being charged with low-level offenses and incarceration (Clay, 2000).

Other related factors include substance abuse, which, when coupled with depression, increases risk because it encompasses poor judgment, impulsiveness, and the loss of social resources. Intoxication is associated with at least 50 percent of all suicides (NIMH, 2001).

APPROACHES TO SUICIDE PREVENTION

It is necessary to be aware of what factors protect young African-American males and contribute to the risk reduction. Suicide prevention and intervention initiatives generally focus on reducing the risk by increasing protective factors.

Protective Factors

Protective factors for suicide are those factors that are pathways to mental stability, balance, and safeguards against social ills within the communities. Within African-American communities there are many pathways that can lead to suicide prevention and intervention. Given that the use of firearms is the leading method of suicide among males of all age groups, a logical and reasonable action would involve means restriction or difficult accessibility as an important protective factor. It has been shown that guns being available to youths can quickly be viewed as the solution to emotional pain and discomfort (Kresnow et al., 2001). This is true because many youth are impulsive and can decide within minutes that death is an option. According to Baca-Garcia et al. (2004), the decision to suicide is an impulsive act. Other factors of importance are spirituality, cultural strengths, and concerned adults.

Spirituality

The concept of spirituality includes a belief in a higher power, positively influencing relationships with others, and peace, calm, and centeredness, as well as efforts to manage adversity through support, and relates to people of African descent (Mattis, 2000). Spirituality has also incorporated a conviction about spiritual power and the unquestionable belief that something greater than us is obtainable and can provide relief (Brisbane & Womble, 1985). Several studies suggest that spiritually may buffer many African Americans from the destructive effects of risk factors that are associated with suicidal behavior (Lester, 1998; Shaffer, Gould, & Hicks, 1994). It has also been found that individuals with religious faith and practices appear to have a sizable and a lower risk of suicide, less criminal activity, and less use and abuse of drugs and alcohol (Strawbridge, Cohen, Shema, & Kaplan, 1997). However, there is also a need to investigate the presence of other protective factors that could be related to African-American cultural strengths.

Cultural Strengths

Researchers that explore African-American male youth health disparities such as homicide and drug-related violence are encouraged to utilize a broad definition of culture. It is recommended that this definition include recognition of a common heritage or set of beliefs and norms as well as the acknowledgment that culture is dynamic in nature (U.S. Department of HHS, 2001). Research supports efforts to maximize the strengths of vulnerable youth and promote their healthy development, and the incorporation of cultural strengths and values into prevention programs (Banks, Hogue, Timberlake, & Liddle, 1996; Delgado, 1997; Harvey & Rauch, 1997). The socialization of African Americans in ways that promote Africentric values has also been suggested as a protective process that can inoculate at-risk youth against self-destruction. Conceptually, an Africentric perspective on health argues that the internalization of Africentric values, such as spirituality, by young African-American males creates individuals that are healthier and more resistant to self-destructive behaviors (Akbar, 1981; Oliver, 1989).

Concerned Adults

It is theorized and research supports that there is a need for parents, concerned adults, and role models to be available to young people. Their presence results in it being far more likely that young people will develop into healthy, successful adults (Furstenberg, 1993; Garmezy, 1985; Rutter, 1987; Werner & Smith, 1992). Research also suggests that mentoring could be a valuable resource for the healthy development of African-American children as they have been particularly successful in reducing the likelihood African-American children will use drugs (Tierney & Grossman, 2000). For example, the Kuumba Mentoring Group out of Memphis, Tennessee, is an innovative culturally centered group mentoring intervention. It was piloted with African-American boys in a relative caregiver program (Washington, Johnson, Jones, & Lang, 2007). The integration of the Africentric conceptual framework has been promoted for therapeutic work with African Americans and was utilized with a group of at-risk urban youth (Asante, 1991; Schiele, 2000). The implementation strategy included attempts to influence spirituality and other values of the participants via a core Afrocentric group discussion strategy. Spirituality was emphasized as a potential key protective factor and was examined via a unique short questionnaire. The perceptions of the relative caregivers are also measured in an attempt to gauge influence of the intervention. Outcome findings included a slight increase in spiritual orientation among the youth and improved school and home behavior.

The limitations of this culturally centered group mentoring effort include a small group size and the lack of control for extraneous variables. However, if spirituality is a suicide protective factor that warrants enhancement in African-American boys, this culturally centered group mentoring approach may be helpful in looking at ways to integrate spirituality into prevention programs.

Developing and Disseminating Strategies

Suggested strategies for developing stakeholder support in the area of suicide prevention include programs and services that promote educational awareness of mental disorders that can lead to suicidal attempts and completions. It is also important to promote awareness of ways to recognize the signs of an individual in suicidal crisis. If families and their communities are educated and made aware of the issues related to suicide, collectively they can work toward saving the lives of our young Black males. When there is neither recognition of risk nor a clear meaning of suicide or mental illness in a community, members will not work together at developing facilities for suicide prevention, intervention, and postintervention (after the fact).

Dissemination strategies should also focus on risk factors such as increased drop-out rates, teen pregnancy, substance use, unemployment, and protective factors such as family and community support networks, expanded secondary education, employment, sex education and family planning, as well as access to culturally sensitive drug prevention and treatment, and mental health counseling. Given that a large number of Black youth end up in the criminal justice system, efforts for identifying youth at risk should be located not only in the educational system, but in the juvenile and adult criminal justice systems (Gibbs & Hines, 1989). A systems-care approach needs to be established in the school systems to allow for a broader assessment of mental health conditions. This includes the existence of poor grades and absenteeism.

There are many youth suicide prevention programs designed for the schools such as the Yellow Ribbon Program, Living Works Education, Inc., and QPR, Inc. These programs are varied but all provide general information on suicide, and give simple crisis management techniques, and some teach how to detect suicidal intent in peers. These programs are significant and need to be utilized in inner city schools. There are several crisis hot lines that are also available to youth, such as the newly developed hotline owned by the government (800-273-TALK). In addition, the following are key points to consider when working with potentially suicidal young African-American males:

1. Learn to ask the suicide question. It is critical that those who work with young African-American males and females feel comfortable and confident in asking about the presence of suicidal thoughts, feelings, plans, and history of suicidal behavior. For example, "When you say 'They'll be sorry' when you're gone, I wonder if that means you're thinking of committing suicide?"
2. Develop a knowledge base of the signs of depression so that one can begin to recognize when someone is suffering from depression. For example, these may include in addition to those listed earlier, significant weight loss, insomnia or hypersomnia, fatigue or loss of energy, feelings of hopelessness, worthlessness, guilt, and self-reproach, recurring thoughts of death, and depressed mood.
3. Many youth feel suicidal when they are feeling desperate, angry, guilty, worthless, lonely, sad, hopeless, and helpless. Help them to be able to get in touch with these feelings.

Allow youth to grieve their losses without expecting them to "get over it." Youth do not know how to grieve. It is a process that is learned. Help them get through the grief-work when they lose a classmate, parent, or relative to acts of violence or an illness, or when their parents break up. When they experience any kind of loss, it is essential to allow for the mourning or grieving of the loss.

CONCLUSION

Recent dramatic fluctuations in suicide rates should not be ignored especially when the causes for the increases are unclear. New research has been proposed and the findings of these empirical studies should be implemented into practice recommendations and policy that impact African-American communities. In the meantime, because young African-American males are at risk, it is necessary to immediately begin promoting risk factor awareness information into protective factor information and preventive intervention initiatives, and existing outreach and treatment programs.

CHAPTER SUMMARY

This chapter discussed the suicidal rates and behaviors, risks and protective factors of suicide prevention, and strategies for solving suicidal behaviors amongst the young African-American males. As indicated, suicide rates have increased among the African-American males and are the third leading cause of death after homicide. This increase is due in part to high rates of homicide, drug abuse, and alcoholism prevalent in many African-American communities. In addition, other factors such as unemployment, crime, poverty, and oppression play a great role in the recent increase. As documented, slaves will choose to commit suicide rather than being taking away from Africa.

Practitioners and family members are encouraged to be aware of the risk factors for suicide among the young African-American males. These include availability of guns in the community, major loss in the family, clinical depression, substance abuse, and poverty. These factors can contribute to self-destructive behavior of an African-American male youth. The knowledge and importance of spirituality in the lives of many African-American males contribute to their unhealthy attitudes, because spirituality positively influences the relationship amongst individuals.

Some strategies to prevent suicidal behaviors among young African-American males include programs and services that promote educational awareness of mental disorders that can contribute to suicidal behaviors. Efforts should be made to identify the risk factors earlier, such as increased drop-out rates, teen pregnancy, substance abuse, and unemployment, and to utilize the protective factors already in place to help African-American youth, such as family and community support networks, expanded education, family planning, drug prevention, and treatment.

GROUP OR CLASSROOM ACTIVITIES

1. Set up a depression screening program every six months within your organization or institution. There are organizations, such as certain chapters of the Delta Sigma Theta Sorority, Inc., for example, which will assist an organization with depression screening. Locate a Delta Sigma Theta Sorority chapter in your area; create a partnership with the chapter for establishing an ongoing screening program.
2. This exercise is intended to assist participants in asking the suicide questions. In groups of five, role-play different responses to an affirmative response from a young man to your question: "When you say, 'They'll be sorry' when you're gone, I wonder if that means you're thinking of committing suicide?"

REFERENCES

Akbar, N. (1981). Mental disorder among African-Americans. *Black Books Bulletin,* 7(2), 18-25.

Asante, M. K. (1991). *Afrocentricity.* Trenton, NJ: Africa World Press.

Baca-Garcia, E., Diaz-Sastre, C., Garcia-Resa, E., Blasco, H., Braquehais-Consea, D., Oquendo, M., et al. (2004, November 19). Suicide attempts and impulsivity. *European Archives of Psychiatry Clinical Neuroscience, 255*(2), 152-156.

Banks, R., Hogue, A., Timberlake, T., & Liddle, H. (1996). An Afro-centric approach to group social skills training with inner-city African American adolescents. *Journal of Negro Education, 65*(4), 414-423.

Barnes, D. H., & Bell, C. C. (2003). Paradoxes of Black suicide. *Preventing Suicide, 2*(1), 2-4.

Brisbane, F., & Womble, M. (1985-1986). Treatment of black alcoholics. *Alcoholism Treatment Quarterly, 2*(3/4), 1-11.

Centers for Disease Control and Prevention. (1992). *Youth Suicide Prevention Programs: A Resource Guide.* Atlanta: US Department of Health and Human Services, Public Health Services.

Center for Disease Control and Prevention. (1998a). Suicide among African American youths: United States, 1980-1995. *Morbidity and Mortality Weekly Reports, 47,* 193-196.

Centers for Disease Control and Prevention. (1998b). Suicide among black youths—United States, 1980-1995. *Morbidity and Mortality Weekly Report, 47,* 193-196.

Clark, R., Anderson, N. B., Clark, V. R., & Williams, D. R. (1999). Racism as a stressor for African Americans. *American Psychologist, 54,* 805-816.

Clark, D. C., & Fawcett, J. A. (1992). An empirically based model of suicide risk assessment for patients with affective disorders. In D. G. Jacobs (Ed.), *Suicide and Clinical Practice* (pp. 55-73). Washington, DC: American Psychiatric Press.

Clay, R. (2000, Spring). Jail diversion programs enhance care. *Substance Abuse and Mental Health Services Administration, SAMHSA News, 8*(2).

Delgado, M. (1997). Strengths-based practice with Puerto Rican adolescents: Lessons from a substance abuse prevention project. *Social Work in Education, 19*(2), 101-112.

Early, K. E. (1992). *Religion and Suicide in the African American Community.* Westport, CT: Greenwood Press.

Fawcett, J., Clark, D. C., & Scheftner, W. A. (1991). The assessment and management of the suicidal patient. *Psychiatry Medicine, 9*(2): 299-311.

Furstenberg, F. F. (1993). Divided families. *Journal of Social Policy, 22,* 130-131.

Garland, A. F., & Zigler, E. (1993). Adolescent suicide prevention: Current research and social policy implications. *American Psychologist, 48*(2), 169-182.

Garmezy, N. (1985). Stress-resistant children: The search for protective factors. In J. E. Stevenson (Ed.), *Recent Research in Development Psychopathology.* Oxford: Pergamon Press.

Gibbs, J. T. (1997). African American suicide: A cultural paradox. *Suicide and Life Threatening Behavior, 27,* 68-79.

Gibbs, J., & Hines, A. (1989). Factors related to sex differences in suicidal behavior among black youth. *Journal of Adolescent Research, 4,* 152-172.

Goldsmith, S., Pellmar, T., Kleinman, A., & Bunney, W. (Eds.). Committee on Pathophysiology & Prevention of Adolescent & Adult Suicide, Board on Neuroscience and Behavioral Health, Institute of Medicine. (2002). *Reducing Suicide: A National Imperative.* Washington, DC: The National Academies Press.

Harvey, A. R., & Rauch, J. B. (1997). A comprehensive Afrocentric rites of passage for Black adolescents. *Health and Social Work, 22,* 30-37.

Holmes, C. (1977). An ethnographic look at black upward mobility as it relates to internalization versus externalization factors in the increase in black suicide. *Dissertation Abstracts International, 33B,* 902.

Joe, S., & Kaplan, M. (2001). Firearm-related suicide among young African-American males. *Psychiatric Services, 53*(3), 332-334.

Joe, S., & Marcus, S. C. (2003). Trends in race and gender in suicide attempts among US adolescents, 1991-2001. *Psychiatric Services, 54,* 454.

Kresnow, M. J., Ikeda, R. M., Mercy, J. A., Powell, K. E., Potter, L. B., Simon, T. R., et al. (2001). An unmatched case-control study of nearly lethal suicide attempts in Houston, Texas: Research methods and measurements. *Suicide and Life Threatening Behavior, 32*(1), 7-20.

Lawson, W. B. (2002). *Suicide and Bipolar in African Americas.* Presented at the National Organization for People of Color Against Suicide, Fifth Annual Conference, Durham, North Carolina, February 3.

Lester, D. (1998). *Suicide in African Americans.* Philadelphia: Nova Science Publishers, Inc.

Mattis, J. (2000). African-American women's definitions of spirituality and religiosity. *Journal of Black Psychology, 26,* 101-122.

Miller, D. B., Webster, S. E., & MacIntosh, R. (2002). What's there and what's not: Measuring daily hassles in urban African American adolescents. *Research on Social Work Practice, 12*(3), 375-388.

National Institute of Mental Health. (2001). Dying for a drink. Global suicide prevention should focus more on alcohol use disorders. *British Medical Journal, 323*(7317), 817-818.

New Freedom Commission on Mental Health (NFCMH). (2003). *Achieving the Promise: Transforming Mental Health Care in America.* Rockville, MD: Office of The President's New Freedom Commission on Mental Health.

Nisbet, P. (1996). Protective factors for suicidal Black females. *Suicide and Life-Threatening Behavior, 26,* 325-341.

Okwumabua, J., & Wong, S. P. (2003). *Anger Expression Mode, Depressive Symptoms, Decision Making, and Hopelessness Among African American Adolescents.* Presented at the American Academy of Health Behavior Scientific Conference, St. Augustine, Florida, March 16.

Oliver, W. (1989). Black males and social problems: Prevention through Afrocentric socialization. *Journal of Black Studies, 20*(1), 15-39.

Owens, L. (1976). *This Species of Property.* New York: Oxford University Press.

Poussaint, A. (1975). Black suicide. In R. A. Williams (Ed.), *Textbook of Black-Related Diseases* (pp. 707-714). New York: McGraw-Hill.

Poussaint, A., & Alexander, A. (2001). *Lay My Burden Down: Unraveling Suicide and the Mental Health Crisis Among African-Americans.* Boston: Beacon Press.

Primm, A.B. (2005). *Your Blues Ain't Like Mine: Depression Across the Life Cycle.* Presentation at the annual Lonnie B. Mitchell Conference, Baltimore, Maryland.

Prudhomme, C. (1938). The problem of suicide in the American Negro. *Psychoanalytic Review, 25,* 187-204, 372-391.

Rodney, H., & Mupier, R. (1999). Behavioral differences between African American male adolescents with biological fathers and those without biological fathers in the home. *Journal of Black Studies, 30*(1), 45-61.

Rodney, H., Tachia, H., & Rodney, L. (1999). The home environment and delinquency: A study of African American adolescents. *Families in Society, 80*(6), 551-559.

Rutter, M. (1987). Psychosocial resilience and protective mechanisms. *American Journal of Orthopsychiatry, 57*(3), 316-331.

Saluja, G., Iachan, R., Scheidt, P., Overpeck, M., Sun, W., & Giedd, J. (2004). Prevalence of and risk factors for depressive symptoms among young adolescent, *Archives of Pediatrics and Adolescent Medicine, 158*(8), 760-765.

Schiele, J. H. (2000). *Human Services and the Afro-Centric Paradigm.* Binghamton, NY: The Haworth Press.

Shaffer, D., Gould, M., & Hicks, R. C. (1994). Worsening suicide rate in Black teenagers. *American Journal of Psychiatry, 151*(12), 1810-1812.

Shelton, D. (2002). Health status of young offenders and their families. *Journal of Nursing Scholarship, 32,* 173.

Strawbridge, W. J., Cohen, R. D., Shema, S. J., & Kaplan, G. A. (1997). Frequent attendance at religious services and mortality over 28 years. *American Journal of Public Health, 87*(6), 957-961.

Tierney, J., & Grossman, J. B. (2000). *What Works in Promoting Positive Youth Development: Mentoring.* Philadelphia, PA: Public/Private Ventures.

U.S. Department of Health and Human Services. (2001). *Mental Health: Culture, Race, and Ethnicity/A Supplement to Mental Health: A Report of the Surgeon General.* Rockville, MD: Office of the Surgeon General.

Wallace, J. M., Brown, T. N., Bachman, J. G., & Laveist, T. A. (2003). The influence of race and religion on abstinence from alcohol, cigarettes and marijuana among adolescents. *Journal of Studies on Alcohol, 64*(6), 843-848.

Washington, G. (2003). *An Analysis of the Influence of Afrocentric Values and the Drug Attitudes of Young African-American Males.* Unpublished doctoral dissertation, Clark Atlanta University, Atlanta, Georgia.

Washington, G., Johnson, T., Jones, J., & Langs, S. (2007). African-American boys in relative care: A culturally centered group mentoring approach. *Journal of Social Work in Groups.*

Werner, E., & Smith, R. (1992). *Overcoming the Odds: High-Risk Children from Birth to Adulthood.* Ithaca: Cornell University Press.

Willis, L. A., Coombs, D. W., Drentea, P., & Cockerham, W. C. (2003). Uncovering the mystery: Factors of African American Suicide. *Suicide and Life Threatening Behavior, 33*(4), 412-429.

Wilson, A. N. (1978). *The Developmental Psychology of the Black Child.* New York: Africana Research Publications.

Chapter 11

Social Supports
of Elderly African Americans
with Mental Health Concerns

Brenda K. J. Crawley

In the past, the mental health problems of elders have remained un-treated across all cultural groups. It is common knowledge that elders do not use community mental health centers and only a small percentage (less than 5 percent) of older adults seek help from mental health professionals. When they do have mental health complaints, most elderly seek help from a primary care physician. Minority elders are often reluctant to seek help because of their cultural backgrounds and beliefs about mental illness. Yet, it has been suggested that 15 to 25 percent of all elders older than 65 have some mental health concerns that are serious enough to require treatment. The lack of usage of mental health services by minority elders continues to be a concern for health providers (Wykle, 1999, p. 127).

This description bodes both an ill future as well as a hopeful one. In general, an elderly person's mental health concerns will continue to be plagued by an avoidance of mental health professionals and services. On the other hand, the past can serve as a wake-up call to undertake a rigorous plan of action backed by adequate resources to serve the geriatric mental health care needs of all elderly accompanied by a commitment to serve disenfranchised, vulnerable, and minority elders (Biegel, Jonsen, & Shafran, 1997; Neighbors & Jackson, 1996a,b; Pickett-Schenk, 2002). This chapter addresses some of the issues facing senior Black Americans with mental health care needs and their social supports. Not only have cultural background and beliefs about mental illness affected their limited use of mental health services but their experiences with culturally insensitive and incompetent

Mental Health Care in the African-American Community
© 2007 by The Haworth Press, Inc. All rights reserved.
doi:10.1300/5364_11

social/human/health/mental health service professionals have also influenced them. The following case study is illustrative of factors that influence help-seeking behaviors and the role of family, friendship networks, and religious support systems.

CASE STUDY

Mr. Carlton could be found sitting in his favorite chair near a window with a blank stare. He was responsive when spoken to, but rarely broached engagement with others. His family had come to accept his behavior and modes of interaction, or lack thereof, almost from the start twenty years ago. When he was clinically diagnosed as depressed (often an unusual diagnosis for African Americans who are more frequently diagnosed with more profound non-affective mental illnesses), his wife and four children, although shocked and disbelieving that this "illness" (attitude factor) had struck their family (a social support system), made a pact to stand by him at all costs to keep the family together and strong. This was not an easy decision, because the family members were afraid of emotional and mental illness. The stigma, the lack of knowledge about mental illness, the lack of experience with persons who had mental health concerns, preconceived negative ideas about mental health practitioners and services, fear of the medical costs, and more, created enormous barriers they were willing to face and overcome in their commitment to help their husband and father.

For the Carltons, it was and is a family affair (social support factor). They supported him by helping him take his medications and they read up on his illness to keep up with advances in treatments and medications. They occasionally attended events with him at the community health center (social support factor); even though they never attended his group sessions, they always made certain that he kept his appointments.

Mr. Carlton experienced a welcomed and needed response from his family. His experience, however, was uncommon for many families in general and for African-Amrican families in particular. We discuss several features of Mr. Carlton's diagnosis and familial response, which are unique, in the following.

PROFILE OF OLDER AFRICAN AMERICANS

This brief profile of older African Americans is taken from the National Caucus and Center on Black Aged, Inc. (2003), which reflects the latest census data, and uses their age definition as 65 years and older. Older African Americans constitute 8.8 percent of all persons age 65 and older. In 2002, there were 3 million older African Americans, and, as would be expected, there are more older females (60.5 percent) than males (39.5 percent). It is projected that by 2012 there will be close to 4 million older African Americans and there will be a shift in the proportion of males (40.2 percent) and females (59.8 percent). Income from two retirement programs, Social Security and Supplemental Security Income (SSI), account for "one of every two dollars of support for this population" (p. 5). On sum, over one half (56.4 percent) of all Black Americans 65 years of age or older were either poor, marginally poor, or economically vulnerable (p. 7). Although no data were cited for mental health status perceptions of older Blacks, the statistics for physical well-being were 42.5 percent of older men and 42.5 percent of older females reported their health as poor or fair. Finally, for noninstitutionalized older African Americans, although 40.4 percent lived with a spouse, the remaining nearly 60 percent lived either alone (33.2 percent), with a relative other than a spouse (23.2 percent), or with a nonrelative (3.2 percent) (p. 18).

LITERATURE REVIEW

Mental Health Care for the African American Elderly

African-American elderly are a subgroup of the larger elderly population and although the mental health care and social support issues they face reflect their subgroup, they reflect how society responds to the mental health care issues and needs of elderly as a whole.

Defining mental health is a challenge. However, defining it is essential to developing a response. Although definitional controversies abound, two definitions are used in this chapter. One definition focuses on the person's ability to function: Ruiz (as cited in Stanford, 1999) describes ". . . mental health as the ability to function effectively in spite of social demands and expectations. . . . mental disorder is viewed as a state characterized by symptoms that hamper or disrupt the person's ability to respond effectively to the social demands of society." Fellin (1996) cites Blumberg's functional orientation, ". . . at any given phase of the life cycle, mental health generally may be defined as a state in which the individual is in proximate balance with the environment and reasonably able to cope with life's goals, activities, and vicissitudes" (p. 239).

A functional definition both helps and challenges understanding the mental care help status of older persons. As functional capacities and abilities decline in older age, the elderly are simultaneously having demands placed on them to occupy a lesser-valued role in a society that values youth. Elderly persons who are or become unable to keep up or function in meeting the demands of society because of diminished emotional and/or psychological/mental health conditions are especially vulnerable. These individuals possess a double stigma, old and mental health-challenged. When the impact of race, in a race-based society like the United States, is factored in, a triple societal-induced stigma exists against individuals who are, for example, older, mental health challenged, and Black Americans. Of course, quadruple-stigmatized and quintuple-stigmatized statuses exist when additional socioeconomic and/or gender factors are included (Murray & Peacock, 1996; Poussaint & Alexander, 2000). The complexity of the issue of mental health functioning in old age combined with multiple stigmas produces a general population group of people who are often ignored in the mental health care system. These individuals are considered to have lived their lives. Resource paucity does play a large part in deciding which populations to serve, at what point/stage in their lives, with what resources, and at what cost (USDHHS, 1999). When the general older population is less valued than younger groups and is more negatively stigmatized as a group (like African Americans who are additionally stigmatized), it can be reasonably expected to fare less well. As will be noted, the need of social support(s) becomes even more critical for this group of elders.

The plethora of topics affecting the mental health care of older African Americans cannot be adequately captured in a chapter. These include, but are not limited to, help-seeking behaviors; addictions; stereotyping; prejudice, discrimination and racism; coping knowledge and skills; service delivery issues and concerns; diagnostic systems and diagnoses; barriers to services; culturally competent professionals; the role of culture in identifying, defining, and treating mental illness; the mental health-mental illness continuum; prevention and treatment; social supports; issues of equality and equity; sociocultural context of mental health and mental illness; voluntary and involuntary commitment; research; evidence-based practices; and more (Biegel et al., 1997; Neighbors & Jackson, 1996a,b; USDHHS, 1999). This chapter covers insurance coverage, attitudes toward mental illness and mental health issues, availability of mental health culturally relevant practitioners, use of mental health services, and social supports.

Insurance Coverage

African-American elderly in general lack insurance coverage for mental health services. This lack takes the form of either no insurance coverage or modest coverage for health or mental health services (Poussaint & Alexander,

2000; USDHHS, 1999). These elderly are dependent on public services for mental health care. Even those who have some type of insurance coverage may find it insufficient as a result of the mental health parity situation (Boden, Cochand, Nelson, & Potter, 2004; Fellin, 1996; Poussaint & Alexander, 2000). Moreover, whether with or without insurance coverage, factors such as attitudes toward mental illness, availability of culturally aware mental health professionals, and other factors interact with access to and use of mental health care services. For example, Mr. Carlton is not poor; in fact, he is solidly middle-income level. He would not have been able to initially obtain mental health care services without his health insurance. Even with health insurance, the coverage for mental health/behavioral services is so limited that care for any other situation is available to him only via local public services. Given that about one half of older Black Americans receive their income from Social Security and SSI, they have extremely limited or no means for securing mental health service beyond the "safety net" provisions of the overwhelmed public mental health services system (NCBA, 2003).

ATTITUDES TOWARD MENTAL ILLNESS/ MENTAL HEALTH ISSUES

African Americans in general, and African-American elderly in particular, are much more likely to attribute emotional, psychological, and mental symptoms to physical ailments and conditions (Biegel et al., 1997; Neighbors, 1985; Neighbors & Jackson, 1996b). A diagnosis of mental illness of any type remains highly stigmatizing for Black American individuals, families, and communities (Biegel et al., 1997; Mays et al., 1996; Poussaint & Alexander, 2000; USDHHS, 1999). A long history of prejudice, discrimination, stereotypes, and racism has produced adaptive, survival, and *thriving* skills and ways not understood by dominant group members (Denby, Rocha, & Owens-Kane, 2004; Gibson & McCoy, 2004). Black America's varied and many multifaceted adaptive patterns have not been added into the general lexicon or the extensive mental health and mental illness research literature. Also, as a highly stigmatized race/ethnicity within this country, African Americans are reluctant to attract further negative attention to themselves by using a stigmatized system such as mental health/ mental illness programs and services (Biegel et al., 1997; Mays et al., 1996; Neighbors, 1985; Poussaint & Alexander, 2000; USDHHS, 1999).

Because of demands for multiple adaptive and/or resistive perspectives and responses in all areas of daily living, along with limited resources to address so-called "abnormal" and "deviant" thoughts and behaviors, Black American individuals, families, and communities have been forced to accept a much broader range of nontraditional speech, thinking, and behavior (Biegel, 1997; Poussaint & Alexander, 2000). Threatening behavior to oneself or others has always had to be dealt with, but the overall range of expressions and behaviors have been and continue to be very broad. As a heterogeneous subgroup, African Americans do not possess monolithic responses or perspectives as to "normal" thinking or behaviors (Freeman & Logan, 2004; Mays et al., 1996; Neighbors & Jackson, 1996a,b; Poussaint & Alexander, 2000). Blumberg's functional orientation as identified previously precludes some kind of "proximate balance" with a racist environment, whether that environment is described in terms of "old fashioned racism" or "modern-quiet racism" (Lowy, 1991). It is the environment within which African Americans find themselves. It would be clearly maladaptive to accept being comfortable with having all aspects of one's group's culture, for example, language, dress, color, body size, entertainment, belief systems, and more, historically and routinely marginalized and negatively criticized.

Elderly African Americans have trained themselves to be stoics, stalwarts, and resisters to the norm of adapting to their marginalized status in society. Having a "breakdown" emotionally or mentally was not an option; one simply kept going, one made the best of things. Both men and women were expected to be strong. Black women, however, like women almost everywhere, were allowed a much broader range of affective expressions than males. Broman (1996), using the National Survey of Black America data, found that women use prayer as a coping means. In contrast, males were more likely to use drinking or getting high as a strategy (p. 127).

Mental health status is not only related to race-based experiences, but is also significantly influenced by socioeconomic and cultural factors. What is stressful for one group may not be perceived as stressful or debilitating to another person or (sub)cultural group society in society. Older Black Americans have experienced subcultural cohort events and conditions that profoundly affect what constitutes an intrapersonal, interpersonal, and/or (sub)cultural group problem(s), distressful situations, external help-seeking behavior, and more. Adaptive coping styles were passed down from previous generations. Hence, attitudes about mental health, mental illness, and coping strategies are reflected in today's senior African-American views about mental health care. Mays, Caldwell, and Jackson (1996) speak of African Americans' reluctance to seek help as not being consistent to African-American cultural coping styles, which emphasize the use of informal systems and the ability to "do it" oneself (p. 163).

AVAILABILITY OF CULTURALLY RELEVANT
MENTAL HEALTH PRACTITIONERS

It is not simply a matter of having adequate numbers of mental health practitioners available. It is also critical that there exist mental health professions who can accurately diagnose and provide culturally relevant services to older African Americans. Poussaint and Alexander (2000) note "For example, in many instances, white mental health practitioners—conditioned by years of cultural stereotypes depicting blacks as leading emotionally uncomplicated lives—have trouble acknowledging depression in black Americans. Consequently, severe clinical depression is often under diagnosed among black Americans" (p. 16).

African-American mental health professionals represent a miniscule proportion of professional mental health providers; only 2 percent of psychologists, 2 percent of psychiatrists, and 4 percent of social workers are in the mental health fields (USDHHS, 1999). It is certainly not the case that all or most of the professionals represented by these data are interested in or have specialized in serving elderly individuals or groups. According to Myers (cited in Thornton & Tuck, 2000), the Black elderly will more than likely represent 33 percent of the total population by the year 2050 (p. 192). As their numbers swell, there will be even greater demand for African-American mental health care professionals as well as a broad range of culturally relevant mental health professionals.

It should not be assumed, of course, that all senior Blacks will want same-race practitioners, but in a race-based society it is important to keep the focus on both groups, that is, same race *and* culturally relevant and culturally sensitive mental health professionals. What African-American elders will want are competent and culturally relevant professionals who provide quality mental health services (Mills, 2000; Neighbors & Jackson, 1996a,b). It is critical to undertake action now to develop mental health providers who can serve the aged African Americans. Serving a triple-stigmatized group will require specialized knowledge, perspectives, and skills.

USE OF MENTAL HEALTH SERVICES
AND AFRICAN-AMERICAN ELDERLY

Use patterns of mental health care services are impacted by several factors. Any single factor can be overwhelming for an older African-American consumer of mental health services. Any combination of factors suggests an almost impossible effort in obtaining and using mental health care services.

Factors include availability of programs and services, past experiences with public social/human services systems, means of payment, location of services, and treatment modalities.

There are not enough mental health care programs and services available for all age groups. It is reported, for example, that one in five children have mental health care needs, but not enough programs and services or practitioners are available (USHDDS, 1999). In addition, the Surgeon General's report calls for more mental health services for all age groups (USHDDS, 1999). Past experience in using mental health care services is limited for the majority of older Blacks. Not only have attitudes toward mental illness affected use of services, but many have extrapolated the results of their experiences with the general public health care system into their views about using mental health care services. Experiences with long waits, rude staff, dull and unattractive settings, assignment to interns and not to seasoned skilled physicians, and medications with severe side effects pose barriers to using services already in place.

As already noted, there is a difference in patterns of use based on gender. Older African-American males are less likely to use mental health care services. In addition, socioeconomic status impacts use or nonuse. Although relatively small in number, higher income African-American males are more likely to use private therapist services. For all other older African-American males, public programs serve as a safety net and are used primarily when symptoms are severe and an emergency exists. As noted, African-American men are more likely to self-medicate through alcohol and/or drug use as a response to stressful conditions, including mental health symptoms. Neighbors (1985) pointed out in his study of Black Americans' use of health and mental health services that "very few black respondents who had a serious personal problem [sought] help within the mental health sector" (p. 161). Neighbors speculated that the stigma of having a mental health problem may be an important factor. Age and gender can be intervening factors, as well; for example, older African-American women are less likely to use mental health services than any other age group (Mays et al., 1996, p. 170). This included private therapists, community mental health centers, and others. Older Black women use ministers and other church-related persons and services, and prayer. Overall, use is predicated on culturally relevant and respectful service provision; that is, "individuals who feel understood, in terms of language, background, and inherent beliefs, will be more trusting of mental health approaches, more responsive to treatment, and will obtain more favorable mental health and social outcomes" (Siegel et al., 2000, p. 104).

Social Supports

Approximately one-third of older Black Americans live alone, four out of ten live with their spouses, and of the remaining proportion of noninstitutionalized older Blacks, 23.2 percent live with a relative and 3.2 percent live with a nonrelative. Aside from dementia-related mental health problems, there are rarely studies that examine the social supports of *elderly* African Americans with mental health care needs. Studies that do reference elders and families (Biegel et al., 1997; Crawley, 2004; Guarnaccia, 1998; Neighbors & Jackson, 1996a,b; Pickett-Schenk, 2002; Stanford, 1999) reflect that families employ a variety of clinical and nonclinical interventions, such as talking through and talking out problems and difficulties (e.g., emotional support, assisting the loved one to seek help, invite the loved one to social activities, assisting with functional activities such as taking medications, helping with finances, providing transportation to medical appointments, and assisting with activities of daily living such as personal care and eating). There is also a consistent theme in decades of research on the social supports of elderly African Americans to the effect that spouses, family (siblings, nieces, nephews, cousins, aunts and uncles, and others), friendship networks, church, and church-related persons are available to provide a variety of services to their elderly. Services include financial assistance, emotional and moral support, transportation, and more, as cited previously. It has been documented that these familial supports apply as well to older African Americans with mental health challenges.

NEW OR EXPANDED APPROACHES

The Reach One, Reach All Program

Reaching out to elderly African Americans with mental health needs cannot be separated from their familial and/or community roots. African Americans who live in institutions are not considered in this chapter. This population at least benefits, at varying levels of quality care, from organizational oversight of any mental health problems or concerns experienced by residents. Those elderly African Americans living alone, with family or relevant others, and in senior citizen housing, are the target of the "new" approach indicated. The approach runs counter to U.S. historical responses to social issues and problems. The approach is intended to be both *preventative* as well as responsive to existing issues as stated in the literature review section. In the course of its administration, the "new" approach will inform many current generations with whom the elderly live about the importance of mental health care and services. As well, it will capture those social support networks that assist the elderly with chores within the elderly person's home.

The nature of the *Reach One, Reach All Program* reveals less that is "new" and more that is focused in prioritizing, combining past and present efforts, committing large resources, and promoting a comprehensive approach to addressing the mental health care of older African Americans, while acknowledging that this cannot be successfully accomplished without addressing the cultural context of this group. Characteristics include large resource commitment, labor intensive efforts, a three-year time commitment, use of information and education products, involvement of community persons/residents, and use of community organizations and businesses.

The *Reach One, Reach All Program* attempts to reach households each month with a packet of information regarding mental health and mental illness, what services are available, and service contact information. Every six months, 15 percent of the recipients in each community are visited and asked about their responses to the materials. The responses to the one-page brief survey are logged into a database and distributed to mental health programs to help them keep current with respondents' input. Door knob drop-off packets are used. Each packet contains a one-page graphically attractive write-up on a topic related to mental health/illness (similar to the AGE Page used by the Administration on Aging), a pencil and/or pen with contact information for the local mental health agency(ies), a map with a photograph and directions to the local mental health agency(ies), and several grocery and pharmaceutical store coupons, all contained in a reusable, recycled plastic bag. The bag does not signify that its sole use is to carry mental health literature. The point is to associate the bag with its contents while having it perceived as functional for other purposes. The mental health care information and education bag must not contain too much information; rather, it should contain just enough to allow residents to be comfortable with the product and with receiving the product monthly. In addition, the bags will be distributed at churches, libraries, senior centers, restaurants, pharmacies, and other relevant spots. The duplication and overlap is intentional.

It should be obvious that there are several goals to the use of this approach. One goal is to provide mental health care information on a regular basis to populations/groups that would not usually visit a mental health services agency or attend seminars, workshops, or training in this topic. Another goal is to target geographical areas, as identified by federal, state, and local census and population data where concentrations of persons fifty-five years of age and older are located. Another goal is to provide visibility to a stigmatized service in as many nonthreatening ways as possible. The writing implements are designed to leave a reminder-source for residents to use services in the future if needed. The three-year window of distribution is intended to provide a sustained effort for topic/subject and agency recognition. This is necessary for a group that has a history of negative experiences with public service agencies. Further, many older African Americans will more than likely have to use public mental health services for their safety net sometime in the near future, so it is important that the *Reach One, Reach All Program* has a focused and concentrated effort to both educate and serve this population. Another goal is to work closely with community resources, a recognized social support for numerous older Black Americans. In addition, family and friends, ministers, and church-related persons can be effective in helping persons to seek services using information from the bags. This is and will by no means be a simplistic achievement. There are religious sects and religious leaders who believe that all matters can be addressed and cured through prayer and divine intervention only. And although these faith positions need to be honored, there are sufficient religious leaders and laity who are open to God or the divine working thorough recognized trained helpers, including those involved in mental health. It is also the goal to impact the emerging baby boomer crop of retirees expected over the next decade (NBCA, 2003). Not only are the numbers of such persons huge already, but every subgroup will experience noticeable increases as the years progress. By being further exposed and educated about mental health care in later life (the reason for using geographical concentrations for those fifty-five years of age and older), African-American baby boomers can be targeted as well.

It is not expected that all outreach efforts or programs and services are going to be able to reach 100 percent of any group. The *Reach One, Reach All Program* hopes to target the greatest possible number of older African Americans and their support networks. It is extremely important that local mental health programs and services impacted by the *Reach One, Reach All Program* insure their services are up to date and capable of handling increased demands for service. It is critical that calls for increased training and culturally relevant mental health service professionals be addressed (Siegel et al., 2000). It is also necessary for calls to be heeded by federal, state, and local governments to increase the numbers and quality of mental health care programs and services for seniors (USDHHS, 1999).

The underlying assumptions of this program draw from the information and data presented in the literature review section. Of particular note are African-American attitudes toward and beliefs about mental illness, combined with low mental health care service utilization rates for a variety of reasons, and the likely scenario that these things will not change soon. It is important to think of long-term sustained efforts. Thus, in the absence of a committed and sustained (three years) outreach information and education effort backed by sufficient resources (money and people), it is unclear whether any net can be wide enough to reach the targeted population. Even improvements in existing programs and the new generation of more programs and services will fail without a paradigm shift in this population's awareness of, beliefs about, and use of such services. In short, under the best-case scenario for improving this population's awareness and use of mental health care as needed, a prerequisite paradigm shift is needed.

As with any consumer information and education program, it is ultimately the consumer who decides whether the "product" is sufficiently desirable, wanted, or needed enough to take steps to buy and/or use it. In the absence of knowing about or having as much information as possible regarding a product, however, a consumer cannot even begin the selection process. This does not suggest a total lack of information or knowledge about mental health and mental illness on the part of African Americans and their support systems. The *Reach One, Reach All Program* is designed to inform and educate over time, for example, three years, with a view to shifting views (however slightly or greatly) about mental health problems and care while simultaneously identifying resource availability.

On first glance the *Reach One, Reach All Program* appears untenable because of potential costs and the sheer enormity of the undertaking. Mental health care sought at early onset accompanied by proper diagnosis, management skill training for handling one's condition and/or medication, and providing periodic monitoring and follow-up services may be shown to be sufficiently less expensive than the costs of responding to chronic conditions, and remediation required from the harm done to relationships and social networks through stress of caring for loved ones.

Policymakers should explore this type of information and education approach for a population with the background of reluctance to use mental health care services and avoidance of engaging mental health practitioners and programs. It may not fit a textbook case of rational policymaking and/or program development, but it fits with the marketing blitz increasingly used by numerous sectors in society, such as hospitals, drug companies, human/social service agencies, and others. This blitz is designed to saturate the potential customer base. One of its downsides is customer fatigue at the onslaught of mail received almost daily from many sources seeking the customer's business, brand loyalty, and relationship with products. The upside is that the *Reach One, Reach All Program* gives and informs without direct cost to the "consumer." Researchers can certainly simulate models based upon this approach or variants of it to determine cost-to-implementation outcomes. The most effective cost-to-implementation model can be used. Educators, especially in courses on aging/gerontology, should ask students to critique the approach using criteria such as thoroughness of the concept, political and economic feasibility, areas needing improvement or modification in the model, and the development of alternative information and education models for older African Americans with mental health care concerns and their social networks.

CONCLUSION

Mental health professionals, human services professionals, social workers, psychologists, psychiatrists, and others interested in reaching elderly African Americans with mental health care needs may find it increasingly necessary to share common information and educational outreach efforts. Although the model suggests high costs for implementation, one way to recoup such charges is to seek combining interdisciplinary resources for this common purpose. Short of going into the homes of each person affected directly or indirectly and conducting one-on-one discussion sessions, it seems that previous information and education efforts have not been successful, thus, the under-utilization rates. The zone between one-on-one information and education sessions and maintaining the current arrangement can be bridged by the *Reach One, Reach All Program* or some variant of it. What is certain is that in the absence of a more sustained, rigorous, time-focused, and costly information and education outreach effort, the status quo is guaranteed a long history. It is, however, hoped that society will embrace a new direction in providing information and education on mental health and mental illness for older African Americans who, with their families and communities, are in need of this resource.

SUGGESTED CLASSROOM ACTIVITIES

Activity #1: Visit an agency/organization in your community whose mission is to serve the elderly with the purpose of ascertaining its knowledge of and practice with the mental health issues and challenges faced by its clientele. For example, you might ask questions such as (a) Does your agency/organization serve the elderly with mental health challenges? (b) What mental health challenges/conditions of the elderly do you work with? (c) What interventions or practices do you use with the elderly? (d) How, if at all, does intervention/practice with the elderly differ from that with the non-elderly? (e) Are your professional staff specifically trained in working with the mental health problems/challenges/conditions of the elderly? Are staff trained gerontological mental health practitioners?

Activity #2: Go into an Internet search engine and discover what information it can provide regarding mental health and the elderly. For example, place terms such as (a) mental health and the elderly, (b) mental illness and the elderly, (c) gerontological mental health training, (d) psychology and the elderly. Be creative and insert terms you think will produce results for a search that focuses on mental health and the elderly.

Activity #3: Interview parents, grandparents, and older relatives in an effort to determine their views about mental health issues affecting the elderly. In addition to creating questions with your instructor or fellow students, probe questions such as (a) Do you think seniors/the aged/older persons have mental health issues or problems? (b) If not, why? Does the interviewee think that age and experience has prepared older persons to handle problems and avoid ill mental health? (c) If so, what sorts of mental health challenges/problems do the elderly have? (d) Should mental health/psychological services be made available for the aged/elderly/seniors? Why or why not?

Activity #4: Interview young persons (about ages 22 to 35 years of age) and ask the same questions as in Activity #3.

Activity #5: Compare and contrast the responses from interviews #3 and #4 and make the findings available to the class via a presentation and/or paper.

Activity #6: Write a three- to five-page paper on how you think your family might respond to an elderly family member being diagnosed with a mental illness. Some diagnoses will have greater impact on a family than others. Specify which elderly member might incur the condition; a family might respond differently to a grandparent with a diagnosis and an elderly uncle with a diagnosis. Other factors to cite include age, assume the elderly family member will live in your home, how each member of the family might react, how the total family system will be impacted (will someone have to give up her/his job, a bedroom, will family routines be altered and how), and so forth.

REFERENCES

Biegel, D. E., Johnsen, J. A., & Shafran, R. (1997). Overcoming barriers faced by African-American families with a family member with mental illness. *Family Relations, 46*(2), 163-178.

Boden, B., Cochand, B., Nelson, C., & Potter, R. (2004). Mental health parity: Past, present and future. *Praxis, 4,* 59-68.

Broman, C. L. (1996). Coping with personal problems. In H. W. Neighbors & J. S. Jackson (Eds.), *Mental health in Black America* (pp. 117-129). Thousand Oaks, CA: Sage Publications.

Crawley, B. K. J. (2004). Research on social support systems of the Black elderly: Informal and formal resources. In E. M. Freeman & S. L. Logan (Eds.), *Reconceptualizing the Strengths and Common Heritage of Black Families: Practice, Research, and Policy Issues* (pp 221-233). Springfield, IL: Charles C Thomas Publishers, Ltd.

Denby, R., Rocha, C., & Owens-Kane, S. (2004). African American families, mental health, and living cooperatives: A program and research analysis. In E. M. Freeman & S. L. Logan (Eds.), *Reconceptualizing the Strengths and Common Heritage of Black Families: Practice, Research, and Policy Issues* (pp 72-94). Springfield, IL: Charles C Thomas Publishers, Ltd.

Fellin, P. (1996). *Mental Health and Mental Illness: Policies, Programs, and Services.* Itasca, IL: F. E. Peacock.

Freeman, E. M., & Logan, S. L. (2004). Common heritage and diversity among Black families and communities: An Afrocentric research paradigm. In E. M. Freeman & S. L. Logan (Eds.), *Reconceptualizing the Strengths and Common Heritage of Black Families: Practice, Research, and Policy Issues* (pp. 5-24). Springfield, IL: Charles C Thomas Publishers, Ltd.

Gibson, P. A., & McCoy, R. G. (2004). Cultural maintenance: Building on the common heritage of Black families. In E. M. Freeman & S. L. Logan (Eds.), *Reconceptualizing the Strengths and Common Heritage of Black Families: Practice, Research, and Policy Issues* (pp. 237-265). Springfield, IL: Charles C Thomas Publishers, Ltd.

Lowy, R. (1991). Yuppie racism: Race relations in the 1980s. *Journal of Black Studies, 21*(4), 445-464.

Mays, V. M., Caldwell, C. H., & Jackson, J. S. (1996). Mental health symptoms and service utilization patterns of help-seeking among African American women. In H. W. Neighbors & J. S. Jackson (Eds.), *Mental Health in Black America* (pp. 161-176). Thousand Oaks, CA: Sage Publications.

Mills, T. L. (2000). Depression, mental health and psychosocial well-being among older African Americans: A selective review of the literature. *African American Research Perspectives, 6*(2), 93-104.

Murray, C. B., & Peacock, M. J. (1996). A model-free approach to the study of subjective well-being. In H. W. Neighbors & J. S. Jackson (Eds.), *Mental Health in Black America* (pp. 14-26). Thousand Oaks, CA: Sage Publications.

National Caucus and Center on the Black Aged, Inc. (NCBA). (2003). *Demographic Profile of the African American Elderly.* Washington, DC: Author.

Neighbors, H. W. (1985). Seeking professional help for personal problems: Black Americans' use of health and mental health services. *Community Mental Health Journal, 21*(3), 156-166.

Neighbors, H. W., & Jackson, J. (1996a). Changes in African American resources and mental health: 1979-1992. In H. W. Neighbors & J. S. Jackson (Eds.), *Mental Health in Black America* (pp. 189-212). Thousand Oaks, CA: Sage Publications.

Neighbors, H. W., & Jackson, J. (1996b). Mental health in Black America: Psychosocial problems and help-seeking behavior. In H. W. Neighbors & J. S. Jackson (Eds.), *Mental Health in Black America* (pp. 1-13). Thousand Oaks, CA: Sage Publications.

Pickett-Schenk, S. A. (2002). Church-based support groups for African American families coping with mental illness: Outreach and outcome. *Psychiatric Rehabilitation Journal, 26*(2), 173-180.

Poussaint, A. F. M. D., & Alexander, A. (2000). *Lay My Burden Down: Unraveling Suicide and the Mental Health Crisis Among African-American.* Boston: Beacon Press.

Siegel, C., Davis-Chambers, E., Haugland, G., Banks, R., Aponte, C., & McCombs, H. (2000). Performance measures of cultural competency in mental health organizations. *Administration and Policy in Mental Health, 28*(2), 91-105.

Stanford, E. P. (1999). Mental health, aging, and Americans of African Descent. In M. L. Wykle & A. B. Ford (Eds.), *Serving Minority Elders in the 21st Century* (pp. 160-179). New York: Springer Publishing.

Thornton, K. A., & Tuck, I. (2000). Promoting the mental health of elderly African Americans: A case illustration. *Archives of Psychiatric Nursing, XIV,* 191-198.

U.S. Department of Health and Human Services (USDHHS). (1999). *Mental health: A report of the surgeon general.* Rockville, MD: US Department of Health and Human Services, Substance Abuse and Mental Health Services Administration, Center for Mental Health Services, National Institutes of Health, National Institute of Mental Health. Accessed March 22, 2007, from http://www.mentalhealth.samhsa.gov/features/surgeongeneralreport/home.asp.

Wykle, M. L. (1999). Section Two: Mental health. In M. L. Wykle & A. B. Ford (Eds.), *Serving Minority Elders in the 21st Century* (pp. 127-129). New York: Springer Publishing.

PART IV:
MENTAL HEALTH RESEARCH,
POLICY INITIATIVES,
AND EVIDENCE-BASED PRACTICE

Chapter 12

Conceptualizing Soul
As a Mental Health Resource
in the Black Community

Nicholas Cooper-Lewter

Because we are, I am.

Akan and Ashanti Proverb

African Americans have enjoyed the distinction of being called "soul brothers and soul sisters." For many, soul is about a style of cooking (soul food), a way of speaking (Ebonics), or a genre of music (R&B or hip-hop). Beyond the popular views, soul is really about a world view, realizing potential and experiencing an evolving and resilient approach to life. Soul is about thoughts, feelings, personality characteristics, the self, desires, passions, and the behaviors that demonstrate the strength and potential of "a living soul." A "fully alive soul" has resilience built into its core belief that puts unavoidable suffering to good use by making sense out of the world and its diverse offerings.

Resilience is a strength expressed. The most promising expression of soul can be found in the manner in which many soul sisters and soul brothers successfully process trauma. Believing that doing springs from being, ancient soul healers used this concept as major foci to support growth and to prevent immediate or long-term damage to self-esteem or identity. The spirit or soul within rituals was based in the belief that facing challenges should instruct, strengthen, mature, and heal. For African Americans, soul healing initially was designed to counter the immediate effect of chattelization and the long-term effects of "slave residues" (Cooper-Lewter, 1998).

Mental Health Care in the African-American Community
© 2007 by The Haworth Press, Inc. All rights reserved.
doi:10.1300/5364_12

Forced segregation and enforced Jim Crow etiquette created the need for unique forms of resilience in African Americans, and this chapter examines the concept of soul and resilience and what has been learned from past experiences of African Americans. The chapter will look at what kind of future potential exists for African Americans as well as what daily choices faced by African Americans suggest about their ability to "thrive."

REVIEW OF LITERATURE

Interest in resilience continues to grow in the social sciences. Available literature suggest that many clinical practitioners are interested in helping children and families to be more resilient (Karapetian & Johnson, 2004). Definitions of resilience are numerous. It has been defined as the ability to withstand and rebound from disruptive life challenges, and as the positive pole of an individual's response to stress and adversity (Rutter, 1990; Walsh, 2003).

The value of positive religious faith and spirituality has begun to catch the eye of health care professionals (Pardini, Pante, Sherman, & Stump, 2000). The research suggests that spirituality and religion are not necessarily synonymous. In both cases a more optimistic life orientation and greater perceived social supports seem to support lower levels of anxiety. According to Mackay (2003), researchers have historically been interested in children. The focus has been on attributes of children that are associated with positive adaptation under adverse circumstances (e.g., academic competence or a sense of self-efficacy).

The question of high achievement raises the question of the effect of chronic stress on resilience. Loehr and Schwartz (2001) point out that consistently high achievement requires physical and emotional resilience as well as a sharp intellect. They believe that chronic stress without recovery reduces energy reserves, causes burnout and breakdown, and eventually erodes performance. The internal world of energy reserves and intellect suggests that people need an "opportunity to develop" internal models of security about the world. Childhood is the natural time to develop a sense of emotional well-being. It is believed that healthy and supportive interpersonal relationships with adults would tend to encourage well-being and psychological resilience in children (Siegel, 1999b).

Interest in resilience or the capacity to bounce back from setbacks has produced a number of new therapeutic perspectives. The strengths perspective, for example, which owes its early development to practitioners and researchers who worked with African-American families, has been adopted by the profession of social work (Boyd-Franklin, 1989; McAdoo, 1997; Miller, 1987). The strengths perspective is way of viewing presenting concerns by focusing on identifying how the client system has coped with hardship in the past and on helping different systems use these discovered "strengths" to support needed change. Traditional psychological research has focused on the avoidance of negative outcomes, but interest has been growing in the nature of well-being or positive outcomes in human beings. The idea of "flourishing" has caught the eye of leaders in the field of psychology (Keyes & Haidt, 2003b). According to Selignman (2003), building competency rather than correcting weakness in prevention has become an emerging focus because psychological researchers have discovered that human strengths act as buffers against mental illness.

The strength perspective, coupled with the emphasis in resilience research, has produced different ways of viewing human development. For example, languishing in life or living lives of quiet despair is viewed as more prevalent than major depression in adults. Those who languish or who are running on empty are increasingly being considered "neither mentally ill nor mentally healthy" (Keyes & Haidt, 2003a, p. 11). The following section will discuss the biology, psychology, sociology, and spirituality of resilience.

The Biology of Resilience

Temperament and social experiences help shape the future resilience of a person. "The mind develops at the interface of neurophysicological processes and interpersonal relationships" (Siegel, 1999a, p. 21). This insight suggests that world view and a group's way of "doing culture" should be considered in researching resilience. For example, groups that view the identity within the family as more important than individual identity could have very different interpersonal relationship standards than those groups who champion individualism over family.

Brain research has opened the door for a more holistic understanding of the connection between biology and human behavior in the social environment. "For the growing brain of a young child, the social world supplies the most important experiences influencing the expression of genes, which determines how neurons connect to one another in creating neuronal pathways which give rise to mental activity" (Siegel, 1999a, p. 20).

The Psychology of Resilience

Resilient individuals have a mindset or set of assumptions that help them feel in control of their lives, stand against stress, feel empathic, effectively communicate, problem solve and make decisions, establish goals, learn from experiences, contribute to society, take responsibility for their actions, feel good about themselves, and encourage others to feel good about themselves (Brooks & Goldstein, 2004, p. 3). Resilient people are considered to have habits that make them "highly effective" and their effectiveness is enhanced because they focus on what they can control (Covey, 1989).

The Sociology of Resilience

Recent research has supported the importance of the family and social relationships in the pursuit of realizing potential. Fischer and Rose (1998) suggest that brain development involves a recurring growth cycle of neural networks and learning in which a child learns skills and concepts and then relearns and reworks them anew at each successive optimal level. According to these authors, there is remarkable resilience and plasticity in this growth when children live and learn in adequate environments (Fischer & Rose, 1998).

The Spirituality of Resilience

Spirituality is generally expressed in concepts such as making sense out of nonsense, finding one's voice, discovering a person's purpose, connecting the dots, discovering meaning, and keeping the lifeline open to the divine. Further, it is generally accepted that spirituality is a broader concept than religion, and spiritual expression may or may not involve a particular religious faith or religious institution (Hutchison, 2003). According to Banerjee and Pyles (2004), spirituality in the lives of women of color suggests a vital source of resilience for them.

Analysis of the Research on Resilience in the Context of the African-American Experience

An appreciation of the strength of African-American resilience can be found in nearly every phase of the African-American experience. Clues to the depth of effective family preservation (resilience) models for African Americans are to be found in the strategies already employed by this group (Denby, 1996). Researchers and practitioners have begun to view resilience as a dynamic process of adaptation utilizing protective factors or strengths in the face of risk factors. As suggested earlier, resilience is a dynamic process highly influenced by protective factors. Protective factors are specific competencies that are necessary for the process of resilience to occur (Dyer & McGuinness, 1996).

Increasingly, research on family resilience has become more concerned with protective factors, which reflects an emphasis on family strengths. This emerging focus fits the collective we-ness of the African and African-American world view. Forgetting one's personal and cultural identity has often been unforgivable because the expectation of support by others in times of adversity has been a given in the African-American family. Therefore, examinations of dynamics such as protective factors must include an assessment of possible bias in traditional developmental frameworks (Howard, 1996). Interest in family resilience is a welcome change from the conventional search for the few individuals who seem to thrive while others languish. It is necessary to recognize that without the collective strength and bio-psycho-socio-spiritual health legacies there would be even less examples of "survival" and certainly less "successes" in the face of adversity in the African-American family experience.

The Bio-Psycho-Socio-Spiritual Health Legacies

The study of biology, in general, and anatomy and physiology, specifically, reveals that under stressful conditions hormones are produced to assist the fight or flight response. In a stressful fight or flight response, the body secretes adrenaline. Adrenaline stimulates the liver to produce more glucose and export it into the blood stream for use by the muscles. Stress is placed on the liver because adrenaline keeps the liver from breaking down glucose for its own energy needs. In addition, other stress-related hormones such as growth hormone and cortisol, which counteract the effects of insulin and increase insulin resistance, are produced. Insulin resistance is a primary factor in type 2 diabetes (Becker, 2001).

Today, diabetes mellitus is one of the most serious health challenges facing over 30 million African Americans. Compared to White Americans, African Americans experience higher rates of three diabetes complications: blindness, kidney failure, and amputations. They also experience greater disability from these complications (BlackHealthCare.com, 2000). Even with traditions of resilience, African Americans remain far behind the majority culture in issues of health and mental health (Chapter 1). The subject of Black health and health care is a sensitive discussion because of the multigenerational legacies of racism and discrimination.

In 2000, six of the ten leading causes of death for all age groups in the United States of America were behaviorally based, but carried implications for mental health: diet, stress, sedentary lifestyle, smoking, violence, and accidents (Caucus, 2004). Public education campaigns have shown connections between tobacco and alcohol consumption, obesity, inadequate physical activity, unprotected sex, poor nutrition and heart disease, diabetes, stroke, disease of the liver and lung, acquired immune deficiency syndrome (AIDS), and yet, African-American communities in the fifty states and territories of the United States lead in health-related disparities when compared with the general population. "Current reports suggest that blacks still have the highest death rates among all groups" (Logan & Freeman, 2000, p. 8). Socioeconomic differences may explain some of the disparities, however, even at equivalent education and income levels, the health and mental health of African Americans still reflect unacceptable levels. These ongoing differences suggest that even though members of African-American communities may be resilient in surviving, something essential to realizing their full potential is missing.

THE PSYCHOLOGY OF HEALTHY CORE BELIEF

It is said that "sticks and stones may break my bones, but names will never hurt me"; however, the truth is that names and certainly the experiences that accompany name calling have hurt African Americans. Internalized insults to identity touch in places that, if untreated, tend not to heal. Modern science can now demonstrate the power of words and their cousins, thoughts, on the health and hopes of a people. According to Amen (1998, pp. 56-57), "Most people do not understand how important thoughts are and leave the development of thought patterns to chance. Thoughts have actual physical properties. They have significant influence on every cell in your body." Sara Little, an authority on belief systems and the design of Christian education, says that belief systems: (1) help persons find meaning and make sense of life; (2) help maintain community, identity, and continuity; (3) give Christians direction to life; and (4) link the individual and the community to ultimate reality and purpose (Little, 1983). Among descendants of ancestors who were transformed into property by the process of chattelization and other major stresses, belief systems can give healing and authorize resilience.

Core beliefs that give power to resilience are much more than easily mouthed shibboleths or creeds. They are the bedrock attitudes that govern all deliberate behavior and relationships and all spontaneous responses to crises. These responses reflect beliefs that have been learned in some way. Core beliefs are working opinions about whether life and God can be trusted.

Core beliefs are often mistaken for innate characteristics because they are buried so deep. However, they are not inherited or beyond the influence of training or discipline. They have been acquired through life experiences, and they can be altered likewise. Core beliefs are perhaps most authentically expressed when uttered spontaneously in crisis situations (Cooper-Lewter & Mitchell, 1991).

Core belief that empowers resilience has to do with the response of all sectors of consciousness (rational, intuitive, and emotive in concert) to the slings and arrows of outrageous misfortune, and to the life abundant as well. The issue is not the correctness of formulation, but the adequacy of resolve as evidenced by the ability to keep moving beyond life's unpleasant experiences and realize potential. The resilient ask in word and deed, Are the beliefs we have about ourselves strong enough to change our world? Simply, at the point where core beliefs critically operate, either one has core belief superior to the challenges of life, or one does not.

THE SOCIOLOGY OF THE COLLECTIVE "WE"

Transplanted Africans believed that a healthy whole village was needed to rear children. "To function effectively, every human being needs to feel wanted, connected, accepted, and affiliated . . ." (Cross, 1998, p. 397). Hood (1994) states that in the old world, before negative color consciousness became of such importance, Africans were free to uphold their traditions of relationship management. They were able to determine the proper use of resources in a spirit of community collaboration built on extended family traditions that celebrated shared patterns of belief, feelings, and adaptations, and guided conduct and defined reality. This spirit of the "collective we" has reflected the perils and possibilities of two primary responses to grief—coping and overcoming. African traditions considered intrauterine life as crucial to the development of a child, thus resilience ideally began in the womb. Sweeten the amniotic fluid, and a fetus will increase its swallowing of this fluid. At six months, a fetus has rapid eye movement (REM) in sleep, the kind associated with dreaming; and a fetus feels pain and responds to familiar music, soft soothing sounds, which produces slower heart and breathing rates. A newborn also prefers its mother's voice. The archetype of God as a wise nurturing older female paralleled the Hebrews' use of words for "womb" to mean compassion. For soul brothers and sisters, the presence of compassion meant the soul was conscious of its makeup and connection to God. In the final analysis, the womb could be either a nurturing place or a hostile environment; whichever predominated or affected the unborn the most set the foundation for resilience. The family and the community were extensions of the womb. Individualism existed within the context of family. "Because we are, I am," say the Akan and Ashanti of Africa. In the purest sense, family membership was presumed until proved otherwise. The frequency of greetings such as "Brother" and "Sister" or "Uncle" and "Auntie" provide testimony to the pervasiveness of the belief.

Learning from the past, planning for the future, and living fully in the present with a purpose required understanding the "collective we" history. Just as African ancestors chanted or sang their history, tribal laws, proverbs, and folk stories, their North American progeny have kept the traditions in notable forms such as "moaned bluesy hollers," "whooped street cries," and "black preaching" (Spencer, 1990, p. 228). "The sum of our memories and experiences is responsible for our sense of identity and connectedness to those around us, as well as our character" and ". . . how well we learn from our mistakes depend greatly what we recall from the past" (Amen, 2002, p. 91). Supported by core beliefs that made a person at home in his or her own body and made manifest the understanding that the body and spirit were one, an appreciation for arts, music, and dance was essential. The use of musical affirmations in the form of rhythm, tone, texture, silence, and dance for healing in soulfully therapeutic and liberating ways remains a gift to the global village.

Hidden within these adaptive, counter-aggressive, interrelated, highly therapeutic, psychological response traditions are ways of healing the soul (Cooper-Lewter, 1996). Oral traditions, then and now, could promote healthy relationships because they required a relationship and time shared to pass on stories that impart history, analyzed problems, and provided reality checks. Combining oral traditions with relationships assures times for expression, re-interpretation, reeducation, reinforcement, encouragement, support for rage and anger, counseling, relaxation, and identity building.

THE SPIRITUAL

Ancients understood and modern descendants out of Africa understand that spirit is the soul's purest form. After all, the creator's true form is spirit. Adult or child, each person is a child of God. Closeness and connection to God is the way of the wise. Only the immature or foolish believe that they need neither God nor others. God sees all possible future events in each present choice or demonstration of will. If asked, God would offer guidance, if not, so be it. God as source and foundation is unchanging, whereas God in creation specializes in change or growth. Therefore, soulful children of God are to be hosts for the providential spirit of God and not a hostage to their "earthly" experiences (Cooper-Lewter & Mitchell, 1991, p. 14).

The family accepted custody of its members, believing children were gifts "no matter the circumstances of birth" (Lincoln & Mamiya, 1990, p. 311). If they survived to birth, the family welcomed them. Family members "stood between them" and those "who sought to control them psychologically and to break their wills to resist" (King, 1996, p. 1). Everyone had a certain role to play. One had to accept what happened and find the blessing even in the horrendous. Thus, maternal and paternal roles were more important than marital opportunities. Informal adoptions would take place even when formal ones were denied. Adoption was both an ideal and a standard of collective caring.

Family elders expected that properly nurtured members would develop "something within" that could heal what negative rhetoric could hurt. Mentors reminded family members that they could and should endure in their identity through applied faith and knowledge gained by overcoming the odds. The God within provided the power to endure and develop greatness of soul. No child of God should surrender to the pressures of life or give up in despair. God accepted and used all of a human being for the whole of one's life.

Family love and acceptance could not be earned but were blessings; therefore, the family was to be a place where love, grace, and justice thrived. The family was to be a safe place. "African Americans feel good about themselves when they have good relations with family and friends" (Billingsley, 1992, p. 235). The actions of a providential God engendered gratitude no matter the circumstances. Thus, such things as "waking up in one's right mind" and leaving yesterday behind deserved thanksgiving (Cooper-Lewter & Mitchell, 1991).

Collective resilience has always meant a struggle with two dialectical opposites, a responsive gospel of good news with a movement beyond comfort zones toward potential and an anesthetizing gospel of comfort that puts potential at risk with the sedation of coping mechanisms. "Every black person has participated in making compromises between resistance and accommodation" (Lincoln & Mamiya, 1990, p. 14). In spite of miracles that can be credited to African-American resilience, the latest trends bear witness to increasing numbers of stress-related disorders like diabetes, high blood pressure, and obesity (BlackHealthCare.com, 2000). The current state of health and mental health of Black America suggests that these compromises continue to challenge Blacks in their efforts to overcome the residues of chattelization, Jim Crow etiquette (Kennedy, 1959, 1990), and American

Slave Codes (Goodell, 1853), as well as optimizing their bio-psycho-socio-spiritual health legacies.

THE ROOTS OF RESILIENCE IN BLACK SPIRITUALITY

Science tells us human life began in Africa. And "long before the religion of the crescent or the religion of the cross arrived on the African continent, Africa was at worship, its sons and daughters were at prayer. The universe and the force of life are all manifestations of God" (Mazrui, 1986, p. 135). Resilience was rooted in pre-Christian African spirituality. African spirituality did not require scriptures to be written or holy books to be canonized. Core belief was recorded in the history, hearts, and experiences of the people. "Unlike Christianity and Islam, traditional African religions exhibited an enviable spirit of toleration towards different world views, philosophies, and religion." (Paris, 1995, p. 68). Resulting religious expressions were expected to be pragmatic and honor those who went before. Core beliefs were handed down from one generation to another with the freedom to make changes to suit current circumstances of life.

African spirituality traditionally taught that people were spiritual beings having human experiences. Loss or death of the body (the human vehicle for spiritual expression) was not the death of the person. Therefore, departed family members were invited and expected to take part in the ongoing life of the community. This was often called ancestor worship by outsiders instead of a more accurate characterization of ancestor appreciation. African spirituality was called religion when expressed in practices of ritual, symbols, festivals, art, music, dance, proverbs, riddles, names, myths, legends, customs, rites of passage, ceremony, and daily life (Mbiti, 1975, 1991).

Good religion was based on healthy spirituality and healthy spirituality required empowering core belief. Core beliefs, central to resilience, were expected to do the following (Cooper-Lewter, 1996):

- Enable a person to function at full capacity physically, intellectually, emotionally, and spiritually.
- Allow a person to adapt to various situations using self-control and discipline.
- Allow a person to develop and maintain a continuing sense of security despite hardships and traumatic change.
- Allow a person to maintain a sense of her or his own unique identity and purpose.

- Allow a person to develop and maintain a sense of confidence and safety, which makes possible positive humor and comfortable relationships with others.
- Allow a sense of *OK*-ness when alone, and balance day-to-day lifestyle and effectiveness in independent or cooperative roles.
- Allow the experience of *happiness* along with the ability to compete where appropriate and to compromise without feeling undone.
- Allow feelings of empowerment that support an ability to affirm all genders, ethnicities, and peculiar personhoods with the capacity for other centered giving of self.
- Develop and maintain dependability without being rigid but with a capacity for dispensing balanced emotions.
- Develop and nurture a positive sense of relationship to God and God's creation however stated or envisioned.

Transported to the Americas, the collective's application of empowering or healthy core beliefs met the need of slaves to feel included and soothed amidst unremitting assaults on their souls.

The Historical Need for Resilience

Soul as a core concept and its part in the resilience of African Americans requires a historical context to be fully appreciated. This context includes one's individual identity and the interplay of multiple systems. Among these are the biological, the intrapsychic, and the interpersonal. The systems dynamically coexist along the time dimension to create a continuous conception of life from past through present to the future. "Exposure to trauma causes a rupture . . ." (Danieli, 1998, p. 7). Thus, trauma can shake the foundation of what makes the world safe and secure and how one perceives oneself. Chattelization is the traumatic process of convincing people that they are things or property. Chronic and acute episodes of terror are essential tools for scraping away the resolve of people to resist the affects of kidnapping, sexual and domestic abuse, and educational or religious indoctrination. "African Americans have been taught to feel ashamed of slavery" and to "forget 400 years of rapes, lynchings, beatings, and murders" (Browder, 1996, p. 112). The Maafa is a Kiswahili term for "disaster" or "terrible occurrence" and has been adopted by many to keep in mind the trauma of the African holocaust (colonization, chattelization, and slavery) and their commitment that it will never happen again (Ani, 1994). This remembering and commitment is part of the need to rebuild one's assumptive world. This is an essential ingredient in resilience.

Africans were kept in dungeons before they were tightly packed on slave ships for the journey to the New World. Children were easier to transport and more economical. They were smaller and less rebellious than adults. A child traumatized early in life will have an alteration in physiological response, such that small stressors lead to large hormonal responses (Siegel, 1999a, p. 20). Thus, their middle passage experience was an endurance race punctuated by stress-related hormonal changes. They were packed and chained into every little space on the slave ships for the six- to eight-week journey across the Atlantic Ocean. There were revolts; many future chattel died, some committed suicide, others went insane, whereas others endured.

People can become grief-stricken simply because of frustrations or deprivations exceeding the limits of individual tolerance. The early symptoms of grief include common emotions such as sadness, despair, fear, guilt, longing, and a lack of interest in life's potential. The Maafa did not end with the voyage to the New World. The experiences of Mary Turner are one example of the lingering legacy of the "terrible occurrence" (Ani, 1994).

> After learning of the lynching of her husband, Mary Turner, in her eighth month of pregnancy, vowed to find those responsible, swear out warrants against them, and have them punished in the courts. For making such a threat, a mob of several hundred men and women were determined to "teach her a lesson."
>
> After tying her ankles together, they hung her from a tree head down. Dousing her clothes with gasoline, they burned them from her body. While she was still alive, someone used a knife ordinarily reserved for splitting hogs to cut open the woman's abdomen. The infant fell from her womb to the ground and cried briefly, whereupon a member of this Valdosta, Georgia, mob crushed the baby's head beneath his heel. Hundreds of bullets were then fired into Mary Turner's body. (Allen, Als, Lewis, & Litwack, 2000, p. 14)

The silence of perpetrators, victims, and witnesses does not alleviate the need to heal insulted souls and provide meaningful answers to experiences of repeated terror. For Mary Turner, the cultural context in which the trauma took place was not unpredictable. Naiveté or hopefulness may have been Mary Turner's greatest mistake, but her crime was believing that Jim Crow etiquette afforded her the same justice enjoyed by her torturers and executioners (Kennedy, 1959, 1990).

Whispers about Mary Turner and others in the form of "sacred secrets" are still transmitted in Valdosta, Georgia. Multigenerational transmission of trauma is an integral part of human history. Transmitted in word, writing, body language, and even in silence, it is as old as humankind. Nevertheless, only scant attention has been paid in religious and classical literary texts to the intergenerational transmission of victimization (Danieli, 1998).

African-American resilience can be seen in the mass migrations north to urban centers. African-American slaves and freemen had lived in New York since colonial times. The 1890s through the 1920s showcased "a dynamic community" emerging in Harlem. This dynamic community was home to the Harlem Renaissance. In the years before the Great Depression, "Harlem . . . represented for many the aspirations and possibilities of a people in the midst of one of the greatest migrations in American history. Harlem now connotes violence, crime, and poverty" (Huggins, 1971, p. 4).

There were the writers like Countee Cullen, Langston Hughes, Zora Neale Hurston, and James Weldon Johnson, and artists like Aaron Douglas and later Romare Bearden (artist and social worker).

New York's Northside Center, the dream of Kenneth and Mamie Clark "was a microcosm of the world the Clarks wanted: a world of social equality, humanity, integration, and caring for all children and their families, without regard to race and circumstance. It was a place where children, in particular, could learn to value their own worth and abilities and believe that they could shape their own future" (Markowitz & Rosner, 1996, p. 250). Yet, "in many ways, the crisis today is as bad, if not worse, than fifty years ago" (Markowitz & Rosner, 1996, p. 250).

Ironically, a hellish life can produce an antagonist to multigenerational legacies of grief as well as multigenerational legacies of resilience. African Americans sing gospel in church and sing it so well; it is a form of the blues (Spencer, 1990, pp. vii-viii). There has always been healing to be experienced and potential to be realized in the balmy singing and moaning styles that soothed their indigenous grandparents and great-grandparents. Although coping is a valid response in extreme situations of survival, for potential health sake, one must eventually "move beyond the things that crucify potential." Coping core belief, without "moving beyond" core belief, results in people being unable to extricate old grief within self and community sufficiently enough to enter a new, sustainable "promised land." "What cannot be talked about can also not be put to rest; and if not, the wounds continue to fester from generation to generation" (Bettelheim, 1984, p. 166).

NEW OR EXPANDED APPROACHES
TO SOUL RESILIENCE AND THE CONCEPT OF SOUL

A positive view of creation among indigenous African ancestors was rooted in sensitivity to God's movement in the world: the birds flying, rivers roaring, flowers spreading their scent, yams sharing their nutrients, and human beings sharing their love. This external world affirmed what the inner self understood, even from that initial merge of egg and sperm. Within the womb, as a dependable and nurturing attachment grew, and as the sense of touch, taste, and hearing emerged, each developing life listened to the rhythm of the mother's heartbeat and the contrapuntal beating of her or his own heart amid the whooshing sounds of embryonic fluid and the assorted audible expressions of the mother's gastrointestinal tract and respiratory system. Muted but definite voices emanated from the world outside the womb, that first biological Garden of Eden. The reassuring sound from the outside world was mother's voice, accompanied by the sensations of rushing blood, adrenaline surges, near weightlessness, the freedom of swimming, the taste of embryonic fluid, and caresses. Then came rhythmic contractions, the pressure of the push through the vaginal canal, the release of birth, the rush of inspiration, the reconnection felt in bonding, the warmth and sustenance of the mother's milk, and the cheers of the family. Deep within the subconscious of each human life, the bio-psycho-socio-spiritual origins of soul therapy are planted!

The "initial environmental experience" of the womb, those pre-intrauterine (with God) and intrauterine experiences of safety, security, and stability, form the basis of the invisible psycho-spiritual and visible sociobiological understandings of the ancestor's indigenous celebrations of creation, whole-self communion, transcendence, and overall connection with the world and its maker, the alpha and omega. This indigenousness is the existential conceptualization of soul as an intervention tool, as it seeks to organize health information in a manner that will help souls prevent, counteract, cope with, and overcome the insults to their humanity. It is the foundation of healthy self-esteem and a necessary ingredient in resilience.

High self-esteem turns mere life into a liveliness that seeks challenges by establishing meaningful and demanding goals, provides energy for coping with and overcoming problems, fuels the ambition to realize full potential, expresses inner riches, supports openness and honesty, attracts one to nourishing instead of toxic relationships, encourages eating to live, and takes the chip off one's shoulder because people and their opinions are no longer fatally threatening.

The African-American community often served as mediator between people and the dominant culture. One example of indigenous resilience are the Gullah of the Georgia and South Carolina coast who nursed their West African culture in an especially fertile environment of few Whites and a number of African medicine men, and fearlessly passed on their African roots (Pinckney, 2000).

In its religious forms, the indigenous community of soul therapists assisted souls in developing a resilient self-concept that could fend off the lethal intrusions of the master culture. This sort of church was an extended family or group of extended family networks with therapeutic value and potential, whose goal of spiritual maturity and emotional health was implemented by verifying an understanding of God (collective lessons of life validated by experience and passed on in sacred/secular forms) within the context of family and community relationships.

The indigenous among the enslaved forebears of today's legacy chattel, sensitive to the psychological effects of chattelization, never took for granted that all slaves could be trusted. For reasons of psychological health, there is a need to trust and a need for trust. But those early protectors of soul routinely held these opposites in tension, constantly shifting between the polarities as events dictated. Embracing the soul concept as a treatment tool requires that individuals speak plainly about the positive and negative—good people have come out of Africa, but not everyone who was out of Africa was "good." Africans enslaved in America have been depicted as very weak, yet the way indigenous forebears dealt with their needs, choosing healthy core beliefs, surviving and thriving, testifies to how they were able to discern aspects of living that were of lesser value than their highest needs—spiritual well-being and sustenance. The chattelization process was developed to make human beings from Africa accept the condition of enslavement. Soul as a treatment tool promoted oral and behavioral traditions that connected people to an energizing past. The healing role of the soul therapist included a vision of a community in which everyone was a responsible and healthy participant. Therapeutic music was used to plant, cultivate, and support the soul making it through the troubles of this world. Rites of passage were used to transfer the essential values needed to nurture a just environment. Progress had to be measurable, and the expectations for passage made the state of progress clear.

Helpers who embrace this concept are expected to understand and help the community practice beliefs and strategies designed to counteract all forms of injury, and to recognize the wide variety of reactions and responses to trauma within the community. Further, it is expected that they understand that problems of survival can be met by relinquishing a lesser need and emphasizing the restorative functions of healthy core beliefs.

CONCLUSION

The demonstrated resilience soul sisters and soul brothers who survive and thrive in the African-American experience deserves more appreciation. The residuals of healthy "therapy for the soul" remain. At the same time, the courage to accept the obvious connections between unhealthy core belief and behavior in the forms of community draining consumerism, tobacco and alcohol consumption, obesity, inadequate physical activity, unprotected sex, heart disease, diabetes, stroke, disease of the liver and lung, and AIDS without a protective narcissistic knee jerk reaction is an essential step. There is a need for more "passaged" soul healers (those who have successfully conquered their own self-limiting core beliefs and habits) to accept "the call to resilience" by confronting the destructive outer forces and inner voices that still grieve the soul brothers and sisters. Actually, soul healing is available to "all people" who want to realize their innate potential.

CHAPTER SUMMARY

This chapter focuses on conceptualizing soul as a useful resource in the African-American community. The author argues that soul healing was initially designed to counter the immediate as well as the long-term effects of enslavement. Reliance is coupled with soul to provide an empowerment, strength-based perspective for framing an expanded way of thinking and talking about African-American mental health. Core beliefs are central to resilience from a historical as well as present-day perspective.

GROUP AND CLASSROOM ACTIVITIES

1. In groups of five, brainstorm as many key words and phrases that reflect the term/concept of resilience.
2. What have African Americans learned from past experiences that, if shared, would benefit the larger society?
3. What behaviors suggest daily choices that enhance or challenge African Americans' ability to "thrive" or experience the present resources fully?
4. Discuss the concept of soul as a mental health intervention.

REFERENCES

Allen, J., Als, H., Lewis, J., & Litwack, L. F. (2000). *Without Sanctuary: Lynching Photography in America.* Washington, DC: Twin Palms Publishers.

Amen, D. G. (1998). *Change Your Brain: Change Your Life.* New York: Three Rivers Press.

Amen, D. G. (2002). *Healing the Hardware of the Soul.* New York: The Free Press.

Ani, M. R. (1994). *Let the Circle Be Unbroken: The Implications of African Spirituality in the Diaspora.* Trenton, NJ: Red Sea Press.

Banerjee, M. M., & Pyles, L. (2004). Spirituality: A source of resilience for African American women in the era of welfare reform. *Journal of Ethnic & Cultural Diversity in Social Work, 13*(2), 45-70.

Becker, G. (2001). *Type 2 Diabetes: An Essential Guide for the Newly Diagnosed.* New York: Marlow & Company.

Bettelheim, B. (1984). Afterword to C. Vegh (R. Schwartz, Trans.). In *I Didn't Say Goodbye: Interviews with Children of the Holocaust* (pp. 166-171). New York: Dutton.

Billingsley, A. (1992). *Climbing Jacob's Ladder: The Enduring Legacy of African-American Families.* New York: Simon & Schuster.

BlackHealthCare.com. (2000). Diabetes in African Americans? Retrieved July 24, 2005, from http://www.blackhealthcare.com/BHC/Diabetes/Description.asp.

Boyd-Franklin, N. (1989). *Black Families in Therapy: A Multisystems Approach.* New York: Guilford.

Brooks, R., & Goldstein, S. (2004). *The Power of Resilience: Achieving Balance, Confidence, and Personal Strength in Your Life.* Chicago: Contemporary Books.

Browder, A. T. (1996). *Survival Strategies for Africans in America: 13 Steps to Freedom.* Washington, DC: The Institute of Karmic Guidance.

Caucus, C. B. (2004, September 8-11). *National Coalition on Health and Behavior.* Paper presented at the Congressional Black Caucus 34th Annual Legislative Conference, Washington, DC.

Cooper-Lewter, N. (1996). *Spiritual Healing/Soul Therapy: A Response to Spiritual Abuse.* Richmond, VA: Virginia Cluster for Pastoral Education in Association with Virginia Union University, School of Theology.

Cooper-Lewter, N. (1998). *Soul Therapy: A Response to Abuse.* St. Paul, MN: American Academy of Religion Society of Biblical Literature Societies Upper Midwest Regional Meeting.

Cooper-Lewter, N., & Mitchell, H. H. (1991). *Soul Theology: The Heart of American Black Culture.* Nashville: Abingdon Press.

Covey, S. (1989). *The 7 Habits of Highly Effective People: Restoring the Character Ethic.* New York: Simon & Schuster.

Cross, W. E., Jr. (1998). Black psychological functioning and the legacy of slavery: Myths and realities. In Y. Danieli (Ed.), *International Handbook of Multigenerational Legacies of Trauma* (pp. 387-400). New York: Plenum Press.

Danieli, Y. (Ed.). (1998). *International Handbook of Multigenerational Legacies of Trauma.* New York: Plenum Press.

Denby, R. W. (1996). Resiliency and the African American family: A model of family preservation. In S. Logan (Ed.), *The Black Family: Strengths, Self-help, and Positive Change* (pp. 144-163). Boulder, CO: Westview Press.

Dyer, J. G., & McGuinness, T. M. (1996). Resilience: Analysis of the concept. *Archives of Psychiatric Nursing, 10*(5), 276-282.

Fischer, K. W., & Rose, S. P. (1998). Growth cycles of brain and mind. *Educational Leadership, 56*(3), 56-60.

Goodell, W. (1853). *The American Slave Code: In Theory and Practice, Its Features Shown by Its Statutes, Judicial Decisions, and Illustrative Facts.* New York: American and Foreign Anti-Slavery Society.

Hood, R. E. (1994). *Begrimed and Black: Christian Traditions on Blacks and Blackness.* Minneapolis: Fortress Press.

Howard, D. E. (1996). Searching for resilience among African-American youth exposed to community violence: Theoretical issues. *Journal of Adolescent Health, 18*(4), 254.

Huggins, N. I. (1971). *Harlem Renaissance.* New York: Oxford University Press.

Hutchison, E. (2003). *Dimensions of Human Behavior: Person and Environment* (2nd ed.). Thousand Oaks, CA: Sage Publishers.

Karapetian, A. M., & Johnson, G. J. (2004). Enhancing resilience in children: A proactive approach. *Professional Psychology: Research and Practice, 36*(3), 238-245.

Kennedy, S. (1959, 1990). *Jim Crow Guide: The Way It Was.* Boca Raton, FL: Atlantic University Press.

Keyes, C., & Haidt, J. (2003a). Introduction: Human flourishing—The study of that which makes life worthwhile. In C. Keyes & J. Haidt (Eds.), *Flourishing: Positive Psychology and the Life-Well-Lived* (pp. 3-12). Washington, DC: American Psychological Association.

Keyes, C., & Haidt, J. (Eds.). (2003b). *Flourishing: Positive Psychology and the Life Well-Lived.* Washington, DC: American Psychological Association.

King, W. (1996). *Stolen Childhood: Slave Youth in Nineteenth-Century America.* Bloomington, IN: Indiana University Press.

Lincoln, C. E., & Mamiya, L. H. (1990). *The Black Church in the African American Experience.* Durham, NC: Duke University Press.

Little, S. (1983). *To Set One's Heart.* Atlanta: John Knox Press.

Loehr, J., & Schwartz, T. (2001). The making of a corporate athlete. *Harvard Business Review, 9*(1), 120-128.

Logan, S., & Freeman, E. M. (2000). An empowerment and health prevention framework for understanding and transforming the health care outcomes of African Americans. In S. Logan & E. M. Freeman (Eds.), *Health Care in the Black Community: Empowerment, Knowledge, Skills, and Collectivism* (pp. 7-22). Binghamton, NY: The Haworth Press.

Mackay, R. (2003). Family resilience and good child outcomes: An overview of the research literature. *Social Policy Journal of New Zealand, 20*, 98-118.

Markowitz, G., & Rosner, D. (1996). *Children, Race, and Power: Kenneth and Mamie Clark's Northside Center.* Charlottesville: University Press of Virginia.

Mazrui, A. A. (1986). *The Africans: A Triple Heritage*. London: BBC Publications.

Mbiti, J. S. (1975, 1991). *Introduction to African Religion* (2nd ed.). Oxford: Heinemann International Literature and Textbooks.

McAdoo, H. (Ed.). (1997). *Black Families* (3rd ed.). Thousand Oaks, CA: Sage.

Miller, D. (1987). *Helping the Strong: An Exploration of the Needs of Families Headed by Women*. Siver Springs, MD: NASW Press.

Pardini, D. A., Plante, T. G., Sherman, A., & Stump, J. E. (2000). Religious faith and spirituality in substance abuse recovery: Determining the mental health benefits. *Journal of Substance Abuse Treatment, 19*(4), 347.

Paris, P. J. (1995). *The Spirituality of African Peoples: The Search for a Common Moral Discourse*. Minneapolis: Fortress Press.

Pinckney, R. (2000). *Blue Roots: African-American Folk Magic of the Gullah People*. St. Paul, MN: Llewellyn Publications.

Rutter, M. (1990). Psychosocial resilience and protective mechanisms. In J. Rolf, A. S. Masten, D. Cicchetti, K. H. Neuchterlein, & S. Wientraub (Eds.), *Risk and Protective Factors in the Development of Psychopathology* (pp. 181-214). New York: Cambridge University Press.

Seligman, M. E. P. (2003). Foreword: The past and future of positive psychology. In C. Keyes & J. Haidt (Eds.), *Flourishing: Positive Psychology and the Life Well-Lived* (pp. xi-xx). Washington, DC: American Psychological Association.

Siegel, D. J. (1999a). *The Developing Mind: How Relationships and the Brain Interact to Shape Who We Are*. New York: The Guilford Press.

Siegel, D. J. (1999b). Relationships and the developing mind. *Child Care Information Exchange, 130*, 48-51.

Spencer, J. M. (1990). *Protest & Praise: Sacred Music of Black Religion*. Minneapolis: Fortress Press.

Walsh, F. (2003). Family resilience: Strengths forged through adversity. In F. Walsh (Ed.), *Normal Family Processes: Growing Diversity and Complexity* (pp. 399-423). New York: The Guilford Press.

Chapter 13

Mental Health Policy: Implications for African Americans

Carrie Jefferson Smith

The response to African Americans in the mental health policy arena is a clear example of the deleterious impact of racism—both historical and contemporary. The mental health system has demonstrated that U.S. mental health policy is plagued with the "baggage of bigotry" (Bush, 2005) in both its implementation and its results for African Americans. Systemic change is needed to overcome the legacy of racism and to dismantle continuing patterns of discrimination that result in disparate mental health outcomes for African Americans.

This chapter uses a policy-practice framework to address disparities in mental health care for African Americans. In addition, several *high-need* groups are identified along with specific social policies that have critical implications for people of color. Although these policies do not ordinarily fall under the general context of mental health policy, they are being used here as exemplars with implications for positive mental health. The chapter then presents a conceptual model for policy analysis pertaining to African Americans. The social policies of the Temporary Assistance to Needy Families legislation (TANF), a part of PL No. 104-193, Personal Responsibility and Work Opportunity Reconciliation Act (PRWORA) of 1996, and the 1997 Adoption and Safe Families Act (ASFA) are examined as a part of this model. A discussion of how African Americans have fared since the implementation of the Community Mental Health Centers Act concludes the chapter.

Mental Health Care in the African-American Community
© 2007 by The Haworth Press, Inc. All rights reserved.
doi:10.1300/5364_13

233

LITERATURE OVERVIEW

The field of mental health is a conundrum of services, policies, practices, and financing structures fraught with controversies and conflicts that often challenge efforts to promote the mental and physical well-being of citizens. Yet mental disorders are among our most prominent health concerns. According to the Campaign for Mental Health Reform (2003), the prevalence of mental disorders, nationally and world wide, is higher than that of any other class of chronic conditions and they impose a significant burden on individuals, their families, and health care systems. Furthermore, in the United States the majority of health expenditures are concentrated on persons with one or more chronic conditions. As measured by the economic burden it creates, mental illness, including depression and manic depression, is among the top five such conditions. As such, the report states, "it is good public policy to ensure that individuals with mental disorders receive early and effective treatment. Failure to provide the effective treatments that now exist burdens both the health system and other social services" (p. 1).

Good public policies, however, do not always result in positive implementation of programs and services. Negative results in policy implementation are the result of myriad issues and a complete discussion is beyond the scope of this chapter, but it is clear that policy is only as good as its implementation. Lipsky (1980) has suggested that those who are tasked with implementing a policy may be confronted with a variety of conflicts, including personal values, inadequate resources and involuntary clients, that may result in agencies performing or engaging in practices that are contrary to their stated policies. The result may be inadequate or unsuccessful policy implementation. Evidence suggests that the implementation of mental health policies in the United States has not been successful for most Americans and has proved to be even less adequate for ethnic minorities. "One of every two Americans who need mental health treatment do not receive it, and the rate is even lower—and the quality of care poorer—for ethnic and racial minorities," according to the Campaign for Mental Health Reform (2003, p. 1).

Inadequate implementation of mental health policy and the resulting inequality in mental health care delivery for people of color have been reiterated in a number of recent reports. In 1999, the U.S. Surgeon General, David Satcher, issued a special report, *Mental Health: A Report of the Surgeon General,* on the status of mental health in America. In it he states: "Even more than other areas of health and medicine, the mental health field is plagued by disparities in the availability of and access to its services. These disparities are viewed readily through the lenses of racial and cultural diversity, age, and gender" (USDHHS, 1999, p. vi). In 2001, a follow-up report, *Mental Health, Culture, Race and Ethnicity,* more clearly identified some of the inequalities in mental health care for ethnic minorities. Specifically, the report noted that African Americans:

1. are less likely to receive mental health services than Whites (estimates are that only one in three who need mental health care receives services);
2. are overrepresented in emergency departments and psychiatric hospitals as a result of referrals from primary care providers rather than referrals from specialists;
3. are more likely to be misdiagnosed with serious mental disorders, such as schizophrenia and mood disorders, than their White counterparts;
4. are less likely than Whites to receive appropriate treatment for anxiety and depression; and
5. are more likely to lack health insurance and thus are more likely to rely on "safety net" services that experience uncertain or limited funding resources.

In addition, the Surgeon General indicated that African Americans, more than any other ethnic minority, are likely to be members of vulnerable "high need" groups that may be underserved by traditional mental health services. High need groups include those on welfare, the homeless, the incarcerated, and children in the child welfare system. The American Psychological Association, in its Resolution on Poverty and Socioeconomic Status, adopted on August 6, 2000, also acknowledges the additional risk for mental health issues faced by members of oppressed groups. Poverty is detrimental to psychological well-being, with National Institute of Mental Health (NIMH) data indicating that low-income individuals are two to five times more likely to suffer from a diagnosable mental disorder than those of the highest socioeconomic status group (Bourdon, Rae, Narrow, Manderschild, & Regier, 1994; Regier et al., 1993), and poverty poses a significant obstacle to getting help for these mental health problems (McGrath, Keita, Strickland, & Russo, 1990); low-income groups are the targets of discrimination based on their socioeconomic status as well as other social indicators such as race/ethnicity and gender (APA, 2005, p. 1; Lott, 2001).

As a result of the increased probability for African Americans' membership in high need groups, special attention must be given to the interlocking effect of social policies that may not be traditionally viewed as mental health policies. These policies impact high need groups and contribute to patterns of environmental stress and inaccessibility to quality mental health services.

Another report, *Achieving the Promise: Transforming Mental Health Care in America,* was released in July of 2003 by George W. Bush's President's Freedom Commission *on Mental Health.* This report also recognized the inadequate implementation of mental health policy by acknowledging the need for improving mental health services and eliminating disparities in mental health service delivery for racial and ethnic minorities.

These and other recent reports indicate a continuing pattern of disparities in mental health treatment and outcomes for African Americans and other "racial and ethnic minority" populations in the United States. It is time to move beyond reporting disparities and take action to resolve the conditions that create and contribute to such disparities. To redress these inequities, it is essential to understand the importance of social policy, and to conduct policy analysis that cogently examines the impact of mental health policy on the African-American community.

HISTORICAL UNDERPINNINGS OF MENTAL HEALTH POLICY FOR AFRICAN AMERICANS

Social policies grow out of human efforts to control civil, political, social, and economic environments that impact the ability to meet basic human needs. Social policies reflect the dominant values of a society and often express attempts to remedy deficits that exist in the environment or "to remediate the perceived shortcomings of previous programs" (Hudson & Cox, 1991, p. 8). Definitions of social policy vary from the simplistic, "Anything that government chooses to do, or not do, that affects the quality of life of its people" (DiNitto, 2005, p. 2), to the complex:

> Social policies are guiding principles for ways of life, motivated by basic and perceived human needs. They were derived by people from the structures, dynamics, and values of their ways of life, and they serve to maintain or change these ways. Social policies tend to, but need not be codified in formal legal instruments. All extant social policies of a given society at a given time, constitute an interrelated, yet not necessarily internally consistent, system of social policies. (Gil, 1992, p. 24)

The majority of African Americans can trace their heritage to the institution of slavery. Thus, the mental health experience of African Americans and public policy response can only be fully understood and appreciated within the historical context of the legacy of slavery and oppression (Jackson, 1999; U.S. DHHS, 2004). Mental health policy toward Blacks in America has been shaped by the events, attitudes, and practices of the past 250 years. The African-American experience in the mental health system evolved from a state of virtual exclusion from the system, with slave owners responsible for their mentally ill slaves who were chattel property, and only limited access to services (usually segregated) by freeborn Blacks, to a status of over-representation in the system due to influences of "long-standing societal beliefs about racial inferiority and worth" (Davis, 2003 p. 116), as well as misdiagnosis and scientifically flawed data on race and mental illness.

Guided by the work of Jarvis (1844) and Snowden and Cheung (1990), Davis has posited five phases or time periods of mental health ideology that focused public policy response regarding African Americans. Between 1763 and 1844, the prevailing mental health ideology was that only property owners could experience mental illness, and thus African slaves and freeborn Blacks were immune from mental illness. From 1845 to 1863, freedom and citizenship were considered harmful to African Americans, who were also viewed as morally inferior. From 1864 to 1964, African Americans were believed to be highly vulnerable to mental illness and the ranks of Blacks in institutions increased significantly; this phase was fueled by post–Civil War fears about large numbers of freed/mentally ill Blacks roaming the countryside and the perceived need to institutionalize them to protect White citizens. From 1964 to 1980, mental health theorists suggested that concentrations of African Americans in urban centers, as a result of migration from the rural south, would increase vulnerability to mental illness; disproportionate numbers of admission of African Americans to mental hospitals ensued. From 1981 to the present studies have shown no significant difference in rates of mental illness by race, and have attributed societal beliefs about poverty and race to the disproportionate rates of admissions of African Americans to mental health facilities. Evidence also suggests high rates of misdiagnoses for African Americans (Davis, 2003). At no time during these ideological timeframes were African Americans treated with parity compared with their White counterparts. In fact, from the beginning, African Americans have experienced disparate and inferior treatment in the mental health system.

NEW OR EXPANDED APPROACHES TO MENTAL HEALTH POLICY ANALYSIS FOR AFRICAN AMERICANS

Crucial to the discussion about expanded approaches to services and activities to alleviate mental disorders and promote mental well-being in the African-American community is an understanding of what mental illness is and is not. There are many complexities in defining both mental health and mental illness, and there is growing acceptance of combining biological and psychosocial factors to determine healthy functioning (Lin, 1995). "Health may be conceptualized as the ability to live and function effectively in society and to exercise maximum self-reliance and autonomy; it is not necessarily the total absence of disease" (Harper, 1990, p. 229). Mental illness represents the clustering of behavioral signs and symptoms that become disruptive of the individual's ability to function effectively in the mainstream of his or her family and community (Harper, 1990, citing Menolascino, 1986).

The definition should also take into account cultural factors that define behavior that may be misinterpreted by professionals outside of the culture. This fact is recognized in the most widely used resource for the classification of mental illness in America, the *Diagnostic and Statistical Manual of Mental Disorders,* Fourth Edition (DSM-IV), (American Psychiatric Association, 1994). However, the competency of mental health professionals in the application and understanding of "culture-bound syndromes" in actual practice and the reliability of the overall system of classification have been questioned (Lin, 1995). The appropriate use of the DSM-IV and issues of cultural competency should be a part of any discussion about future policy directions in mental health.

Although it is not my intention to duplicate recommendations here, issues that should be addressed in new approaches include the numerous recommendations made in the reports by the Surgeon General and the President's Freedom Commission. In addition, see Harper, 1990; Lin, 1995; and Davis, 2003, for specific mental health policy recommendations for African Americans and other ethnic minority communities. Key recommendations can be summarized as follows:

1. Determine in what ways the knowledge from the Surgeon General's and similar reports actually finds its way into public discourse and is implemented in various local, state, and federal planning strategies. Consideration of funding tactics is an essential component of such strategic planning.
2. Determine what approaches in current mental health intervention and research are effective with African Americans and other communities of color and which ones have negative impacts. Opportunities for culturally competent training and research are needed.
3. Engage an array of mental health advocates, including mental health organizations and other providers, family members, researchers, and educators, in broad-based advocacy and legislative lobbying activities to increase access to culturally competent services that address

the needs of African Americans and other historically oppressed populations in a community context and with representative numbers of providers of color.

4. Implement public education strategies that are rooted in community needs and that use culturally appropriate educational and media approaches in order to reduce social stigma and promote awareness of available treatment and support.

Another necessary part of the framework for action associated with social policies for African-American communities is *social impact assessment* or *policy analysis*. Policy analysis may be defined as "learning about the consequence of public policy" (DiNitto, 2005, p. 523). Both governments and private entities have expressed growing awareness of the need for analysis and evaluation of policies. The need is especially great in the area of mental health because of the paucity of mental health policy analysis. "Of the prodigious amount of policy analytic studies in existence, especially those studies appearing in mainstream professional journals, only a relatively small proportion concern themselves with mental health policymaking" (Rochefort, 1997, p. 13). The need for a critical consciousness with regard to policy analysis is imperative. African Americans and other populations of color suffer when there is a lack of attention to indigenous mores and emotional realities.

African Americans may in general be viewed as living in a "hostile environment" in which they confront a condition of *mundane extreme environmental stress*. This syndrome is the experience of chronic unpredictable overt and covert acts of racial discrimination, neglect, and oppression (McCreary, Slavin, & Berry, 1996; Peters & Massey, 1983; Pierce, 1978) that require them to live in two worlds, one Black and one White, with each mandating different ways of functioning. This double existence contributes to a sense of persistent anxiety and stress. As one African-American woman explains, "Once you're used to living in a hostile environment and you get good at it, and you understand the rules, it's hard to let down your guard" (Jones & Shorter-Gooden, 2003, p. 79). In addition to the mundane stress in the environment, African Americans are more likely to be exposed to violence-related trauma while living in poor and dangerous communities. For a variety of reasons, in such communities random violence may be common, fostering a sense of nihilism. West (1993) refers to a "nihilistic threat" or the danger of violence due to a sense of hopelessness and lovelessness that is spawned by the lived experience of oppression.

Also contributing to inadequate health care for African Americans is a deep sense of mistrust of the medical community because of real and perceived misdeeds by medical professionals (e.g., The Tuskegee Syphilis Experiment). Combined with the lack of trust of the medical community that negatively impacts access to mental health services for African Americans, is the stigma of mental illness in the Black community that results in strong reluctance to acknowledge mental illness and to seek mental health services. Concerns about negative stereotypes of African Americans' mental functioning also create a stigma and fear regarding a diagnosis of mental illness. In a conversation with this author, a prominent African-American writer noted "We in the African American community are more likely to tell someone that we have a relative in prison or on drugs than we are to tell anyone that we have one with a mental illness" (T. Williams, personal communication, May 18, 2005).

African Americans also experience widespread lack of trust of social service systems that exist to assist people in need. Such distrust extends to the child welfare and criminal justice systems. These systems have been identified as those serving "high need" populations and African Americans are overrepresented in them. The next section briefly examines the Temporary Assistance to Needy Families legislation (TANF) and the Adoption and the Safe Families Act (ASFA) as nontraditional policies that have interlocking mental health implications for the African-American community.

TANF AND ASFA IMPACTS ON MENTAL HEALTH POLICY FOR AFRICAN AMERICANS

Welfare reform has had a profound impact on the African-American community, and the interaction of policies (e.g., TANF and ASFA) designed to protect children and families intersect in ways that have implications for mental health and well-being. The following discussion and conceptual model for policy analysis examine the impact of these policies on African-American families.

To understand Figures 13.1 and 13.2, conceptual model for policy analysis, attention should be directed to the following terms as identified by Segal and Brzuzy (1998) and modified in this chapter to address issues that are confronted by African-American communities. These terms make up the elements of the conceptual model for policy analysis.

Social Issue: What is the social issue to be addressed by the policy (i.e., poverty, substance abuse, or a shortage of affordable housing)? Moreover, what are the specific concerns that promote the need for intervention (such as large numbers of people who are not self-sufficient and who are dependent on public support)? In addition, who defines the problem and how does the

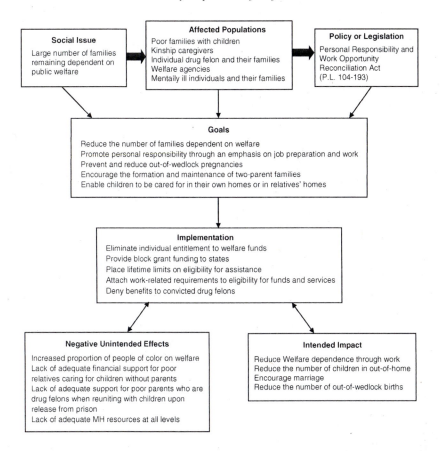

FIGURE 13.1. Conceptual model for policy analysis of TANF pertaining to African-American families.

issue impact the African-American community? Policy creation and analysis is not a linear process nor is it stagnant. It should be an ongoing process so one should ask these questions in both historical and contemporary terms.

Goals: What are the aims of the policy? What is to be achieved by its implementation? Will poverty be reduced or is the aim simply to reduce public spending? How will the goals impact the quality of life of African Americans?

Policy or Legislation: What is the specific policy or legislation that is needed or that is to be to implemented, that is, The Adoption and Safe Families Act (ASFA) or the Temporary Assistance to Needy Families (TANF)

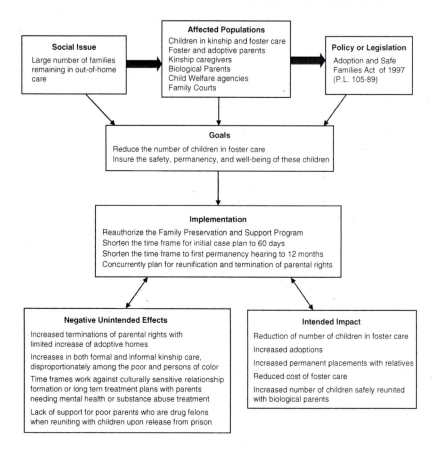

FIGURE 13.2. Conceptual model for policy analysis of ASFA pertaining to African-American families.

legislation? With regard to African-American families, one should ask whether there is a hidden agenda in the proposed policy in relation to the well-being of African Americans. In addition, might the phrasing of the title of the legislation be offensive to the people it is intended to serve? For example, personal responsibility may imply to African Americans that they have not taken responsibility in addressing their own needs and it may be interpreted as ignoring the realities of privation. Furthermore, the wording "personal responsibility" ignores the collectivistic cultural approaches that exist for many African Americans. Mutual aid and communalism have long been viewed as helping mechanisms in the African-American community. This example speaks to an emphasis on "the collective" verses "the individual" or a decidedly Eurocentric versus an Africentric perspective (Schiele, 1997).

Implementation: What specific types of programs and tasks will be initiated to meet the goals of the policy or legislation? For example, will people be required to meet new admission or eligibility requirements? Will benefits be reduced or eliminated or in other ways modified? With regard to the African-American community, will the procedures be implemented in a socially just way and by culturally competent practitioners?

Affected Populations: Who is the identified target of the new legislation or policy and who will be actually impacted? In the African-American community, issues of disproportionate representation may be a concern. In other words, will particular subgroups in the African-American community be disproportionately affected by the legislation? For example, will African-American grandparents be asked to care for dependent children and then not provided with needed financial and social support to adequately care for the children? Will African-American inner city teenagers be dealt a blow because of insufficient employment prospects in their communities? Lastly, will African-American males be profiled more acutely because of inadequacies or inconsistencies associated with the Rockefeller drug laws?

Negative Unintended Effects: Are there unintended outcomes? Consider the possibility of negative (short-term and long-term) consequences that may be unexpected outcomes of the policy. Will such consequences provoke negative reactions or renewed distrust from the African-American community or will the policy/legislation cause additional hardship for members of the community? For example, will poor African-American families be faced with additional caregiver burdens by aiding homeless mentally ill family members or by caring for children whose parents are dropped from welfare roles because they are unable to meet work requirements?

Figure 13.1 outlines the negative unintended consequences of TANF for African-American families. Among the negative effects are increased numbers of people of color on welfare. It has been reported that Blacks and Latinos make up less than 25 percent of the U.S. population and approximately 60 percent of the welfare roles (Crewe, 2003). In 2000, African Americans made up the largest cohort (39 percent) of TANF recipients (U.S. DHHS, 2000). Another negative impact of TANF for the African-American community is an increased reliance by the child welfare system on unpaid kinship caregivers. To some professionals, transferring responsibility for childcare from the welfare system to relatives without adequate compensation represents a sleight of hand for the child welfare roles. In some instances, children have simply been reclassified from "prior AFDC cases to kinship care"

(Crewe, 2003, p. 83) and moved from welfare to poor relatives. Keigher and Fendt (1998) refer to such practices as "policy obfuscation" (p. 226). This practice can undermine the mental health of the children, their parents, and the caregiver relatives.

Intended Impact: Are the goals of the policy addressed as intended? For example, is poverty actually reduced or are families simply pushed into other systems. In Figure 13.2, one of the intentions of ASFA is identified as *"Increased numbers of children safely returned to biological parents."* However, for many children, shortened time limits do not allow adequate time to achieve reunification with incarcerated parents or those requiring treatments for mental illness or substance abuse (Smith & Young, 2003). In addition, in the African-American community, one should consider how positive consequences (the intent) will be sustained over time. If, for example, innovative programming that results in positive outcomes is not financially supported so that it may be sustained, it may be viewed as another "set up" by a biased political system. Alford (2003) posits that prolonged programming in the form of culturally specific human service intervention has a lasting impact for African-American adolescent males who face omnipresent risk factors, but such programs may struggle for financial support.

TANF and ASFA are not normally thought of as policies with mental health implications. However, being able to take care of one's needs and provide for the basic needs of one's family has enormous mental health consequences. Few issues are more upsetting to parents than being unable to care for their children, and few problems cause more anguish to children than being separated from their parents. When one is unable to provide such basics as food, shelter and clothing, he or she can easily fall into a state of mental turmoil. In addition, mental illness, substance abuse, and addiction are major contributing factors to domestic violence and child abuse/neglect, and impair parents' ability to care for their children. Furthermore, inadequate resources to meet the mental health needs of children who are in foster care contribute to delays in returning children to their families, especially poor families that lack resources to access services independently of the child welfare agency. Here lies the interlocking relationship of social policies and mental health realities for ASFA and TANF.

THE COMMUNITY MENTAL HEALTH CENTERS ACT

Like TANF and ASFA, the Community Mental Health Centers Act of 1963 had unintended consequences and negative impacts for African Americans (Figure 13.3). This legislation (CMHC Act, Title II of Public Law 88-

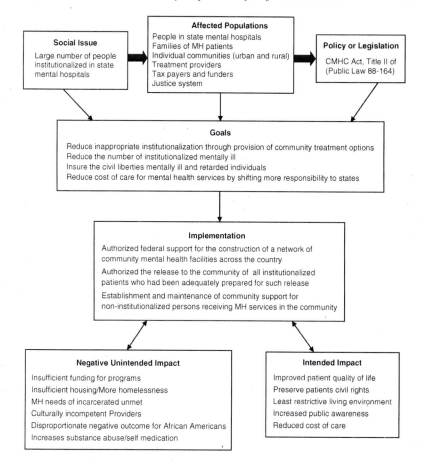

FIGURE 13.3. Conceptual model for policy analysis of CMHC act pertaining to African-American families.

164) was seen as a watershed policy of its era. It was signed into law by President John F. Kennedy and authorized federal support for the construction of a network of community mental health facilities across the country.

The policy emphasized deinstitutionalization and community-based treatment that continues today (Rochefort, 1997). A number of forces converged to promote the passage of the CMHC legislation (see Grob, 1991; Rochefort, 1997 for a detailed discussion). Chief among these forces in the African-American community was the Civil Rights movement that focused attention on the unequal and often unfair treatment of African Americans. In addition, according to Rochefort (1996), the concept of *community* influenced lawmakers to consider the possibility that social problems were the result of the breakdown of family and community (Moynihan, 1970). In mental health the notion was further advanced by the belief that the family and relationships in the community served to foster bonds that had the potential to mitigate the negative impact of mental illness.

The concept of community is significant to the African-American culture in that the family, houses of worship, and mutual aid organizations have been hallmarks of support, and African Americans, who were historically excluded from formal human services programs, sought refuge in their own cultural traditions. Also significant was the concept "maximum feasible participation," which was in vogue at the time CMHC was passed. This concept meant that clients who were impacted by programs and policies must be engaged in the development and implementation of such programs and policies. Suffice it to say, there has been, and continues to be, a strong need for increased participation by African Americans in the implementation of community-based mental health services.

The CMHC has been amended many times since it was passed in 1963, and has contributed to the advancement in humane treatment, as well as the rights of the mentally ill. On the other hand, the policy has not resulted in adequate numbers of programs and services for those in need. In fact, the rise of the nation's homeless population has been associated with the widescale deinstitutionalization of the mentally ill. This fact is keenly felt in the African-American community. "Proportionally, 3.5 times as many African Americans as white Americans are homeless" (U.S., DHHS, 2001, p. 9). In addition, the policy has not resulted in delivery of culturally competent services and has not sufficiently involved the African-American community in the planning and implementation of approaches to address gaps in service.

CONCLUSION

African Americans compose approximately 12 percent of the population of the United States (U.S. Census Bureau, 2001), yet they represent a disproportionate number of high-need groups that are underserved by the mental health system. Although the Surgeon General's 2001 supplemental report states that Blacks experience mental disorders at the same rate as Whites, "What does differ by race and ethnicity is diagnosis, help-seeking, access to services, utilization of mental health services, and participation in research studies" (Davis, 2003, p. 112). Akbar (1991) reminds us that sanity should not be defined by normative standards. Understanding the rudiments of mental well-being and the barriers that impede it is essential. A prevailing issue that needs to be addressed concerning behavior observed in any oppressed group is whether the behavior is a response to the conditions of the oppression experienced by the group (Bell, Bland, Houston, & Jones, 1983). What is often viewed as pathological behavior exhibited by African Americans may, in fact, be a survival adaptation given an often unjust world. Policy makers and human service practitioners must educate themselves on issues of cultural competence, actively engage in culturally competent practices, and participate in ongoing policy analysis in order to alleviate disparities in the diagnosis and treatment of mental illness among African Americans.

CHAPTER SUMMARY

This chapter has presented information on some of the implications of mental health policy for the African-American community, examining issues that are not traditionally thought of in the context of mental health policy. A brief review of the literature affirms ongoing health disparities for ethnic minorities and demonstrates that African Americans are particularly at risk for negative outcomes. Furthermore, an examination of the historical underpinnings of mental health policy for African Americans reveals that, from the beginning, African Americans have experienced disparate and inferior treatment in the mental health system.

Citing recent studies such as the Surgeon General's report and the President's Freedom Commission on Mental Health, this chapter acknowledges the importance of those recommendations and highlights the need to examine the implications for mental health policy in legislation that impacts high-need populations, such as those on welfare or in the foster care system. A conceptual model for policy analysis borrowed from Segal and Brzuzy (1998) is presented to analyze TANF and ASFA as exemplars of nontraditional policies that should be considered in addressing the mental health needs of African Americans. In addition, the conceptual framework is applied to the Community Mental Health Centers Act to assess its impact on the African-American community.

Finally, the chapter provides a list of additional reading resources on the issue of mental health policy, and suggests class activities to assist students to further explore the issue of mental health needs and policy issues for African Americans and other ethnic minorities.

SUGGESTED GROUP OR CLASSROOM ACTIVITIES
(ALL ASSIGNMENTS MAY BE DONE
IN SMALL GROUPS OR TEAMS)

1. *Poster Session on Mental Health Policies*. Ask students to present a poster session on selected mental health policies (e.g., Americans With Disabilities Act). The conceptual framework can be used as an outline for significant content. Special attention should be given to the differential impact of the policy implementation on ethnic minorities and African Americans in particular. Students are then asked to do a five-minute class presentation on their posters. This assignment may be given to individuals or small groups.

2. *Newspaper Assignment*. Engage students in discussions of current event articles that have implications for mental health policy: for example, child abuse and post partum depression, the mentally ill homeless, mental health needs of children in the child welfare system, and the mental health needs of the incarcerated. Ask students to read the newspaper or news magazines and do brief reaction papers to articles that deal with issues that have implications for mental health and mental health policy (e.g., grandparents raising grandchildren—What are some mental health needs and what are some implications for mental health policy?). Special attention should be given to issues that may differentially impact ethnic minorities and African Americans in particular. The conceptual model for policy analysis may be used as an outline for significant content areas.

This assignment might also be extended to pop literature/culture. Students might be asked to journal on the ways in which mental illness is portrayed in pop culture (TV, magazines, comic strips, music) and then asked to explore policy implications for reducing the social stigma of mental illness.

3. *Mapping Mental Health*. To demonstrate the complexity of mental health services, students may be asked to map the number of places in the community where a person might enter the mental health system: for example, school, hospital, substance abuse services, church, and so on. Students might be asked to pair the entry point for services with possible payment sources for each. The second part of the assignment might require an outside of class research component that calls for students to search the Internet and/or contact community agencies for information on payment for mental health services. Finally, students in a policy class might be asked to identify what policies authorize the delivery of services and the payment of services in the various locations where mental health services are provided. Address issues of the differential access of mental health services for ethnic minorities and African Americans in particular.

4. *The Chronology of Mental Health Policy*. Ask students to locate and review a chronology of mental health policies (e.g., see National Institute of Mental Health (NIMH)—Chronology at http://www.nih.gov/about/almanac/organization/NIMH.htm#chronology and Davis, 2003, p. 102). Ask students to explore the social climate of the various time frames in terms of attitudes toward mental health and toward African Americans. Ask students to discuss their thoughts on how such attitudes might impact the implementation of services for ethnic minorities and African Americans in particular. Then ask students what measures might be taken to remedy any identified concerns regarding the negative impact on African Americans and other ethnic minorities.

5. *Create a Table of Mental Health Concerns in the African-American Community*. Ask students to create a three-column table that lists mental health concerns that have been identified in the African-American community (e.g., increased risk of misdiagnosis). In a second column, identify some possible policy implications for the particular concern (e.g., the need for more culturally competent practitioners). In the last column, students should identify how various professionals might respond to the particular issue based on professional policy statements or codes of ethics (e.g., review the National Association of Social Workers policy statement on Mental Health). Other columns might be added depending on the learning goals of the class or interests of the instructor and students.

READING RESOURCES

Anderson, J. E. (2002). *Public Policy Making* (3rd ed.). New York: Praeger.

Broskowski, A., Marks, E., & Budman, S. *Linking Health and Mental Health*. Beverly Hills, CA: Sage Publications.

Dohrenwend, B. P., Dohrenwend, B. S., Gould, M. S., Link, B., Neugebaur, R., & Wunsch-Hitzig, R. (1980). *Mental Illness in the United States: Epidemiological Estimates*. New York: Praeger.

Harper, M. S. (1987). Public policy and long term care: Domestic and international. In H. J. Altman (Ed.), *Alzheimer's Disease: Problems, Prospects, and Perspectives* (pp. 371-387). New York: Plenum Press.

McGuire, T. (1981). *Financing Psychotherapy: Costs, Effects, and Public Policy*. Cambridge, MA: Ballinger Publishing Company.

Mechanic, D. (1980). *Mental Health and Social Policy* (2nd ed.). Englewood Cliffs, NJ: Prentice Hall.

Rubin, J. (1978). *Economics, Mental Health and the Law*. Lexington, MA: Lexington Books.

Ruiz, S. S., & Comer, J. P. (Eds.) (1990). *Handbook of Mental Health and Mental Disorder Among Black Americans*. New York: Greenwood Press.
U.S. DHHS (2001). Mental Health: Culture, Race and Ethnicity: A Supplement to Mental Health: A Report of the Surgeon General. Rockville, MD: US Department of Health and Human Services, Substance Abuse and Mental Health Services Administration, Center for Mental Health Services.

REFERENCES

Akbar, N. (1991). Mental disorder among African Americans. In R. Jones (Ed.), *Black Psychology* (pp. 339-352). Berkeley, CA: Cobb & Henry.
Alford, K. (2003). Cultural themes in rites of passage: Voices of young African American males. *Journal of African American Studies, 7*(1), 3-26.
American Psychiatric Association. (1994) *The Diagnostic and Statistical Manual of Mental Disorders* (4th ed.), Washington, DC: Author.
American Psychological Association. (2005). *Resolution on Poverty and Socioeconomic Status*. Public Interest Directorate, Washington, DC: Author. Retrieved August 17, 2005, from http://www.apa.org/pi/urban/povres.html.
Bell, C. C., Bland, E., Houston, E., & Jones, B. E. (1983). Enhancement of knowledge and skills for the psychiatric treatment of black populations. In J. Chunn, C. Dunston, & F. Ross-Sheriff (Eds.), *Mental Health and People of Color: Curriculum Development and Change* (pp. 205-238). Washington, DC: Howard University Press.
Bourdon, K. H., Rae, D. S., Narrow, W. E., Manderschild, R. W., & Regier, D. A. (1994). National prevalence and treatment of mental and addictive disorders. In R. W. Mandershild & A. Sonnenschein (Eds.), *Mental Health: United States* (pp. 22-51). Washington, DC: Center for Mental Health Services.
Bush, G. W. (2005). *Presidential Inaugural Address, January 20*. Retrieved January 21, 2005, from http://abclocal.go.com/kfsn/news/012005_inauguration_speech_txt.html.
Campaign for Mental Health Reform. (2003). *Whither Medicaid? A Briefing Paper on Mental Health Issues in Medicaid Restructuring*. Retrieved August 17, 2005, from http://www.mhreform.org/policy/whithermedicaid.htm.
Crewe, S. (2003). From paper to people: An analysis of critical welfare reform issues affecting the black community. In T. B Bent-Goodley (Ed.), *African-American Social Workers and Social Policy* (pp. 69-92). Binghamton, NY: The Haworth Press.
Davis, K. (2003). The policy implications of the Surgeon General's report on mental health, race, culture, and ethnicity. In T. B. Bent-Goodley (Ed.), *African-American Social Workers and Social Policy* (pp. 93-122). Binghamton, NY: The Haworth Press.
DiNitto, D. M. (2005). *Social Welfare: Politics and Public Policy*. New York: Pearson, Allyn and Bacon.

Gil, D. G. (1992). *Unraveling Social Policy: Theory, Analysis, and Political Action Toward Social Equality* (5th ed.). Rochester, VT: Schenkman Books.

Grob, G. N. (1991). *From Asylum to Community: Mental Health Policy in Modern America*. Princeton, NJ: Princeton University Press.

Harper, M. S. (1990). Mental health and social policy. In S. S. Ruiz & J. P. Comer (Eds.), *Handbook of Mental Health and Mental Disorder Among Black Americans* (pp. 229-251). New York: Greenwood Press.

Hudson, C. G., & Cox, A. J. (1991). Introduction: Analysis of state mental health policy. In Hudson, C. G. & Cox, A. J. (Eds.). *Dimensions of State Mental Health Policy* (pp. 1-14). Westport, CT: Praeger Publishers.

Jackson, V. (1999). *An Early History: African American Mental Health*. Retrieved January 26, 2005 from http://academic.udayton.edu/health/01status/mental01.htm.

Jarvis, E. (1844). Insanity among the colored population of the free states. *American Journal of the Medical Sciences, VII*, 71-83.

Jones, C., & Shorter-Gooden, K. (2003). *Shifting: The Double Lives of Black Women in America*. New York: Perennial, Harper Collins Publishers.

Keigher, S., & Fendt, P. (1998). Welfare at ground zero: Having to fly without a safety net. *Health and Social Work, 23,* 223-321.

Lin, M. P. (1995). Mental health overview. In R. L. Edwards (Ed.), *Encyclopedia of Social Work* (pp. 1705-1711). Washington, DC: NASW.

Lipsky, M. (1980). *Street-Level Bureaucracy*. New York: Russell Sage Foundation.

Lott, B. (2001). Low income parents and the public schools. *Journal of Social Issues, 57*(2), 247-260.

McCreary, M. L., Slavin, L. A., & Berry, E. J. (1996). Predicting problem behavior and self-esteem among African American adolescents. *Journal of Adolescent Research, 11*(2), 216-234.

McGrath, E., Keita, G. P., Strickland, B. R., & Russo, N. F. (1990). *Women and Depression: Risk Factors and Treatment Issues*. Washington, DC: American Psychological Association.

Moynihan, D. P. (1970). *Maximum Feasible Misunderstanding: Community Action in the War on Poverty*. New York: Free Press.

New Freedom Commission on Mental Health. (2003). *Achieving the Promise: Transforming Mental Health Care in America. Final Report*. U.S. DHHS Pub. No. SMA-03-3832. Rockville, MD: Author.

Peters, M., & Massey, G. (1983). Mundane extreme environmental stress in family stress theories: The case of Black families in White America. *Marriage and Family Review, 6*(1/2), 193-225.

Pierce, C. (1975). The mundane extreme environment and its effect on learning. In S. Brainard (Ed.), *Learning Disabilities: Issues and Recommendations for Research*. Washington, DC: National Institute of Education.

Regier, D. A., Farmer, M. E., Rae, D. S., Myers, J. K., Kramer, M., Robins, L. N., et al. (1993). One-month prevalence of mental disorders in the United States and sociodemographic characteristics: The epidemiologic catchment area study. *Acta Psychiatrica Scandinavica, 88,* 35-47.

Rochefort, D. A. (1997). *From Poorhouse to Homelessness* (2nd ed.). Westport, CT: Greenwood Publishing Group.

Schiele, J. H. (1997). An Afrocentric perspective on social welfare philosophy and policy. *Journal of Sociology and Social Welfare, 24*(2), 21-39.

Segal, E. A., & Brzuzy, S. (1998). *Social Welfare Policy, Programs, and Practice.* Itasca, IL: F. E. Peacock Publishers.

Smith, C. J., & Young, D. S. (2003). The multiple impacts of TANF, ASFA, and mandatory drug sentencing for families affected by maternal incarceration. *Children and Youth Services Review, 25*(7), 535-552.

Snowden, L., & Cheung, R. (1990). Use of inpatient mental health services by members of minority groups. *American Psychologist, 45,* 291-298.

U.S. Census Bureau. (2001). *Overview of Race and Hispanic Origin: Census 2000 Brief.* Retrieved June 28, 2001, from http://www.census.gov/population/www/socdemo/race.html.

U.S. DHHS. (1999). *Mental Health: A Report of the Surgeon General.* Rockville, MD: US Department of Health and Human Services, Substance Abuse and Mental Health Services Administration, Center for Mental Health Services, National Institutes of Health, National Institute of Mental Health. Retrieved December 15, 2004 from http://www.surgeongeneral.gov/library/mentalhealth/chapter6/sec4.html.

U.S. DHHS. (2001). *Mental Health: Culture, Race and Ethnicity: A Supplement to Mental Health: A Report of the Surgeon General.* Rockville, MD: US Department of Health and Human Services, Substance Abuse and Mental Health Services Administration, Center for Mental Health Services, National Institutes of Health, National Institute of Mental Health. Retrieved December 15, 2004, from http://www.surgeongeneral.gov/library/mentalhealth/chapter6/sec4.html.

U.S. DHHS. (2004). *Health, United States, 2004. With Chartbook on Trends in the Health of American* (p. 9). Retrieved January 28, 2005 from http://www.cdc.gov/nchs/data/hus/hus04.pdf.

U.S. DHHS, Administration for Children and Families. (2000). *Temporary Assistance to Needy Families (TANF) Program: Third Annual Report to Congress.* Washington, DC: Author.

West, C. (1993). *Race Matters.* New York: Vintage Books.

Chapter 14

Rural African-American Families and Their Mental Health Needs: South Carolina As an Exemplar

Sadye M. L. Logan

Mental illness accounts for five of the ten leading causes of disability worldwide. In the United States and other developed countries, it is the second leading cause of disability and premature mortality. It is estimated that over half of the population in the United States will experience a mental illness in their lifetime. Available data suggest that the prevalence of mental illness varies little between rural and urban settings in the general population in the United States (Rosenthal & Fox, 2000; Hartley, Bird, & Dempsey, 1999; USDHHS, 1999). Although the prevalence of mental illness may not vary between these two broad geographical categories (urban and rural), the major differences are in access and availability of mental health care and services. It is the intent of this chapter to discuss access to and availability of mental health care in rural areas in general, with specific focus on South Carolina.

Given that the South Carolina mental health care system is viewed as being in crisis and that the state is among the five southern states (including Georgia, Alabama, Mississippi, and Louisiana) that have the greatest rural (non-metro) African-American population, it seems appropriate to use South Carolina as an exemplar for discussing rural mental health in Black America. It also is important to note that 69 percent of all African Ameri-

The author would like to thank Stephanie Cooper-Lewter, PhD candidate, for her assistance with this chapter.

Mental Health Care in the African-American Community
© 2007 by The Haworth Press, Inc. All rights reserved.
doi:10.1300/5364_14

cans living in rural areas live in South Carolina and the other four states. Figure 14.1 reflects the African-American population by region. In total, 5 million rural residents are African American. The age distribution in this population reflects a high proportion of all persons falling between 18 and 44 years of age or younger. It follows that such a significant young population will place high demands on education and child care services. Moreover, in socially oppressed and economically depressed rural areas, quality education and child care are generally not available or available only at a substandard level.

According to available data, the majority of African Americans live in counties that have less than 7 percent of the labor force in agriculture. This percentage of rural African Americans tends to reside in counties where significant portions of the economy are in manufacturing. Despite the movement from household or commercial cleaning jobs to sales and technical positions, rural African-American workers reside in smaller rural towns that have become a poverty trap with high rates of unemployment. Overall, approximately 33.8 percent of the rural African-American population lives below the poverty line and is highest in Mississippi, Georgia, North Carolina, Louisiana, Alabama, and South Carolina. Seventy percent (69.9 percent) of all poor, rural African Americans live in these six states, and more specifically, in the state of South Carolina (see Table 14.1) (Mckinnon, 2003).

LITERATURE OVERVIEW

The literature on the mental health specific to African Americans in rural communities is limited. Although recognition has grown that the neighborhood context impacts a number of facets of individual lives, including

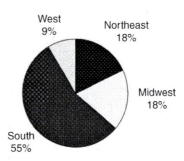

FIGURE 14.1. African American population by region: 2002.

TABLE 14.1. South Carolina rural Black population.

Total population	4,012,012,000	
Total Black population	1,185,216,000	30%
Total rural Black population	1,163,483,480	29%
Total very rural population	1,604,804,800	40%

mental health practices (Cutrona, Russel, & Brown, 2005), the application of this in examining mental health in rural African-American communities is sparse. What we do know is that high rates of poverty and limited insurance in rural communities has created a "triple jeopardy" where a large population has been neglected and underserved in mental health services (Blank, Tetrick, Brinkley, & Doheny, 1994).

The provision of mental health services to rural African Americans present unique challenges and barriers. In particular, the effects of poverty, ethnicity, and the social isolation linked to southern rural life are hard to ignore (Blank et al., 1994). In general, rural communities have limited resources and mental health services, which result in fewer opportunities to provide a broad array of services in comparison to their urban counterparts. Thus mental health service availability is of great concern within rural communities.

In addition, service utilization and access in rural African-American communities is also a significant challenge. Generally speaking, African-American rural populations are less likely to access mental health services as they tend to rely upon their own networks of support within their family system, church, or community. This raises concerns around the accuracy of information being provided in terms of mental health needs. Because service utilization of supportive service among rural communities is limited (Bane, 1991), African American are more likely to be invisible to mental health service providers. Barriers to adequate service utilization and access primarily include the lack of both transportation and insurance (Rasheed & Rasheed, 2003; Bane, 1991). As a result, a strong reliance upon health protective behaviors and an informal network of care or the Black helping tradition has remained (Rasheed & Rasheed, 2003; Wilson-Ford, 1992). In one sense an ongoing cycle is perpetuated: because there are limited services in rural communities, African Americans rely more on their extended networks, maintaining their invisibility within the service system.

Another barrier faced by rural African-American populations in accessing mental health services includes lack of insurance (Blank et al., 1994), which can prevent access to appropriate mental health services, as well as inhibit ability to maintain the medications necessary to cope with their illness. Lack of insurance impacts children, adults, and elderly populations, and as a result, African-American individuals and families in need of services or ongoing mental health treatment may not able to maintain mental health services as necessary.

Culturally sensitive and culturally responsive service providers may also be limited or lacking in rural communities. Bane (1991) noted that "sensitivity to cultural differences on the part of service providers is needed, as is commitment to eliminating access problems and cultural barriers" (p. 64). For example, cultural mistrust of White mental health clinicians among African Americans with severe mental illness has been noted (Dembling, Rovnyak, Mackey, & Blank, 2002; Whaley, 2001; Blank et al., 1994). Blank et al. (1994) examined the impact of racial matching on service provision in the rural south among seriously mentally ill populations. The study results concluded that African-American clients were more likely to be assigned to African-American case managers. Over time, Blank et al. (1994) found that there was a greater number of client visits when racial matching occurred. However, within this study, the authors also noted failed visits also occurred among racially matched case managers, perhaps the result of a stronger reliance on informal care and supportive networks (Blank et al., 1994).

Differences in parenting styles among African-American parents and their children in rural communities is another area where cultural differences can emerge between the mental health practitioner and clients. A high level of parental control and a no-nonsense approach among African-American parents is often considered a sign of parental involvement and concern, particularly within the context of academic expectations (Brody & Flor, 1998). Recognition that "the task of creating and maintaining supportive family relationships is perhaps more difficult in rural families because of the lack of support systems and amenities" (Brody, Stoneman, & Flor, 1995, p. 577) is necessary among practitioners.

Elderly African Americans in rural settings face an increased rate of poverty of 46.5 percent when compared to their non-Black peers (Bane, 1991). For example, poverty rates among African-American elderly women living alone are 79.9 percent (Bane, 1991). As a result, disparities among older rural African-American mental health status are great in comparison to elderly Whites (Rasheed & Rasheed, 2003).

Concentrated effort and further research are needed to ensure that culturally competent and culturally responsive services are provided. Comprehensive strategies to effectively include the natural helping traditions of the church, increased mental health service opportunities, and the elimination of access and transportation barriers are needed to increase the utilization of mental health services among rural African Americans. In addition, further training is needed in preparing mental health practitioners for working with the diverse and varied needs of this population.

MENTAL HEALTH ISSUES IN SOUTH CAROLINA

Not unlike stakeholders of mental services everywhere, those in rural South Carolina cite lack of *availability* and *access* as the two main concerns impacting good mental health care. Holzer, Goldsmith, and Ciarlo (1998) defined *availability* as a concept that captures the presence, volume, and range of services providers. *Presence* denotes the existence of mental health providers in the vicinity. *Volume* suggests the number of service providers in comparison with the population most likely to use the providers. *Range* is intended to define the diversity among service providers, such as social workers, psychologists, psychiatrists, and those in the medical sector such as nurses, family practice physicians, and others. *Accessibility* on the other hand is conceptualized by Aday (1974) to represent the potential and actual entry of a given population group to the health care delivery system. Further, *access* is usually defined by the geographical, time, and cost factors associated with a consumer reaching the service delivery systems or the service delivery system reaching the consumer.

The following voices of three stakeholders resonate across rural communities everywhere:

> *The voice of the first stakeholder:* Living in a rural area makes receiving services difficult—if not impossible. We lack transportation services over county lines. We lack choice of providers. Staff turnover in rural areas are high, people leave to find better paying jobs in larger cities. (The President New Freedom Commission on Mental Health, 2003, p. 12)

> *The voice of rural providers:* The number one comment I hear from our consumers is that being in a rural area, it is difficult to travel to and from appointments for services. In our rural area, our nearest provider is approximately 45 miles away. (The President New Freedom Commission on Mental Health, 2003, p. 12)

> *A family member of a mental health consumer:* I am just sick and tired of the poor quality of care that seems to be all that we ever get. (A focus group member from a very rural area in SC)

In addition to access and availability, stakeholders are also concerned with barriers resulting from lack of qualified service providers, including peer support specialists, social workers, psychiatrists, and nurses. Coupled with the inadequate numbers of qualified service providers is the ongoing and more pronounced issue of providing culturally sensitive practice. In rural areas the number of culturally diverse consumers is increasing. Language and other cultural and social factors are confounding challenges for consumers and service providers. It should also be noted that many of South Carolina rural counties still lack 911 systems, thereby blocking quick access to Emergency Medical Services (EMS) (Watkins, 2001).

Shrinking resources is an issue impacting quality mental health care. This is especially true in rural and very rural areas of South Carolina (see Table 14.1). According to NAMI (National Alliance for Mental Illness) (2006), the South Carolina Department of Mental Health since 2001 has lost $30 million in funding, even as the cost of programs increases by more than $45 million. In addition, Partners in Crisis, a South Carolina coalition advocating for responsible mental health and substance abuse services, described the South Carolina mental health system as being in crisis because of the elimination of long-term psychiatric beds and outpatient services in local communities (Lott & McCullough, 2006). Given the state of mental health care in rural South Carolina, it is believed that it would be appropriate to define this as a crisis.

At the consumer level, poverty and lack of insurance are persistent problems for rural African Americans. It is not clear to what extent the Children's Health Insurance Plan (CHIP) under Medicaid has effectively impacted the health and mental health needs of African-American children. However, given their lack of access and availability, it is expected that impact would be limited. Rural children of color are also less likely to receive care for behavioral or other mental disorders (Watkins, 2001). Consumers with disabilities and those who are older are underserved in South Carolina rural areas. It is important to note that rural areas have a greater proportion of people aged 65 or older. As discussed in Chapter 11, physical and mental disability increases with age. Therefore, it is expected that elderly persons in rural areas will become more dependent and functionally limited. Declining or unavailable community supports and services place older rural residents at risk for clinical or major depression along with chronic illness and disability. Overall, concerns for anxiety, disability, stress, depression, suicide, and access are repeatedly identified as major rural health concerns.

AN EXPANDED APPROACH TO RURAL SERVICES

NAMI, in grading the South Carolina mental health system, commended it for improvements in its system of care. These included South Carolina demonstrating commitment to providing evidence-based practices (EBP) or best practices and peer specialist. It appears that the state went beyond federal requirements to develop and implement an Assertive Community Treatment (ACT). This is a service-delivery model that provides comprehensive, locally based treatment to people with serious and persistent mental illness. ACT provides highly individualized services directly to consumers. ACT recipients receives services from a multidisciplinary team 24 hours a day, 7 days a week, 365 days a year in their home and community. The ACT team members trained in the areas of psychiatry, social work, nursing, substance abuse, and vocational rehabilitation.

Peer specialists are paraprofessionals who provide expertise in self-help and peer support in outpatient sites. Their focus is to empower individuals who receive mental health services to regain personal control over their lives and their recovery process (NAMI, 2006; New York State Office of Mental Health, 2006). South Carolina has also supported employment progress, housing initiatives, and other programs that meet fidelity standards.

Given the compelling problems with access and availability in rural areas, a critical question is whether it is possible for ACT to be effective in rural communities, specifically in South Carolina. Although available data show that ACT is effective in rural states in the midwest, research is needed to determine the extent of planning for effective implementation in rural South Carolina.

Lynette Studer, an ACT team leader for ten years at the Monroe, Wisconsin Green County Program, defines rural in relation to ACT as fewer people with severe mental illness in the service area who need the comprehensive outreach services provided by ACT (NAMI, 2006). However, effectiveness is dependent on having enough staff and adequate funding.

It is generally acknowledged in rural areas that the primary care doctor is often the main contact for mental health concerns (Hartley et al., 1999). However, for African Americans in rural South Carolina, primary care physicians as well as rural hospitals are simply non-existent (Watkins, 2001).

Vanek (2002) reemphasized several creative strategies for improving access and educating and encouraging help seeking behavior in rural communities. One strategy is the use of local radio and television public service announcements on mental health topics (depression, anxiety, chemical dependency, attention deficit/hyperactivity disorder, post-traumatic stress disorder, and suicide). The aim of the announcements would be educational and informative, and symptoms and treatment options would be described. The intent would be to demystify and debunk the belief that experiencing mental illness is shameful.

The second strategy involves outreach and connection with local support systems and informal community networks. These would include churches, social service agencies, local schools, community volunteers, and community activists. These support systems would be used for the purpose of linking community residents with available services. Finally, where possible, available technology may be used to maintain contact via telecommunication.

CONCLUSION

Structural and financial barriers serve to differentiate mental health care in rural and urban areas. Structural barriers to care include poverty, access, and shortage of mental health specialists and services. Residents of rural and very rural areas of this country marginalized by higher rates of poverty and disability become further marginalized by the various structures responsible for programs and policy development. Essentially, our rural residents are supported by advocacy groups and favorable legislation.

CHAPTER SUMMARY

This chapter demonstrates that the need for mental health services varies very little between rural and urban geographical categories. The major differences are in access and availability.

The chapter further demonstrates that the majority of African Americans live in the southern region of the United States in counties where a significant portion of the economy is in manufacturing with low wages, and live in smaller rural towns that are poverty traps with high rates of unemployment. Rural areas are especially disadvantaged in meeting the needs of the elderly and children with serious mental problems. Both groups are at risk. Rural areas are disadvantaged due to shortages in mental health infrastructure and availability of mental health professionals.

GROUPS AND CLASSROOM EXERCISES

1. This is a two part exercise. In part one, you are to conduct a modified version of the survey conducted by the South Carolina Department of Mental health on attitudes, beliefs, knowledge, and perceptions of the residents of your local community. Collect data on the participants responses to the following questions:
   - If mental illness were in my family, I would not want people to know.
   - Individuals who have a mental illness and are receiving competent treatment are no more dangerous than the general population.
   - How familiar are with your state Department of Mental Health?
   - If you thought you or someone close to you were mentally ill, would you contact the local mental health program run by the Department of Mental Health in your state?

2. Part two:
   - Divide into groups of four and discuss and compare your findings from the survey, then report your integrated findings to the class as a whole.
   - As an entire class, discuss the implications of your findings for additional research and mental health practice and intervention.

3. The class will be divided into two debate teams. The focus of both teams will center on the question of whether locating a group home or apartment for people with mental illness in a residential area will harm property value.
   - *The debate focus for team #1:* Someone being diagnosed with cancer, diabetes, or heart disease will not change property value, but one cannot argue the same for someone with mental illness.
   - *The debate focus for team #2:* People with mental health problems are capable of full community participation. We should accept, support, and encourage their recovery, and allow them to live wherever they wish.

4. Identify, discuss, and propose solutions to the various structural barriers to effective mental health care in rural African-American communities.

REFERENCES

Aday, L. A. (2001). *At Risk in America: The Health Care Needs of Vulnerable Populations in the United States* (2nd ed.). San Francisco, CA: Jossey-Bass Publishers, 2001.

Bane, S. D. (1991). Rural minority populations. *Generations, 15*(4), 63-65.

Blank, M., Tetrick, F., Brinkley, D., & Doheny, V. (1994). Racial matching and service utilization among seriously mentally ill consumers in the rural south. *Community Mental Health Journal, 30*(3), 271-281.

Brody, G., & Flor, D. (1998). Maternal resources, parenting practices, and child competence in rural single-parent African American families. *Child Development, 69*(3), 803-816.

Brody, G., Stoneman, Z., & Flor, D. (1995). Linking family processes and academic competence among rural African American youth. *Journal of Marriage and the Family, 57*(3), 567-579.

Dembling, B., Rovnyak, V., Mackey, S., & Blank, M. (2002). Effect of geographic migration on serious mental illness prevalence estimates. *Mental Health Services Research, 4*(1), 7-12.

Hartley, D., Bird, D., & Dempsey, P. (1999). Rural mental health and substance abuse. In Ricketts, T. C. (Ed.), *Rural Health in the United States* (pp. 159-178). New York: Oxford University Press.

Holzer, C. E., Goldsmith, H. F., & Ciarlo, J. A. (1998). *Effects of Rural-Urban County Type on the Availability of Health and Mental Health Care Providers.* U.S. DHHS Pub. No. (SMA) 99-3285 (pp. 204-213). Washington, DC: Superintendent of Documents, US Government Printing Office.

Lott, L., & McCullough, A. (2006). It's time to address mental health crisis: The State. Available at http://www.the state.com/mld/state/news/opinion/14109738 .htm. Accessed March 16, 2006.

McKinnon, J. (2003). The Black population in the United States. March 2002. *Current Population Report,* Series P20-541. Washington, DC: U.S. Census Bureau.

NAMI. (2006). Grading the States: A report on America's health care system for serious mental illness. Available at http://www.nami.org. Accessed March 2, 2006.

New York State Office of Mental Health. (2006). Peer Specialists First year formative for them, co-workers and recipients. Retrieved May 3, 2006, from http://www.omh.state.ny.us/omhg.

President's New Freedom Commission on Mental Health. (2003). Achieving the promise: Transforming mental health care in America. Final report. U.S. DHHS, Pub. No. SMA-03-3832, Rockville, MD: Author.

Rasheed, M., & Rasheed, J. (2003). Rural African American older adults and the Black helping tradition. *Journal of Gerontological Social Work, 41*(1/2), 137-150.

Rosenthal, T. C., & Fox, C. (2000). Access to health care for the rural elderly. *Journal of the American Medical Association, 284*(16), 2034-2036.

U.S. Department of Health & Human Services. (1999). *Mental Health: A Report of the Surgeon General.* Rockville, MD: Substance Abuse and Mental Health Services Administration, National Institutes of Health.

Vanek, D. (2002). *Rural Facts.* Montanta: The University of Montana Rural Institute. Retrieved November 30, 2005, from http://rtc.ruralinstitute.umt.edu/mental health.htm.

Watkins, J. R. (2001). *Development of a Research Agenda on the Issues of Access in Care and Reduction of Health Status Disparities of Rural African Americans in South Carolina.* Columbia, SC: South Carolina State Office of Rural Health.

Whaley, A. (2001). Cultural mistrust of white mental health clinicians among African Americans with severe mental illness. *American Journal of Orthopsychiatry, 71*(2), 252-256.

Wilson-Ford, V. (1992). Health-protective behaviors of rural black elderly women. *Health & Social Work, 17*(1), 28-36.

Chapter 15

Kinship Care
As a Mental Health Intervention
for African-American Families

Priscilla A. Gibson

The literature presents kinship care in three interrelated ways: as an informal caregiving tradition in some minority communities, especially in the African-American community; as a child welfare service; and as an intergenerational parenting context with distinct family dynamics. Kinship care is defined as the caregiving of dependent children by a relative or close family friend when the biological parents are unavailable, unable, or unwilling to care for the child(ren) (Child Welfare League of American [CWLA], 1994). In the African-American community, kinship has traditional roots in slavery, in which children were taken into the homes of relatives and friends when their biological parents were sold. Contemporarily, the phrase kinship care emerges from the work of Stack (1974), who found that in an African-American community, the extended family network is an important social support strategy. Kinship care also has moved from a traditional informal caregiving arrangement in the African-American community to a formal child welfare service. There are two types of kinship care arrangements: informal, which is an agreement among family members, and formal, which is facilitated in the child welfare system. Currently, a subsystem of formal service, kinship foster care, has evolved, in which children live with relatives and are under the jurisdiction of the child welfare system. Foster kinship care is the fastest growing out-of-home living arrangement. It is difficult to assess the prevalence of informal kinship care arrangements, but it is assumed to exceed formal kinship care arrangements.

Mental Health Care in the African-American Community
© 2007 by The Haworth Press, Inc. All rights reserved.
doi:10.1300/5364_15

As an informal tradition in the African-American community, kinship care assures contact among family members. In kinship care, children have an opportunity to live in the most familiar environment as promoted by the Indian Child Welfare Act of 1978, which is the first policy that supported kinship care (Hegar, 1999). Therefore, kinship care translates into family preservation (Danzy & Jackson, 1997).

Kinship care translates into a unique form of intergenerational parenting, which is different from biological parents establishing their own families (McGoldrick, 1999) and making their families a priority (Boszormenyi-Nagy & Spark, 1973). The literature on kinship support in the African-American community discussed how young single mothers are helped by older women in their community (McDonald & Armstrong, 2001). In the context of this chapter, kinship caregiving is seen as an alternative arrangement where parenting is performed by an older generation (parents, grandparents, aunts, and uncles to the biological parents) or in more rare cases, relatives in the same (sibling of the biological parents) or a younger (older children of the biological parents caring for their younger siblings) generation. Thus, family structure and roles are changed and become more complex. For example, grandparents' relationships include the role of parents and grandparents. For grandmother caregivers, Gibson (2002) documented how this complex process affects family relationships with grandchildren, parents of the grandchildren, and the other adult children. In addition, Gibson (2005) found that grandmothers who assume this role also develop specific parenting strengths in the context of kinship care.

As a child welfare service, kinship care functions as a viable child placement arrangement alternative to foster care with strangers, thus saving states millions of dollars because kinship placements cost less compared to stranger foster care payments (Berrick, Barth, & Needell, 1994; Scannapieco, Hegar, & McAlpine, 1997). In fact, kinship care is described as a solution to the out-of-home arrangement problem encountered by child welfare in the twenty-first century (Brown, Cohon, & Wheeler, 2002). It is also congruent with the least restrictive environment philosophy in child welfare that promotes family preservation and child safety (Smith & Devore, 2004). Moreover, federal legislation such as the 1996 Personal Responsibility and Work Opportunity Reconciliation Act and Adoption Safe Families Assistance Act of 1997 (ASFA) explicitly recognize relative caregiving as a preferred option for children in need of care (Lorkovich, Piccola, Groza, Brindo, & Marks, 2004).

These three conceptualizations of kinship care, while not mutually exclusive, result in a narrow view, which is not inclusive of the healing properties inherent in it. Kinship care has been promoted as (1) a safety net for children in care, (2) beneficial to relatives, and (3) valued by the community.

For African Americans, kinship care can be viewed as a mental health intervention that is beneficial to the dependent child in care, the biological parents, the caregiving relative, and the community.

The purpose of this chapter is to set forth an argument for a view of kinship care as a mental health intervention in the African-American community. This chapter provides a review of the literature on kinship care and an expanded view that analyzes the mental health intervention properties of kinship care. The chapter concludes with ancillary materials to be used as classroom activities. Although experts concur that there are both risks and benefits in kinship care (Child Welfare League of America, 1994; Dubowitz, 1994; Gibson, 1996; Meyer & Link, 1990), there seems to be more of a focus on risks than on benefits. In this chapter, kinship care and relative caregiving will be used interchangeably.

LITERATURE REVIEW

Kinship care is most prevalent in African-American families (Goodman & Silverstein, 2001) and the gap in prevalence continues to widen between this group and other racial groups (Gleeson, 1999). Smith and Devore (2004) explain that the pattern of overrepresentation of African-American children in foster care has now shifted to kinship care. According to the latest census figures, there are over 6 million children in kinship care, 52 percent of which are African Americans (U.S. Census, 2000). African-American grandmothers disproportionately assume the role of caregivers followed by aunts, great-grandmothers, uncles, and grandfathers.

Kinship care does not always translate into benefits for those involved. In fact, much has been written about the negative influence on the health, well-being, and finances incurred by relatives, especially grandmothers who assume the role (Burnette, 1997; Emick & Hayslip, 1999; Fuller-Thompson & Minkler, 2000; Kelley, Whitley, Sipe, & Yorker, 2000). Experts have voiced concerns about permanence for children in kinship care, especially when caregivers decide not to legally adopt. However, despite the social and financial costs, increasingly relatives are accepting the roles of caregivers, especially in the African-American community. Not all African-American grandmothers accept the role (Gibson, 1996), yet experts have noted that African-American grandmothers cope better with their caregiving responsibilities than their counterparts in other racial groups (Caputo, 2001; Goodman & Silverstein, 2001). One reason may be a sense of mutual obligation and collective identity in the African-American community

(Schiele, 2000). It may also point to sociopolitical factors experienced in the lives of African Americans because of their race.

INTERVENTION PROPERTIES OF KINSHIP CARE

To detail the intervention properties of kinship care, a definition of an intervention is in order. An intervention is defined by Thomas (1984) as:

> A planned intrusion into the life or environment of an individual, couple, family, or other target unit that is intended to bring about beneficial changes for the individuals or others involved. The interventive action is the most conspicuous and central element in producing the desired outcomes of the helping effort, but it does not stand-alone. It is, or should be part of a helping strategy in which the other components help shape the interventive action and have an influence on the outcome achieved. (p. 29)

Shilling (1997) agrees with the beneficial characteristics in an intervention and notes that in social work, an intervention ought to enhance or maintain the functioning and well-being of individuals, families, groups, communities, or populations (p. 2). Fisher, Ellis, and Chamberlain (1999) call for interventions that are designed to enhance the development of children. Others have applied this view to children in out-of-home living arrangements. Specifically Ruff, Blank, and Barnett (1990) urge a view of foster care as an active intervention. Finley (1999) describes formal adoption as an effective intervention. Allowing a dependent child to live with a relative has occurred historically in the African-American community because of the benefits that will be incurred by children and families. It has been described as a "resilient, natural system of childrearing" (Scannapieco & Jackson, 1996, p. 194), a preventive tool (Freundlich, Morris, & Hernandez, 2003), a key form of family preservation (Child Welfare League of America, 1994; Danzy & Jackson, 1997), and a protective factor (Ruiz & Carlton-LaNey, 1999). Ehrle, Geen, and Clark (2001) note that most experts are in agreement that kinship care is beneficial for children. In addition, Testa and Slack (2002) found that kinship foster care has an inherent reciprocal relationship between the caregiver and the child that is beneficial to both. In this chapter, the beneficial effects of kinship care will be presented for the family and community as well.

EXPANDED APPROACH

Life Course Perspective

Life course perspective is one of the most appropriate lenses in which to view kinship care as an intervention. Germain and Gitterman (1986) describe the life model as "(1) a conceptual framework (an ecological perspective) that provides a simultaneous focus on people and environments; and (2) a method of practice that integrates practice principles and skills for work with individuals, families, and groups within an organizational, community, and cultural context" (p. 619). It is also called the ecological model and emphasizes potential for growth in clients and their environment (Germain & Gitterman, 1986). Life course perspective is an approach to studying changes in families over time at the micro- and macrolevels (Bengtson & Allen, 1993). These authors suggest the importance of five themes: (1) temporal, (2) multiple social context, (3) development, (4) heterogeneity in structures and process, and (5) multidisciplinary perspective on development.

Interventive Qualities of Kinship Care

Other experts have noted the beneficial nature of kinship care. Ruiz and Carlton-LaNey (1999) state that the positive influence of kinship care is a recurrent theme in the literature. Kinship care is one method that supports the survival of African-American families and is congruent with the role flexibility and interchangeability of parent roles in African-American families (Hill, 1997). It has become so typical with grandparents that it is has been labeled as a normative experience for certain groups (Force, Botsford, & Holbert, 2000). Rosenfeld, Pilowsky, Fine, and Thorpe (1997) suggest kinship care as a means of reducing adjustment problems for children in out-of-home placements. Testa (2001) succinctly summarizes kinship care as an intervention by noting, "kinship does matter" (p. 39).

MENTAL HEALTH PROPERTIES
OF KINSHIP CARE FOR CHILDREN IN CARE

Using a combination of Shilling (1997), Fisher et al. (1999), and the life course perspective approach, the mental health properties for children in kinship care indicate how their development, functioning, and well-being are improved by living with relatives. Numerous experts have indicated that for African-American children, living with a relative may result in many benefits (Courtney & Needell, 1997; Gleeson, O'Donnell, & Bonecutter,

1997; Iglehart, 1994; Scannapieco et al., 1997). Thus kinship care acts as a mental health intervention for children in placement in the following ways:

1. *Preserve culture and identities.* Kolomer (2000) states that the context of kinship care is ideal for preserving children's multiple social identities including personal, cultural, and ethnic. Kinship care keeps children in the most culturally familiar family environment. Children remain with family members who accept them in their homes and confirm their connection to them. These two factors combine to support social identity. In addition, identifying with one's ethnic group promotes self-esteem. Scannapieco et al. (1997) note that in kinship care, transmission of family identity is possible. Moreover, this living arrangement provides an opportunity to infuse racial dignity and pride. Given the values that most African Americans place on religion and spirituality, children also learn to live by faith-based rules (Timberlake, Stukes, & Chipungu, 1992).

2. *Confirm acceptance and value of the child.* Kinship care is seen as informal adoption in the African-American community (Hill, 1977). Children experience feeling loved, being cared about, and enjoying acts of kindness that are offered to them (Altshuler, 1999). This acceptance is salient because of the absence of the biological parents and the possibility of supporting self-esteem.

3. *Maintain in familiar environment.* Kinship care is so familiar to some children that Brown et al. (2002) conclude that it is "neither novel or disruptive" (p. 53). Actually, it is viewed as reducing the negative feelings of being separated from biological parents and facilitates connections to siblings (Gibbs & Muller, 2000). Unlike in stranger foster care, where children are generally placed in a different community, which translates into a different school, neighborhood, and other forms of newness, children in kinship care are afforded a level of comfort in the familiar. Being with a familiar adult also reduces trauma to the child (Sannapieco et al., 1999).

4. *Support well-being.* Whether kinship care is positively associated with child well-being is controversial. However, there is strong evidence that it can be beneficial. For example, Iglehart (1994) found that adolescents in kinship care were less likely to experience mental health problems. Solomon and Marx (1995) found no significant difference in health and school function between children in kinship care and those living with their biological parents.

5. *Promote emotional healing.* Although the trauma of being separated from biological parents is lessened when in kinship care, children do

experience intense emotional feelings. Being in the care of a relative provides an opportunity for children to share their feelings about being separated from their biological parents. Both the caregiving relative and the children have close affectional connections to the absent biological parents and as such, the stigma of the situation is lessened.

6. *Increase feelings of safety and security.* Generally, the feelings of safety for children in kinship care have been compromised because of prior maltreatment. Children in kinship care, although disliking having to change caregivers, expressed that the removal from their biological parents was necessary (Altshuler, 1999). In addition, Berrick et al. (1994) found that the biological parents are usually the only family members who have maltreated the children. Gibson (1996) found that grandmothers monitor the interactions between biological parents and grandchildren when safety is a concern. Moreover, when living with a relative, children's lives become more routine and predictable, which also increases feelings of security.

7. *Social support from other relatives.* Other noncaregiving relatives such as aunts, uncles, and cousins may provide emotional and social support to the children in care. This kind of support is congruent with the African Proverb, "it takes a village" to raise a child. Gibson (1996) found that when the grandmother's other adult children are supportive of the caregiving arrangement, they provide both social and financial support to the children in care.

8. *Increase contact with siblings.* When living with relatives, children in kinship care are more likely to have contact with their siblings than are children in stranger foster care (Chipungu, Everett, Verdulik, & Jones, 1998). Maintaining these relationship connections are important to the child's well-being.

MENTAL HEALTH PROPERTIES
OF KINSHIP CARE FOR RELATIVE CAREGIVERS

Whereas caregivers in kinship care vary widely in their demographic factors, most would agree that they serve as a buffer for the children in their care (Brown-Standridge & Floyd, 2000), which has a beneficial effect on them (Ruiz & Carlton-LaNey, 1999). Despite the stresses that are inherent in the role of primary caregivers, relatives overwhelmingly expressed their support of this living arrangement. Although relative caregivers experience costs and benefits when accepting the role as kinship caregivers, they continue seemingly because the benefits outweigh the costs. Most of the research on the benefits of kinship care has been conducted on grandmothers. The following list contains the mental health properties of kinship care for relatives.

1. *Enhance well-being.* In their research on the well-being of grandmother caregivers, Goodman and Silverstein (2001) found that African-American grandmothers in their study were more satisfied with life and less negatively affected than grandmothers in other racial groups. Some of the benefits reported by grandmothers include nurturing and cultivating family legacies (Burton & Bengston, 1985), new awareness of their strengths and feelings of being blessed (Gibson, 1996), and grandchildren's positive presence, good qualities, and accomplishments (Gibson & Lum, 2003), purpose for living (Jendrek, 1993), and enhanced sense of meaning and hopefulness (Burton, Dilworth-Anderson, & Merriwether-deViers, 1995).

2. *A second chance at parenting.* Grandparents have an opportunity to try different parenting strategies than those used with their biological children. Roe and Barnwell (1994) found that they could correct past parenting mistakes. Berrick et al. (1994) concluded that kinship caregivers have higher expectations for the future of the child than caregivers working within the foster care system. This increased level of expectation may produce positive results.

3. *Increase peace of mind.* These caregivers enjoy a peace of mind due to the knowledge that their young dependent relatives are receiving quality caregiving. They no longer worry about the vulnerable child being maltreated. They also have a level of control over the rearing of their children and values imparted to them. Ehrle and Day (1994) found that grandparents have a commitment to the well-being of their grandchildren.

4. *Pride in the achievements of the children in care.* Gibson and Lum (2003) and Minkler and Roe (1993) found that grandmothers experienced positive feelings including satisfaction from their grandchildren's accomplishments.

5. *Increase in hope for biological parents.* For some relatives, caregiving is seen as giving respite for the biological parents, who then have a period of time in which to work through their social difficulties. At the same time, grandparents maintain hope that the biological parent will return as an effective caregiver (Weber & Waldrop, 2000). This hope provides another level of positive feelings.

6. *Increase parenting skills.* Caregivers must deal with different concerns when raising nonbiological children and, often, learn new skills as parents. Gibson (2005) found that grandmothers develop parenting strengths to help their grandchildren succeed. These skills also help

structure the activities of the grandchildren with the hope that they will bypass the social problems their biological parents are experiencing.

MENTAL HEALTH PROPERTIES OF KINSHIP CARE FOR BIOLOGICAL PARENTS

Little research exists on the biological parents of the children in kinship care and accompanying mental health benefits they incur. Literature on biological parents describes them as the absent middle generation (Dressel & Barnhill, 1994) and absent parents (Smith & Devore, 2004). The social problems of these parents affect their children, relatives, and family dynamics (Gibson, 1996, 2002), yet they are an essential component in the lives of their children and relatives. Their importance has been acknowledged by ASFA, which mandates that if a child is in kinship care, then parental rights are not terminated. Kinship care functions as an intervention for biological parents in the following ways:

1. *Increased contact with child.* Physical contact between biological parents and their children is more frequent in kinship care (Meyer & Link, 1990). African-American caregivers are more likely than Whites or Hispanics to arrange for visitation by biological parents (Berrick et al., 1994).
2. *Motivation to resolve difficulties and return to effective parenting.* With their children in the care of relatives and not legally adopted, the rights of biological parents are not terminated. Maintaining these parental rights allows an opportunity for these parents to return to their role as parents. It may assist in parents' motivation to tackle their social problem.
3. *Experience a sense of relief because their children are being cared for by a family member.* Although there may be conflicts between the biological parents and relative caregivers (Grant, 2000), being placed with relatives provides the biological parents with a level of knowledge about the child that is not feasible in stranger foster care.

MENTAL HEALTH PROPERTIES OF KINSHIP CARE FOR THE AFRICAN-AMERICAN COMMUNITY

Mental health properties of kinship for the African-American community can be viewed in various ways. First, the African-American community has a tradition of collective responsibility for its children (Schiele, 2000). It is not unusual to hear concerns about children from adults in the community regardless of their relationship to the child. Second, it also functions as a reciprocal relationship between the community and its members and among members in the community. In addition, each also acts as a resource to the other. As such, each entity contributes to the well-being and capacity building of the other. Components include valuing its members, providing social support to them, and members giving back to the community. Details about those functions are listed here:

1. *Placing a priority on valuing children.* Winston (2003) notes that the African-American community values family caregiving. In the African-American community, assisting families and friends as well as the community is a norm and has been described in various ways. McDonald and Armstrong (2001) describe solidarity, responsibility, and accountability as three qualities of this community norm. Collins (1990) discusses the ethics of caring in which African-American women display three interrelated qualities as (1) individual uniqueness, (2) emotions in dialogue, and (3) capacity for empathy. This latter quality can be seen in kinship care.

2. *Following the self-help tradition.* The African-American community has a strong self-help tradition. Informal kinship care is seen as following that tradition. The African-American community, in which belongingness is prized and children are seen as a responsibility of all adults, can properly fulfill its role. It can support relative caregivers in their roles as primary caregivers.

3. *Growing community resources.* Kinship care functions to maintain children in their communities where they can learn about their culture while living with family members. Given that African-American children constitute a disproportionate number in child welfare, kinship care functions as an intervention to keep these children in the African-American community where they can potentially grow to be community resources as well. The reciprocal relationships between the African-American community and its members are enhanced because of kinship care. Maintaining children in kinship, thus having them in the community, increases the possibility that the community will then assist the children. Members work together to support each other, which adds to community resources. This is congruent with the Afrocentric view of belongingness and collectivity. In response, children who develop into successful, productive adults function in the capacity of human capital and can be a resource to their communities.

PRACTICE INCORPORATING A LIFE COURSE PERSPECTIVE OF KINSHIP CARE AS AN INTERVENTION

Effective direct and indirect (community) social work practice strategies with kinship care families must involve a framework that values the context of kinship care as an aspect of culture in the African-American community. Thus the inclusion of context is essential (Bengtson & Allen, 1993), as well as an acknowledgment of the strengths of natural helpers such as the extended family system. Ruiz and Carlton-LaNey (1999) voice that relative caregivers help not only the African-American community, but also society at large. Given the disproportionality of African-American children in the foster care system, kinship care removes a large number of children from the child welfare system, which results in financial savings to this system (Berrick et al., 1994; Scannapieco et al., 1997).

CONCLUSION

Kinship care is a complex living arrangement that influences the mental health of all significant parties. Although much has been written about the benefits of kinship care, viewing this living arrangement as a mental health intervention is new. The literature discusses benefits of kinship care primarily for the children in care. This chapter provides a more inclusive conceptualization incorporating the life course model to discuss the interventive factors in kinship care for the caregiver, biological parents, and the community.

Although there is no doubt that kinship care serves as a mental health intervention, if it is to function effectively, certain factors must be addressed. One important recommendation is the recognition of the benefit of kinship care not only to the children in care, their caregivers, and the African-American community but also to the child welfare system. Kinship care ought to be recognized as a solution for children in out-of-home placement and as an example of the resilience in African-American families (Danzy & Jackson, 1997; Poindexter & Linsk, 1999). One barrier that continues is the attitude of child welfare workers who are concerned about (1) the quality of parenting, (2) intergenerational transmission of poor parenting, (3) re-abuse because of close ties to the biological parents who previously abused the child, (4) whether the caregiver will obtain social and mental health services needed by the child in care, and (5) functioning abilities for older caregivers.

A second recommendation is increased financial and social support for the practice. Experts agree that the policies regarding governmental financial assistance to caregivers must be revisited with an eye toward increasing the amounts closer to that received by foster care providers. When reviewing the characteristics of caregivers, it is clear that they generally have limited financial resources.

Those who assume the role of primary caregivers to their young relatives must be adequately compensated by the child welfare system. Demonstration projects are being funded on small levels nationwide with research components to assess the benefits of such compensation. Support is needed not only from the African-American community, but also from legislation and professionals. A salient factor is the lack of support from formal social service agencies and systems that do not understand the phenomenon of kinship care in the African-American community. Another issue is the history of negative relationships between professionals and kinship caregivers (Ruiz & Carlton-LaNey, 1999). Children and caregivers must be respected and valued rather than seen as burdens on the system.

Third, more attention ought to be given to the biological parents of the children in care. Increased information from their perspectives would assist social workers in enhancing their involvement in parents' mental health well-being, that of their children, and the caregivers of the children.

CHAPTER SUMMARY

This chapter introduces a different philosophical view of kinship care. It espouses a view of kinship care as a mental health intervention instead of a service and provides examples of its benefits to children in care, caregivers, biological parents, and the community. As kinship care continues to grow, it is suggested that this living arrangement ought to be supported by public policy and supportive services to increase the relatives' capacities in their role as kinship caregivers.

CLASSROOM ACTIVITIES

To assist social work students in applying the aforementioned conceptualization into practice, the following suggestions are offered for classroom activities.

Activity I: Advocacy for Kinship Care

Divide the class into three groups representing advocates for children in care, caregivers, and biological parents. Give the groups 20 minutes to prepare their arguments about the benefits of kinship care to a legislative body that must decide whether to increase funding to caregivers. Groups need to make a list of benefits that can be objectively assessed by the policymakers. In each group, members will need to critically select their arguments.

Activity II: Understanding Complex Views on Kinship Care

Discuss the following:

- What are the major differences in the views on kinship care? What theoretical models are underlying those views (strengths perspective, pathological model, etc.)?
- List the mental health benefits of kinship care for the adult children of grandparent caregivers.
- Discuss the importance of culture in the context of kinship care. What skills emerged from the discussion that are essential to the provision of culturally competent social work services to this group?
- This chapter presented information on the interventive quality of kinship care for community. Identify possible costs to the community because of kinship care. If there are no costs, provide a logical argument.

Activity III: Training for Context Sensitive Social Work Services to Kinship Care Families

Providing effective service delivery to kinship care systems (child, caregivers, biological parents, and the community) is essential and complex. This exercise requires students to develop a training program for social workers, regardless of their setting, to provide services in such a manner. Instruct students to divide into four groups representing the aforementioned groups (child in care, caregivers, biological parents, or community). They will have 20 minutes to meet to list social work skills, attitudes, knowledge base, and values needed. Then all groups will convene into the larger group to write their list on the broad, which will be then prioritized.

Activity IV: Legal Adoptions in the Kinship Care Living Arrangements

Social workers generally encourage relative caregivers to legally adopt the children in their care in support of permanency. Yet, some relatives are not in favor of legal adoption because the children are already members of their families, not wanting the rights of the biological parents to be terminated, and being unclear about how the legal adoption would affect the family dynamics.

In this individual-focused activity, instruct students to list at least five reasons to support and oppose legal adoption for relative caregivers. Allow about five minutes for a listing of the reasons. Then facilitate a class discussion in which students will share their views. As students share, list their comments on a board. After 20 minutes of sharing, summarize the comments.

Activity V: Openness in Kinship Care for Biological Parents

Will the mental health status of the children in care be enhanced by contact with their biological parents? Divide students into four discussion groups: (1) relative caregivers, (2) biological parents, (3) children in care, and (4) social workers from the child protection system. Allow the groups to convene separately to take a position on this issue. Then allow each group to present its respective position. After all positions have been presented, allow groups to asked question and engage in a discussion.

REFERENCES

Altshuler, S. J. (1999). The well-being of children in kinship care. In J. P. Gleeson & C. F. Hairston (Eds.), *Kinship Care: Improving Practice Through Research* (pp. 117-143). Washington, DC: CWLA Press.

Bengtson, V. L., & Allen, K. R. (1993). The life course perspective applied to families over time. In P. G. Boss, W. J. Doherty, R. LaRossa, W. R. Schumm, & S. K. Steinmetz (Eds.), *Sourcebook of Family Theories and Methods: A Contextual Approach.* New York: Plenum Press.

Berrick, J. D., Barth, R. P., & Needell, B. (1994). A comparison of kinship foster homes and foster family homes. *Children and Youth Services Review, 16,* 35-63.

Boszormenyi-Nagy, I., & Spark, G. (1973). *Invisible Loyalties: Reciprocity in Intergenerational Family Therapy.* New York: Harper & Row.

Brown, S., Cohon, D., & Wheeler, R. (2002). African American extended families and kinship care: How relevant is the foster care model for kinship care? *Children and Youth Services Review, 24*(1/2), 53-77.

Brown-Standdrige, M. D., & Floyd, C. W. (2000). Healing bittersweet legacies: Revisiting contextual family therapy for grandparents raising grandchildren in crisis. *Journal of Marital and Family Therapy, 26*(2), 185-197.

Burnette, D. (1997). Grandparents raising grandchildren in the inner city. *Families in Society, 78,* 489-499.

Burton, L., & Bengston, V. L. (1985). Black grandmothers: Issues of timing and continuity of roles. In V. L. Bengston & J. F. Robertson (Eds.), *Grandparenthood* (pp. 61-77). Beverly Hills, CA: Sage.

Burton, L. M., Dilworth-Anderson, P., & Merriwether-Devries, C. (1995). Context and surrogate parenting among contemporary grandparents. *Marriage and Family Review, 20,* 349-366.

Caputo, R. (2001). Depression and health among grandmothers co-residing with grandchildren in two cohorts of women. *Families in Society, 82*(5), 473-483.

Child Welfare League of America. (1994). *Kinship Care: A Natural Bridge.* Washington, DC: Child Welfare League of America.

Chipungu, S., Everett, J., Verduik, M. J., & Jones, J. (1998). *Children Placed in Foster Care with Relatives: A Multi-State Study.* Washington, DC: Department of Health and Human Services, Administration on Children, Youth, and Families.

Collins, P. H. (1990). *Black Feminist Thought* (2nd ed.). New York: Routledge.

Courtney, M., & Needell, B. (1997). Outcomes of kinship care: Lessons from California. In J. D. Berrick, R. P. Barth, & N. Gilbert (Eds.), *Child Welfare Research Review, Volume II* (pp. 130-149). New York: Columbia University Press.

Danzy, J., & Jackson, S. (1997). Family preservation and support services: A missed opportunity for kinship care. *Child Welfare, 76,* 31-44.

Dressel, P. L., & Barnhill, S. K. (1994). Reframing gerontological thought and practice: The case of grandmothers with daughters in prison. *The Gerontologist, 34,* 685-691.

Dubowitz, H. (1994). Kinship care: Suggestions for future research. *Child Welfare, 72,* 153-169.

Ehrle, J., Geen, R., & Clark, R. (2001). *Children Cared for by Relatives: Who Are They and How Are They Faring.* Washington, DC: Urban Institute New Federalism Report. Series B-28.

Ehrle, G. M., & Day, H. D. (1994). Adjustment and family functioning of grandmothers rearing their grandchildren. *Contemporary Family Therapy, 16,* 67-82.

Emick, M. A., & Hayslip, B. Jr. (1999). Custodial grandparenting: Stresses, coping skills, and relationships with grandchildren. *International Journal of Aging and Human Development, 48*(1), 35-61.

Finley, G. E. (1999). Children of adoptive families. In W. K. Silverman & T. H. Ollendick (Eds.), *Developmental Issues in the Clinical Treatment of Children* (pp. 358-370). Needham Heights, MA: Allyn and Bacon.

Fisher, P. A., Ellis, B. H., & Chamberlain, P. (1999). Early intervention foster care: A model for preventing risk in young children who have been maltreated. *Children's Services: Social Policy, Research, and Practice, 2*(3), 159-182.

Force, L. T., Botsford, A., Pisano, P. A., & Holbert, A. (2000). Grandparents raising children with and without a developmental disability: Preliminary comparisons. *Journal of Gerontological Social Work, 33*(4), 5-19.

Freundlich, M., Morris, L., & Hernandez, C. (2003). *Kinship Care: Meeting the Needs of Children and Families of Color: A Position Paper of the Race Matters Consortium.* Retrieved March 10, 2006, from http://www.racemattersconsortium .org/docs/whopaper5.pdf.

Fuller-Thomson, E., & Minkler, M. (2000). African American grandparents raising grandchildren: A national profile of demographic and health characteristics. *Health and Social Work, 25,* 109-118.

Germain, D. B., & Gitterman, A. (1986). The life model approach to social work practice. In F. J. Turner (Ed.), *Social Work Treatment: Interlocking Theoretical Approaches* (3rd ed., pp. 618-658). New York: Free Press.

Gibbs, P., & Muller, U. (2000). Kinship foster care moving to the mainstream: Controversy, policy, and outcome. *Adoption Quarterly, 4*(20), 57-87.

Gibson, P. A. (1996). The Lived Experience of Kinship Care: African American Grandmothers and their Grandchildren. Unpublished doctoral dissertation, University of Denver, Colorado.

Gibson, P. A. (2002). Caregiving affects family relationships of African American grandmothers as new mothers again: A phenomenological perspective. *Journal of Marital and Family Therapy, 28*(3), 341-353.

Gibson, P. A. (2005). Intergenerational parenting from the perspective of African American grandmothers. *Family Relations, 54*(2), 280-297.

Gibson, P. A., & Lum, T. Y. (2003). *Informal Kinship Care in Minnesota: A Pilot Study* (Final Report to the Minnesota Kinship Caregivers Association). University of Minnesota School of Social Work, MN: St. Paul.

Gleeson, J. P. (1999). Kinship care as a child welfare service: What do we really know. In J. P. Gleeson & C. F. Hairston (Eds.), *Kinship Care: Improving Practice Through Research* (pp. 3-34). Washington, DC: CWLA Press.

Gleeson, J. P., O'Donnell, J., & Bonecutter, F. J. (1997). Understanding the complexity of practice in kinship foster care. *Child Welfare, 76*(6), 801-826.

Goodman, C. C., & Silverstein, M. (2001). Grandmothers who parent their grandchildren. *Journal of Family Issues, 22*(5), 557-578.

Grant, R. (2000). The special needs of children in kinship care. *Journal of Gerontological Social Work, 33*(3), 17-33.

Hegar, R. L. (1999). The cultural roots of kinship care. In R. L. Hagar & M. Scannapieco (Eds.), *Kinship Foster Care: Policy, Practice, and Research* (pp. 17-27). New York: Oxford Press.

Hill, R. (1977). *Informal Adoption Among Black Families*. Washington, DC: National Urban League.

Hill, R. (1997). *The Strengths of African American Families: Twenty-Five Years Later.* Washington, DC: R & B Publishers.

Iglehart, A. P. (1994). Kinship foster care: Placement, services, and outcome issues. *Children and Youth Services Review, 16,* 107-122.

Jendrek, M. P. (1993). Grandparents who parent their grandchildren: Effects on lifestyle. *Journal of Marriage and the Family, 55,* 609-621.

Kelley, S. J., Whitley, D., Sipe, T. A., & Yorker, B. C. (2000). Psychological distress in grandmother kinship care providers: The role of resources, social support, and physical health. *Child Abuse & Neglect, 24*(3), 311-321.

Kolomer, S. R. (2000). Kinship foster care and its impact on grandmother caregivers. *Journal of Gerontological Social Work, 33*(3), 85-102.

Lorkovich, T. W., Piccola, T., Groza, V., Brindo, M. E., & Marks, J. (2004). Kinship care and permanence: Guiding principles for policy and practice. *Families in Society, 85*(2), 159-164.

McDonald, K. B., & Armstrong, E. M. (2001). De-romanticizing Black intergenerational support: The questionable expectations of welfare reform. *Journal of Marriage and Family, 63*, 213-223.

McGoldrick, M. (1999). Women through the family life cycle. In B. Carter & M. McGoldrick (Eds.), *The Expanded Family Life Cycle: Individual, Family, and Social Perspectives* (3rd ed., pp. 106-123). Needham Heights, MA: Allyson & Bacon.

Meyer, B. S., & Link, M. K. (1990). *Kinship Foster Care: The Double Edge Dilemma.* Rochester, NY: Task Force on Permanency Planning for Foster Care.

Minkler, M., & Roe, K. M. (1993). *Grandmothers as Caregivers: Raising Children of the Crack Cocaine Epidemic.* Newbury Park, CA: Sage.

Poindexter, C. C., & Linsk, N. L. (1999). "I'm just glad that I'm here": Stories of seven African American HIV-affected grandmothers. *Journal of Gerontological Social Work, 32*(1), 63-81.

Roe, K., & Barnwell, R. (1994). The assumption of caregiving: Grandmothers raising the children of the crack-cocaine epidemic. *Qualitative Health Research, 4*(3), 281-303.

Rosenfeld, A. A., Pilowsky, D. J., & Thorpe, M. (1997). Foster care: An update. *Journal of the American Academy of Child and Adolescent Psychiatry, 36*, 448-457.

Ruff, H. A., Blank, S., & Barnett, H. L. (1990). Early intervention in the context of foster care. *Developmental and Behavioral Pediatrics, 11*, 265-268.

Ruiz, D. S., & Carlton-LaNey, I. (1999). The increase in intergenerational African American families headed by grandmothers. *Journal of Sociological & Social Welfare, 16*(4), 71-86.

Scannapieco, M., Hegar, R., & McAlpine, C. (1997). Kinship care and foster care: A comparison of characteristics and outcomes. *Families in Society, 78*(5), 480-488.

Scannapieco, M., & Jackson, S. (1996). Kinship care: The African American response to family preservation. *Social Work, 41*(2), 190-196.

Schiele, J. H. (2000). *Human Services and the Afrocentric Paradigm.* Binghamton, NY: The Haworth Press.

Schilling, R. F. (1997). Developing intervention research programs in social work. *Social Work Research, 21*(3), 178-180.

Smith, C. J., & Devore, W. (2004). African American children in the child welfare and kinship system: From exclusion to over inclusion. *Children and Youth Services Review, 26*(5), 427-446.

Solomon, J. C., & Marx, J. (1995). "To grandmother's house we go": Health and school adjustment of children raised solely by grandparents. *The Gerontologist, 35*(3), 386-394.

Stack, C. (1974). *All Our Kin: Strategies for Survival in a Black Community.* New York: Harper and Row.

Testa, M. F. (2001). Kinship care and permanency. *Journal of Social Service Research, 28*(1), 25-43.

Thomas, E. J. (1984). *Designing Interventions for the Helping Professions.* Beverly Hills: Sage.

Timberlake, E. M., & Stukes-Chipungu, S. (1992). Grandmotherhood: Contemporary meaning among African American middle-class grandmothers. *Social Work, 37,* 216-222.

U.S. Census Bureau (2000). *Supplementary Survey Summary Tables.* Retrieved January 20, 2006, from http://factfinder.census.gov/home/en/datanotes/exp_c2ss .html.

Weber, J. A., & Waldrop, D. P. (2000). Grandparents raising grandchildren: Families in transition. *Journal of Gerontological Social Work, 33*(2), 27-46.

Winston, C. A. (2003). African American grandmothers parenting grandchildren orphaned by AIDS: Grieving and coping with loss. *Illness, Crisis & Loss, 11*(4), 350-361.

Chapter 16

Mental Health Needs of Multiethnic Families and Children

Chandra F. Brown

Multiracial families, families composed of people from different racial or ethnic groups, and multiracial individuals, persons whose parents are from two separate races or cultures, are a rapidly growing population in the United States. These individuals have a unique history and continue to face a number of challenges in today's society. This chapter will focus on issues related to families and children who have one Black parent and one White parent. Although there are several other racial pairings that can occur, historically, it has been the case that Black and White unions have held the greatest controversy in the United States (Brown, 1987; Davidson, 1992).

Historically, multiracial families and individuals have had to face a tremendous amount of discrimination, and negative societal perceptions and attitudes. This oppression has not only been perpetuated by society, but by government and political institutions as well. As early as the mid-1600s, antimiscegenation laws were placed in effect, making multiracial unions illegal and punishable by imprisonment. It was not until 1967 in the landmark Supreme Court Case *Loving v. Virginia,* that these laws were declared unconstitutional. Although it was no longer illegal to marry across races, several states maintained these laws on their books. It was not until November of 1998 that South Carolina removed their antimiscegenation laws, and the final state, Alabama, removed their antimiscegenation laws in 2000.

Despite this history of discrimination, the population of multiracial families and children continues to grow. According to the U.S. Census 2000, 2.4 percent (6.8 million people) of the U.S. population identified as having

Mental Health Care in the African-American Community
© 2007 by The Haworth Press, Inc. All rights reserved.
doi:10.1300/5364_16

more than one race. Further, the census data indicated that 6 percent of married households were multiracial (approximately 1.6 million couples) (U.S. Census, 2003). According to Kelley (2002), the numbers of multiracial marriages has increased 10 times since the 1960s. Also, according to the census, 10 to 12 percent of unmarried couples were in multiracial relationships. This growing trend in multiracial relationships and marriages clearly indicate that this is rapidly becoming the new face of America. Despite this massive population growth, multiracial families and individuals continue to face a myriad of challenges in today's society.

Multiracial families encounter several barriers within the course of their relationship development and family growth, especially from extended family and peers who do not approve of multiracial unions (Gibbs, 1987; Stephan & Stephan, 1991; Wardle, 1989). This animosity toward multiracial relationships often transfers to the children of these relationships, resulting in some extended family members rejecting both the multiracial relationship and the child (Wardle, 1989).

McRoy and Freeman (1986) acknowledge that in order for biracial individuals to develop a positive racial identity, their families must nurture both Black and White backgrounds, and provide role models from both Black and White racial cultures, as well as expose children to peers in the community and school that are from both racial cultures. This can be difficult if families or children feel a sense of rejection not only from their families but also from one or both cultures (Stephan & Stephan, 1991). Thus, multiracial families have the unique challenge to raise their children in a social environment that may not be supportive of the achievement of positive mental health (Ladner, 1984). As a result of this animosity, some multiracial families face difficulty finding a place to fit in. Many have found some degree of acceptance and have chosen to align with Black communities (Billingsley, 1992; Buttery, 1987), although according to Billingsley, some Black/White families have chosen not to side with any particular racial community (Billingsley, 1992).

The rationale for this chapter is to provide knowledge and direction for working with multiracial families' and children's unique mental health needs by exploring literature both historically and recently, as well as provide a strengths-based life perspective approach for addressing the needs of this rapidly emerging population. Empirically based studies and results will be presented and analyzed based on their cultural relevance, and suggestions will be offered for families, practitioners, educators, researchers, and policy makers.

REVIEW OF THE LITERATURE

Historically, the literature pertaining to multiracial families and individuals has been largely deficit oriented. Multiracial families have been depicted as fraught with problems, high divorce rates, and having ulterior motives for entering into multiracial relationships (Davidson, 1992; Kato, 2000; Logan, Freeman, & McRoy, 1987; Nakashima, 1992; Spickard, 1989; Wardle, 1989, 1991). Some of the myths that have been perpetuated include rebelliousness (Davidson, 1992; Foeman & Nance, 1999; Kato, 2000; Kelley, 2000; Spickard, 1989), selling out of own race (Nakashima, 1992; Wardle, 1991), hypergamy, or status seeking (Davidson, 1992; Foeman & Nance, 1999; Kato, 2000; Kelley, 2000; Wardle, 1989), unable to attract a mate within own race (Kato, 2000; Kelley, 2000), racial self-hatred (Kelley, 2000; Nakashima, 1992), sexual curiosity, dominance or acting out (Davidson, 1992; Foeman & Nance, 1999; Kato, 2000; Kelley, 2000; Wardle, 1989), and insecurity and low self-esteem (Davidson, 1992; Kelley, 2000). Multiracial families have been portrayed as abnormal or outcasts (Foeman & Nance, 1999; Logan et al., 1987; Nakashima, 1992), having a high divorce rate (Spickard, 1989), and breaking "a fundamental taboo" (Brown, 1987, p. 24).

Multiracial individuals, the offspring of these "abnormal" relationships, were equally negatively portrayed. Myths abounded, indicating that multiracial individuals were marginal people (Brown, 1987; Kerwin & Ponterotto, 1995; Nakashima, 1992; Park, 1928; Stonequist, 1937); had to select the identity of the minority parent or be considered a sell out to their race (Brown, 1987; Kato, 2000; Kerwin & Ponterotto, 1995; Wardle, 1991); were genetically inferior (Nakashima, 1992); have problems in school, society, and with their personalities (Wardle, 1991); suffer low self-esteem; and are psychologically maladjusted and confused about their racial identity (Buttery, 1987; Gibbs, 1987; Park, 1928; Stephan & Stephan, 1991; Teicher, 1968). Interventions that were applied were usually developed to work with individuals from one race, most often, interventions for African Americans (Poston, 1990).

More recently, researchers have begun to take a closer look at these myths and beliefs pertaining to multiracial families and individuals. Through qualitative and quantitative studies, many of the findings have run contrary to the earlier literature base on this population. Current findings are more strengths focused, discovering their uniqueness rather than their maladjustments. As such, theories pertaining to multiracial families and children have been developed that reflect the unique changes which can occur throughout the development of a relationship/family and of an individual.

MULTIRACIAL FAMILIES

One recent theory pertaining to the developmental process of a multiracial relationship was formulated by Foeman and Nance (1999). Foeman and Nance proposed a four-stage model that begins with racial awareness.

Stage one: During this stage, the couple develops awareness of both similarities and differences between them. Foeman and Nance report that the couple will have a heightened sensitivity to the role race has in their lives (Foeman & Nance, 1999). During this stage, and subsequent stages, open communication is important for successful navigation to the next stage.

Stage two: Coping with social definitions of race includes the couple coming together to deal with negativity from society. According to Foeman and Nance, during this time, the couple begins to develop strategies to protect the relationship and may avoid situations where potential conflicts could arise (Foeman & Nance, 1999). The couple will either develop a strong bond or may be unable to deal with the societal pressure and end the relationship (Foeman & Nance, 1999).

Stage three: Identity emergence is when the multiracial couple define themselves within their relationship and take charge of their new identity (Foeman & Nance, 1999). In addition, the couple begins to appreciate their uniqueness and the strengths of their relationship (Foeman & Nance, 1999).

Finally, *stage four* is maintenance of stage three development.

MULTIRACIAL CHILDREN

Several theories have emerged over the years to describe the process in which a multiracial child develops a racial identity. Earlier models focused on the deficits of multiracial individuals, particularly a sense of marginalism (Stonequist, 1937). The first developmental theory was introduced by Stonequist in 1937. Stonequist's theory focused on developing an awareness of marginality, never indicating a sense of an integrated identity. Stonequist's developmental theory was deficit-oriented, focusing on the multiracial person being maladjusted and having a problematic identity development process (Poston, 1990). Since Stonequiest's model, several others have proposed developmental models that have moved away from a deficit approach and focused more on strengths and influence of external factors. These newer models often incorporate an ecological approach taking into account intrapersonal, family, community, and societal factors.

In 1977, Jacobs presented a biracial identity development model based on empirical research from a doll play study utilizing ten Black/White children ages 3 to 8. From his findings, Jacobs presented a three-stage theory of development mostly focused on awareness of color (Jacobs, 1992). W. Carlos Poston (1990) presented a five-stage model based on past literature incorporating many environmental factors. Although mostly strengths based, Poston's model did suggest that a multiracial person will go through periods of maladjustment and guilt before arriving at an integrated identity (Kerwin & Ponterotto, 1995).

More recently, in 1995, Kerwin and Ponterotto developed a model for bi-racial identity development, based on their own empirical research and empirical studies of others. This six-stage model begins at pre-school and culminates with adulthood, utilizing a life-course perspective. During stage one, preschool, which occurs usually up to age 5, racial awareness develops and the child begins to recognize similarities and differences in people's appearances (Kerwin & Ponterotto, 1995). Entry into school, stage two, is distinguished by the use of labels and color terms to define self and family. Kerwin and Ponterotto recognize that parents' use of a biracial label, role models, and school can all influence the child during this stage (Kerwin & Ponterotto, 1995). Increased awareness of skin color differences and use of labels based on race and ethnicity characterize stage three, preadolescence. Adolescence, stage four, includes a feeling of pressure to identify with one racial group. Development of a more secure sense of self and a growing acceptance of biracial identity describes stage five, college/young adulthood. Kerwin and Ponterotto specify that there may still be an identification with one parent's race identity at this time, however, the individual begins to gain insight into pros and cons of an integrated identity (Kerwin & Ponterotto, 1995). Finally, during stage six, adulthood, there is continued development of an integrated identity as well as development of skills to maneuver within different cultures and situations (Kerwin & Ponterotto, 1995).

CRITICAL ANALYSIS OF THE LITERATURE

As a result of the literature that often described multiracial families and individuals in a negative context as well as the models of relationship and identity formation, many researchers sought to validate or invalidate these ideas. As a result, an increasing body of empirical evidence has emerged.

Multiracial Relationships and Families

Yancey and other researchers conducted several studies (Qian, 1999; Yancey, 2002; Yancey & Yancey, 1998) examining these myths and theories for why people enter multiracial relationships. In a study employing a nationwide sample of 2561, Yancey found that integrated schools led to increased incidences of interracial dating and found no evidence of entering interracial relationships to increase social status (Yancey, 2002). Yancey and Yancey (1998) reported that familiarity with the other race was a likely predictor for entering an interracial relationship per the results of a content analysis.

Lewis, Yancey, and Bletzer (1997) also examined factors that played a role in partner selection. Through a mail-out questionnaire of 371 participants, it was found that personal and sexual attraction and easy conversation were the most important factors in partner selection in interracial relationships. Further, in a study by Qian (1999) using data from the 1980 and 1990 census, findings showed that the main factor in interracial mate selection was education compatibility.

Some studies have examined outside forces and acceptance levels of multiracial relationships and families. Killian (2002) conducted a qualitative study on ten Black/White couples in order to assess family history, experiences together, and types of discussions on racial and ethnic differences. Killian found that issues of race and racism were not commonly discussed within the relationship (Killian, 2002). Furthermore, close friends and relatives often discouraged the relationship (Killian, 2002). Also examining the factor of acceptance, Mills, Daly, Longmore, and Kilbride (1995) conducted a study utilizing a sample of 142 college undergraduate students, and found Whites had a greater degree of negativity and prejudice toward multiracial relationships than Blacks (Mills et al., 1995).

Contrary to the myth that people enter multiracial relationships because they are a sell-out or are confused about their own racial identity, Kerwin, Ponterotto, Jackson, and Harris (1993) found in their qualitative study of nine Black/White multiracial children and their families that parents had a secure sense of their own racial identity. In addition, parents reported having open discussions on race. Further, for the participating families in this particular study, no one identified as being alienated from their extended family as a result of entering a multiracial relationship (Kerwin, Ponterotto, Jackson, & Harris, 1993).

Multiracial Children

Although some research has been carried out on multiracial children and individuals since the late 1960s (Teicher, 1968), a surge in studies has transpired over the past decade, particularly dissertation work. Many studies have sought to gain a general understanding of this population, however, several have examined the myths that abound surrounding multiracial persons. Myths that have often been assessed and will be discussed include a sense of marginality, adjustment problems, self-esteem problems, and the most commonly discussed myth, identity selection.

In a qualitative study of nine Black/White children and their families, Kerwin et al. (1993) found that contrary to the marginality myth, children did not see themselves as marginal. In fact, the children were identified with having the strength of showing sensitivity to views and beliefs of both parental cultures. Tizard and Phoenix (1995) also examined the myth of marginality. Using a sample of 58 biracial adolescents, they found that only one-fifth expressed feelings of marginality. In addition, Tizard and Phoenix reported that the participants actually had strength of being able to see things from a dual perspective and felt that their family was "a witness against racism" (Tizard & Phoenix, 1995, p. 1407).

Not all findings have been as positive as the studies listed above. Gibbs and Moskowitz-Sweet (1991), led a study involving intensive case studies of 20 multiracial/multicultural adolescents and concluded that participants did experience social marginality, and were willing to make value concessions in order to fit into a peer group (Gibbs & Moskowitz-Sweet, 1991).

Johnson and Nagoshi (1986) examined the myth of multiracial children having adjustment problems. In their quantitative study comparing monoracial and multiracial persons, they found few differences between the two groups, and not much difference in adjustment, which runs contrary to the belief that multiracial children are maladjusted (Johnson & Nagoshi, 1986). In addition, Jones' (2000) dissertation research involving 251 participants found no significant differences between multiracial and monoracial youth in their psychological adjustment.

Milan and Keiley (2000) also explored the myth of marginality. Using a nationally representative database to obtain a sample of monoracial and multiracial adolescents, results showed that multiracial youth were indeed vulnerable to delinquency, school problems, and lowered self regard (Milan & Keiley, 2000). In addition, Cooney and Radina (2000) conducted a study on adjustment issues through the use of data from a subsample of the National Longitudinal Study of Adolescent Health. Findings showed that multiracial adolescents had higher rates of problems consisting of school problems, delinquency, and depression (Cooney & Radina, 2000).

Stephan and Stephan (1991) studied the myth that multiracial persons had low self-esteem. In a study of 497 persons, 180 being multiracial, results indicated that being raised in a multiracial family had no negative effects, and furthermore, multiracial participants did not have low-self esteem, feel alienated, or experience greater stress (Stephan & Stephan, 1991). In a dissertation study, Van Kirk (2003) used a sample of 83 multiracial participants to examine self-esteem and adjustment. Findings showed that multiracial participants scored higher on self-esteem than monoracial participants (VanKirk, 2003). Further, Jones' dissertation study on 251 participants found no significant differences between multiracial and monoracial youth in self-esteem (Jones, 2003).

The most widely studied myth is that regarding identity development. Myths regarding this issue have asserted that multiracial individuals are confused about their identity, that their identity development process is problematic, and that a multiracial person, if Black and White, had to select the race identity of the Black parent (Brown, 1987; Buttery, 1987; Gibbs, 1987; Kato, 2000; Kerwin & Ponterotto, 1995; Park, 1928; Teicher, 1968; Wardle, 1991). One of the first studies on identity of multiracial children was led by Teicher (1968). Results from Teicher's study of 50 multiracial families illustrated children were unable to identify with their parents and had identity-related problems (Teicher, 1968).

Bracey, Bamaca, and Umana-Taylor also studied ethnic identity among multiracial adolescents versus monoracial adolescents. Findings showed that although multiracial youth scored higher than Whites on ethnic identity, they scored lower on this measure than Blacks, Asians, and Hispanics (Bracey et al., 2004). In addition, in their study of 20 multiracial/multicultural adolescents, Gibbs and Moskowitz-Sweet (1991) found participants often overidentified with the minority parent and displayed ambivalence over their racial identity.

Conversely, in their two-year study of 12 multiracial adolescents and their families, Gibbs and Hines (1992) found that 75 percent of their study participants felt positive about their identity and only 25 percent showed psychological adjustment problems possibly as a result of ambivalence over their racial identity. In addition, in Kerwin et al.'s qualitative study of nine Black/White children and their families, results showed that more open discussion on race led to a higher likelihood of an integrated racial identity (Kerwin et al., 1993).

Although children of dual heritages are more likely to select a multiracial identity (Kerwin et al., 1993; Suzuki-Crumley & Hyers, 2004), some studies have also pointed to a trend in identity selection that is not as clear cut as Black, multiracial, or White (Rockquemore & Brunsma, 2002; Tizard & Phoenix, 1995). Using survey data from a sample of 177 multiracial respondents to study racial identity choices, Rockquemore and Brunsma found that respondents had a multidimensional approach to identity selection (Rockquemore & Brunsma, 2002). Respondents made various choices based on different locations or social networks. Choices selected included exclusively Black; exclusively White; exclusively biracial; exclusively biracial, but experiencing the world as Black; Black, White, and biracial (fluid) depending on social context; and lastly, transcendent (not bound to any category) (Rockquemore & Brunsma, 2002). Finally, in their study of 58 multiracial adolescents, Tizard and Phoenix found that more than half of participants identified as multiracial, but would identity as Black at times, based on the situation (Tizard & Phoenix, 1995). Half of the participants did indicated that in the past, they wanted to be a different color, however, only 14 percent still had that desire (Tizard & Phoenix, 1995).

IMPLICATIONS FOR INDIVIDUALS, FAMILIES, AND COMMUNITIES

These findings, although not conclusive, provide a basis for shifting the old paradigm of viewing multiracial families and children as abnormal and laden with problems to a new view of healthy families and children who as individuals and cohesive units are not necessarily maladjusted, but do face unique barriers and challenges within their perspective communities and larger society. Myths perpetuated by resistant family members and communities on why people should not enter multiracial relationships or bear children, are now challenged with supporting evidence that these myths are not indeed facts.

Despite this growing body of literature supporting the normalcy of this population, multiracial families and children still face a number of challenges within their families, communities, and society. Although problems faced by multiracial families and individuals often result from interactions with family, peers, community, and society's negative attitudes and behaviors (Brown, 1990; McFadden, 2001), it is important for multiracial families to settle in neighborhoods and communities that don't oppose their existence. Integrated communities will have to come to grips that due·to availability, multiracial dating is likely to occur. Community agencies and schools will be challenged to accept the dual heritage of multiracial children rather than to automatically assign the label of "Black" to a child raised as "biracial," or even "White." This will be particularly challenging for the Black community because there may be an underlying fear that if multiracial children assert this dual heritage, the Black population will decrease, thus affecting their political power to address social and economic disparity in the Black community (Brown, 1995; Wardle, 1991).

Public policy and strengths-based interventions have particularly been affected by past practices. Public policy surrounding this population has largely been in the form of classification systems. Formal and informal policies, such as one-drop rules, have caused problems for multiracial individuals at all levels. Because of this policy, individuals have often been socialized in the past to identify as Black if they have one drop of Black blood in them (Kerwin & Ponterotto, 1995). Families have frequently been pressured to label their multiracial children as Black. Children and families who have to complete forms asking for demographic data in order to visit a doctor or clinic, enroll in school or seek community help, have been forced to classify their children as Black or as an "other" (Wardle, 1991).

Policies regarding classification systems have frequently been inconsistent. The Federal Office of Budget and Management, which sets classification standards, previously indicated that multiracial persons should be classified based on the racial category that their community views that person (Ferrante & Brown, 1998). The National Center for Health Statistics, however, was categorizing multiracial children based on the racial category of the mother (Ferrante & Brown, 1998). This same center, before 1989, classified multiracial children on the racial status of the non-White parent, and if both parents were non-White, then the racial status of the father (Ferrante & Brown, 1998).

As a result of the myths surrounding multiracial families and children, practitioners are faced with having to challenge assumptions that multiracial families are abnormal and multiracial children are maladjusted. Instead of automatically assuming any problems within the relationship or the child's behavior stems from race conflict or racial confusion, practitioners are going to have to make a paradigm shift and look at strengths and supports (Kelley, 2002; Oriti, Bibb, & Mahboubi, 1996; Wardle, 1989). Focus should be directed at a multiracial family's strengths to overcome racism and adversities and the multiracial child's uniqueness and dual worldviews (McFadden, 2001; Oriti et al., 1996). Also, strengths-based interventions would now address family, community, and society support factors that enhance family cohesion and identity development over the family's life course, as well as the child's development throughout childhood, adolescence, and adulthood.

EXPANDED APPROACH

Although multiracial families and children have been researched and some methods have been addressed for working with this population, other than identity development, few approaches have been suggested. Recently, discussions have begun to explore strengths-based approaches focusing on multiracial individuals' adaptability (Oriti et al., 1996) and ecological approaches focusing on the influence of family and environmental factors (Kelley, 2002; Logan et al., 1987; McRoy & Freeman, 1986; Milan & Keiley, 2000). These approaches are most useful when addressing mental health needs for this population; however, as a result of multiracial families and children's historical and political oppression, an empowerment approach is needed as well.

With foundations in systems and ecological theories, an empowerment approach would encourage and assist multiracial families and individuals to take more control over their lives and the issues that may affect them socially and politically (Gutierrez, Parsons, & Cox, 1998). Although often applied to other minority and oppressed or disadvantaged groups, it has been minimally explored for its application to multiracial families and children. This approach would also help affect change in public policy and community supports for upcoming multiracial generations. Gutierrez et al. (1998), outline the components of an empowerment process as attitudes, values, and beliefs; shared experience; knowledge and skills for critical thinking; and action throughout the life span. Problems are conceptualized based on the interaction with the social system. The goal of interventions are to increase power of a person at the personal, interpersonal, and environmental levels so that they can take a more active role in their lives (Gutierrez et al., 1998). This approach is applicable to multiracial families and children as it is recognized that many of the mental health problems they may experience are the result of interactions with family, community, and society members who do not accept them (Kelley, 2002; Oriti et al., 1996). Further, as a result of the history of one-drop rules and antimiscegenation laws, this population has felt a large degree of oppression.

Increasing knowledge, a key component of empowerment theory, would be supported by educators at all levels. During elementary and high school years, the focus should be to include the history of multiraciality in the United States, by providing print materials and visual aids that include images and information on multiracial families and children (McFadden, 2001). Multiraciality should be normalized within the classroom milieu. Multiracial role models should be presented along with role models from other groups (McRoy & Freeman, 1986). At the higher education level, history of antimiscegenation laws, classification systems, and history of oppression should be discussed and critically analyzed (McFadden, 2001; Oriti et al., 1996). Research should be presented that debunks myths in order to raise consciousness of students.

Practitioners also have a vital role in promoting empowerment-based approaches across the life cycle. Oriti et al. (1996) identify that it is important for practitioners to use a strengths-based approach when working with multiracial populations to prevent perpetuation of oppression. Moreover, they suggest that practitioners should help to promote visibility of this population as well as political power (Oriti et al., 1996).

Kelley (2002) stated that practitioners at the micro level should develop services that are culturally appropriate to meet the needs of this population and provide support through use of multiracial community networks and at the macro level be agents of change against forms of sociopolitical oppression. McFadden (2001) provides suggestions for empowering multiracial families to include open and honest communication, understanding own racial background, development of a positive sense of self, and an increased awareness of cultural, social, and political issues that may affect them. Furthermore, practitioners can incorporate ecological techniques such as eco-maps and cultural genograms to explore supports within families and communities as well as increase awareness of own family history regarding both parental cultures (Logan et al., 1987; Milan & Keiley, 2000).

Based on this expanded approach, in order to gain support from stakeholders such as families and communities, education is the first step. It is vital to help families and communities move past myths and stereotypes regarding multiracial families and children. This can be done through presentation of evidenced-based literature that speaks to the normalcy of multiracial families and children. There are scores of multiracial community networks and agencies throughout the United States and they play a crucial role in disseminating information to families and communities, and in lobbying Congress to affect public policy.

One influential group is the Association of Multi-Ethnic Americans (AMEA). This group played a key role in petitioning the Office of Management and Budget to change race categories for the Census 2000 so that multiethnic Americans could select more than one race category. Other organizations include National Advocacy for the Multi-Ethnic (NAME), I-PRIDE, Swirl, People in Harmony, and the Center for the Study of Biracial Children. A number of magazines, online communities, and local support groups have also emerged to support the multiracial community. Some of the larger magazines both online and print include Mavin, which is an internationally distributed online magazine, Interracial Voice, the Multiracial Activist, New People, and InterRace. Further, many online communities had surfaced such as Mixedrace.com. Lastly, numerous local support groups have emerged in various states around the United States.

Researchers also play a pivotal role in continuing to study and disseminate information about multiracial families and children. Root recognized the difficulty in conducting research with multiracial families and individuals (Root, 1992). According to Root, researching this population can be challenging in numerous ways, such as locating an adequate sample size, making sure to avoid further oppression by using inappropriate labels or forcing an agenda, and the importance of qualitative research with this population to give voice to their unique experiences (Root, 1992).

Although qualitative research is vital, this is still an area with a limited amount of research, and it is critical that researchers seek to overcome barriers to obtaining a sample size and put more efforts into conducting quantitative, empirical studies as well, as this is what will drive clinical interventions (Root, 1992). There is an emerging body of literature developing around multiracial individuals; however, there is only a very limited body of evidence-based literature pertaining to multiracial families. Furthermore, there is only limited information on evidenced-based approaches and interventions for both multiracial families and children.

Researchers have the responsibility to continue to challenge myths and stereotypes as well as explore culturally specific issues and interventions to support optimal well-being of this population. This information gets trickled down to practitioners who support evidence-based practice, educators, lobbyists, and support groups, all of whom are critical to overcome the oppression that multiracial families and children still face in today's society.

CONCLUSION

Multiracial families and children are a rapidly growing segment of the U.S. population. Historically, multiracial families have been viewed as abnormal and that these types of unions were forged with ulterior motives. Multiracial children have been considered marginal, confused, and maladjusted. An emerging body of research is beginning to present a counter view depicting families as normal and children as well adjusted as their monoracial peers.

Practitioners, researchers, educators, policy formulators, families, and communities are now challenged to shift their thinking from focusing on deficits to focusing on the strengths of multiracial families and children. A multidimensional approach that utilizes empowerment theory, an ecological and strengths-based approach, is key to address the diverse issues of this population in the context of their long history of sociopolitical oppression.

CHAPTER SUMMARY

Multiracial families and individuals have had a history of oppression and discrimination in the United States, which has resulted in mental health care needs to promote family cohesion and identity development. This chapter has four main themes that address these issues and needs. First, is the history of discrimination toward multiracial families and individuals. The United States has had a long history of legislation against interracial unions from the first antimiscegenation laws of the 1600s to the Supreme Court ruling on the *Loving v. Virginia* case of 1967. As late as 1998 and 2000, South Carolina and Alabama had antimiscegenation laws on their state law books, although not enforced. Second, multiracial families and individuals still face many barriers in today's society. These include continued lack of acceptance by families and society, stigma, and a plethora of myths such as marrying for increased social status or selling out to multiracial individuals lacking self-esteem and a healthy self-identity. Third, several stage theories have emerged to help understand family and individual development over the life span. Foeman and Nance developed a four-stage model to gain better insight into the developmental process of multiracial relationships. Several models of identity development of individuals have emerged from more marginal or deficit-oriented models to recent models that promote a more positive developmental process. One such model is a six-stage model from Kerwin and Ponterotto. Fourth, intervention models have been proposed to support development of multiracial families and individuals. Ecological approaches are helpful to look at family systems and social supports within the community. Empowerment approaches are helpful for multiracial families and individuals to take more control of their lives through education and consciousness raising. Finally, strengths approaches seek to normalize experiences and enhance factors that support families and individuals to overcome racism and adversity (Exhibit 16.1).

EXHIBIT 16.1. Historical Time Line

- **1662**—Christians were banned from having relationships with a Negro. This was punishable by a fine or whipping.
- **1691**—Racial intermarriage between Whites and Negro, Mulatto, or Indian was illegal, punishable by banishment from Virginia forever.

- **1780**—Pennsylvania repeals bans on interracial marriage
- **1785**—Any one with one-fourth Negro blood is considered mulatto
- **1866**—Any one with one-fourth Negro blood is labeled as colored
- **1883**—*Pace v. State of Alabama*—Section 4189 in Alabama State Code made interracial marriages between Black and White illegal.
- **1895**—South Carolina enacted interracial ban
- **1910**—Anyone with one-sixteenth Negro blood should be considered colored
- **1924**—Virginia Act on racial integrity
- **1950**—Bob Jones University in Greenville, South Carolina, had a disciplinary rule banning interracial dating
- **1964**—Civil Rights Act
- **1967**—*Loving v. Virginia.* Interracial couple married in Virginia in 1958 and arrested in 1959. Went to Supreme Court. June 12, Chief Justice Earl Warren declared ban on interracial marriages unconstitutional according to the Fourteenth Amendment.
- **1987**—Mississippi removed wording related to ban on interracial marriages from its state constitution.
- **1997**—October 30, the Federal Office of Management and Budget, which determines the standards for classification of racial and ethnic data under its Directive Number 15, declared that people with more than one racial background should have the option to select more than one racial category on forms collecting race data.
- **1998**—South Carolina voted to remove wording related to ban on interracial marriages from the state constitution. Passed by 62 percent of the voters.
- **2000**—Bob Jones University removes ban on interracial dating.
- **2000**—Census 2000—Americans allowed to select more than one category when reporting race. Nearly 7 million Americans reported two or more races as a result.
- **2000**—Alabama removed wording on ban on interracial marriages from state constitution.

Source: Adapted from Roberts (1994). Sollors (2000), Spickard (1989).

Note: Fourteen states did not have bans on interracial relationships, including Alaska, Connecticut, District of Columbia, Hawaii, Illinois, Iowa, Kansas, Minnesota, New Hampshire, New Jersey, New York, Vermont, Washington, and Wisconsin (Spickard, 1989).

DISCUSSION POINTS

1. What are some challenges that multiracial children face during childhood and adolescence? What role does the family play in handling these challenges?
2. What are some of the unique challenges that multiracial families face in their communities?
3. How has history influenced the lives of multiracial families and children?
4. A multidimensional approach to addressing the mental health needs of multiracial families and children has been suggested. How could this be helpful?
5. Recommended activities: Obtain a handful of popular magazines to review. Identify how often multiracial families are depicted. Review movies such as *Guess Who's Coming to Dinner* and *Jungle Fever.* Discuss how issues of multiracial relationships are dealt with.

REFERENCES

Billingsley, A. (1992). *Climbing Jacobs's Ladder: The Enduring Legacy of African American Families*. New York: Simon & Schuster.

Bracey, J., Bamaca, M., & Umana-Taylor, A. (2004). Examining ethnic identity and self-esteem among biracial and monoracial adolescents. *Journal of Youth and Adolescence, 33*(2), 123-132.

Brown, J. A. (1987). Casework contacts with black-white couples. *Social Casework: The Journal of Contemporary Social Work, 68*(1), 24-29.

Brown, P. (1990). Biracial identity and social marginality. *Child and Adolescent Social Work, 7*(4), 319-337.

Brown, U. (1995). Black/white interracial young adults: Quest for a racial identity. *American Journal of Orthopsychiatry, 65*(1), 125-130.

Buttery, T. (1987). Biracial children: Racial identification, self-esteem and school adjustment. *Kappa Delta Pi Record, 23,* 50-53.

Cooney, T. M., & Radina, M. E. (2000). Adjustment problems in adolescence: Are multiracial children at risk? *American Journal of Orthopsychiatry, 70*(4), 433-444.

Davidson, J. R. (1992). Theories about Black-White interracial marriage: A clinical perspective. *Journal of Multicultural Counseling and Development, 20*(4), 150-157.

Ferrante, J., & Brown, P., Jr. (Eds.) (1988). *The Social Construction of Race and Ethnicity in the United States*. New York: Longman.

Foeman, A. K., & Nance, T. (1999). From miscegenation to multiculturalism: Perceptions and stages of interracial relationship development. *Journal of Black Studies, 29*(4), 540-557.

Gibbs, J. T. (1987). Identity and marginality: Issues in the treatment of biracial adolescents. *American Journal of Orthopsychiatry, 5*(2), 265-278.

Gibbs, J. T., & Hines, A. M. (1992). Negotiating ethnic identity: Issues for Black-White biracial adolescents. In M. P. P. Root (Ed.), *Racially Mixed People in America* (pp. 223-238). Newbury Park, CA: Sage Publications.

Gibbs, J. T., & Moskowitz-Sweet, G. (1991). Clinical and cultural issues in the treatment of Biracial and Bicultural adolescents. *Families in Society: The Journal of Contemporary Human Services, 72,* 579-591.

Gutierrez, L., Parsons, R., & Cox, E. (Eds.) (1998). *Empowerment in Social Work Practice: A Sourcebook.* Pacific Grove, CA: Brooks/Cole Publishing Company.

Jacobs, J. H. (1992). Identity development in biracial children. In M. P. P. Root (Ed.), *Racially mixed people in America* (pp. 190-206). Newbury Park, CA: Sage Publications.

Johnson, R., & Nagoshi, C. (1986). The adjustment of offspring of within-group and interracial/intercultural marriages: A comparison of personality factor scores. *Journal of Marriage and the Family, 28,* 279-284.

Jones, J. (2000). Multiethnic identity development, psychological adjustment and parental attachment in adolescence. *Dissertation Abstracts International, 60,* 5227.

Kato, S. (2000). Coats of many colors: Serving the multiracial child and adolescent. *Journal of Family and Consumer Sciences, 92*(5), 37-40.

Kelley, K. (2002). Counseling interracial couples and multiracial individuals: Applying a multicultural counseling competency framework. *Counseling and Human development, 35*(4), 1-13.

Kerwin, C., & Ponterotto, J. (1995). Biracial identity development: Theory and research. In J. Ponterotto, J. Casas, L. Suzuki, & C. Alexander (Eds.), *Handbook of Multicultural Counseling* (pp. 199-217). Thousand Oaks, CA: Sage Publications.

Kerwin, C., Ponterotto, J., Jackson, B., & Harris, A. (1993). Racial identity in biracial children: A qualitative investigation. *Journal of Counseling Psychology, 40*(2), 221-231.

Killian, K. (2002). Dominant and marginalized discourses in interracial couples' narratives: Implications for family therapists. *Family Process, 41*(4), 603-619.

Ladner, J. (1984). Providing a healthy environment for interracial children. *Interracial Books for Children Bulletin, 15*(6), 7-8.

Lewis, R., Jr., Yancey, G., & Bletzer, S. (1997). Racial and nonracial factors that influence spouse choice in black/white marriages. *Journal of Black Studies, 29*(1), 60-79.

Logan, S., Freeman, E., & McRoy, R. (1987). Racial identity problems of bi-racial clients: Implications for social work practice. *Journal of Intergroup Relations, 15,* 11-24.

Married-couple and unmarried partner households: 2000. (2003). http://www.census.gov/prod/2003pubs/censr-5.pdf.

McFadden, J. (2001). Intercultural marriage and family: Beyond the racial divide. *Family Journal: Counseling and Therapy for Couples and Families, 9*(1), 39-42.

McRoy, R., & Freeman, E. (1986). Racial-identity issues among mixed-race children. *Social Work in Education, 8,* 164-174.

Milan, S., & Keiley, M. K. (2000). Biracial youth and families in therapy: Issues and interventions. *Journal of Marital and Family Therapy, 26*(3), 305-315.

Mills, J., Daly, J., Longmore, A., & Kilbride, G. (1995). A note on family acceptance involving interracial friendships and romantic relationships. *Journal of Psychology, 129,* 349-351.

Nakashima, C. L. (1992). An invisible monster: The creation and denial of mixed race people in America. In M. P. Root (Ed.), *Racially Mixed People in America* (pp. 162-178). Newbury Park, CA: Sage Publications.

Oriti, B., Bibb, A., & Mahboubi, J. (1996). Family-centered practice with racially/ethnically mixed families. *Families in Society: The Journal of Contemporary Human Services, 77*(9), 573-582.

Park, R. (1928). Human migration and the marginal man. *The American Journal of Sociology, 33*(6), 881-893.

Poston, W. S. C. (1990). The biracial identity development model: A needed addition. *Journal of Counseling and Development, 69,* 152-155.

Qian, Z. (1999). Who intermarries? Education, nativity, region and interracial marriage, 1980 and 1990. *Journal of Comparative Family Studies, 30*(4), 579-598.

Roberts, R. E. (1994). Black-white interracial marriages in the United States. In W. R. Johnson & D. M. Warren (Eds.), *Inside the Mixed Marriage: Accounts of Changing Attitudes, Patterns, Perceptions of Cross-Cultural and Interracial Marriages* (pp. 25-80). Lanham, MD: University Press of America.

Rockquemore, K. A., & Brunsma, D. (2002). Socially embedded identities: Theories, typologies, and processes of racial identity among black/white biracials. *The Sociological Quarterly, 43*(3), 335-356.

Root, M. P. (1992). Back to the drawing board: Methodological issues in research on multiracial people. In M. P. Root (Ed.), *Racially Mixed People in America* (pp. 181-189). Newbury Park, CA: Sage Publications.

Sollors, W. (Ed.), (2000). *Interracialism: Black-White Intermarriage in American History, Literature and Law.* New York, NY: Oxford University Press.

Spickard, P. (1989). *Mixed Blood: Intermarriage and Ethnic Identity in Twentieth-Century America.* Madison, WI: The University of Wisconsin Press.

Stephan, W. G., & Stephan, C. W. (1991). Intermarriage effects on personality adjustment and intergroup relations in two samples of students. *Journal of Marriage and the Family, 53,* 241-250.

Stonequist, E. (1937). *The Marginal Man: A Study in Personality and Culture Conflict.* New York: Russell & Russell.

Suzuki-Crumly, J., & Hyers, L. (2004). The relationship among ethnic identity, psychological well-being and intergroup competence: An investigation of two biracial groups. *Cultural Diversity and Ethnic Minority Psychology, 10*(2), 137-150.

Teicher, J. (1968). Some observations on identity problems in children of Negro-White marriages. *The Journal of Nervous and Mental Disease, 146*(3), 249-256.

Tizard, B., & Phoenix, A. (1995). The identity of mixed parentage adolescents. *Journal of Child Psychology, 36*(8), 1399-1410.

Van Kirk, M. (2003). Self-esteem and psychological adjustment of multiracial people. *Dissertation Abstracts International, 63,* 4929.

Wardle, F. (1989). Children of mixed parentage: How can professionals respond? *Children Today, 18*(4), 10-14.

Wardle, F. (1991). Raising interracial children. *Mothering, 58,* 110-118.

Yancey, G. (2002). Who interracially dates: An examination of the characteristics of those who have interracially dated. *Journal of Comparative Family Studies, 33*(2), 179-196.

Yancey, G., & Yancey, S. (1998). Interracial dating: Evidence from personal advertisements. *Journal of Family Issues, 19*(3), 334-349.

PART V:
IMPLICATIONS FOR AN INTEGRATED, HOLISTIC APPROACH TO MENTAL HEALTH SERVICES

Chapter 17

African-American Males and the Rites of Passage Experience

Keith A. Alford

Adolescence, customarily known as the teen years, is one of the most exciting as well as precarious periods in the life cycle. The social and familial supports available and accessible to help successfully transition individuals to the next developmental stage play a crucial role during adolescence. Teenagers typically explore their relationships to peers, family, social surroundings, and impending young adulthood. They also attempt to cement their identity and seek to nurture their self-esteem. Adolescence is obviously a vulnerable time in a young person's life and social acceptance, various influences on behavior, and critical thinking skills all impact a teen's sense of well-being. This chapter discusses adolescent Black males and their general psychological and emotional well-being. The term "Black" is used as opposed to African American because it encompasses individuals of color living in the United States who trace their ancestry to Africa, the Caribbean, and other parts of the world. For the purposes of this chapter, the term Black also includes individuals who see themselves as biracial or multiracial and are comfortable identifying as Black.

Adolescent Black males, although hailed with many strengths, continue to face numerous micro and macro challenges. Urban adolescent Black males, in particular, face overwhelming socioeconomic odds. This chapter reviews the definition of high-risk youth and the role that pseudo rites of passage have played in the lives of many urban adolescent Black males. In particular, applicability of contemporary rites of passage (RITES) to this population and the Africentric perspective as a paradigm of practice are explored. Selected programmatic components of RITES are also explained.

Mental Health Care in the African-American Community
© 2007 by The Haworth Press, Inc. All rights reserved.
doi:10.1300/5364_17

What are the benefits of RITES for improving the outlook of young Black males? To answer this question, the affirming nature of RITES with respect to racial identity, racial socialization, and positive emotional well-being is addressed, followed by a chapter summary and discussion questions.

HIGH-RISK YOUTH AND PSEUDO RITES OF PASSAGE, AND EMOTIONAL WELL-BEING

Drug and alcohol involvement, sexual promiscuity, poor school performance, criminal activity, gang activity, and community violence have become transitional markers for many urban youth. These markers have become a pseudo rite of passage, allowing some adolescent youth to pass through their teen years with low-level competencies and poor outcomes. For adolescent Black males who may not have the support base of extended family bonds, teachers who exhibit tough love, youth programs like the Boys and Girls Clubs of America, or even neighborhood recreation centers, the ability to buffer negative transitional markers is significantly reduced. Consequently, the likelihood of greater gang involvement and run-ins with the law increases, and life becomes a war of survival. However, there are select groups of youth living in urban environments that find strength to overcome their social surroundings. The trajectories of these youth should be studied so that practitioners might learn from their stories and appropriately offer their knowledge to others (Alford, McKenry, & Gavazzi, 2001).

McWhirter, J.J., McWhirter, B.T., McWhirter, E.H., and McWhirter, R.J. (2004) have identified five characteristics that differentiate low-risk and high-risk youth. These characteristics include critical school competencies; concept of self and self-esteem; connectedness; coping abilities and control regarding decision making; and purposeful planning. Adolescent youth who are deficient in one or more of these areas can easily fall into the category of high risk. The absence of strong familial and social supports is also a barometer of directional courses for adolescent youth. Families that are ravaged by substance abuse, physical or mental illness, or other serious problems are less likely to be stalwarts for their younger members. In these circumstances youth often take on adult roles in caring for other family members and maintaining the household. They may also find refuge in the streets via feelings of belonging and connectedness through gang membership. Such gangs provide economic benefits—albeit illegal activities—and leadership opportunities that elevate gang member status. In reality, the coping abilities of these youth often dictate which route they will take.

Responsible adults intervening in the lives of young Black males in a way that opens doors of communication to help usher healthy coping behaviors and foster resilience is necessary for progress with this population. Allowing open exchange without imposing social judgments and highlighting the strengths of these young men are keys to the development of resilience. In an effort to promote resilience in children, Garbarino, Dubrow, Kostelny, and Pardo (1992) state that supportive individuals are especially effective when they can supply a caring, stable, and structured environment. Allowing too much freedom and permissiveness in familial roles can send the wrong message to adolescent youth. Appropriate amounts of structure and accountability send a message that young people are valued, their whereabouts are important, and they should be age appropriately monitored. Having at least one caring parent or other adult makes a world of difference in an adolescent's life (Miller & McIntosh, 1999; White & Cones, 1999; Gavazzi & Blumenkrantz, 1993; Quinn, Newfield, & Protinsky, 1985).

We will learn later in this chapter how RITES programming supports emotional well-being in adolescent Black males, but first it should be noted that RITES is not a panacea (Alford et al., 2001; Hill, 1992). RITES programming is not meant to replace therapeutic services for adolescent Black males when such services are warranted. When a multiaxial assessment from the *Diagnostic and Statistical Manual of Mental Disorders* has been rendered for a youth, the treatment process should unfold as planned. RITES programming should work in tandem with human service professionals but not in lieu of psychiatric or other forms of therapeutic treatment. The RITES elder or leader who is assigned to work with the youth should be kept abreast of treatment goals, milestones, and setbacks so as to coordinate any RITES activity that will complement the course of therapy. Participation on a multidisciplinary treatment team would be another option for the assigned elder or leader. In all cases, the adherence to confidentiality must be honored.

THE SURGE OF YOUTH VIOLENCE

Human service professionals must always look for reasons behind the behavior in the clients they see. For many violent and aggressive youth, loss has pervaded their lives. Loss comes in many forms such as abandonment, death, or termination of relationships. It also comes as a part of economic and social disenfranchisement. Hardy and Laszloffy (2005) note that for adolescents, loss of physical safety in the form of molestation, accidentally being shot by a stray bullet in a drive by shooting, or being beaten during a hate crime could have a lasting impact on the youth's functioning capacity if the trauma is left untreated. These experiences of loss are compounded when race enters the picture. "African American adolescents are an especially vulnerable population for experiencing stressful life events, because they negotiate the developmental tasks of adolescence within a race-conscious society" (Caldwell, Zimmerman, Bernat, Sellers, & Notaro, 2002, p. 1324). There is a sense of cultural loss that happens when Black youth experience racism and discrimination. These ills are associated with social disenfranchisement, which is equated with second-class citizenship. The hip-hop movement has provided a haven for many Black youth, but some members of the generation publicly acknowledge that they do not feel a connection to the larger society. Feelings of marginalization are felt by many youth of color particularly adolescent Black males. Consequently, apathy and discontent abound in a number of urban youth circles (Caldwell et al., 2002).

Hardy and Laszloffy (2005) discuss the notion of rage that manifests itself in violent and aggressive youths. Cultural rage is a result of the devaluation of people of color. This devaluation has also transmitted to the many losses experienced by violent youth. These youth may have witnessed a murder or are living in communities where killings occur regularly. Hardy and Laszloffy (2005) postulate that there is a dehumanization of loss as a result of its regularity. In one example of a youth's emotionally unexpressed loss they cite, "He recounted the horrific murder of his father without the slightest hint of emotion. Had we not understood the words he was saying, we could have assumed he was talking about the weather forecast" (Hardy & Laszloffy, 2005, p. 78). Helping young Black males who have suffered multiple losses grieve is critical, whereas helping these males believe again in the value of human life is vital. The world, because of classism, racism, and economic disenfranchisement, has taught them that they are subordinates. The streets have taught them to be tough and to never show any vulnerability. Rehumanizing human life for Black males who are caught in the throes of street life and urban existence and reclaiming the cultural interconnectedness that has sustained people of color through the years will be the mandate of the twenty-first century practitioner.

Practitioners must become adept at helping youth who are victims (and perpetrators) of violent crimes rehumanize their losses. The concern is that if the rehumanization does not occur, the likelihood of these youth committing additional acts of violence increases. Transitional markers of criminal activity are not pro-social and hold no redemptive value for the adolescent Black males. This proliferation of community and gang violence has trickled down to individual family dwellings (McWhirter et al., 2004). The rehumanization that is needed cannot happen soon enough. Mason, an Ohio

RITES participant living in out-of-home care, called for a unified effort to stop the violence. He poignantly articulates this sentiment:

> We found a lot of our Black brothers and sisters out on these blocks, you know, selling dope, peddling dope, whatever, but you find others that are determined to make something out of themselves. I'm happy and proud that our Black brothers and sisters are making something out of themselves. Being lawyers, judges, firemen, police officers, or whatever. . . . I would like to see African American brothers and sisters come together as one instead of fighting and killing each other off. . . . (Alford, 1997, p. 84)

CONTEMPORARY RITES OF PASSAGE STEEPED IN AFRICENTRICITY

Contemporary RITES programming involves several components. Each component is designed to facilitate a positive, well-grounded transition from old behaviors and ways of knowing to new, more enriching, and culturally validating behaviors and thinking patterns. Building on the importance of ritualistic ceremony with the acquisition of knowledge and skill is fundamental to RITES programming. There is a psychoeducational emphasis that permeates the RITES experience. Primary components of RITES programming include the following:

1. *Inculcation of values consistent with the Africentric perspective.* Values that support interconnectedness, mutual aid, spirituality, and cultural pride, are central to the RITES experience. These values are key elements of the Africentric perspective. Of these values, interconnectedness is central because it promotes the idea that all things in the universe are interdependent (Schiele, 1996; Asante, 1988). There is no survival without the collective harmony and positive relations that are necessary parts of relational activity (Warfield-Copppock, 1990). This perspective differs greatly from the survival of the fittest notion in which every person fends for him or herself. Africentricity touts the belief that there can be social unity among people sharing a particular time and space but that cultural uniformity is not essential (Schiele, 1996; Asante, 1988). Africentric thought also gives assent to the notion that affect (feelings or emotions) is a valid source of knowing. Thoughts are no more superior to feelings than emotions are to thoughts (Schiele, 1996).

2. *Life skills training for survival is taught as part of the RITES curriculum.* Life skills training involves learning the basics of cooking, job interviewing, banking, budgeting, study habits, time management, hygiene maintenance, and conflict resolution. Substance abuse prevention, HIV/AIDS prevention, and health awareness tips are taught to young RITES participants. Other curriculum areas may include discovering what it means to be a man. This involves helping RITES participants to understand the importance of honoring humanity, which is inclusive of teaching respect and appreciation for others. Success, the role of spirituality, recognizing when you have a problem beyond your immediate control, and learning about your heritage are among the other curricula areas that adolescent Black males are required to master. It may be several months or years before compete mastery is obtained and the skill acquisition ceremony is convened. Lee (1996) says that it is better to start before the onset of adolescence with young Black males because the influence that the elder or leader may have on younger children is often greater. Nonetheless, beginning at any point in the life of young Black males and maintaining through the duration is just as important. Lee (1996) also reminds practitioners that RITES programming must be creative, and the use of music, poetry, and other literary work is acceptable and highly recommended. He offers the example of playing the rhythm and blues hit, "Pappa was a rolling stone—wherever he laid his hat was his home," to facilitate discussion with young Black males regarding their opinions of fatherhood and the role of a man in caring for his family.

3. *The Nguzo Saba, also known as the Seven Principles, are in concert with the practice of Africentricity and are taught to RITES participants experientially.* The Nguzo Saba (Seven Principles) adds credence and application to daily interactions. The Swahili terms that define the Nguzo Saba, designed by Karenga (1988) in the mid-1960s, are at the heart many RITES initiatives (Gavazzi, Alford, & McKenry, 1996). They include Umoja (unity)—striving and maintaining unity in the family, community, nation, and race; Kujichagulia (Self-Determination)—defining and molding ourselves from a strengths-oriented perspective as opposed to being incorrectly defined or spoken for by others; Ujima (Collective Work and Responsibility)—working collectively toward resolving problems and maintaining our community; Ujamaa (Cooperative Economics)—building and preserving our stores, shops, and businesses in an effort to jointly profit from them; Nia (Purpose)—making a concerted attempt to build, develop, and cultivate our community in order to reclaim the inherent greatness of our peo-

ple; Kuumba (Creativity)—thinking of and executing ways to improve our community both intrinsically and aesthetically; and Imani (Faith)— having steadfast determination and belief in ourselves, parents, teachers, and leaders, all of whom have struggled for racial justice and equality (Harvey & Hill, 2004; Alford, 2003; Warfield-Coppock, 1990). It is not uncommon for RITES participants to operationalize the principle of Ujima, for example, by organizing a neighborhood clean-up drive and involving as many people as possible to help the cause. Charles Lee Johnson, a leading authority on RITES programming in Los Angeles, said that young men need the experience of doing; if we tell them what not to do, then we must give them the experience of what to do. The application of Nguzo Saba provides a culturally specific learning experience that is grounded in interconnectedness and cooperation.

4. *Acquiring an appreciation of one's cultural heritage is essential for developing a secure sense of self.* This tenet directly correlates with self-identity. Living in a society where European influence is omnipresent, Black youth are sometimes uncertain about where their Blackness fits in. Blackness is noted here in an affirming tone to mean one's cultural roots and present-day mores and customs. Adolescent Black males have been said to be the most susceptible to racial backlash as a result of historic devaluation and degradation of this population. They are also the group most vulnerable to school failure, incarceration, and being placed in out-of-home care. Finding one's Blackness in a society that still struggles with racial equality is not an easy task. Hence, teaching Black history as part of the RITES experience facilitates learning that is well rounded as opposed to traditional western history where an occasional reference to a Black leader is mentioned or read. Unfortunately, despite efforts from groups within and outside various public school districts across the country, Black history continues to be relegated to one month out of the school year and familiar names of notable Black Americans like civil rights champion Dr. Martin Luther King, Jr., Supreme Court Justice Thurgood Marshall, and United States Congresswoman Shirley Chisholm are repeated time and time again. The RITES experience goes beyond what is familiar and brings to the forefront Black heroes and heroines who have made enormous contributions to the sciences, the arts, politics, and education. Adolescent RITES participants often hear, for the first time, about such great Black Americans as Garrett Morgan, inventor of the smoke inhalator and the stop signal, which is now known as the traffic light; Dean Dixon, symphony conductor; Ralph Bunche, United

Nations mediator; and Mary Church Terrell, human rights activist. For many adolescent Black males, sports figures in football, basketball, and baseball are well known to them. It is not uncommon for impressionable young Black boys to want to emulate star athletes like Shaquille O'Neal or Donavan McNabb. But the terrain of Black Americans who have achieved professional prominence in sports is vast. Thanks to other athletes like tennis pro Arthur Ashe, golfing great Tiger Woods, and speed skating sensation Shani Davis, young Black males see role models in diverse sporting arenas that have not traditionally been occupied by Blacks. Teaching Black history facilitates racial pride, a key ingredient for proactive cultural socialization.

5. *Excursions to historical sites that promote the accomplishments and strengths of Black people.* Examples of such excursions would be visitation to the National Black History Museum, King Center for Nonviolent Social Change and/or cultural events/festivals that celebrate the Black experience in America. The emphasis placed on trips to historical sites is twofold. First, being able to see where Harriett Tubman once lived and walk through her home in Auburn, New York, for example, provides a living pictorial that cannot be adequately captured by viewing it in a book. Second, for many urban youth, traveling outside their immediate community is a new and fresh experience. This becomes even more enlightening when the trip is to a place that affirms Blackness and highlights the contributions of people who look like them.

6. *Mentoring by elders and leaders remains a key part of RITES programming.* The elders and leaders of a RITES program have a very demanding job that is vital to the life of the program. They provide the instructional help and offer paraprofessional counseling to RITES participants. Eldership is usually reserved for men over 50 and leaders are younger men, but both sets have received training for their positions and take they jobs seriously. The elders may decide that a youth is ready to advance to another content area (Alford, 2003). Often there is more than one elder who works with a RITES group. Both elders and leaders are like mentors and in some programs are called mentors. Their mentoring supports the notion of resiliency and builds on the belief that forming solid and close relationships with RITES participants is synonymous with securing "social capital," that combination of social and economic potential embodied in human relations (Clinton, 2002). The sacrifice of time and participation in other activities is freely given by elders and leaders of RITES programs because the dividends are paid back to them through the participant's

successful acquisition and incorporation of knowledge and skills vis-à-vis daily living.

7. *Rituals are required for RITES programming.* RITES signify that there is some public expression in the form of a ceremony or event which underscores the term "Rites." "Passage" indicates the actual transition to the next phase of life, as is the case of an adolescent male being transitioned or symbolically moved to the developmental level of young adulthood. Recognizing the significance of maturational transitions or markers is paramount. RITES programming includes celebratory recognition because such recognition sends a message to the youth that he is valued and his achievement is monumental. When achievement in the aforementioned component areas has been reached and sanctioned by the elders, a community celebration of RITES occurs. African regalia are often worn, and African artifacts used, to add to the pageantry of the event and to signify that the event is special.

RACIAL IDENTITY AND ADOLESCENT DEVELOPMENT

Erik Erikson (1950) elaborates on his stages of human development during his examination of the life cycle. He notes that a primary issue during adolescence is identity versus identity confusion. Living in a constant state of "becoming" can be unsettling. Given this, how is identity formed for adolescents? Familial, peer, and social influences play pivotal roles, but often these roles compete with one another when the adolescent is torn by whether allegiance should be paid to one influence over another. High-risk adolescent Black males often have the conundrum of navigating the stressors of poverty, social disorganization, and troubled families (Bennett & Miller, 2006). These overwhelming socioeconomic odds are coupled with the likelihood that racism will be perpetrated against them by virtue of the color of their skin. Racism may present itself through job discrimination, racial profiling, racial stereotyping, differential treatment by store personnel, and other race-based bias that is manifested in daily life. Second chances do not easily come to young Black males if they have a past prison record, have been terminated from previous jobs, or do not possess the competencies to positively engage others. Erikson's notion of identity confusion is more apparent in these instances because race cannot be easily separated from the equation. A race-conscious society does not easily forgive or forget past wrongs of Black males and may observe indigenous mannerisms, speech, and gestures as deficient compared to those of mainstream America (Denby & Alford, 1996; Majors, 1991). Ironically, the essence of such communicative behaviors lies in the guardedness that some Black males express as a result of racial ordering and racial inequities still present in this society. Majors and Billson (1992) discuss such behaviors and even reference them categorically as "cool pose" (p. 16). Identity issues may surface when adolescent Black males have to mentally place themselves on guard while at the same time safeguard their social standing for good or bad within their own peer group.

Human service providers should work to insure that support structures like RITES programming are in place to constructively assist in the building of racial identity and racial socialization efforts. Miller (2003) notes that the socialization process is not the same in all African-American families, and for some families it may be direct or indirect, verbal or nonverbal. Modeling of behaviors, sharing stories of cultural significance, and exposing children to culturally edifying material and relevant activities are some of the means that parents can employ to facilitate socialization. When the family is unable to perform these tasks for various reasons, RITES programming can fill in the gap, not as a replacement but more as a supplement, executing functions that will increase racial awareness, which, in turn, will bolster racial socialization and strong racial identity (Miller, 2003; Parham, 1993; Cross, 1971).

The following passage is from the field notes of this book chapter's author when he interviewed Cresswell, an Ohio RITES participant living in out-of-home care. The following highlights the strong racial identification Cresswell has adopted for his life's course:

> I ate lunch at Tower City with one of the RITES participants. Tower City is a large mall located in downtown Cleveland. At the participant's request, I conducted most of the interview with him there. At first, I thought the noisiness and combustion in the mall would hamper my ability to facilitate an open-ended interview, but I was wrong. Cresswell, as he will be referred to for the purposes of this study, talked boldly about how the AA-RITES program taught him how to live in a racist society.
>
> After lunch we walked around the mall and his gait reflected an air of confidence and self-assurance. He began to freely tell me which merchants were culturally friendly to African Americans and which ones were not. We later walked around downtown Cleveland, and though he condemned Black on Black crime, he shared with me certain areas in which "one must wear heavy boots." Literally, according to Cresswell, the shoes you wear may make a difference as to whether you will be a target of crime. It was obvious that Cresswell knew how

to physically take care of himself and how to emotionally protect himself. It also seemed apparent that he knew how to socially navigate the racial and cultural idiosyncrasies of our society.

When we went into the stores, he interacted with the merchants in a proactive fashion. Basically, his rationale was that you engage the merchant up front so that he does not label you as a thief or thug. Cresswell had a lot of what I call "people skills." His engaging personality has been a shield for him in maneuvering his way through some tough and physically rough situations. Basically, Cresswell intimated that the way to stay out of trouble is know what trouble looks like. We spent the majority of the afternoon together, and he gave quick analyses of various sites, which assured me that he knew the streets of Cleveland and the ways of the world. More importantly, he knew that the negativity of this world is off limits to him. (Alford, 1997, pp. 68-69)

Identity issues in general are linked to emotional well-being. For people of color, racial identity, racial socialization, and emotional well-being are intertwined because of the very reasons that were exhibited by Cresswell's deportment in the mall, in the store, and in his neighborhood. There is a bifurcated mindset that many Black males have to endure. One set of behaviors is acceptable in venue A and another in venue B, and it is rare that both are accepted in the same place, but both are needed for societal survival. The reality is that all Black males do not follow this code. Some are unaware of it, and others have difficulty mastering it. These concerns give rise to issues of emotional well-being that only people who have experienced oppression and racial disdain fully understand. Although there is strength associated with being able to live biculturally, there are degrees of pain associated with it as well.

CONCLUSION

There are a number of RITES programs across the country for girls and boys. Some RITES programs are subject specific and others have a particular functional focus. Warfield-Coppock (1992) posits that RITES programs may fall under such typologies as community-based, agency-based, school-based, church-based, therapeutic-based, or family-based. For instance, an agency- or organizationally-based RITES will use RITES programming with a target population within their own structure (Harvey & Hill, 2004; Warfied-Coppock, 1992). One such program is located in Dallas, Texas.

The West Dallas Community Center's staff, parents, and community members work with a select group of young people for several years at a time, concentrating on the study and practice of African and African-American history, the arts, and life skills with male and female RITES participants (Prevention Programs for Youth and Communities, SAMHSA, 1997). Typically, all RITES programs have the aim of building self-esteem and racial pride while simultaneously promoting pro-social values with the end goal of producing contributing and responsible adults. Training and certification are required before launching a RITES program. The National Rites of Passage Institute (NROPI) in Cleveland, Ohio, under the leadership of Paul Hill, provides training to prospective adult leaders and elders on Afrocentricity and how to implement a RITES curriculum. RITES initiatives have positive mental health outcomes (Harvey & Hill, 2004; Alford, 2003; Wilcox, 1998). Participants leave the program schooled and counseled in ways and matters germane to their culture. Many also leave with newfound support systems because of lasting friendships they have made with fellow participants. The Afrocentric tenet of collectivity has new meaning for RITES participants because of the trusted bond established with their peers, RITES leaders, and elders. Renewed familial ties become a by-product of RITES participation, because birth and foster family members and fictive kin are all invited to participate in auxiliary activities and celebratory rituals of the program. RITES programming is a model for practice that is culturally specific. With ever-increasing media attention on the negative behaviors of adolescent Black males and the reality that Black males are overrepresented in almost every corrective governmental domain, it is time to refocus our efforts as human service professionals on culturally competent programming. When intervention is guided by an appreciation of the client's cultural roots, there is a higher chance that curative effects will occur.

CHAPTER SUMMARY

Adolescence is filled with uncertainty and vibrancy. However, adolescent Black males from urban settings have many social and contextual challenges. Affirming their realities while acknowledging their resilience are important steps toward offering professional assistance. Rites of Passage (RITES) programming, although not a substitute for familial socialization, seeks to support this population through Afrocentric teachings and skill acquisition. RITES is a proactive measure used to enhance the lives of young Black males.

Resisting the pull of negative peer influences, adolescent Black males can find refuge in the interconnectedness of RITES programming. Living in a race-conscious society, Black youth need to learn "who they are" and "what they should be about" (Alford, 2003). When birth family members are not able to provide life skill training, RITES programming can fill in the gap. Learning one's cultural history and acquiring basic living skills like cooking, cleaning, and banking, while also learning how to buffer the impact of racism, are all components of the RITES experience. Knowing and appreciating the magnitude of what many urban adolescent Black males face on a daily basis helps one to understand the interplay of emotional well-being, positive racial socialization, and strong racial identification. These elements require the support of programs such as RITES that provide culturally specific intervention and service delivery.

DISCUSSION QUESTIONS AND POINTS

1. What are three primary concerns that urban adolescent Black males face?
2. How does a RITES program offer help toward facilitating a strong sense of racial identity?
3. What did Cresswell teach the researcher interviewing him about living in a race-conscious society?
4. Explain the interplay of emotional well-being, racial socialization, and racial identification for adolescent Black males.

REFERENCES

Alford, K. (1997). A Qualitative Study of an Africentric Rites of Passage Program Used with Adolescent African American Males in Out-of-Home Care: Looking for Uunexpected Themes. Unpublished doctoral dissertation, The Ohio State University, Columbus, OH.

Alford, K. (2003). Cultural themes in rites of passage: Voices of young African American males. *Journal of African American Studies, 7*(1), 3-26.

Alford, K., McKenry, P., & Gavazzi, S. (2001). Enhancing achievement in adolescent black males: The rites of passage link. In R. Majors (Ed.), *Educating Our Black Children: New Directions and Radical Approaches* (pp. 141-156). London: Routledge Falmer.

Asante, M. (1988). *Afrocentricity.* Trenton, NJ: Africa World Press.

Bennett, M. D., Jr., & Miller, D. B. (2006). An exploratory study of the urban hassles index: A contextually relevant measure of chronic multidimensional urban stressors. *Research on Social Work Practice, 16*(3), 305-314.

Caldwell, C. H., Zimmerman, M. A., Bernat, D. H., Sellers, R. M., & Notaro, P. C. (2002). Racial identity, maternal support, and psychological distress, among African American adolescents. *Child Development, 73*(4), 1322-1336.

Clinton, G. (2002). Mentoring programs for at-risk youth. *The Prevention Researcher, 9*(1), 1-3.

Cross, W. (1971). The Negro to Black conversion experience: Toward a psychology of Black liberation. *Black World, 20,* 13-27.

Denby, R., & Alford, K. (1996). Understanding African American discipline styles: Suggestions for effective social work intervention. *Journal of Multicultural Social Work, 4*(3), 81-98.

Erikson, E. H. (1950). *Childhood and Society.* New York: Norton.

Garbarino, J., Dubrow, N., Kostelny, K., & Pardo, C. (1992). *Children in Danger: Coping With the Consequences of Community Violence.* San Francisco: Jossey-Bass Publishers.

Gavazzi, S., & Blumenkrantz, D. (1993). Facilitating clinical work with adolescents and their families through the rites of passage program. *Journal of Family Psychotherapy, 4*(2), 47-67.

Gavazzi, S., Alford, K., & McKenry, P. (1996). Culturally specific programs for foster care youth: The sample case of an African American rites of passage program. *Family Relations, 45*(2), 166-174.

Hardy, K. V., & Laszloffy, T. A. (2005). *Teens Who Hurt: Clinical Interventions to Break the Cycle of Adolescent Violence.* New York: The Guilford Press.

Harvey, A., & Hill, R. (2004). Africentric youth and family rites of passage program: Promoting resilience among at-risk African American youths. *Social Work, 49*(1), 65-74.

Hill, P. (1992). *Coming of Age: African American Male Rites-of-Passage.* Chicago: African American Images.

Karenga, M. (1988). *African American Holiday of Kwanzaa.* Los Angeles: Sankore Press.

Lee, C. C. (1996). *Saving the Native Son: Empowerment Strategies for Young Black Males.* Greensboro, NC: ERIC Counseling and Student Services Clearinghouse.

Majors, R. (1991). Non-verbal behaviors and communication styles among African Americans. In R. Jones (Ed.), *Black Psychology* (pp. 269-294). Berkeley, CA: Cobb & Henry.

Majors, R., & Billson, J. M. (1992). *Cool Pose.* New York: Lexington.

McWhirter, J. J., McWhirter, B. T., McWhirter, E. H., & McWhirter, R. J. (2004). *At-Risk Youth: A Comprehensive Response for Counselors, Teachers, Psychologists, and Human Service Professionals.* Belmont, CA: Brooks/Cole-Thomson Learning.

Miller, D. (2003). Racial socialization and racial identity: Can they promote resiliency for African American adolescents? *The Prevention Researcher, 10*(1), 11-13.

Miller, D., & MacIntosh, R. (1999). Promoting resilience in urban African American adolescents: Racial socialization and identity as protective factors. *Social Work Research, 23*(3), 159-169.

Parham, T. A. (1993). *Psychological Storms: The African American Struggle for Identity.* Chicago: African American Images.

Quinn, W. H., Newfield, N. A., & Protinsky, H. O. (1985). Rites of passage in families with adolescents. *Family Process, 24,* 101-111.

Schiele, J. H. (1996). Afrocentricity: An emerging paradigm in social work practice. *Social Work, 41*(3), 284-294.

Substance Abuse and Mental Health Services Administration (SAMHSA). (1997). *West Dallas Community Centers, Inc., Rites of Passage.* Prevention Programs for Youth and Communities. DHHS Pub No. 97-4195. Rockville, MD.

Warfield-Coppock, N. (1990). *Afrocentric Theory and Applications, Vol. I: Adolescent Rites of Passage.* Washington, DC: Baobab Associates.

Warfield-Coppock, N. (1992). The rites of passage movement: A resurgence of African-centered practices for socializing African American youth. *Journal of Negro Education, 61*(4), 471-482.

White, J. L., & Cones, J. H. (1999). *Black Man Emerging: Facing the Past and Seizing a Future in America.* New York: Routledge.

Wilcox, D. (1998). The Rites of Passage Process for African American Youth: Perspectives of Eight Elders. Unpublished doctoral dissertation, Kent State University.

Chapter 18

African-American Women: Mental Health and HIV/AIDS

Kendra P. DeLoach

In the United States, HIV/AIDS continues to be a health epidemic for African Americans. They compose only 12.3 percent of the United States population, but they account for 368,169 (40 percent) of the 929,985 estimated AIDS cases diagnosed since the epidemic began (CDC, 2003). According to CDC (2003), African Americans account for 42 percent of people living with AIDS in the United States. Although HIV/AIDS affects the entire African-American community, it affects African-American women more.

HIV/AIDS is one of the top four leading causes of death for African-American women between the ages of 20 and 54 years old. It is the number one cause of death of African-American women between the ages of 25 and 34 years old. However, in 2003, the rate of HIV cases decreased 2 percent among females. Despite the 2003 decrease, African-American women have consistently higher rates of infection of HIV/AIDS and appear to be more vulnerable than women of other racial and ethnic groups (Jones, 2004, p. 60). Thus, African-American women not only endure HIV/AIDS, but also mental health conditions related to issues of race (Lichtenstein, Laska, & Clair, 2002), sex (Braithwaite & Thomas, 2001; Williams, Ekundayo, & Udezulu, 2003), class (Ickovics et al., 2002; Quinn, 1993), and socioeconomics (Elwood, Williams, Bell, & Richard, 1997; Lichtenstein, Laska, & Clair, 2003).

Given the AIDS epidemic within the United States, it is imperative that public policy, social support, community-based programs, research, and strengths-based interventions be developed to reduce the rate of HIV/AIDS infection. To understand better the affects of these issues on the lives of

Mental Health Care in the African-American Community
© 2007 by The Haworth Press, Inc. All rights reserved.
doi:10.1300/5364_18

African-American women and those African-American women living with HIV/AIDS, we must first seek to understand all of the environmental factors that are involved. Therefore this chapter provides an overview of the literature on the mental health of African-American women living with HIV/AIDS by using evidence-based practice and a life course perspective. This will demonstrate how the integration of sociocultural issues, mental health, and HIV/AIDS affects the quality of life of African-American women.

The total effect of HIV/AIDS in the African-American community creates physical health issues in addition to mental health issues. If we want to seek better health and well-being within the African-American community, we must address the multiple effects of HIV/AIDS. This chapter includes a discussion of historical and current approaches, a case example, and a conceptual framework for addressing HIV/AIDS in a holistic context. Included will be a focus on practice, research and policy, mental health issues, strategies for developing stakeholder support, and the dissemination of information for impacting family, community, and system changes.

IMPACT ON INDIVIDUALS

As indicated earlier, HIV/AIDS continues to thrive among African-American women. As a result, African-American women are faced with many problems that affect their mental health. They endure more mental health conditions, such as anger, depression, anxiety, substance abuse, and post-traumatic stress disorder (PTSD) (Jipguep, Sanders-Phillips, & Cotton, 2004; Mellins et al., 2002). Despite their mental health conditions, African-American women lack seeking medical or mental health services. They often do not seek these services because of the stigma associated with HIV infection, fear (Lichtenstein et al., 2002; Linsk et al., 2002), and lack of health insurance (Lam, Wechsberg, & Zule, 2004). In addition, structural issues, such as living in impoverished neighborhoods, raising children alone, enduring financial strain, and caring for extended family members (Gilbert, 2003), are a few responsibilities that African-American women must face while living with the affects of HIV/AIDS. These structural issues deter African-American women from obtaining optimal health and well-being, which become even more difficult when the woman must deal with her HIV status.

Within the African-American community, African-American women have been known to put the needs of others before themselves (hooks, 1981). They will care for children, spouses, intimate partners, and extended family (Williams et al., 2003) and neglect themselves. Because of tending to other priorities, they often suffer poor physical and mental health. After years of neglect, their health slowly deteriorates, negatively affecting how their family functions.

Seeking mental health services is not well accepted in the African-American community (Myers & Durvasula, 1999). Other issues such as, distrust, misperception, spirituality (Eugene, 1997; Mattis, 2002), and alternative coping strategies deter African Americans from obtaining mental health services. Thus, they are susceptible to mental health problems that become exacerbated by the physical health problems of HIV infection. Their mental and physical health conditions impede their ability to receive the necessary services to promote their health and well-being. In addition, issues of mental and physical health are exacerbated by economics, poor housing, lack of education, and caring for others. These issues extenuate circumstances in an African-American women's life, which does not lead to a balanced and stress-free existence. Because African-American women are primarily responsible for sustaining the functioning of their families, issues of mental and physical health become a family matter.

Living a balance existence with HIV/AIDS becomes a problem for African-American families on multiple levels. Given that a significant number of African-American women with HIV/AIDS are between the ages of 20 and 34, the primary age of childbearing, it is no surprise that more infants are being born who are infected with HIV (CDC, 2003). This presents an additional problem to women who are living with HIV/AIDS. They must deal with their own physical problems resulting from the disease, in addition to dealing with their child's physical problems. This can be a major source of several dilemmas in the lives of African-American women living with HIV/AIDS.

The first dilemma is a generation of babies being born to women who are infected with HIV; thus, this generation needs a lot of medical attention (Feldman, 2003). Better drug therapy exists today, which has improved the quality of life and life expectancy of babies born with HIV (Feldman, 2003).

The second dilemma is that young mothers who are living with HIV must deal with their own illness, in addition to the illness of their child(ren). The emotional, economic, and psychological stress of multiple hardships worsens the mental health of these women and their families (Gilbert, 2003). The children of these families experience these hardships along with the heightened awareness of their mother's illness and possible death related to the disease. Making matters worse, if they are living with the disease they must deal with their own issues of illness and death (Gilbert, 2003). Many of these children will experience disruption in their families, subjecting them to having to live in arrangements outside of their immediate family.

The third dilemma relates to the living arrangements of children of women who die from complications related to AIDS. In families that have both mother and father living in the home, the child can rely on the support of her or his father. However, for children living in single female–headed households, living arrangements can become much more difficult, resulting in them needing other living arrangements.

The following case example will illustrate the above dilemmas:

> During a routine visit to the doctor's office, Tonya, a 35-year-old African-American recently divorced woman living with AIDS, learns that her health is declining. She is the mother of three small children who were all born HIV-positive. The physician informs her that her T cells are deteriorating at a rapid rate and that she should begin thinking about end-of-life issues. The physician prescribes her two more medications that she will add to her pill collection. She currently takes over eighteen pills a day and her children take over six pills a day. Tonya receives some financial assistance from HIV/AIDS medicine assistance programs; however, they do not cover the total cost of the medicines. Her finances are strained from purchasing her and her children's monthly prescription of medicines.
>
> Before she goes to the pharmacy to fill her prescription, she goes to the neonatal intensive care unit (NICU) of the hospital to visit her 8-month-old child, who is experiencing complications as a result of being born HIV-positive. Currently, a respirator assists his breathing and he possesses a weak pulse. The medical staff informs Tonya that her son's prognosis is poor and that he will slowly decline over time.
>
> Tonya begins to sob loudly, prompting the medical staff to request a social worker to speak to her. Upon social work intervention, Tonya states that she cannot deal with her failing health and impending death, along with her son's poor prognosis. She asks the social worker several questions: "Who will take care of my children, especially my son who is struggling for his life in the NICU, when I become too weak to care for them? Where will my children live when I become too weak to care for them or when I die? Who will make my son's funeral arrangements, if I die before him?" Tonya fears that she will not be able to answer these questions.

Historically, African-American women have accepted the responsibilities of caring for children of other family members when those members died or became incapacitated (Brown & Boyce-Mathis, 2000). When African-American women die from the complications of AIDS, it is likely that other family members will assume the care of the children left behind. However, this is not always true, which results in some children becoming a part of the foster care system. Regardless of the living arrangements, both extended family members and foster care parents caring for HIV-infected children or children whose mothers have died from complications of AIDS will have to obtain special training to provide them with the best physical and mental health care.

The fourth dilemma is the promotion of drugs that increase male and female sexual functioning in older adults. With the discovery of drugs that improve sexual activity in older adults, more adult women over the age of 44 years of age have contracted HIV (CDC, 2003). This presents a new problem in the fight against the spread of HIV/AIDS, because most HIV/AIDS services do not target this population. This can be a devastating problem in the African-American community, because the number of grandparents raising their grandchildren over the past decade continues to grow (Gibson, 2005; Winston, 2003). Approximately 760,000 African-American children are living with their grandparents in the United States (Gibson, 2005). HIV infection among this older population will greatly affect the care of African-American children, families, and communities. Thus, the risk of HIV infection presents several dilemmas for children, parents, grandparents, and service providers.

STRENGTHS AND EVIDENCE-BASED PRACTICE

The pandemic of HIV/AIDS in the United States over the past 20 years has encouraged many agencies and officials to develop programs that will reduce the spread of the disease. Although many programs exist, some researchers do not feel that they are rooted in science-based practice, thus, their effects are minimal.

Over the course of two decades, many programs have emerged that aimed to reduce the risk of HIV/AIDS. Some programs have demonstrated success in terms of decreasing the rate of HIV/AIDS within particular populations, whereas other programs have failed. Programs that have been successful at reducing the rate of HIV/AIDS have three common characteristics: (1) they target specific populations (i.e., males who have sex with males, intravenous drug users [IDU], crack-cocaine users) (Gilbert, 2003); (2) use culturally sensitive or responsive, and appropriate materials (Herek et al., 1998; Sterk, Theall, Elifson, & Kidder, 2003); (3) focus on gender-specific issues (Jones, 2004; Wechsberg, Lam, Zule, & Bobashev, 2004); and (4) address the mental health issues related to living with HIV/AIDS. Because of the complexity of the disease, it is increasingly evident that programs in general, but especially those working with African-American women, need a more comprehensive focus on specific issues of disease reduction. There-fore, the impact of psychosocial issues related to living with HIV/AIDS on African-American women is not surprising. Despite the advances in HIV treatment, many people still associate HIV with issues of grief and loss, fear, uncertainty, difficulty disclosing to family members, friends, and em-ployers, drug regimens, and various treatment strategies (Linsk et al., 2002). These issues are greatly exacerbated by the situation of African-American women within the intersection of race, sex, and class.

Issues of race, sex, and class place African-American women in con-ditions that make them more susceptible to contracting HIV (McNair & Prather, 2004). Structural issues such as poverty, poor housing, lack of educa-tion, and economic strain coupled with social factors such as male-female sex ratio and negative attitudes toward condom use within the African-American community place African-American women at greater HIV risk (McNair & Prather, 2004). Other factors that are unique to understanding each woman's experience would consist of her personal history of child abuse, sexual trauma (Gilbert, 2003), interpersonal power in relationships (McNair & Prather, 2004), and substance abuse (Jones, 2004; McNair & Prather, 2004).

As suggested by the statistics and the case example, African-American women living with HIV/AIDS suffer from high rates of mental illness and anxiety (Myers & Durvasula, 1999), anger (Jipguep et al., 2004), depression (Jipguep et al., 2004; Johnson, Cunningham-Williams, & Cottler, 2003; Jones, O'Connell, Gound, Heller, & Forehand, 2004), mood disorders (Myers & Durvasula, 1999), and substance abuse (Johnson et al., 2003). However, several factors contribute to mental health issues of African-American women living with HIV/AIDS. These include substance abuse; poverty; historical oppression—sexism, racism, and classism; health dispari-ties—medical and mental health; trauma and victimization; incarceration; and stigma and distrust, the leading issues that affect African-American women. Stigma, invisibility, and denial are characterizations that represent people who are living with HIV/AIDS. For African-American women liv-ing with HIV/AIDS, the burden of race, class, gender, and HIV status affect how legislators and agency directors create HIV/AIDS social policy (Perry, 2003). Although the total number of AIDS cases among African-American women reported to the CDC (2003) increased as compared to their White counterparts, few HIV/AIDS policy-related programs exist.

In a study of African Americans (n = 234) who were older than the age of 18 years old, experienced low socioeconomic status, and were affected by HIV/AIDS, 135 women demonstrated a high prevalence of psychiatric dis-orders with anxiety spectrum disorders (38 percent), mood disorders (23 percent), depression (20 percent), and significant symptoms of post-traumatic stress disorder (PTSD; 50 percent) most prevalent among the women (Myers & Durvasula, 1999). The results of the study suggested that among the women, mental health issues were associated with low social support, low income, poor education, and substance abuse. These contraindications in the study suggest that multiple factors contribute to mental health issues of African-American women living with HIV/AIDS. Because African-American women are the heart of the family in the Black community, issues of mental health and HIV/AIDS affect not only them, but also their families. The findings of the research study indicated that an important intervention in preventing panic or psychiatric disorders in African-American women living with HIV/AIDS might be establishing or improving social support networks.

PUBLIC POLICY

One of the first federal aid policy of HIV/AIDS-related policies to exist is the Ryan White Comprehensive AIDS Resources Emergency Act (CARE). It is the most comprehensive AIDS-related policy, enacted when an adolescent, Ryan White, presented his story to the White House in the early 1980s. Although African Americans, especially African-American women, are overrepresented in the population of people contracting HIV infection annually, the CARE initiative did not address issues specific to them (Perry, 2003). Because research has historically excluded ethnic groups of color, it is no surprise that HIV/AIDS programs did not target African-American women and other women of color. To account for this exclusion, legislators formed two major governmental offices—Women's Health and the Office of AIDS Research—ensuring that women of all ethnicities be included in all HIV/AIDS research. Despite this push to address women's health care needs, the Women's Health and the Office of AIDS Research still experienced difficulties including African-American women in their HIV/AIDS research. Some of their difficulty occurred because of the historical relationship that African Americans have with scientific research. Government experiments and research, such as the Tuskegee Experiment, are not distant memories to the African-American community. During this experiment, the government officials infected African-American men with syphilis and did not explain to the men the effects of the disease. They did not provide them with medicine to treat it once the government knew the ramifications of the disease. They only provided them with a placebo. Many African-American men endured horrific physical and mental results related to this experiment, ultimately affecting their families and the community. The African-American community has not forgotten this and remains distrustful of research and experiments. Because of the African-American community's unwillingness to participate, researchers now have few scientific results to help influence social policy.

Public policy programs that exist in the United States do not focus primarily on the African-American community, but focus on the larger population of people who are living with HIV/AIDS (Perry, 2003). Policies that benefit this population are referred to as benefit and status-conferring policies. Social Security Disability Insurance (SSDI), Medicaid, Housing Opportunities for People with AIDS Act (HOPWA), and the Alcohol, Drug Abuse and Mental Health Administration Reorganization (ADAMHA) are benefit-conferring policies that ensure that eligible recipients receive monetary or resource compensation.

Status-conferring policies support benefit-conferring policies by offering antidiscrimination protection and legal compensation for people living with HIV/AIDS (Feldman & Fulwood, 1999). Vocational Rehabilitation Act (VRA) of 1973, the Fair Housing Act (FHA) of 1988, and the Americans with Disabilities Act (ADA) of 1990 are status-conferring policies. Programs that provide protection to African Americans, particularly women with children living with HIV/AIDS, against "discrimination in employment, education, housing, transportation, public accommodations, and social services," (Perry, 2003) play an important role in their physical health and well-being.

A program in Harlem, New York, addresses sociocultural factors within an evidence-based framework. Harlem Dowling-West Side Center (HDWC) comes from the merging of two historical agencies that provided services to Black children since the early nineteenth century. In 1989, Harlem Dowling Children's Services and West Side Center merged to form one of the oldest child advocacy centers for at-risk children and Black families. Although the center does not solely focus on HIV/AIDS services, a large component of its services focus on children and families affected by HIV/AIDS (Butler & Smith-McKeever, 2003). This type of program located within the heart of Harlem, predominately an African-American community, attempts to provide services to families affected by HIV/AIDS while reducing the stigma associated with HIV/AIDS. Other programs attempt to achieve these same goals.

The Balm in Gilead is another program developed in the African-American church that provides holistic services to Black families affected or infected by the HIV/AIDS disease. The program acknowledges that people living with the disease are suffering in many areas of their lives. This program provides educational, physical, and spiritual support for members in the HIV/

AIDS ministries (Munke-Pittman & Venturini, 2003). It provides palliative care, prevention measures, opportunities for collaborations, HIV/AIDS advocacy, and opportunities to increase the cultural competence of HIV/ AIDS practitioners (Eugene, 1997).

More programs like these, as well as programs that acknowledge the strengths of the African-American community, in addition to the socio-cultural factors that deter the community from health and well-being, need to be developed and implemented. These programs empower the individuals of the community to continue creating and participating in programs that improve the health and well-being of those individuals in the community who are living with HIV/AIDS.

EXPANDED APPROACHES

Practice, Policy, and Research

Harvey and Bird (2004), in an exploratory study, interviewed 22 young African-American women at risk of contracting HIV or an unintended pregnancy, in an attempt to understand the meaning of power in heterosexual relationships, women's feelings of power in relationships with men, and sexual and reproductive decision-making in relationships. The study suggested that women shared reproductive and sexual decisions with their partners and that relationship power was linked to control, security, and positive relationship characteristics. Programs that address HIV/AIDS reduction must also address power differentials among women and men. The difference of power within a relationship affects women's ability to protect themselves from HIV/AIDS (Harvey & Bird, 2004).

The fight against HIV/AIDS will have to address several factors that undergird the spread of HIV/AIDS in the African-American community. According to Fitzpatrick, McCray, and Smith (2004), four main issues have emerged that mental health workers, practitioners, and advocates must address to eradicate the spread of HIV/AIDS. First, service personnel will have to understand the psychological underpinnings and develop effective interventions that will reduce risk-taking behavior, self-denial, and HIV-related stigma. Second, mental health personnel must learn how to "assist the effective, long-term delivery of antiretroviral and opportunistic infection-preventive medicines. . . ." Third, personnel who work with children must develop better and more effective assessment tools and strategies that will deal with the growing numbers of "orphaned, fostered, and inadequately cared for children and youth." Fourth, the mental health system must develop better training opportunities for mental health workers (Fitzpatrick et al., 2004).

In addition to these main issues, another issue is that programs must be rooted in science and research. Some programs do not have a strong science background because of other structural issues. The exclusion of sociocultural factors—race, sex, and class economics (Cargill, Stone, & Robinson, 2004)— and programs not derived in evidence-based methods (Gordon, Forsyth, Stall, & Cheever, 2005), have been the reason some HIV/AIDS programs have failed. Programs that embody these characteristics demonstrate better results in reducing the spread of HIV/AIDS and treating African Americans who are living with the disease.

Discussions on HIV/AIDS need to address issues such as family stigma, prevention efforts, societal acceptance of HIV-infected individuals (Clark, Lindner, Armistead, & Austin, 2003), cultural specificity (Herek et al., 1998), gender specificity (Lichtenstein et al., 2002), and oppressive structures that affect African-American women (Quinn, 1993). Discussions that embody these major concepts must be the focus for educators, practice, research, and policy development.

Logan, Cole, and Leukefeld (2002) found that programs that focused on culture, race, and social factors increase the effectiveness of HIV interventions for African-American women. More researchers need to conduct research that examines cultural and social factors associated with HIV infection. Researchers have stressed the need for interventions that integrate social and cultural factors (McNair & Prather, 2004). Factors related to individual risks do not need to be included with social and cultural factors to understand the unique experience of African-American women who live with HIV/AIDS. Developing and implementing programs that are holistic in assessing individual risk factors, social factors, and cultural factors will be the best strategy for reducing the spread of HIV infection.

Stopping the spread of HIV infection will take a holistic approach that addresses the uniqueness of the African-American community. This approach will have to be sensitive to the social forces that affect all members of this community who are living with or affected by HIV/AIDS. Although the focus of this chapter is African-American women, strategies that address HIV/AIDS must address all members of the community. Thus, HIV/AIDS advocates must take on a multifaceted approach that increases support of HIV/AIDS-related programs and policies. Educators, researchers, and policy makers must attempt to create programs that deal with all of the social forces that affect people living with HIV/AIDS within the African-American community.

The social forces that hit hardest within the African-American community are inappropriate or scarce housing, addiction, unemployment/underemployment, stigma, and other oppressive issues: racism, classism, sexism, and homophobia. To help African Americans living with HIV/AIDS, advocates must help them to address all of the social forces that can become more burdening on their lives than the disease itself. Advocates can help African Americans living with HIV/AIDS by empowering them and advocating on their behalf for programs and policies that will benefit them.

Programs and policies that will be most useful to this population must embrace two central goals. First, they must aim to prevent the spread of HIV transmission. Second, they must aim to provide treatment, support, and social services to individuals, families, and communities affected by the disease (Stockdill, 2003). No longer can programs operate under an either/or dichotomy where programs provide either prevention services or treatment services. Programs and policies must avoid this false dichotomy and provide holistic services that integrate both goals for individuals and the larger community.

To integrate these goals, programs and policies must embrace the social realities that affect African Americans living with HIV/AIDS at all ages. Dialogues about their social realities have to be framed within the context of how HIV/AIDS affects babies, infants, adolescents, adults, and older adults. Dialogues that focus on how HIV/AIDS affects all ages within the African-American community must be at the forefront of any HIV/AIDS-related program and policy.

Educating the community through workshops, public protests, arts, and presentations will provide the community with a forum to be active participants in these dialogues. They will provide them with an opportunity for their voice to be heard, which is problematic in most communities of color. In addition, they will be able to provide the larger community a more distinct understanding of the issues that plague their community while seeking resources that address their issues.

Another strategy is developing ways to empower members of the community infected or affected by HIV/AIDS. Empowerment strategies must be holistic and embrace the specific obstacles encountered by this population. For example, social service agencies that serve a rural population of African-American women infected or affected by HIV/AIDS must identify the sociocultural factors that affect them (i.e., the imbalance of power within heterosexual relationships, ideas about family, and inaccessibility to medical services), provide HIV/AIDS education (prevention, intervention, and maintenance), provide support for family members affected by HIV/AIDS, and referral to other community services for issues not directly related to

HIV/AIDS infection (i.e., homelessness, poverty, discrimination, economic disparity, and social injustice). In addition, advocates must empower the community on ways to resolve these issues and provide resources that create social change and social justice.

Empowerment strategies must not focus solely on the individual level, but must also focus on the family and community level. These strategies should provide individuals with a more expanded system of care and resources that aid psychosocial, biological, and spiritual needs. They should also address the family and community level through HIV/AIDS education, resource acquisition education, and advocacy. These strategies must include petitioning, activities focused on consciousness-raising, culturally specific programming, advocating (especially for legislators to develop and implement social policies that focus on stopping the spread of HIV transmission), and providing resources for those living with HIV/AIDS. For example, the Women's Center, a program located in Bronx, New York, addresses these issues for women living with HIV/AIDS, their children, family members, and friends (Pivnick, 2003). Thus, the program attempts to broaden the HIV/AIDS infected and affected individuals' knowledge of services provided by the local service provider and the broader community.

Existing programs need to focus more on the unique needs of people of color versus their White counterparts. Because the community plays an important role in the lives of African Americans, programs that specifically incorporate cultural traditions, rituals, and customs of the African-American community would better serve this population. Programs that include family members to participate in the prevention or intervention services of those infected or affected by HIV/AIDS promote stakeholder support. This includes them in this process and helps to destigmatize HIV/AIDS. In addition, family members can become educated about HIV/AIDS, learn ways to support their family members who are living with the disease, and learn ways to become community educators, and HIV/AIDS advocates. Their heightened sense of understanding the disease on a micro- and macrolevel can help them to influence policymakers, thus encouraging policymakers to develop and implement programs that will better serve HIV/AIDS affected communities.

Programs that focus on African Americans must also focus on the marginalized group of African Americans who exist within the African-American community: lesbian women, lesbian women with children, and gay men. Despite their ethnic identity, they are often times relegated to a lesser status within this ethnic community (Lichtenstein et al., 2003). They share the burden of all of the social forces that other African Americans endure along with the social forces that affect them because of their sexual identity. For HIV/AIDS related programs to be truly successful, they must address various aspects, such as sexual identity, gender, homophobia, lack of social support, race, and class that affect this population.

CONCLUSION

Because no cure or immunization for HIV exists, interventions must be aimed toward reducing or preventing the spread of HIV infection. Educators, researchers, and practitioners must improve their strategies of educating the larger community and the smaller communities, (i.e., African-American community). More importantly, policymakers, practitioners, educators, and researchers must work together to develop approaches that target the African-American community. Researchers must conduct more research and be able to translate research findings so that the results are accessible to the community (Jones, 2004). It is only through local, state, and national level efforts that major steps will be made in reducing the rate of HIV/AIDS infection in the lives of African-American women, assisting people infected and affected by HIV/AIDS, and eradicating the sociocultural issues that affect their quality of life.

CHAPTER SUMMARY

These are the key themes to be gleaned from the chapter:

- *HIV/AIDS is the fourth leading cause of death among African-American women between the ages of 20 and 54.* The high infection rate of HIV/AIDS on this population has major implications on the individual, family, community and society. This physical health condition also affects their mental health conditions.
- *African-American women living with HIV/AIDS endure multiple problems affecting their mental health and physical health.* African-American women living with HIV/AIDS experience a greater risk of negative mental and medical health than do women of other ethnic cultures. In addition, they experience other structural issues, such as child care, family care, housing, and lack of finances.
- *Empowerment programs that provide holistic services are the most successful at reducing the rate of HIV/AIDS.* These programs proved to be successful because they target specific populations, use culturally sensitive or responsive and appropriate materials, and address issues of race, class, sex, and sexuality.

- *Practitioners and educators must develop culturally specific interventions and prevention strategies that will garner support and help to educate individuals and the community.* Practitioners, educators, and policymakers must establish social and political collaborations of all agents within the community that provide direct services to this population. These agencies must include social service agencies, grassroots programs, churches, and other community-based organizations. Collectively they must all fight for local, state, and national policies and programs that eradicate issues of stigma, racism, sexism, classism, spiritual ostracism, addiction, and harmful sexual risk-taking behavior that plague this community.

GROUP/CLASSROOM ACTIVITIES

1. Identify a community service agency that addresses issues related to women. Interview a professional from that agency and solicit the following information:
   - Services provided
   - Demographics of target population
   - The effects of HIV/AIDS on population
   - The challenges and rewards of addressing the effects of HIV/AIDS on population
2. As a class, discuss the challenges and the rewards that affect a community service agency which is located within a community with a high HIV/AIDS infection rate.
3. In a small group of four to five students, compare and contrast the risk and protective factors of
   - African-American lesbian women living with HIV/AIDS
   - African-American lesbian women living with HIV/AIDS and caring for small children

Discuss how their tripled marginalized status (i.e., African American, female, and lesbian) affects their well-being. Identify interventions for working with this population.

REFERENCES

Braithwaite, K., & Thomas, V. G. (2001). HIV/AIDS knowledge, attitudes, and risk-behaviors among African-American and Caribbean college women. *International Journal for the Advancement of Counselling, 23*(2), 115-129.

Brown, D. R., & Boyce-Mathis, A. (2000). Surrogate parenting across generations: African American women caring for a child with special needs. *Journal of Mental Health and Aging, 6*(4), 339-351.

Butler, M., & Smith-McKeever, C. (2003). Focus on solutions: Harlem Dowling-West Side Center for children and family services: A comprehensive response to working with HIV-affected children and families. In D. J. Gilbert & E. Wright (Eds.), *African American Women and HIV/AIDS: Critical Responses.* Westport, CT: Praeger Publishers.

Cargill, V. A., Stone, V. E., & Robinson, M. R. (2004). HIV treatment in African Americans: Challenges and opportunities. *Journal of Black Psychology, 30*(1), 24-39.

CDC. (2003). HIV/AIDS among African Americans. Retrieved January 1, 2005, from http://www.cdc.gov/hiv/pubs/Facts/afam.htm.

Clark, H. J., Lindner, G., Armistead, L., & Austin, B.-J. (2003). Stigma, disclosure, and psychological functioning among HIV-infected and non-infected African-American women. *Women & Health, 38*(4), 57-71.

Elwood, W. N., Williams, M. L., Bell, D. C., & Richard, A. J. (1997). Powerlessness and HIV prevention among people who trade sex for drugs ("strawberries"). *AIDS Care, 9*(3), 273-284.

Eugene, T. M. (1997). There is a Balm in Gilead: Black women and the black church as agents of a therapeutic community. *Women & Therapy, 16*(2-3), 55-71.

Feldman, M. (2003). The challenges of working with perinatally infected adolescents: Clinical and concrete possibilities. In B. I. Willinger & A. Rice (Eds.), *A History of AIDS Social Work in Hospitals: A Daring Response to an Epidemic* (pp. 277-286). Binghamton, NY: The Haworth Press, Inc.

Feldman, R. H., & Fulwood, R. (1999). The three leading causes of death in African Americans: Barriers to reducing excess disparity and to improving health behaviors. *Journal of Health Care for the Poor and the Underserved, 10*(1), 45-71.

Fitzpatrick, L., McCray, E., & Smith, D. K. (2004). The global HIV/AIDS epidemic and related mental health issues: The crisis for Africans and Black Americans. *Journal of Black Psychology, 30*(1), 11-23.

Gibson, P. A. (2005). Intergenerational parenting from the perspective of African American grandmothers. *Family Relations: Interdisciplinary Journal of Applied Family Studies, 54*(2), 280-297.

Gilbert, D. (2003). The sociocultural construction of AIDS among African American women. In D. J. Gilbert & E. Wright (Eds.), *African American Women and HIV/AIDS: Critical Responses.* Westport, CT: Praeger Publishers.

Gordon, C. M., Forsyth, A. D., Stall, R., & Cheever, L. W. (2005). Prevention interventions with persons living with HIV/AIDS: State of the science and future directions [(Special Issue: Prevention with Persons Living with HIV)]. *AIDS Education and Prevention, 17*(Suppl A), 6-20.

Harvey, S. M., & Bird, S. T. (2004). What makes women feel powerful? An exploratory study of relationship power and sexual decision-making with African Americans at risk for HIV/STDs. *Women & Health, 39*(3), 1-18.

Herek, G. M., Gillis, J. R., Glunt, E. K., Lewis, J., Welton, D., & Capitanio, J. P. (1998). Culturally sensitive aids educational videos for African American audiences: Effects of source, message, receiver, and context. *American Journal of Community Psychology, 26*(5), 705-743.

hooks, b. (1981). *Ain't I a Woman: Black Women and Feminism.* Boston, MA: South End Press.

Ickovics, J. R., Beren, S. E., Grigorenko, E. L., Morrill, A. C., Druley, J. A., & Rodin, J. (2002). Pathways of risk: race, social class, stress, and coping as factors predicting heterosexual risk behaviors for HIV among women. *AIDS and Behavior, 6*(4), 339-350.

Jipguep, M.-C., Sanders-Phillips, K., & Cotton, L. (2004). Another look at HIV in African American women: The impact of psychosocial and contextual factors. *Journal of Black Psychology, 30*(3), 366-385.

Johnson, S. D., Cunningham-Williams, R. M., & Cottler, L. B. (2003). A tripartite of HIV-risk for African American women: The intersection of drug use, violence, and depression. *Drug and Alcohol Dependence, 70*(2), 169-175.

Jones, D. (2004). HIV risk-reduction strategies for substance abusers: Effecting behavior change. *Journal of Black Psychology, 30*(1), 59-77.

Jones, D. J., O'Connell, C., Gound, M., Heller, L., & Forehand, R. (2004). Predictors of self-reported physical symptoms in low-income, inner-city African American women: The role of optimism, depressive symptoms, and chronic illness. *Psychology of Women Quarterly, 28*(2), 112-121.

Lam, W. K. K., Wechsberg, W., & Zule, W. (2004). African-American women who use crack cocaine: A comparison of mothers who live with and have been separated from their children. *Child Abuse & Neglect, 28*(11), 1229-1247.

Lichtenstein, B., Laska, M. K., & Clair, J. M. (2002). Chronic sorrow in the HIV-positive patient: Issues of race, gender, and social support. *AIDS Patient Care and STDs, 16*(1), 27-38.

Lichtenstein, B., Laska, M. K., & Clair, J. M. (2003). The politics of invisibility: HIV-positive women who have sex with women and their struggle for support. *Journal of the Association of Nurses in AIDS Care, 14*(6), 37-47.

Linsk, N. L., Mitchell, C. G., Despotes, J., Cook, J., Razanno, L., Grey, D., et al. (2002). Evaluating HIV mental health training: Changes in practice and knowledge for social workers and case managers. *Health and Social Work, 27*(1), 67-70.

Logan, T. K., Cole, J., & Leukefeld, C. (2002). Women, sex, and HIV: Social and contextual factors, meta-analysis of published interventions, and implications for practice and research. *Psychological Bulletin, 128*(6), 851-885.

Mattis, J. S. (2002). Religion and spirituality in the meaning-making and coping experiences of African American women: A qualitative analysis. *Psychology of Women Quarterly, 26*, 309-321.

McNair, L. D., & Prather, C. M. (2004). African American women and AIDS: Factors influencing risk and reaction to HIV disease. *Journal of Black Psychology, 30*(1), 106-123.

Mellins, C. A., Havens, J. F., McCaskill, E. O., Leu, C. S., Brudney, K., & Chesney, M. A. (2002). Mental health, substance use and disclosure are significantly associated with the medical treatment adherence of HIV-infected mothers. *Psychology, Health, Medicine, 7*(4), 451-460.

Munke-Pittman, P., & Venturini, V. J. (2003). HIV/AIDS among African Americans in the Mississippi/Louisiana Delta region: A macro-practice empowerment model. In R. J. Mancoske & D. J. Smith (Eds.), *Practice Issues in HIV/AIDS Services* (pp. 177-196). Binghamton, NY: The Haworth Press, Inc.

Myers, H. F., & Durvasula, R. S. (1999). Psychiatric disorders in African American men and women living with HIV/AIDS. *Cultural Diversity & Ethnic Minority Psychology Special Issue: HIV/AIDS and Ethnic Minority Women, Families, and Communities, 5*(3), 249-262.

Perry, T. (2003). HIV/AIDS policy and African American women. In D. J. Gilbert & E. Wright (Eds.), *African American Women and HIV/AIDS: Critical Responses.* Westport, CT: Praeger Publishers.

Quinn, S. C. (1993). AIDS and the African American woman: The triple burden of race, class, and gender. *Health Education Quarterly, 20*(3), 305-320.

Sterk, C. E., Theall, K. P., Elifson, K. W., & Kidder, D. (2003). HIV risk reduction among African-American women who inject drugs: A randomized controlled trial. *AIDS and Behavior, 7*(1), 73-86.

Stockdill, B. C. (2003). *Activism Against AIDS: At the Intersections of Sexuality, Race, Gender, and Class.* Convent Garden, London: Lynne Rienner Publishers.

Wechsberg, W. M., Lam, W. K. K., Zule, W. A., & Bobashev, G. (2004). Efficacy of a woman-focused intervention to reduce HIV risk and increase self-sufficiency among African American crack abusers. *American Journal of Public Health, 94*(7), 1165-1173.

Williams, P. B., Ekundayo, O., & Udezulu, I. E. (2003). An ethnically sensitive and gender-specific HIV/AIDS assessment in African American women: A comparative study of urban and rural American communities. *Family & Community Health, 26*(2), 108-123.

Winston, C. A. (2003). African American grandmothers parenting grandchildren orphaned by AIDS: Grieving and coping with loss. *Illness, Crisis, & Loss, 11*(4), 350-361.

Chapter 19

Counseling African-American Students at a Predominately White University: The Role of Stereotype Threat

Anita-Yvonne Bryant

African-American student matriculation in predominantly White higher education institutions (PWIs) has received significant attention from several academic disciplines. For example, African-American students' contributions to campus diversity and multiculturalism have been illuminated in higher education literature (Gurin, Dey, & Hurtado, 2002; Hurtado, 1992; Hurtado, Millem, Clayton-Pederson, & Allen, 1998). Their academic trajectory has been examined from kindergarten to college and beyond (Bowen & Bok, 1998; Jencks & Phillips, 1998; Massey, Douglass, Charles, Lundy, & Fischer, 2003; Nettles, 1998; Osborne, 1999; Tyson, Darity, & Castillinos, 2003). African-American students' social, academic, climate, and classroom experiences have also received multidisciplinary attention (Mayo, Murguia, & Padilla, 1995; Oliver, Smith, & Wilson, 1989; Stearns, Bonneau, & Buchmann, 2005; Tyson, 2004). Moreover, researchers have systematically explored many factors that influence the academic achievement,

This chapter is based in part on a paper presented at the annual meeting of the American Sociological Association, San Francisco, California. Research support for this chapter was provided by grants from the Andrew W. Mellon Foundation and Duke University. The author bears sole responsibility for the contents of this chapter. Identifying information has been changed to maintain confidentiality. Special thanks to Dr. Lydia P. Buki for her helpful comments and editorial assistance on an earlier version of this chapter.

persistence, and status attainment of African-American students (Ainsworth-Darnell & Downey, 1998; Jencks & Meredith, 1998; Kao & Thompson, 2003; Roscigno & Ainsworth-Darnell, 1999). Recently, researchers have been investigating the differences between predicted and actual educational outcomes for African-American students. These differences are described as the "achievement or performance gap." They occur in highly selective PWIs and are perhaps larger there than in other colleges and universities (Bowen & Bok, 1998).

All of these strands of research have significantly influenced discourse and policy germane to the matriculation of African Americans in PWIs. However, for the university mental health practitioner, their utility is limited. The application of matriculation research is restricted because experimental data and clinical material speak in different dialects. Statistical power and personal narratives have distinct norms, values, and cultures. Thus, without a bridge between psychosocial research and therapeutic application, essential clinical contributions to the educational success of African-American students are lost in translation.

Furthermore, the university clinician remains unaware of a vital therapeutic resource that psychosocial research can offer. Matriculation research illuminates personal, cultural, and environmental factors influencing the successful educational and psychological competencies of African-American students. It highlights key aspects of academic and cultural identity, and environmental sources of psychological distress; all of these factors are important to the African-American student. The research also emphasizes the classroom, extracurricular, and residential domains, ecological variables that are often on the margins of psychotherapy. African-American student matriculation research, if translated, can move the relationship between matriculation experiences and psychological distress towards the center of the treatment framework. The goal of this chapter is to translate one thread of African-American student matriculation research out of the subject pool and into the therapy room. Drawing upon extant literatures in social psychology and sociology, the examination of stereotype threat, a recent contribution to the body of achievement/performance gap literature, will serve as the conceptual framework for this task. First, features of stereotype threat and stereotyping as an academic environmental stressor will be discussed. Quantitative and qualitative examination of the power of stereotyping will follow. The role of anxiety as a mediating variable in the psychosocial research and its salience as a presenting concern for African-American clients will be highlighted. Ways of coping with stereotype threat will be examined. A case study will illuminate the translation of stereotype threat into the therapeutic milieu. Finally, clinical assessment and treatment implications will be discussed.

REVIEW OF THE LITERATURE

Stereotype Threat and the Power of Academic Stereotyping

One thread of matriculation research explores one possible reason underlying the differences in educational outcomes for African-American students. In a relatively novel explanation for these differentials, Steele and his colleagues developed and tested the stereotype threat (ST) construct (Aronson, Fried, & Good, 2002; Aronson, Lustina, Good, Keough, & Steele, 1999; Steele, 1997, 1998, 1999; Steele & Aronson, 1995, 1998; for a review, see Wheeler & Petty, 2001). They have suggested that individuals recognize the existence of negative stereotypes linking performance expectations with membership in a particular group (e.g., women are poor at math, old people are slow, White men can't jump). The possibility of confirming the stereotype evokes a domain specific threat or fear that interferes with performance and leads to lower performance outcomes (Steele & Aronson, 1995; Steele, 1997). The existence of ST is strongly supported in the literature. It has been investigated across racial, gender, economic, and professional groups (see Wheeler & Petty, 2001, for a review). Although the relationship between ST and lowered performance has been clearly established, the process through which performance is lowered remains unclear.

Steele (cf: Rivera, 1996), a pioneer in the area of ST, discussed this construct and underscored the rationale underlying stereotyping. Contrary to the traditional explanations of stereotyping as a method of cognitive shorthand, he noted that stereotyping serves as a warning signal in the environment:

> We are calling it "stereotype threat" now, as opposed to simply "stereotype vulnerability." It is really a threat from the environment, from the situation, as much as or more than something internalized in a person. Stereotype threat locates the source in the situation as opposed to the internal psychology of the person. Stereotype threat is an immediate situational pressure that one could be judged or treated stereotypically, or that one might do something that would confirm the stereotype as self-characteristic. (Cited from Rivera, 1996, p. 8)

This perspective on stereotyping as a purposeful behavior has also been proposed by LaViolette and Silvert (1951). In their seminal discussion on stereotyping, they hypothesized that stereotypes function to reify social differences. "Stereotypes eliminate conditions of social insecurity . . . and emerge from conditions of insecurity and group conflict" (p. 261). Accordingly, when actors (i.e., faculty and students) communicate stereotypes in an environmental setting, the hierarchical structure of that setting is reinforced.

Furthermore, when this hierarchy is threatened or becomes destabilized, stereotyping can serve to restore the equilibrium.

Stereotyping in predominantly White academic settings serves as an environmental cue or warning for African-American students. African-American students receive stereotyped communication from actors in the environment. These stereotypical statements attempt to demarcate "their place" in the academic hierarchy. The types of demarcations communicated include: (1) African-American students are less intelligent than their peers (intellectual inferiority stereotyping), (2) African-American students are lazy or unmotivated (low achievement motivation stereotyping), and (3) African-American students have entered the university solely based on race or affirmative action (token stereotyping). When stereotypes are evoked by faculty and students, they reinforce an academic hierarchy that situates African-American students on the bottom rung (Suarez-Balcazar, Orellana-Damacella, Portillo, Andrews-Guillen, & Rowan, 2003). Through activation, African-American students receive messages that negative judgments about them, their group, and their performance are in effect.

STEREOTYPE THREAT ACTIVATION

In an academic setting, the activation of stereotypes functions as an alert system. To use an analogy, the warning is similar to the familiar Emergency Broadcast System. The viewer or listener hears a series of loud and jarring signals that physiologically activate arousal. Our attention is immediately captured and shifts towards the noxious stimuli.

The activation of stereotyping is an emergency broadcast in the academic environment. Activation alerts students to the potential of being viewed through a stereotype (Steele & Aronson, 1995) and downgraded in the classroom hierarchy. A recent nonexperimental test of ST found that 21 percent of African-American respondents reported that in both their first and second years of college, instructors verbally expressed a lack of confidence in their ability to succeed in class (either sometimes, often, or always). In addition, 15 percent reported that the instructor or students made prejudiced comments that made them feel uncomfortable (Spenner, Bryant, Bonneau, & Landerman, 2004). A sub-sample of these respondents was selected to participate in a focus group investigating experiences of stereotype threat. When asked to report on their classroom experiences, they noted the following:

P1: I've had to respond as the "Black person." Everybody looks at me and forces me to generalize and the professor focuses on you.

P2: I've walked in class and a White guy was like "Hey, boo" trying to talk down to how he thinks Black people speak. . . . Can you speak English please? Am I supposed to lower my speech?

P6: I never had a problem until recently. In September after the first test, a math professor told me he anticipated that I would fail.

P4: White students are offended if you do better on a test. (Bryant et al., 2004)

These quotes illustrate that in the classroom setting, African-American students are exposed to stereotyping from their classmates and professors. The alert system has been activated. Expectations for failure, communicating in hip-hop slang, and being viewed as the token expert are all jarring and noxious signals that may arouse students' awareness of environmental threats.

Other researchers cite stereotyping threats that are similar to and different from those discussed by Spenner et al. (2004). For example, in a diary study of racism, African-American respondents reported that they experienced racism every other week. Incidents that were more ambiguous were estimated to have occurred every week (Swim, Hyers, Cohen, Fitzgerald, & Bylsma, 2003). African-American students have also described experiencing overt questions about their entrance qualifications and receiving comments about being "affirmative action admits." They also expressed that faculty had lower expectations for their achievement (Bryant, 1999). Similar themes of perceived intellectual inferiority, lowered academic expectations, and tokenism have been reported by various investigators (Davis et al., 2004; Schweitzer, Griffin, Ancis, & Thomas, 1999; Solorzano, Ceja, & Yosso, 2000; Suarez-Balcazar et al., 2003).

These are some examples of the ways in which stereotyping flourishes in predominantly White academic settings. Stereotypical judgments and comments are expressed by faculty and classmates in the classroom. Stereotyping sends a potent warning to African Americans. These signals alert them to the perception that they occupy the lower position in the academic hierarchy. How African-American students respond when stereotyping is activated is particularly relevant in the counseling setting.

STEREOTYPE THREAT REACTIONS

The Role of Anxiety

When African-American students are exposed to ST activation, several possible reactions might occur. Psychosocial researchers emphasize the mediating effects of these reactions. Scholars have proposed a range of factors that may influence the relationship between threat activation and lowered performance. They include: evaluation apprehension (Aronson et al., 1999), motivation (Croizet & Claire, 1998), domain identification (Aronson et al., 1999; Leyens, Desert, Croizet, & Darcis, 2000), and anxiety (Osborne, 2001; Stone, Lynch, Sjomeling, & Darley, 1999). From the outset, researchers have hypothesized that anxiety mediated stereotype activation and lowered academic performance in African-American samples (Steele, 1999; Spencer, Steele, & Quinn, 1999; Steele & Aronson, 1995). In one study, the Spielberger State Anxiety inventory was administered. Time spent on each test item was an indicator of anxiety. African-American participants in the diagnostic conditions took longer to answer questions than subjects in other conditions, indirectly consistent with an anxiety type of mediation (Steele & Aronson, 1995, ST Experiment 2). One of the few other nonexperimental studies that found anxiety in ST testing situations mediated between 28 and 39 percent of the differences in achievement between African American and White participants (Osborne, 2001).

When anxiety is not a statistically significant mediator, it still exerts a main effect on both performance and health outcomes. In a survey of students attending a highly selective predominantly White university, researchers (Spenner et al., 2004) found that anxiety produced statistically significant lower grades (by about one-quarter of a letter grade equivalent) in a self-reported most challenging class. Furthermore, 49 percent of the African-American respondents in this study reported experiencing anxiety in their most challenging class. A review of 53 community studies on racism, discrimination, and health reported that, of the 25 studies investigating mental health outcomes, 20 demonstrated that increased discrimination was associated with increased psychological distress. Participants who reported greater degrees of discrimination also reported more psychological distress (Williams, Neighbors, & Jackson, 2003).

Anxiety symptoms such as freezing, withdrawal, hyperviligance, and emotional distress are typical distress reactions to threat (Greenberg & Safran, 1987, p. 184). Anxiety symptoms are consistently in the top two presenting concerns in national surveys of university counseling centers (Clack, 2004; Gallagher, 2004). Stereotyping is an insidious environmental stressor. In the classroom, stereotyping communicates to African-American students that they are viewed as academically inferior. It is hypothesized that this warning process elicits an emergency response reaction for the stereotyped student. The student, in his or her state of arousal, experiences a constellation of symptoms commonly diagnosed as anxiety. How he or she manages this anxiety is the focus of the following section.

Responses and Resources

When an African-American student is the target of ST in the classroom, the research on the relationship between stereotyping, racism, and discrimination reveals that he or she might experience anxiety. How does the student manage or cope with these threat episodes? Traditionally, researchers use a stress and coping model to investigate this relationship. Coping responses influence the relationship between stress and distress (Allen & Britt, 1984; Billings & Moos, 1982; Folkman & Lazurus, 1980; Lazurus & Folkman, 1984).

Recently, an integrative model of coping (Compas, Connor-Smith, Salzman, Thompsen, & Wadsworth, 2001) has been applied to coping with social stigma. The authors propose that stigmatization devalues one's status in a particular setting or context. Because stigmatization is linked with a specific domain, the efficacy of the coping response is contingent upon that environment. An individual copes with stigmatization by using a variety of affective, behavioral, or cognitive strategies. The model implies that for clinicians, one treatment goal would be the assessment and formulation of effective and noneffective coping responses (Miller & Kaiser, 2001).

This model is useful when developing a clinical framework that addresses stereotyping threat, anxiety, and coping responses. Conceptually, stereotyping and stigmatization share status devaluation processes, which are present in the academic setting. Second, the model underscores the transactional relationship between coping responses and the environmental context. From a transactional perspective, the question in treatment is: Under what circumstances is a coping response maladaptive or adaptive? The answer is that coping responses are developed, utilized, and modified based on their efficacy in a particular academic setting. As a result, coping flexibility becomes a characteristic of a productive coping response. Finally, the model includes several affective, cognitive, and behavioral responses to stigma. For the purposes of this discussion, three cognitive restructuring responses will be highlighted: altering performance expectations, altering performance attributions, and altering the importance of one's identity in the stereotyping setting. Each of these coping strategies will be discussed in the following.

ALTERING PERFORMANCE EXPECTATIONS

When an African-American student experiences stereotyping, a stereotype may contain assumptions about his or her ability to achieve in the academic domain. Performance expectations are the goals and associated values that the student, his or her peers, or the faculty has for achievement. For example, in qualitative and quantitative studies reviewed for this chapter, African-American students reported that faculty perceive and communicate lower expectations for their performance. These lowered expectations are relative to their non–African-American classmates. How does a student respond to some variant of "you won't do well because you're African American"? A student may either expend less energy and restructure his or her assessment of achievement, or overexert energy in an effort to disconfirm the perception. Both responses are derived from a cognitive reappraisal of achievement. Modifying these responses serves to reduce the dissonance between personally derived expectations for success and stereotypical expectations for success.

ALTERING PERFORMANCE ATTRIBUTIONS

Like performance expectations, altering one's performance attributions is another way of cognitively coping with ST. Attributions are externally or internally derived reasons that a student may give for his or her success or failure on an academic task. Whether or not the attributions are internal or external or under the control of the student may serve as a cognitive buffer against threat (Miller & Kaiser, 2001).

Under ST, attributions for poor performance should be more likely to include internal attributions (a student perceives that he does not have the skills or did not put forth enough effort). African-American students may minimize their abilities to mirror lowered ability expectations in the academic environment. It is also possible that African-American students identified as gifted attribute their success to hard work. This serves to minimize the "specialness" or "uniqueness" of their academic abilities, a strategy common to these students when they desire to "fit in" with their African-American peers.

IDENTITIES: DOMAIN IDENTIFICATION
AND DISIDENTIFICATION

The final cognitive reframing strategy to be discussed is disidentification (Miller & Kaiser, 2001; Osborne, 1997) or disengagement (Schmader, Major, & Gramzow, 2001). Through this process, a student begins to devalue an environment she previously valued as important. When a student encounters stereotyping that devalues his or her status in an academic setting (i.e., you are here only as a race token), one response is to devalue the setting or members in the setting. The student cognitively diminishes the value and importance of that domain in the matriculation experience.

Stereotyping communication is comprised of coexisting stereotypes about African Americans and achievement. Disidentification involves cognitively reducing the importance of (1) one's racial and ethnic group identity, (2) high achieving student identity, or (3) both. For example, when a student disidentifies from an academic setting, he or she may either divest energy from his or her identity as a student or invest more in another domain (i.e., social or extracurricular). Alternatively, the student may divest from his or her identity as an African American and from academic classes in which aspects of identity will be discussed. These three coping responses, namely adjusting performance expectations, altering performance attributions, and disidentification are cognitive reappraisals in response to stereotype threat. These strategies modulate the dissonance between self-valuations and achievements and environmental devaluation.

Using these three strategies, a student may restructure his or her cognitions. Several normative transitions may be a focal point for restructuring. They include changes in major choice, course selections, grade expectations, or career choice. Others include lowered academic confidence, general academic performance concerns, or a disinterest in the academic domain. For students experiencing ST, it is critically important to assess the cognitive processes underlying a seemingly normative adjustment process. Clinicians may erroneously assume that these changes are developmentally appropriate and thereby mask the discussion of ST and its impact. The following case example highlights how important a thorough assessment of ST, the academic environment, and coping responses is to clinical treatment.

A Case Study of the ST and Its Impact

Leila was a 20-year-old African-American junior from Texas. She presented with the following self-reported symptoms: problems with schoolwork, disagreements at school, irritable feelings, anxiety, worry, and discrimination. The intensity of her symptoms had decimated her self-esteem, academic performance, and daily functioning. During the initial interview, Leila was very agitated. She cried throughout the session and spoke dejectedly about living in a state of psychological paralysis.

Leila had declared a major in a department that had a reputation for its hostility toward African-American students. She described her experience in the environment as "a pernicious sense of hell." Frequently, classroom discussions on politics, economics, and race were loaded with stereotypes about why African Americans do not succeed economically. Leila was treated as the expert on issues of welfare, crime, and affirmative action. Her professors routinely neglected to intervene in these discussions and contributed to the stereotyping.

Group projects were agonizing for Leila. She chronicled multiple instances when her White peers ignored her contributions, attributed them to other group members, or attempted to supervise her portion of group projects. Several times group members were verbally hostile and ignored her outside of group meetings. Leila coped with this by vacillating between attempting to connect with her peers and withdrawing from them and her classes. Her behavior was perceived and experienced as inconsistent. Leila anticipated that any behavior she displayed would confirm negative stereotypes about African-American women as "angry" or "mammies."

Leila had an academic history of racial isolation, harassment, and challenges to her intellectual abilities. Identified as gifted in elementary school, Leila was the proverbial "fly in the buttermilk." She was often the only African-American student in honors and advanced placement classes. High school was particularly difficult for her. Leila's interest in dating piqued with limited opportunities to do so. Leila did experience times of respite when she was involved in summer research and enrichment programs at two historically Black colleges. From these experiences, Leila gained esteem as a talented African-American student. Her sense of communalism flourished and she maintained connections with peers in these programs. In reviewing Leila's symptoms and current academic experiences, conceptualizing the case using a stereotype threat model was useful. Leila described numerous episodes of stereotyping in addition to verbal hostility. She reported that perceptions of intellectual inferiority, low achievement, and token stereotyping were in effect in her classroom settings. Although initially she was able to link her anxiety symptoms as specific to her academic setting, they began to generalize to academic tasks outside of the setting (i.e., studying at home, writing papers for other classes). Further, she was attempting to use physical and academic disengagement as a coping response. Unfortunately, she was not able to use this cognitive behavioral strategy to her benefit. It was beginning to add to her academic jeopardy.

Several factors warranted an initial evaluation for medication. Leila's symptoms were chronic and severe enough to render her academically and psychologically incapacitated. Her class attendance and performance had declined significantly. She was in danger of academic probation. Her symptoms overwhelmed her ability to engage in therapy. Her anxiety symptoms prevented her from being able to discuss her experiences. Therefore, symptom stabilization was the first goal of treatment. Sleep, good hygiene, and exercise were recommended as an adjunct to medication. Once equilibrium was restored, Leila began to painfully explore the injurious experiences of her academic setting, her interpersonal style, and the coping responses that made her feel most vulnerable.

Slowly, Leila was able to describe the feelings of fear, rage, and humiliation that accompanied incidents of stereotyping and hostility. While recounting her experiences in session, Leila also learned how to regulate the anxiety that accompanied her recall of events. She was able to describe painful experiences, regulate her anxiety, and not anticipate being overwhelmed by her anxiety.

Leila learned to recognize that her anxiety responses controlled her interpersonal behavior. Her decisions to connect or disconnect with her peers were driven by anticipatory fear of their reactions to her and actual fear of the stereotyping and verbal hostility. Leila became aware of her environment and her times of strength and vulnerability. With this knowledge, she became more purposeful about when she needed to engage and disengage from her peers. When she had more behavioral coping options available to her, she was able to use them with more internal consistency. Leila was able to identify that, of her three historical coping responses, she only used (and therefore overused) her long-distance social support system. When she reintegrated her spiritual beliefs and church attendance, she had more coping responses at her disposal. She was also able to use her Bible study and priest as additional local support resources. Leila responded favorably to psychoeducation on stereotype threat. She read Steele's 1999 article on stereotype threat, and sessions were devoted to discussing this construct. Through the article and discussion, Leila was able to identify threat experiences in her classes. This ability allowed her to predict when and how it might occur and thus prepare her response. Her feelings of aloneness and invalidation decreased once she recognized that there was a body of research dedicated to studying her experience. This had particular appeal to her intellectual identity. Leila's symptoms continued to decrease. At the end of psychotherapy, we concurred additional development of her spirituality would be her target goal. She decided to engage in spiritual direction with her priest and she continued to utilize check-in appointments as necessary.

EXPANDED APPROACHES FOR ASSESSING AND TREATING STEREOTYPE THREAT

Assessment and Treatment Considerations

Leila's case demonstrates that a ST framework can guide the assessment and treatment of academic environmental stress and its symptoms. When an African-American client presents with concerns that are academically focused, the model helps elucidate environmental factors that may be contributing to distress. The model also links anxiety symptoms to the environment. This allows a client to develop self- and environmental mastery of the symptoms. Finally, the companion article on ST facilitates a contextual understanding of the ST experience for the client. There are several aspects of the ST framework that have direct implications for assessing the client and his environment, how the client modifies coping responses, and the enhancement of the treatment protocol. Each of these will be discussed below.

The extensive research supporting the link between academic domain–specific stressors and psychological functioning for African-American students dictates its inclusion into the assessment protocol. The impact of the academic environment warrants the consideration of, along with intrapsychic, familial and cultural aspects of a client's experience. Specifically, episodes of stereotyping, racism, and discrimination should be assessed. The frequency, duration, and types of stereotyping should be discussed. Leila's presentation included chronic and pervasive stereotyping in the initial intake. Tokenism was present throughout her schooling. From this assessment, the clinician can then determine whether stereotyping is a chronic environmental stressor and manage both the cumulative effects and the current impact. This fact was central in the decision to refer Leila for medication as an adjunct to therapy.

It is also important to assess the global academic experience. An assessment should include the sociocultural demographics of the schooling experience, other racial trauma in educational settings, and an assessment of current educational functioning. Sociocultural demographics of schooling do play a role in the degree of isolation and marginalization that an African-American student may experience. Discrepancies between neighborhood, social, and educational settings also determine how an African-American student transitions between multicultural and monocultural settings. The demographics of teachers, mentors, and other role models can provide insight into where a student might seek help.

Racial trauma, in addition to stereotyping, is also important to explore. African-American students in PWIs may experience verbal and physical harassment from same and other race peers. This contributes to their feelings of isolation, particularly in middle and high school. How students have coped with racial trauma may influence who is in their college social network.

An assessment of the current academic environment might include: college choice, major interests, course difficulties, and classroom climates. Assessment of class attendance, study habits, interaction with faculty, and interactions with classmates can illuminate specific areas of engagement and disengagement for a client. Through the assessment of academic strengths and challenges, a therapist can determine potential strengths and vulnerabilities in the coping repertoire.

The next area of assessment emphasizes clinical assessment of anxiety symptoms. A clinician should be aware of cultural differences in how anxiety might be described and expressed. For example, it is not uncommon for an African-American client to use terms like "having a nervous breakdown" or "having bad nerves" (Neal-Barnett, 2003). Based on clinical experience, the author has found that a direct question of "are you feeling anxious?" elicits less information than asking African-American clients about specific symptoms (i.e., "Do you have an upset stomach? Do you have difficulty sleeping?"). Similarly, localizing the source of anxiety is helpful for African-American clients. Awareness develops that they are experiencing symptoms in one domain of their lives, but perhaps not others. Once the domain is targeted (e.g., the classroom, a professor, a course), coping responses can be designed for that specific domain.

An accurate assessment of the ST domain yields precise information about coping strengths and vulnerabilities. For example, Leila's decisions about engaging and disengaging academically were perceived by her classmates and experienced by her as erratic. It was determined that although disengagement was a feasible strategy, it was driven by her anxiety and thus avoidance. When Leila was able to be choiceful and decide to engage or disengage from the setting, she used this strategy with consistency. This also occurred with her long-distance support network. Driven by anxiety, Leila would use her network frequently. As she learned to assess her needs deriving from stereotyping experiences, she was able to increase her repertoire, and use it flexibly. Assessment of specific ST stressors, general academic functioning, anxiety, and coping responses promotes the development of psychological resiliency and efficacious treatment goals.

The treatment of ST symptoms relies on a thorough and accurate assessment of the domain experiences, symptoms, and coping resources. Based on this assessment, treatment protocols should incorporate: ST normalization and psychoeducation, promotion of affective expression and regulation, awareness of culturally specific and generic coping responses, and development of a healthy and flexible coping repertoire. Individual treatment can be complemented with medical evaluations, workshops, group support, and cultural forms of healing.

Two of the most powerful catalysts for change for an African-American client experiencing ST are normalization and contextualization of the experience and the anxiety. Psychoeducation is particularly helpful in providing a context. The Steele (1999) article appeals to clients because of its ease of reading and research grounding. The article clearly documents the pervasiveness of ST, and provides anecdotal and research evidence.

Similar to other types of threat or trauma, opportunities to express strong feelings associated with the experience facilitate resolving the trauma. Clients discussing ST report a range of feelings and reactions including anxiety, anger, frustration, hopelessness, and humiliation. Emotional catharsis in therapy is necessary to facilitate psychospiritual growth (Elligan & Utsey, 2003). Expressing the intense feelings in the ST setting may lead to further devaluing (Miller & Kaiser, 2001). Therefore, the therapeutic space may be the only place to work through intense emotions. Verbal expression, poetry, music, exercise, and prayer are some ways in which African-American clients can discharge intense feelings during and outside of session.

When clients are safe to discharge powerful emotions, they simultaneously develop skills to manage the intense feelings. The client gains awareness of and competency in managing intense fear or rage without being overwhelmed. Once this occurs, a client develops insight into contextual factors (i.e., particular types of stereotyping, certain environments) that trigger particular emotional reactions. They learn how to express and tolerate the intense feelings related to stereotyping threat.

Self- and environment awareness are two essential building blocks for transforming noneffective coping responses into a healthy coping repertoire. This has been described as the synthesis phase of therapy. This phase consists of integrating awareness and regulation with fine-tuning coping responses (Elligan & Utsey, 1999). This phase of treatment is characterized by a greater degree of insight into the nature of stereotyping; it is personal impact, generating and testing coping strategies, and developing a coping repertoire. A critical aspect of this phase is understanding the transactional nature of ST and the individual's response. Once clients develop this awareness, they can choose from a variety of emotional, behavioral, and cognitive coping strategies. As the repertoire widens, clients learn how to choose and when to use individual or collective means to address ST.

Individual direct methods may involve directly addressing the stereotyping (i.e., speaking with a student, professor, or equity officer). Indirect methods include selectively using engagement or disengagement (behavioral), reframing the experience (using a stereotyping incident as an opportunity to practice coping skills), or "persona shifting" (see Shorter-Gooden, 2004).

Group strategies rely on the power of social support and affirmation. Using local church, fraternity, community, or student organization support is often helpful. For graduate and professional students, joining African-American professional organizations and using outside mentors can be very helpful. In addition, mobilizing for collective action against stereotyping can be very effective.

CONCLUSION

Stereotype threat (ST) is an insidious toxin for African-American students attending PWIs. ST creates a tangled web that reifies social differences and attempts to situate African-American students at the low end of that hierarchy. These threats, whether repeated or intermittent, serve to reinforce the devaluation of the African-American student. When students and professors transmit stereotypes in the classroom environment, African Americans are alerted to the fact that they are being viewed through the lens of that stereotype.

When psychosocial research is translated into a clinical context, clinicians gain awareness that our most academically talented African-American students can become ensnared in a psychological web that depletes vital psychological and academic energy. When we acknowledge the body of research that illuminates the pernicious effects of ST, we can incorporate these findings into clinical practice. Then we are competently equipped to provide a secure therapeutic environment in which client restoration and educational success can thrive.

CHAPTER SUMMARY

This chapter explores the reasons underlying the differences in educational outcomes of African-American students in predominantly White universities (PWIs). Drawing upon the research studies, the chapter examines the stereotype threat (ST), recent contribution on achievement/performance gap, stereotyping as academic environmental stressor, quantitative and qualitative assessment of the power of stereotyping, role of anxiety as a mediating variable in the psychosocial research and its major effects on African-Americans clients, ways of coping with stereotype threat, examples from a case study, assessment, and treatment implications.

Stereotyping in predominantly White academic settings serves as an environmental warning for African-American students. Examples of stereotyping statements are (1) African-American students are less intelligent than their peers, (2) African-American students are lazy or unmotivated, and (3) African-American students were admitted into the university solely based on race or affirmative action. These stereotypical statements define their status in university academic ladder as well as show the perceived intellectual inferiority from the faculty and classmates. However, stereotyping of this magnitude is shown to result in anxiety when an African-American student is exposed to many of these stereotype activations. In addition, anxiety exerts a great effect on performance and health outcomes of African-American students.

Strategies such as an interactive model of coping, altering performance expectations, and cognitive reframing are very useful in developing a clinical framework that addresses threat, anxiety, and coping responses. A case study showing the academic experiences of an African-American student and an expanded approach for assessing and treating stereotype threat were also discussed.

CLASSROOM DISCUSSION QUESTIONS

1. African-American students in predominantly White classrooms experience different stereotypes in different settings. What stereotypes are present in primary, secondary, and post-secondary schools? How would they have a differential impact on student development?
2. What are the types of coping responses that students in these different settings might employ?
3. How might they differ when familial, cultural, and gender influences are taken into account?
4. How would you design a psychological intervention for students at the differing levels of education?

REFERENCES

Ainsworth-Darnell, J. W., & Downey, D. B. (1998). Assessing the oppositional culture explanation for racial/ethnic differences in school performance. *American Sociological Review, 63,* 536-553.

Allen, L., & Britt, D. W. (1984). Black women in American society: A resource development perspective. In A. U. Rickel, M. Gerrard, & I. Iscoe (Eds.), *Social and Psychological Problems of Women* (pp. 61-79). Washington, DC: Hemisphere.

Aronson, J., Fried, B., & Good, C. (2002). Reducing the effects of stereotype threat on African American college students by shaping theories about intelligence. *Journal of Experimental Social Psychology, 38,* 113-125.

Aronson, J., Lustina, J., Good, C., Keough, K., & Steele, C. (1999). When White men can't do math: Necessary and sufficient factors in stereotype threat. *Journal of Experimental Social Psychology, 35,* 29-44.

Billings, A. G., & Moos, R. H. (1982). Conceptualizing and measuring coping resources and processes. In L. Goldberger & S. Breznitz (Eds.), *Handbook of Stress: Theoretical and Clinical Aspects* (pp. 212-230). New York: The Free Press.

Bowen, W. G., & Bok, D. (1998). *The Shape of the River: Long Term Consequences of Considering Race in College and University Admissions.* Princeton, NJ: Princeton University.

Bryant, A-Y. (1991). A Legacy of Survival: Environmental Oppressors and the Resources of African-American Female Students. Unpublished doctoral dissertation, University of Maryland, College Park.

Bryant, A-Y. (1999). Learning From the Teachers: Black Students and Their Experiences at Duke. Unpublished report. Durham, NC: Duke University.

Bryant, A-Y., Spenner, K., & Tyson, W. (2004). *Stereotype Threat and African American College Students: A Qualitative Inquiry.* Manuscript in preparation.

Clack, R. J. (2004). CAPS Annual Report. Unpublished report. Durham, NC: Duke University.

Compas, B. E., Connor-Smith, J. K., Saltzman, H., Thomsen, A. H., & Wadsworth, M. E. (2001). Coping with stress during childhood and adolescence: Problems, progress, and potential in theory and research. *Psychological Bulletin, 127*(1), 87-127.

Croizet, J., & Claire, T. (1998). Extending the concept of stereotype threat to social class: The intellectual underperformance of students from low socioeconomic backgrounds. *Personality and Social Psychology Bulletin, 24*(6), 588-594.

Davis, M., Dias-Bowie, Y., Greenberg, K., Klukken, G., Pollio, H., Thomas, S., et al. (2004). A fly in the buttermilk: Descriptions of university life by successful Black undergraduate students at a predominately white southeastern university. *Journal of Higher Education, 75*(4), 420-445.

Elligan, D., & Utsey, S. (1999). Utility of an African-Centered support group for African American men confronting societal racism and oppression. *Cultural Diversity and Ethnic Minority Psychology, 5*(2), 156-165.

Folkman, S., & Lazarus, R. S. (1980). An analysis of coping in a middle-aged community sample. *Journal of Health and Social Behavior, 21,* 219-239.

Gallagher, R. P. (2004). *National Survey of Counseling Center Directors.* International Alexandria, VA: Association of Counseling Services Inc.

Greenberg, L. S., & Safran, J. D. (1987). *Emotion in Psychotherapy.* New York: Guilford.

Gurin, P., Dey, E. L., & Hurtado, S. (2002). Diversity and higher education: Theory and impact on educational outcomes. *Harvard Educational Review, 72*(3), 330-366.

Hurtado, S. (1992). The campus racial climate: Contexts of conflict. *Journal of Higher Education, 63,* 539-569.

Hurtado, S., Milem, J. F., Clayton-Pederson, A. R., & Allen, W. (1998). Enhancing campus climates for racial/ethnic diversity: Educational policy and practice. *The Review of Higher Education, 21,* 279-302.

Jencks, C., & Phillips, M. (1998). *The Black-White Test Score Gap.* Washington, DC: Brookings Institution.

Kao, G., & Thompson, J. S. (2003). Racial and ethnic stratification in educational achievement and attainment. *Annual Review of Sociology, 29,* 417-442.

LaViolette, F., & Silvert, K. H. (1951). A theory of stereotypes. *Social Forces, 29*(3), 257-262.

Lazurus, R. S., & Folkman, S. (1984). *Stress Appraisal, and Coping.* New York: Springer.

Leyens, J., Desert, M., Croizet, J., & Darcis, C. (2000). Stereotype threat: Are lower status and history of stigmatization preconditions of stereotype threat? *Personality and Social Psychology Bulletin, 26*(10), 1189-1199.

Massey, D. S., Charles, C. Z., Lundy, G. F., & Fischer, M. J. (2003). *The Source of the River: The Social Origins of Freshmen at America's Selective Colleges and Universities.* Princeton, NJ: Princeton University.

Mayo, J. R., Murguia, E., & Padilla, R. V. (1995). Social integration and academic performance among minority university students. *Journal of College Student Development, 36,* 542-552.

Miller, C. T., & Kaiser, C. R. (2001). A theoretical perspective on coping with stigma. *Journal of Social Issues, 57*(1), 73-92.

Neal-Barnett, A. (2003). *Soothe Your Nerves: The Black Woman's Guide to Understanding and Overcoming Anxiety, Panic, and Fear.* New York: Fireside Books.

Nettles, M. T. (1998). *Toward Black Undergraduate Student Equality in American Higher Education.* New York: Greenwood Press.

Neville, H. A., Heppner, P. P., & Wang, L. (1997). Relations among racial identity attitudes, perceived stressors and coping styles in African American college students. *Journal of Counseling and Development, 75,* 303-311.

Oliver, M. L., Smith, A. W., & Wilson, K. R. (1989, Fall). Supporting successful black students: Personal, organizational, and institutional factors. *National Journal of Sociology, 3*(2), 199-221.

Osborne, J. W. (1997). Race and academic disidentification. *Journal of Educational Psychology, 89*(4), 728-736.

Osborne, J. W. (1999). Unraveling underachievement among African American boys from an identification with academics perspective. *Journal of Negro Education, 68*(4), 555-565.

Osborne, J. W. (2001). Testing stereotype threat: Does anxiety explain race and sex differences in achievement? *Contemporary Educational Psychology, 26,* 291-310.

Rivera, J. (1996). Fighting stereotype anxiety. *The Hispanic Outlook in Higher Education, 5*(13), 8.

Roscigno, V., & Ainsworth-Darnell, J. (1999). Race, cultural capital and educational resources: Persistent inequalities and achievement returns. *Sociology of Education, 72,* 158-178.

Schmader, T., Major, B., & Gramzow, R. H. (2001). Coping with ethnic stereotypes in the academic domain: Perceived injustice and psychological disengagement. *The Journal of Social Issues, 57*(1), 93-111.

Schweitzer, A. M., Griffin, O. T., Ancis, J. R., & Thomas, C. R. (1999). Social adjustment experiences of African American college students. *Journal of Counseling and Development, 77*(2), 189-197.

Shorter-Gooden, K. (2004). Multiple resistance strategies: How African American women cope with racism and sexism. *Journal of Black Psychology, 30*(3), 406-425.

Solorzano, D., Ceja, M., & Yosso, T. (2000). Critical race theory, racial micro-aggressions, and campus racial climate: The experiences of African American college students. *The Journal of Negro Education, 69*(1-2), 60-73.

Spencer, C. M., Steele, C. M., & Quinn, D. M. (1999). Stereotype threat and women's math performance. *Journal of Experimental Social Psychology, 35,* 4-28.

Spenner, K. I., Bryant, A.-Y., Bonneau, K., Landerman, D. L., & Thompson, R. (2004). Race, Stereotype Threat, and Classroom Performance: Tests of Social Psychological Mechanisms. Under review (Sociology of Education).

Stearns, E., Bonneau, K., & Buchmann, C. (2005). Do birds of a feather flock together once they leave the nest? Interracial Friendship Networks in the Transition from High School to College. Paper under review at *Social Forces.*

Steele, C. M. (1997). A threat in the air: How stereotypes shape the intellectual identities of women and African-Americans. *American Psychologist, 52,* 613-629.

Steele, C. M. (1998). Stereotype threat and the test performance of academically successful African Americans. In C. Jencks & M. Phillips (Eds.), *The Black-White Test Score Gap* (pp. 401-428). Washington, DC: Brookings Institution.

Steele, C. M. (1999, August). Thin ice: Stereotype threat and Black college students. *The Atlantic Monthly, 284*(2), 44-54.

Steele, C. M., & Aronson, J. (1995). Stereotype threat and the intellectual test performance of African Americans. *Journal of Personality and Social Psychology, 69,* 797-811.

Stone, J., Lynch, C. I., Sjomeling, M., & Darley, J. M. (1999). Stereotype threat effects on black and white athletic performance. *Journal of Personality and Social Psychology, 77*(6), 1213-1227.

Suarez-Balcazar, Y., Orellana-Damacella, L., Portillo, N., Andrews-Guillen, C., & Rowan, J. M. (2003). Experiences of differential treatment among college students of color. *Journal of Higher Education, 74*(4), 428-444.

Swim, J. K., Hyers, L. L., Cohen, L. L., Fitzgerald, D. C., & Bylsma, W. H. (2003). African American college students' experiences with everyday racism: Characteristics of and responses to these incidents. *Journal of Black Psychology, 29*(1), 38-67.

Tyson, K., Darity, W., & Castellino, D. (2003). *Breeding Animosity: The "Burden of Acting White" and Other Problems of Status Group Hierarchies in Schools.* Working Papers Series SAN04-03. Durham, NC: Duke University.

Tyson, W. (2004). Roommate and Residence Hall Racial Composition Effects on Interracial Friendship Among First Year College Students. Unpublished doctoral dissertation. Duke University, Durham, NC.

Wheeler, S. C., & Petty, R. E. (2001). The effects of stereotype activation on behavior: A review of possible mechanisms. *Psychological Bulletin, 127*(6), 797-826.

Williams, D., Neighbors, H., & Jackson, J. (2003). Racial/ethnic discrimination and health: Findings from community studies. *American Journal of Public Health, 93*(2), 200-208.

Chapter 20

Understanding
Mental Health Conditions:
An African-Centered Perspective

Elijah Mickel

A critical factor in wellness is taking ownership and control of the healing process. In order to be well, one must at a minimum articulate an empowering position. This is true in physical, mental, and spiritual health. Health is the goal; wellness is the outcome, whereas healing is the journey. A discourse on the African personality is necessary in the move to wellness.

LITERATURE REVIEW

In order to be healthy one must know self, the environment, and illness. The most important component is to understand self. According to Wilson (1963), "If we don't know ourselves, not only are we a puzzle to ourselves, other people are also a puzzle to us as well. If we don't know who we are then we are whomever somebody else tells us we are" (p. 38). In order to understand self one must begin with a theory that has a foundation in truth. Truth can best be developed through an approach and discourse. A discourse is a knowledge-building exchange among people resulting in an agreement that a position contains truth. An approach is generally viewed as a world view, method, or model. The African-centered approach joins traditional cultural values that are more than 2,000 years old with the focus upon wellness leading to healing. The personality and specifically the African personality are based in theory that focuses on, and provides the parameters for,

Mental Health Care in the African-American Community
© 2007 by The Haworth Press, Inc. All rights reserved.
doi:10.1300/5364_20

the wellness needs of all humans (Ani, 1994; Asante, 1988; Asante & Asante, 1990; Budge, 1960; Diop, 1974, 1987, 1991; Karenga, 1984; Massey, 1970; Mickel, 1991, 2000, 2005).

This chapter provides a descriptive definition of African personality, whereas it continues a discourse on the role of it (which is the only personality) to explain human behavior. All human experiences are interconnected and interrelated. A change in one group's experiences impacts other groups. It should be noted that a Black experience and negritude are not restricted to a single group (Black people) but affects all groups. Therefore, to varying degrees all humans have been impacted by these variables. The strength of impact is determined by culture as shaped by epistemology and axiology. We must remember that racism and separation of people is a relatively new (historically speaking) phenomenon (Felder, 1989). Anthropologically, historically, and genetically the evidence supports Africa as the source of all human life. Culture is the codification of life.

The African personality, for purposes of this chapter, is composed of the Black experience and negritude based on African-centered axiology and epistemology resulting in a spiritually-focused collective consciousness.

NEW EXPANDED APPROACH

Traditionally, personality is defined as patterns of thoughts, feelings, and behaviors. This definition includes an approach that is based on individual behavior (Azibo, 1989; Baldwin, 1986). The objective is to separate and uniquely define a person. The focus is on what is different. This concept of personality is a combination of heredity and environment. Personality is generally thought to either develop over the life course (Schriver, 2004) or to be present at birth. The life course perspective is implicit within the African personality. It is especially manifested in and can be viewed through the impact of the Black experience and the collective consciousness (Hillard, 1995). Time is a most significant variable. The maturation of human beings transforms their perception of the importance of values and knowledge. The person in the environment as well as the environment in the person shapes the form and function of one's life course. All that we are or become is influenced by our relationship with a constraining or liberating environment as well as factors transmitted from the ancestors. Some (1998) notes, "Whether they are raised in indigenous or modern culture, there are two things that people crave: the full realization of their innate gifts, and to have these gifts approved, acknowledged and confirmed" (p. 27).

African personality postulates the unity of the many differences that separate the Black African from the European or the Asian, despite their common humanity (Irele, 1990). Again, this chapter reinforces the existence of the African personality as the only personality. We begin with the understanding that all humans have African roots. These roots provide a glimpse into the early understanding of human behavior. The Human Genome Project (HGP) (2005) reaffirmed what the Black world already knew, we are all interconnected and interrelated. This was the subjective truth (Fanon, 1967) that was transformed into objective reality. Human genomics supported with research that the phenotypical and genotypical as well as the anthropological foundation of human kind is Africa. We are all African people wherever we are on this planet. According to Brown (1990), "Modern man arose, alas, in sub-Saharan Africa. . . . Everyone has recent African roots, whether the leather-faced Indians who first crossed the Bering Strait or the milk-white Swedes" (p. 39). As a result of the HGP, it is accepted, scientifically, that all humans are genetically 99.9 percent alike. Major differences are generally the result of environment. Behavioral differences result from history and culture (Mickel and Liddie-Hamilton, 2003). Life course theory helps to explain the variations in the human family.

Many geneticists are engaged in HGP's search for the basic definition of all life. Collins (2001) relates that the human genome was written in a mysterious language, it was the book of life, history, a blueprint for building a human cell and a transformative textbook. In April 2003, the completion of the final draft of the human genome was announced. Genomic research will provide scientists and policymakers an opportunity to change how society is understood. The HGP created opportunities for research on social issues, including how we define ourselves and each other (Collins, Green, Guttmacher, & Guyer, 2003). The political issues concerning race have thus been laid to rest with not only anthropological evidence but finally with genetic substantiation. Therefore, all discussion of race is moot except as it relates to power configurations. One chooses to be of a particular race as it denotes power or influence to belong. Diop (1991) states, "Race does not exist!" (p. 17). The African personality provides one method to more fully explain how we define ourselves and each other.

In the modern era, Edward Wilmot Blyden first codified African personality in 1893. African personality as a term was used to denote a distinctive physical and moral disposition of the African, and the collective personality of Black people throughout the world (Irele, 1990). Knowledge and values have their roots in African beginnings. Human problem solving was founded in African (human) beginnings. Our African ancestors are the source of the epistemological and axiological platform. Before Freud and the modern personality theorist, Africans mused for thousands of years on the causes and consequences of human behavior. Their studies resulted in the description of the African personality. Among the modern theorists who have defined the African personality are Akbar (n.d.) and Kambon (1998).

Akbar (n.d.) posits the African personality was viewed as extending the life space of all life forms but recently narrowed to mean only the individual characteristics. Kambon (1998) takes the position that the African personality is being directed toward affirmation, self-determination, and actualization. Kambon defines the African personality as "[T]he system of psychogenetic (spiritual, cognitive-emotional, biochemical) and behavioral traits that are fundamental to African people" (p. 525).

The role of culture in the formation of personality is at times not referenced, as if personality is formed in a vacuum. It is important to understand that the African personality exists and impacts the work that one would do with families, especially African-American families. African personality centers culture as an important contributor to the development of personality. In defining culture, one can also define personality. Culture frames reality and within that framework personality is defined (Asante & Asante, 1990; Noble, 1990). Culture does not develop the personality in isolation but is significant to the family's interpretation of the real world. Perception is a significant, if not the most significant, component in understanding behavior. In order to understand the African personality, one must begin with a focus on culture that is founded on an African world view. The basic difference between the African-centered theories and other theories of African personality is that the African-centered theories are based on the African world view and the non-African theories are based on the European world view (Kambon, 1998).

The African personality utilizes the quintessential African way of knowing—intuitive knowledge. This does not obviate the way of science, a priori, experience, authority, and so on. The African personality, which includes the Black experience, negritude, axiology, epistemology, spirituality, and collective consciousness, is the most efficacious method used to explain and explore healing the African way. An explanation of each of these components of the African personality follows.

BLACK EXPERIENCE

An essential component that contributes to an understanding of the African personality is the Black (African-American) experience. The Black experience is transformed into a Black perspective in practice. A Black perspective is a major reference point for planning, implementing, and evaluating services with African Americans and their communities. There is an assumption of an interconnection between the group's status that is race based (being Black), and the problems that may threaten families and communities, especially those that are poor.

The Black experience is a pan-African experience. It is composed of experiences acquired over time through an oppressed group's awareness, observation, and perceptions, resulting in a set of collective behaviors. This experience is codified into a set of cultural behaviors. The Black experience provides a lens through which reality is filtered, altered, and transformed.

The knowledge acquired through the study of the Black experience is significant to a holistic understanding of the interactions among social, psychological, and cultural systems as they affect and are affected by human behavior. The Black experience provides a perspective for the planning, organizing, and implementation of social and economic justice. Incorporating this into practice requires the following:

1. Knowledge of the Black experience is exemplified in Black institutions. If you want to understand the impact of the Black experience, study these institutions (Blassingame, 1979; Mickel, 1999).
2. Develop an understanding of the successful mechanisms to resist and overcome oppression. This blueprint develops a system, which promotes achievement, and a sense of well-being.
3. Understand that self-help is essential to understanding prevention, intervention, and change (Carlton-LaNey, 2001; Mickel, 1999). The value of a Black perspective when working with persons subject to discrimination is that practitioners are required to consider the external factors such as racism and discrimination as they impact persons. Many of the traditional intervention models have failed to include such a requirement (Schiele, 2000; Schriver, 1998, 2004).
4. Learn how the Black experience is associated with the pan-African movement. Africans throughout the diaspora are interconnected. The Black experience began and ends as an African experience. The connection has been reified through the concept of negritude.

NEGRITUDE

Negritude is a central construct contributing to understanding African personality. Negritude recognizes the common humanity of all people but also promotes the acceptance of differences in cultural expressions of Black people. Negritude is the recognition and acceptance of being Black, as related to the destiny, history, and culture of Black people. Practice strategies that adhere to this component include:

1. Knowing the Black world from historical and international perspectives (Irele, 1990). This is a nontraditional, although pan-African, approach to understanding the international Black experience.
2. Awareness of the interconnectedness of people of African descent. These people can be found throughout the diaspora. Whether one looks to Europe or the Americas, African people are there. This is especially true in what is now the United States. Negritude (Irele, 1990) expands the Black experience, adding a pan-African focus.
3. Understanding that the history of humans is the history of the African diaspora. Africans throughout the diaspora were reconnected through the pan-African movement and negritude codified that connectivity.
4. Understanding that cultural and spiritual values are reified by negritude. It was formulated to defend the values of the African culture under attack by colonization and neo-colonization. Negritude recognized and promoted the inner state of the Black experience operationalized into a spiritual way of life.
5. Valuing the connection to Africa. Africa is now valued as contributing to the advancement of world interests. The revaluing of Africa represents a movement toward the recovery of a certain sense of spiritual integrity by Black people. The definition of a Black collective identity derives from new feelings that value African heritage (Irele, 1990).
6. Knowing that this mental structure is a significant contributor to the African personality. Negritude is a reconnecting movement. It has its roots in the movement of the children of Africa reconnecting to the continent. Africans, many of who never left the continent, used this movement to reconnect with those in the diaspora. The pan-African movement was essentially the organizing of the diasporic Africans. This connects the foundation of the African personality. According to Irele (1990), "From Africa, the Negro has inherited those mental traits which more than the biological factor, establish an original bond between him and the African" (p. 72).

AFRICAN-CENTERED EPISTEMOLOGY

Perception is the result of a union of the components of the sensory system. This system is comprised of knowledge filters that are used to interpret the real world. An African-centered perceptual system incorporates many ways of knowing (epistemology) (Mickel, 1993). African epistemology is non–science-dependent and includes intuition, experience, tradition, and a priori (all ancestors related). Convergence, a union of various ways of knowing, is the optimal way. The author agrees with Batson and Bass (1996) that "Epistemologies are systems and thus, if one part is radically changed, other parts are affected as well" (p. 46). All systems, including knowledge systems, are interrelated and interdependent. Using this component, one would:

1. Learn how the basis of knowing has been transformed from one of authority and tradition to science (empirical). The scientific way of knowing has been elevated to truth whereas other forms are relegated to faith. Somehow, the western thought process, through its epistemological base, has denigrated faith (West, 1982).
2. Understand the importance of sources of knowledge. African-centered epistemology uses multiple sources of knowledge (convergence and triangulation—cross-referencing). Knowledge becomes restrictive or culturally exclusive when one is taught that the only "truth" is the way of science. Our knowledge system is composed of our many ways of knowing (convergence). Included in the cross referencing of knowing are: tenacity, authority, a priori, science, common sense, tradition, and intuition (Kerlinger, 1973; Mickel, 1993).
3. Understand the difference between knowledge and values. For the purpose of understanding, knowledge is presented as distinct from values, although they are interconnected and interdependent. One does not exist without the other and impact upon one has a concomitant impact upon the other. Epistemology and axiology are requisite to an understanding of the African personality.

AFRICAN-CENTERED AXIOLOGY

The axiological (values) system is based upon modern and ancient philosophical principles (Mickel, 1993). The value system which is exemplified in the National Association of Social Workers (NASW) code of ethics is generally accepted as exemplifying the social work value system. African-centered axiology includes a connection to the social work code of ethics (see Mickel, 2000, for a detailed explanation). The following concepts need to be included in practice: ancient philosophy (Karenga, 1984, 1990; Mbiti, 1969), basic needs (Glasser, 1984, 1990; Mickel, 1991), social work code, and the Hermetic Principles (Three Initiates, 1988) join together to form the basis for an African-centered axiology.

1. The social work code is composed of six core values (service, social justice, dignity, and worth of the person, importance of human relationships, integrity, and competence).
2. The Hermetic Principles (divine image, perfectibility, essentiality of moral social practice, freewill, and teachability) are historically consistent with the African personality. The African-centered basic needs (love and belonging, power, fun, freedom, survival, and spirituality) represent a modern African-centered value system with the infusion of spirituality (Mickel, 1991, 2005). These areas are interconnected to form an African-centered healing paradigm.

COLLECTIVE CONSCIOUSNESS

Our behaviors are our best attempts to choose our perceptions and are contained within our organizational system. Within this system are the subsystems of organized behaviors and creative behaviors. These behaviors result from the collective conscious' efforts to solve problems and to meet our needs. The collective conscious of the Black community is visibly manifest in self-help organizations that are inclusive of an African-centered perspective (Mickel, 1999). In order to move from the oppressor driven collective conscious (auto-oppression) to the collective conscious (non-oppression) there must be an assessment of the collective consciousness; development of a transformed collective consciousness; transformation of consciousness to action (self-help), and the creation of a non-oppressive environment (need-fulfilling).

In African and African-American history, the most effective means of communication about oppression has been through speech and song. Music provided a system to organize behaviors for the oppressed collective community. Within the music were the messages which provided a foundation necessary to act as a community of one. This community acts collectively to improve its living conditions. Today, at the beginning of the twenty-first century, the music is rap with generally similar outcomes (Mickel & Mickel, 2002). Many would posit that the time for collective consciousness is at an end. This author submits that until the oppressive conditions end, a collective response continues to be required.

The mission of the collective consciousness is to move individuals from dependence to interdependence. The role of the collective becomes paramount. The collective conscious is manifested as collective behavior. Each member acts individually and collectively at the same time, taking on roles and responsibilities for the benefit of the collective body. This interdependence allows for the maintenance of one's autonomy while supporting and maintaining the stability and integrity of the whole. Community roles are at times fluid, as are the roles in families, organizations, and small groups. There is a bonding, a commonality among the community members. Bonding aids in developing stronger membership identification that encourages members to exchange thoughts and ideas and to cement the foundation for an interrelated, interdependent network.

CONCLUSION

There is no personality that is not African. The history of humanity begins in Africa. All personality is therefore a variation of its African roots. The traditional definition of personality is concerned with the individual. Individualistic approaches also focus on non-wellness and mental illness. The African personality is an interconnected, interdependent paradigm. It focuses on the whole rather than components of the whole. The African personality provides a description of the causative factors in the development of collective behaviors. The purpose of African-centered practice is to liberate the individual from the restrictive limits of the constricting environment. African-centered practice attempts to increase perceptual choices, while at the same time maintaining a harmonious relationship within the perceptual world. The African-centered generalist social work practice requires a historic study of the ancestors to learn the way of success. The ancestors left documentation of their struggles to overcome oppression. The ancestors left us monuments, writings, behavioral models, and successful organizations that document that success (Ani, 1994; Browder, 1992; Budge, 1960; Carlton-LaNey, 2001; Some, 1998).

Healers must infuse this knowledge with the chosen theoretical modality to maximize the healing process. This author has chosen to explicate the role of the African personality as a foundation for understanding human behavior in the social environment. It is postulated that this understanding will lead to healing. The change to infusing the perception of the values of the African personality impacts the practices that result. The basic needs provide the foundation upon which values and knowledge infused with the mind, body, and spirit shape the outcomes. African personality undergirds the wellness needs of humans. It focuses and provides the parameters for healing practice. If one would understand the African personality, one must begin with a spiritually-focused collective conscious and its connectors, Black experience and negritude, infused with epistemological and axiological foundations.

The African personality is composed of present, past, and future behaviors, attitudes, beliefs and values. It is the interconnector of all that is human on this planet. Those who profess to be wholistic in treatment cannot in good conscious omit the role of the African personality in understanding human behavior. It is especially significant to those who profess to work with families, particularly families of color.

CHAPTER SUMMARY

From this chapter, one ought to glean the essential components to understanding mental health from an African perspective. These components include the African personality, Black experience, negritude, African-centered epistemology, African-centered axiology, and collective consciousness. To undertake the journey of healing with African Americans, mental health workers must understand the African personality and its components.

ANCILLARY ACTIVITIES

For those who use this chapter with students, the suggested activities will reinforce the information acquired in reading this chapter. The concepts in this section will help clarify those presented in the text. The web sites will further the knowledge of the reader while reifying the knowledge base, helping to compare and contrast the African personality as a healing paradigm.

Classroom Activities

1. Review the following Internet sites:
   - http://www.cric.com/
   - www.africawithin.com/akbar/rhythmic
   - www.gnostic.org/kybalionhtm/kybalion
   - http://www.archives.gov/research_room/research_topics/contem porary_african_art/selelist229.html

   Critique each based on the following:
   - Framework: What did you learn from the site?
   - Has it helped you to understand the African personality? Why? Why not?

- Are you able to apply this information to your understanding of human behavior? Why? Why not?
2. Define the following concepts and provide an example of their use in direct or community practice:
   - Axiology
   - Black Experience
   - Collective Conscious
   - Epistemology
   - Human Genome
   - Negritude
3. Discuss the concepts of epistemology and axiology. Provide examples of family behaviors that reflect these concepts.
4. How would you explain the idea that regardless of socially designated race, humans have a common ancestry in Africa? How would you begin? What evidence would you highlight?
5. Which factors are essential to working within a Black perspective? Provide your rationale for the significance of using this perspective.

REFERENCES

Akbar, N. (n.d.). Rhythmic patterns in African personality. Retrieved March 10, 2004, from http://www.africawithin.com/akbar/rhythmic.htm.

Ani, M. (1994). *Yurugu.* Trenton, NJ: African World Press, Inc.

Asante, M. K. (1988). *Afrocentricity.* Trenton, NJ: African World Press, Inc.

Asante, M. K., & Asante, K. W. (1990). *African Culture: The Rhythms of Unity.* Trenton, NJ: African World Press, Inc.

Azibo, D. A. (1989). African-centered theses on mental health and a nosology of Black/African personality disorder. *The Journal of Black Psychology, 15,* 173-214.

Baldwin, J. A. (1986). African (Black) psychology: Issues and synthesis. *Journal of Black Studies, 16,* 235-249.

Batson, T., & Bass, R. (1996, March/April). Teaching and learning in the computer age. *Change, 28*(2), 42-47.

Blassingame, J. W. (1979). *The Slave Community.* New York: The Oxford Press.

Browder, A. T. (1992). *Nile Valley Contribution to Civilization.* Washington, DC: The Institute of Karmic Guidance.

Brown, M. (1990). *The Search for Eve.* New York: Harper and Row.

Budge, E. A. (1960). *The Book of the Dead.* New Hyde Park, NY: University Books, Inc.

Carlton-LaNey, I. (2001). *African American Leadership.* Washington, DC: NASW Press.

Collins, F. S.,(2001). Remarks at the press conference announcing sequencing and analysis of the human genome. Retrieved March 10, 2004, from http://www .genome.gov/pfv.cfm?pageid=10001379.

Collins, F. S., Green, E. D., Guttmacher, A. E., & Guyer, M. S. (2003). A vision for the future of genomics research. *Nature, 422,* 835-847.

Diop, C. A. (1974). *The African Origin of Civilization: Myth or Reality.* New York: Lawrence Hill Books.

Diop, C. A. (1987). *Precolonial Black Africa.* New York: Lawrence Hill Books.

Diop, C. A. (1991). *Civilization or Barbarism.* New York: Lawrence Hill Books.

Fanon, F. (1967). *Black Skin, White Masks.* New York: Grove Press.

Felder, C. H. (1989). *Troubling Biblical Waters.* Maryknoll, NY: Orbis Books.

Glasser, W. (1984). *Control Theory.* New York: Harper and Row.

Glasser, W. (1990). *The Quality School.* New York: Harper and Row.

Hillard, A. (1995). *The Maroon Within Us.* Baltimore: Black Classic Press.

Irele, A. (1990). *The African Experience in Literature and Ideology.* Bloomington: Indiana University Press.

Kambon, K. K. K. (1998). *African/Black Psychology in the American Context: An African Centered Approach.* Tallahassee, FL: Nubian Nation.

Karenga, M. (1984). *Selections from the Husia.* Los Angeles: Kawaida Publications.

Karenga, M. (1990). *The Book of Coming Forth by Day.* Los Angeles: University of Sankore Press.

Kerlinger, F. N. (1973). *Foundations of Behavioral Research.* New York: Holt, Rinehart and Winston, Inc.

Massey, G. (1970). *Ancient Egypt.* New York: Samuel Weiser.

Mbiti, J. S. (1969). *African Religions and Philosophy.* London: Heinemann.

Mickel, E. (1991). Integrating the African centered perspective with reality therapy/ control theory. *Journal of Reality Therapy, 11*(1), 66-71.

Mickel, E. (1993). Reality therapy based planning model. *Journal of Reality Therapy, 13*(1), 32-39.

Mickel, E. (1999). Self-help in African American communities: A historical review. In B. Compton & B. Galaway (Eds.), *Social Work Processes* (pp. 410-416). Pacific Grove, CA: Brooks/Cole Publishing.

Mickel, E. (2000). African-centered reality therapy: Intervention and prevention. In S. L. Logan & E. M. Freeman (Eds.), *Health Care in the Black Community.* Binghamton, NY: The Haworth Press.

Mickel, E. (2005). *Africa Centered Reality Therapy and Choice Theory.* Trenton, NJ: Africa World Press.

Mickel, E., & Liddie-Hamilton, B. (2003). *Human Genome III. The Human Genome Project and the African Personality.* Workshop conducted at the 35th Annual Conference of the National Association of Black Social Workers, Jacksonville, Florida.

Mickel, E., & Mickel, C. J. (2002). Family therapy in transition: Choice theory and music. *International Journal of Reality Therapy, 21*(2), 37-40.

National Human Genome Research Institute. (2005). Retrieved October 27, 2005, from http://www.genome.gov/.

Noble, W. W. (1990). The infusion of African and African-American content: A question of content and intent. In A. G. Hilliard, L. Payton-Stewart, & L. O. Williams (Eds.), *Infusion of African American Content in the School Curriculum* (pp. 5-26). Chicago, IL: Third World Press.

Schiele, J. (2000). *Human Services and the Afrocentric Paradigm.* Binghamton, NY: The Haworth Press, Inc.

Schriver, J. (1998). *Human Behavior and the Social Environment* (2nd ed.). Boston: Allyn and Bacon.

Schriver, J. (2004). *Human Behavior and the Social Environment* (4th ed.). Boston: Allyn and Bacon.

Some, P. M. (1998). *The Healing Wisdom of Africa.* New York: Penguin Putnam Inc.

The Human Genome Project. (2005). Retrieved October 27, 2005, from http://www.cric.com/.

Three Initiates. (1988). *The Kybalion.* Clayton, GA: Tri-State Press.

West, C. (1982). *Prophesy Deliverance.* Philadelphia, PA: The Westminster Press.

Wilson, A. N. (1963). *The Falsification of Afrikan Consciousness.* New York: Afrikan World InfoSystems.

Epilogue

The Healing Spirit of Our Ancestors:
A Look Toward the Future

Sadye M. L. Logan

There is no doubt that at this time in history,
Western civilization is suffering from a great sickness of the soul

(Malidoma Patrice Somé, 1994, p. 1)

Malidoma Patrice Somé, a writer with great wisdom, also says that westerners are increasingly turning away from their functioning spiritual values with a total disregard for the environment and the protection of our natural resources. He, as well as others, point to our growing intolerance toward multiculturalism and the conditions of our trouble inner cities (Freeman & Logan, 2004; Logan, 2003; Thernstrom & Thernstrom, 2002). The problems of poverty, drugs, crimes, unemployment, and gross economic injustices, are rendering our inner cities inhabitable for families and children residing there, but this is especially true for African-American families and children.

I am convinced that nearly all of the contributors to this book formed their chapter content with some degree of acknowledgment and agreement regarding the conditions of our inner cities and the general state of Black America. The critical question is: Was that enough to support the call for a paradigm shift with respect to the mental health crisis in Black America and the ongoing social and economic conditions exacerbating it? Have we proposed something new and different or are we too enmeshed in the process of living with these conditions to effectively step outside and observe this crisis through a different lens? Somé (1994) has directed his message toward all westerners, but for the African-American community it resonates in many different ways. Much like W. E. B. Dubois' prophetic message about

Mental Health Care in the African-American Community
© 2007 by The Haworth Press, Inc. All rights reserved.
doi:10.1300/5364_21

the future state of Black America in the classic, *The Souls of Black Folk*, I believe that to truly propose and live a paradigm shift regarding the mental health crisis in Black America, it is imperative that we hold triple consciousness regarding where we have been as a people, where we are going, and how we are arriving there.

A LOOK TO THE PAST

In 1903, W. E. B. DuBois (1868-1963) wrote that:

> the Negro is sort of a seventh son, born with a veil, and gifted with second-sight in this American world, a world which yields him no true self consciousness, but only lets him see himself through the revelation of the other world. It is a peculiar sensation, this double consciousness this sense of always looking at one's self through the eyes of others, of measuring one's souls by the tape of a world that looks on in amused contempt and pity. One ever feels his twoness, an American, a Negro, two souls, two thoughts, two unreconciled; two warring ideals in one dark body, whose dogged strength alone keeps it from being torn asunder. The history of the American Negro is the history of this strife—this longing to attain self-conscious manhood, to merge his double self into a better and truer self. (1961, pp. 16-17)

When DuBois wrote the powerfully evocative *The Souls of Black Folk,* the enslaved African in America had been freed for little less than four decades. Although of Black and White parentage and born free, DuBois became very aware of his double consciousness through interacting with his White peers as a young child at school in New England. Over time, he became more cognizant of the fact that he was not White. He felt excluded from the world of his peers. Instead of attempting to tear down the veil of exclusion, he chose instead to hold everyone beyond the veil in contempt, and gained much satisfaction from using his superior intelligence and physical strengths to gain advantage over those he considered to be beyond the veil. Somehow, despite the veil of exclusions, Dubois knew that he would succeed at enjoying some of the opportunities available to his White peers. He also realized that there were other Black boys who were not as fortunate as he. In this regard he wrote: "their youth shrunk into sychophany, or into silent hatred of the pale world about them and mocking distrust of everything white, or wasted in a bitter cry, why did God make me an outcast and a stranger in mine own house?" DuBois, (1961, p. xiv).

It is interesting to note how this 104-year-old document so aptly describes the conditions of life in Black America today. It is also believed that this document not only holds the way to the salvation of African-American people, but for the people of the world. In my thinking, DuBois' experience as captured in *The Souls of Black Folk* serves as a metaphor for better understanding the state of mental health in Black America. Take for example, DuBois' powerful concept of double consciousness for describing the Black/White experience. However, for the Blacks not of DuBois' world and experiences, existence was at least experienced as a triple consciousness. As is commonly known, DuBois' experiences affirmed that all Blacks were defined by the color of their skin. It did not matter that he was a scholar of the first order and educated in the most prestigious universities at home and abroad. Despite his intellectual accomplishments, he was still treated as a second-class citizen, with the same rights and privileges of the newly-freed slaves. The time and events surrounding DuBois' birth and childhood are also significant in developing this metaphor to understand Black mental health. DuBois was born two years after the emancipation and his childhood evolved during the reconstructive period following the Civil War. This was a period of heavy hopefulness and dreams of equality and political power. In the early 1890s, DuBois was convinced that the solution to the oppressive conditions experienced by Black America could be solved by providing thorough systematic investigations and developing quantitative research that was accurate about Black people. He believed that ignorance alone was the cause of race prejudice and that information derived only from scientific research would be sufficient to change prejudicial thinking and behavior. By the late 1890s, the hopes and dreams of the freedmen were shattered by the use of deliberate, premeditated violence (Sterling, 1997). Racial intolerance was the order of the times. The plight of Black Americans has continued to deteriorate and has not recovered.

DuBois also wrote in 1903 that the color line was a great problem in the United States, but that an even greater problem both obscured and implemented the problem of this color line. DuBois surmised that "so many civilized persons are willing to live in comfort even if the price of this is poverty, ignorance, and disease for the majority of their fellowmen; that to maintain this privilege, men have waged wars, until today war tends to become universal and continuous." Sadly, as DeBois predicted, "the excuse for this war continues to be color and race" (p. xiv).

It is amazing that as a leader among leaders of the world this nation has not truly addressed the race and color line issue in an appreciable way. According to Thernstrom and Thernstrom (2002), Americans are in such denial about race questions that it is almost impossible to have a useful dialogue. A major barrier is that those in the conversation are viewing race and the color line through very different lenses. Instead of talking about the issues in ways that produce results, we talk across the issues in ways that suggest commitment and concern, but not results. For example, "equal opportunity" is the most overused and least-defined phase in our conversations on race and the color line. So how might African Americans join in this dialogue in ways that produce results?

REMEMBERING THE HEALING WISDOM OF THE ANCESTORS

We are proposing here that joining in true dialogue will begin with remembering what we have forgotten so long ago. The clues to remembering can be gleaned not only from the chapters in this book, but also from the pages of *The Souls of Black Folk* by DuBois (1961) and *The Healing Wisdom of Africa* by Somé (1994). Central to this remembering is the concept or toll of ritual, which embodies a process that heals and connects people to the ancestors and life's purpose. In his book, Somé focuses on the practice of ritual, healing, and community or connectedness. He defines ritual as "the most ancient way of binding community together in a close relationship with Spirit" (Somé, 1994, p. 141). It is viewed as one of the most practical and efficient ways to facilitate safe and effective healing by individual and community. It is a tool for maintaining balance between spirit and body (Figure E.1). Ritual is intended to restore balance or the essence of health to individual and community. Somé (1994) purports that ritual will only have meaning and produce results if we understand that the elements of the cosmological wheel are its molecular tools and their proportion to one another must be monitored and restored often.

Community or connectedness is an equally important aspect of remembering. We are reminded, however, that building community is extremely difficult, if not impossible, when people are not grounded or centered and have not maintained a sense of balance and focus in their lives. Somé states that when we lose contact with the ground as our point of strength, we tend to focus on the material world. Even when we have obtained all the material things of the world, we still have a sense of being unfulfilled and uncertain about ourselves.

Somé (1994) spoke of the elements identified in Figure E.1 as the embodiment of people and cultures. One or several of the five elements are found within all cultures; the most common of which are fire and water. He states that if a culture does not nurture and monitor these elements through

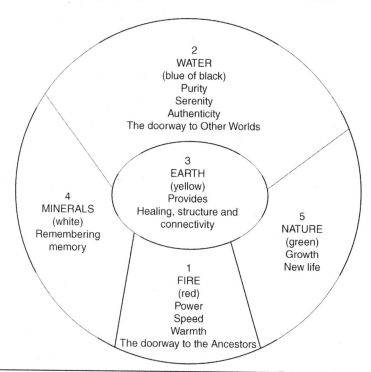

The medicine wheel is a symbolic representation of the relationship between the five elements (earth, water, minerals, nature and fire) that form the cosmos. Earth is at the center and touches all the other elements.

FIGURE E.1. The medicine wheel of Dagara people of West Africa. *Note:* The Dagara people of Burkino Faso, formally Upper Volta, West Africa, are known for their healing abilities and spiritual practices.

ritual, most people will do something else to fill the gap in order to heal. For example, in many cultures, especially the west, people turn to different forms of therapy or drugs and other substance to anesthetize their pains. The bottom line is that ritual is critical to our internal and external healing and transformation.

It is intended that these chapters in this book will begin to move all people, especially the people that are the focus of this book, to reconnect and engage in ritual, to reconnect with the ancestors, and to reconnect with our deepest purpose.

REFERENCES

DuBois, W. E. B. (1961). *The Souls of Black Folk.* New York: CBS Publications.

Freeman, F. M., & Logan, S. L. (2004). *Reconceptualizing the Strengths and Common Heritage of Black Families: Practice, Research and Policy Issues.* Springfield, IL: Charles C Thomas Publishers.

Logan, S. L. (2003). Issues of Multiculturalism: Multicultural practice, cultural diversity, and competency. In Richard A. English (Ed.), *Encyclopedia of Social Work,* (19th ed., 2003 supplement, pp. 95-105). Washington, DC: NASW Press.

Somé, M. P. (1994). *The Healing Wisdom of Africa: Finding Life Purpose Through Nature, Ritual, and Community.* New York: Jeremy P. Tarcher/Putnam.

Sterling, D. (Ed.). (1997). *We Are Sisters: Black Women in the Nineteenth Century.* New York: W.W. Norton.

Thernstrom, A., & Thernstrom, S. (Eds.). (2002). *Beyond The Color Line: New Perspectives on Race and Ethnicity in America.* Stanford, CA: Hoover Institute Press.

Index

Page numbers followed by an *f* or *t* indicate footnotes or tables.